IMPACT OF WESTERN MAN

A Study of Europe's Role in the World Economy 1750-1980

William Woodruff

NIVERSITY
ESS OF
MERICA

University Press of America,® Inc.

4720 Boston Way
Lanham, MD 20706

3 Henrietta Street
London WC2E 8LU England

Printed in the United States of America

Library of Congress Cataloging in Publication Data

Woodruff, William.
Impact of western man.

Reprint. Originally published: New York : St. Martin's Press, 1967, c1966.
Bibliography: p.
Includes index.
1. Economic history—1750-1918. 2. Economic history—1918- . 3. Civilization, Occidental. I. Title.
HC51.W6 1982 337.4 81-40861
ISBN 0-8191-2485-0 (alk. paper)
ISBN 0-8191-2486-9 (pbk. : alk. paper)

All University Press of America books are produced on acid-free paper which exceeds the minimum standards set by the National Historical Publications and Records Commission.

For HELGA

CONTENTS

LIST OF TABLES

PREFACE

BECAUSE I believe that European economic history since the eighteenth century (some would say much earlier) can only be understood in a world context, I have tried to show in this book how the world has been affected by Europe's expansion during the past two hundred years. I have placed emphasis upon the external aspect of European history because ours is a world moulded these past two centuries by the white man's hands.

The story of the expansion of Europe during the past two hundred years is a story of common humanity — the chapter of national, colonial aggrandisement was short-lived. More enduring was the worldwide impact of western attitudes, beliefs and ideas; more enduring was the contribution of Europe's 'huddled masses' who migrated to every part of the earth; more enduring was the widespread investment of European wealth, and the diffusion to all peoples of European agricultural and industrial technology. These forces, coupled with the marvels of western systems of transport and communications, and the establishment of a system of world commerce, have drawn the world together.

To emphasise the study of humanity as a whole is not to decry the intense specialization of recent decades; to emphasize the interconnection between European expansion and the development of a world economy during the past two centuries is not to belittle the importance of national or regional studies. Without them this book could not have been written. I am conscious that the intercontinental view of history which I have presented here will be unacceptable to those who see the past through the changing fate of nations. In any event, anyone who allows his curiosity — as I have done — and perhaps his recklessness in this age of intense specialization to commit him to such a vast inquiry should not be shy of criticism. Yet I make no apology for having tried to illuminate our present dramatic phase of world history in the most general way. In this I follow a respectable tradition which, alas, has fallen out of fashion. In a world where distance is fast disappearing I felt that such a book was needed, and I know of no other work which has already tried to do what I have done here. And I have done it so that the reader need not fall in with my point of view. There are enough facts and figures in this book to enable him to reach his own conclusions.

I look upon my work not as a point of arrival but as a point of departure. In stressing the later expansionist phase of European life I merely hope to direct attention to a field of enquiry from which one might glean additional understanding of the human drama. This is all that any historian can hope to do, and no greater claim is made for what is written here. The tale I have told covers a short episode in the life of man. I suffer no illusions about my ability to re-create even this fleeting moment of time. Of necessity, my views are locational, personal and temporal; they are not likely to be the views of other historians, now or in the future. Each will tell the tale as he sees it. All the various accounts, whatever their origin, will suffer from human fallibility. History is written by men, not by gods. Yet it is only in historical terms that we can ever hope to understand the metamorphosis of the modern world. And it is quite essential that we should try to do so. We are not, as Jean Jacques Rousseau said, 'born free'; we are an inseparable part of a great human concourse reaching to the beginning of time. We are the only species who can learn from the past; we are threatened with extinction if we fail to do so. There has never been an age when the unity of mankind has been so much within our grasp. Yet, as the world shrinks it is increasingly divided by the clash of conflicting ideologies and the political barriers of the emerging nations.

Very early on in my work I had to decide what was meant by Europe. I have followed the usual geographical description by setting the eastern boundary at the Urals. I am aware of the regional differences and variations in Europe to which one can point. Yet, in my mind, Europe exists as an entity in a way that the heterogeneous societies of Africa and Asia can never exist. In order to keep the story of the impact of Europeans in the world within manageable proportions, from a research and writing point of view, I found it necessary to deal primarily with the extrusive aspect of Europeans living in Europe and only in passing with the external aspect of the history of other great white settlements in the world. I decided that a European was someone born of European stock in Europe, and that is the way I have used the word in the book. I made place of birth, not citizenship, my dividing-line. Thus I have neglected the important external impact in the world made by the people of the United States during the past century. Yet most Americans sprang from a European cradle. Experience taught me, however, that the external aspect of the American story should be told separately. It is too important a contribution to be treated as an appendage to the expansion of Europe in the world. Having completed this first volume dealing with the impact of Europeans, I am now concerned in a second volume to trace the external impact of the Anglo-American.

When I speak of the western nations, and the West, I am dealing with those people who belong to a general European cultural pattern, regardless of where they were born or where they reside. Thus, the terms 'western nations' and 'the West' include those living within Europe, as well as those whites living within the great European settlements of the Americas, Australasia and parts of Africa. To those who see 'America' as larger than the 'United States' I apologize for using these terms interchangeably. My plea is that I have followed the general European practice. Where I have used the term 'North America' I mean Canada and the United States. 'Latin America' for me includes the area from the Mexican–United States border to Cape Horn, as well as the West Indies.

In this account I have largely avoided discussing what writers refer to as 'current problems'. Instead I have tried to bring alive an historical situation and to say a little about some of the causal factors underlying the conditions that exist in the world today; if the past is a guide to the future, many of the economic problems which press upon us so heavily today will probably be solved in ways that the wisest among us cannot now predict. I have also shown a reluctance to become involved with the contemporary debate about the 'process of economic growth'. I suspect that economic growth — like so many other aspects of our work that have managed to claim a disproportionate part of our time in the past — is receiving more attention than its true importance warrants. There is nothing fundamentally new about economic growth (or decline) except our present obsession with it. Despite the present high rate of increase in material well-being of certain nations, most men do not face 'self-sustained, continuous economic growth'; they face the problem of survival. For western economists to suggest that they can bestow upon non-western nations a magic formula of economic growth is to foster false hopes. It was a special interaction of forces, a special conjunction of circumstances (not least that earlier great accident of history, the discovery of America) which gave the white man temporary ascendancy in wealth and power. In generalizing from these special conditions we not only deceive others, we delude ourselves.

Perhaps the greatest hazard confronting a European writer engaged in a task of this kind lies not in the breadth of this subject, or its complex nature, but in the fact that he is a European. The story of Europe's recent past is so closely connected with present-day happenings that it must powerfully influence our interpretation of Europe's role. It is easy for us Europeans to forget how brief, how fleeting, when measured against the span of ancient civilizations such as that of the Indus and that of China, the period of European predominance has been; easy for us to stress what Europe has given to the world and overlook the intangible values that the world has lost as a result of European expansion.

* * *

It is not possible to thank individually all those who have helped me during the years that I have been writing this book. It is fairly obvious that no one could pretend to cover such an immense field without the assistance of others. During the past decade I have had occasion to worry a great number of people in many parts of the world, and I very willingly express my thanks for the generous help I have received from them. I hope they will not be disappointed if, in spite of their kindness and their erudition, I have on occasions stuck stubbornly to my own particular point of view.

The introductory chapter on European ideas was read by Professor J. Bowman and Dr. G. Kitson Clark. My writing on the course of European empires benefited from being read by Professor H. Lüthy, who caused me to take a more critical attitude towards the classical descriptions of early European expansion. He also saved me from exaggerating the extent of European world power before the mid-nineteenth century. On European migration generous help was given by the official statisticians of many governments, as well as by members of the Institute of Historical Studies, the Academy of Science, Moscow; acknowledgements have been made on the relevant tables. On the subject of European foreign investment I was fortunate in being able to draw upon the assistance of banking and investment friends who wish to remain anonymous. On western technology and the process of invention I received much help from Dr. S. C. Gilfillan and Professor R. S. Woodbury. I was also able to draw upon the specialized knowledge in mining and agriculture of Professor C. Marshall and Professor D. Williams. Similarly, the chapter dealing with transport and communications benefited from being read by Professor D. P. Locklin and Professor G. R. Taylor. My treatment of the changing pattern of trade was criticized by Mr. R. W. Green of the British Board of Trade, Mr. A. Maddison, and Dr. J. Perkins. In handling the French and German trade figures I received the assistance of Monsieur Schmidlin of the Ministère des Finances, Paris, and Herr Schlüter of the Statistisches Bundesamt, Wiesbaden.

I also owe a debt to the following gentlemen who were kind enough to read the book in typescript: Mr. G. Blainey, Professor D. Carneiro sen., Professor D. Carneiro jun., Professor Sir Douglas Copland, Professor W. H. B. Court, Professor Sir A. Grenfell Price, Professor G. F. Kennan, Mr. J. R. Kirwan, Professor Y. Komatsu, Mr. H. Rhee and Professor J. Ward. The book's shortcomings are mine, not theirs.

I especially want to thank the University of Illinois and the University of Melbourne for providing me with research assistance. Mr E. A. Beever, Mr. J. Fogarty, Mr. K. Slonina, Dr. T. K. Tan, Mr. S. Weiner and Dr. H. Witthöft rendered me assistance in Australia and America for which I am deeply appreciative. Dr. Tan and Mr. Fogarty came to me last of all and upon their very able shoulders fell the hard task of helping to get this book ready for the press. The book was put into final form with the aid of a grant from the Rockefeller Foundation in 1964 which enabled me to set aside my more compelling University teaching and administrative duties. I am most grateful to the Foundation for all their help.

It remains to thank the library staff at Illinois and Melbourne, especially the Reference Librarian at Melbourne University library, Mr. P. Singleton, and the Librarian of the Giblin library at Melbourne, Miss A. Murdoch. All the bibliographical data used in this book was prepared by Miss Murdoch.

Alas, when an author thinks he has finished his work it has only just begun for those who painstakingly try to make the author's work presentable to the public. No one could have had more loyal and efficient assistance in the typing of the successive drafts of this manuscript than I received from Mrs. H. Godfrey, Miss W. Kimpton, Mrs. L. M. Kneale, Mrs. M. Willes and Miss S. Bingley.

The Institute for Advanced Study, Princeton, 1966

WILLIAM WOODRUFF

Chapter I

PROLOGUE: THE IMPACT OF EUROPEAN IDEAS IN THE WORLD

WITHIN the relatively brief space of three or four hundred years Europe transformed the economic and social pattern of much of the world. It did this partly by establishing European communities all over the world, partly by investing great quantities of capital in other lands, partly by developing a system of world commerce, and partly through the enormous improvements made to the techniques employed in agriculture, industry, commerce, transport, and communications. Yet tiny Europe's ability to reach out and impose its will on far greater, far older, and far more cultured civilizations in the world can never be explained in these terms alone. To do so would be to ignore the explosive dynamism of European ideas and beliefs which drove the European across the world and enabled him to leave his indelible impress on every land. In contrast to the general retreat of western domination in Africa and Asia today, the influence of European ideas and beliefs — especially in science and technology — is growing. It has become part of the intellectual heritage of the whole human race and will outlast all the more obvious forms of European impact in the world.

To identify anything so complicated as a civilization with a single idea seems absurd. And yet it is the idea of a continuous, cumulative expansion of man's power over his own environment, and perhaps even over his own destiny, which most sharply distinguishes the European from other civilizations. It is the most powerful idea that Europe has put abroad. It stands in sharpest contrast to the underlying aim of ancient and medieval civilizations: stability. European dynamism has created immeasurable opportunities for man; it has also helped to disrupt and destroy the older cultural and religious patterns of European and non-European societies alike.

The origin of the European idea of progress must be sought in the history of eastern and western science as well as in the history of Christianity. The scientific tradition upon which Europe now builds, and with which it is most closely identified, was inherited from the civilizations found along the banks of the Tigris, the Euphrates, and the Nile. In these communities time was first measured, mathematics and astronomy begun; the basic principles of agronomy, of hydraulics, and pneumatics were evolved. The

Greeks, seeking to discover the precise nature of the phenomena around them, made extraordinary advances in almost every branch of science, particularly in geometry, arithmetic, mechanics, hydrostatics, astronomy, and physiology. In their logical progression of thought lies the origin of the western scientific method. In the history of scientific development the two centuries 330 to 130 B.C. stand out as a great landmark. The Saracen civilization of the early Middle Ages, stretching from the Indus to Spain, added to the almost forgotten scientific legacy of Greece. For long periods the light of learning, scientific inquiry, and intellectual curiosity, which the Arabs kept burning at the Moorish University of Cordoba in Spain, cast its bright rays across a darkened Europe. Arabic scholars introduced to the West 'arabic' numerals, algebra, and other fundamentals of the science of mathematics, some of which they had themselves taken from India; alchemy, astronomy and medicine were also advanced. From the fall of the Roman Empire until the sixteenth century the West was debtor to the East. Then Europe shed its inertia. Slowly, imperceptibly, the tide turned.

The origins of Europe's reawakening reach far beyond the sixteenth century. Medieval Europe did not suddenly emerge from complete darkness. Europe's rise and expansion in the world is seen as an incident in a long chain of events. It was not Europe which created a world economy; all past efforts, all civilizations and cultures, helped to prepare the way for Europe's conquest of so much of the world. The great Christian crusades are but one expression of the growing intellectual and religious ferment at work in Europe. As early as the twelfth century one can detect a quickening of Europe's economic pulse in parts of Italy (in Venice, and later Florence, Genoa, Pisa, and Milan), and Flanders (in Bruges, Ghent, and Ypres), the Netherlands (in Amsterdam and Rotterdam), and in many German cities of the North (among them Lübeck and Hamburg). When the floodgates of Europe's creative energy were opened during the Renaissance there resulted not only a questioning of religious traditions which culminated in the Reformation, but a questioning and re-appraisal of all traditions. The sixteenth, seventeenth, and eighteenth centuries witnessed momentous intellectual and scientific developments. The traditional notions of gravity, space, time, and power were overthrown. Gradually, some of the physical laws that govern the universe were understood. Meanwhile there grew up within Europe industrial and manufacturing power greater than the world had known before and upon which Europe's wealth and influence would eventually rest. There followed first in Europe in the nineteenth and then in the world in the twentieth century, the material and social changes collectively known as the Industrial Revolution. All these changes help to account for the quite unprecedented belief held by Europeans, that man's earthly destiny rests not in God's hands but in his own.

Yet the origins of European civilization and the tradition it has created in the world are religious as well as scientific. Dazzled by the marvels of contemporary science, we Europeans have forgotten that our heritage is the Graeco-Roman culture, fused with Christian rules of conduct, and (for some) the Christian form of worship. Europe's impact in the world during the past two or three centuries cannot be understood without realizing that Christianity did not begin as a purely spiritual religion and was then corrupted to incorporate a material view of the world. The religious influences of early technical developments in the West are manifest. All is touched with the hand of God. The Christian interpretation of history is both a spiritual ideal and a material process. Christian doctrine makes no attempt to separate spirit and matter. It rightly regards such a task as impossible. The 'materialism' of Christianity, the stress on man's earthly as well as his heavenly lot, is there from the very beginning. It is there in the biblical doctrine of Creation and of the sacraments as it is in the materials used for the mystery-rites and for its miracles. In Christian thought man is not a spirit imprisoned, as in certain other religions, within a body: man is a unity of body and spirit. Christian redemption is not simply redemption of the spirit but the resurrection of the body as well. In Christianity the spiritual is highest in the scale of values only because it was believed that the meaning and the purpose of the material element cannot be understood any other way. But there is no necessary conflict in Christianity between matter and spirit. Only in recent generations has there recurred in Europe a conflict between spirit and matter, between science and religion. Western civilization is referred to today as 'materialistic' simply because the earlier Christian order, which placed the spiritual ideal before the material element, has been reversed — material things are now first in the scale of values of the West. The worldliness of Christianity in contrast to Buddhism and Taoism was undoubtedly a factor in the conversion of such seventeenth-century Chinese scholar-officials as Hsü Kuang-ch'i and Li Chih-tsao.[1] To the devout Buddhist it is of little consequence what happens in this world. The Buddhist is encouraged to withdraw from normal social activities in a manner inconceivable to the Christian. To the Christian this world matters intensely. Nor does the Christian suffer an illusion about the actual world as does the Hindu. Nowhere in the *Bhagavad Gita* is there the sense of purpose, the sense of destiny contained in the Old Testament and the New. With examples before us of rapid economic development in non-Christian societies it behoves us not to exaggerate the influence of Christianity (or any other religion) upon economic change. Yet the

[1] Teng, Ssu-yü and J. K. Fairbank *China's Response to the West.* A documentary survey, 1839–1923 (Camb. Mass., 1954) p. 13.

student of economic development cannot help asking himself whether this 'materialistic' element in Christianity helps to explain why modern science and industry first appeared in the West rather than the East.

The impact which the Christian West has had upon the rest of the world springs not only from the 'materialism' of Christianity, but also from its progressiveness and its dynamism. Early Christianity possessed the same explosive vitality which the Prophet of Islam later gave to the Arab people. When it was founded, the Christian religion was completely hostile to all other religions and to the whole spirit of Roman civilization and of Imperial rule. It was not Christ but his apostle Paul who gave Christianity this intolerance of other creeds. Christianity accepted and thrived on martyrdom. In contrast to the ancient paganism, and the paganism of the new oriental religions which by the third century had become dominant in the West as well as in the East, Christianity was a religion of hope looking forward to the second coming of Christ and the establishment of the Kingdom of God on earth. Some of Christianity's spiritual dynamism, its aggressiveness and its intolerance invaded the temporal sphere and helped to provide the basis underlying the material progress of the West.

Christianity was not only 'materialistic' and dynamic, it also thought in terms of a common humanity. This impulse to find common ground with all men precedes the Christian era. Six centuries after the death of Christ the prophet Mohammed repeated the message of human brotherhood. The importance of Christianity is that it made this spirit, to help one's fellow-men, a world force. When Christ came to Jerusalem to fulfil in His person and His works the Law and the prophecies, He looked not to Jerusalem alone but to all mankind. To many Christians the central theme of Jewish history is world history; the crisis of Jewish history — the coming of the Messiah and his rejection by the Jewish leaders — is the crisis of world history. Henceforth, the message was directed not only to the Jews but to all men. This extrusive element in Christianity helps to explain how such a small and relatively recently established civilization in the West could impose its will upon great countries such as China and India which had led a powerful and cultured existence for thousands of years. Whether, as St. Paul tells us, the birth of Christ was 'in the fullness of time', or whether the success of Christianity in becoming a world force is to be explained by a piece of historical good fortune, i.e. the fact that the Graeco-Roman civilization was available to become the vehicle of the Christian message, is of no real consequence here. The outcome was the same: Greek philosophy provided the language through which the Church founded at Jerusalem could speak to all men; the Roman Empire, the greatest Empire until then, provided the channel through which the message of a humble Galilean in a remote province of the Roman Empire could reach all its dominions — a circumstance not without its disadvantage; for once having become identified with the Romans, Christianity found it difficult to pass beyond the frontiers of the Roman Empire.

This idea of a common humanity — of a passion for world brotherhood — is at the back of Europe's nineteenth-century civilizing mission to the world. It can be found in the words of the nineteenth century African explorer, Lieutenant Speke, who in 1855 expressed 'the hope . . . of raising his fellow-men in the scale of civilisation',[1] as it can be found in innumerable other nineteenth-century sources. The idea that under European tutelage all mankind would advance towards growing perfection cannot be dismissed as moral humbug. It is this Christian idea of a common humanity which helps to explain the European attitude towards commerce. In the case of the Portuguese in the sixteenth and seventeenth centuries, with their aim of a world kingdom under Christ, it is quite impossible to divorce religion from trade. Even to the Protestant British, who had no such religious ambitions, nineteenth-century commerce was not a matter of selling cheap European products to reluctant foreign buyers; it was a civilizing medium for the world, ' . . . by that means [the promotion of commerce]', wrote David Livingstone, 'we may not only put a stop to the slave trade, but introduce the Negro family into the body corporate of nations . . . Success in this . . . would lead in the course of time, to a much larger diffusion of the blessings of civilization than efforts exclusively spiritual and educational . . .'.[2] And hear Leopold II, King of the Belgians, speaking at the conclusion of the Berlin Conference of 1885: 'It is from here the light shines forth which for millions of men still plunged in barbarism will be the dawn of a better era. . . . Our cities are gorged with the products of the most diverse industries; nowhere will they find so great a market to absorb them. The most intelligent of our youth demands wider horizons on which to expand their abounding energy. Our working population will derive from the virgin regions of Africa new sources of prosperity and render more in exchange.'[3] The good that Leopold did has largely been forgotten; only his mistakes in the Congo live on.

European dynamism was a strange mixture of God, greed, and glory; of gunpowder and the Gospel. However badly the white man behaved in Africa, the hope that legitimate commerce would one day replace slavery and barbarism never died. Trade in goods should replace the traffic (especially in Africa) in human beings. This view sometimes gave a cloak of respectability to European piratical tendencies. In this respect, what distinguishes European civilization from preceding civilizations is that it

[1] Quoted in Richard F. Burton, *First Footsteps in East Africa* (Everyman's Library, 1924), p. 333.

[2] *Missionary Travels and Researches in South Africa* (London, 1857), p. 28.

[3] G. Oppelt, *Léopold II, Roi des Belges, chef de l'état indépendent du Congo* (Bruxelles, 1885).

hoped not only to exploit the world but to build a better world. The stress in nineteenth-century Europe was not laid on European harmony, but on world harmony. The world view (the-all-things-for all-men attitude) grew in strength in Europe throughout the nineteenth century and expressed itself in the most extraordinary manner. To take only two examples, it can be seen at work in the principles laid down for the use of the European-created Suez Canal, as it can be seen in the terms agreed upon by European nations for the use of the Congo River. The concern for a world system of law and order that would benefit all men alike sprang from Europe's Christian background. It can be found expressed in the deliberations of the Berlin Congress of European powers in 1884–5. The standards proclaimed were largely European orientated, and the acts of the Europeans in their colonial empires often belied their words. Yet during the period of European aggrandizement and expansion it is impossible to separate the religious from the non-religious forces at work. Paradoxically, the Christian Church and its foreign missions had a greater degree of success in transmitting western materialism, with its growing emphasis upon superior weapons, productive methods, and an ever-widening commerce, than it did in transmitting its own spiritual message.

The difficulty, nay, the impossibility, of separating the religious from the material forces from the eighteenth century onwards can be seen in the growing role given to the individual. The new trust placed in the power of the individual in place of the older forms of established authority, such as the family, tribe, clan, church, or feudal system, was partly the result of western economics and western rationalism which tended to dissolve the traditional bonds of these older groups. Under the 'enlightened' revolutions of the eighteenth and nineteenth centuries, right became what the individual conscience determined; truth what the individual reason recognized. This is partly the philosophy expressed in the American Declaration of Independence (1776) and the French Declaration of the Rights of Man (1789). Yet the new emphasis placed upon the role of the individual was also partly the result of Christianity and the Christian missions in the world. To the Christian — and here Christianity is akin to earlier Buddhism — it was the individual soul that was sacred, the highest moments of the Christian's life were those spent in communion with God; man's final and eternal end was life with God; salvation, like guilt, could only be comprehended by the Christian in individual terms. God helped him who helped himself. Until the coming of Christianity the emphasis lay with groups and classes, with monarchs and leaders, with rich men and poor men. It was Christianity which first attached importance to the individual human being on account of his individual human person and for no other reason. Is it possible that in doing so Christianity helped to create the excessive individualism against which it preached?

From these scientific and religious origins was born the western idea of progress: a continuous, cumulative expansion of man's control over his environment. In its vigour, optimism, confidence, egalitarianism, and enterprise this idea reached its peak in Europe before the outbreak of the First World War. A little more knowledge, it was thought, a little more rational spirit of inquiry and understanding, a little more education, a little more science and technology, and there was no limit to what man might achieve. Everything was susceptible to improvement if the laws that govern change were understood. From these origins came the feverish restlessness, insatiable curiosity, diversity, and dynamism of European man. To strive to discover the sources of the waters of the White Nile in the nineteenth century, as Speke did, or to conquer outer space, as European man in America and Russia has done more recently, is to be peculiarly European. Among other things, it was this vigour, this spirit of inquiry, this urge to expand, this sense of adventure, which enabled the European to set his impress upon the world. 'Im Anfang war die Tat',-'in the beginning was action'.[1] This emphasis upon purposive action which Goethe expressed in *Faust* might be used to describe the genius of European civilization. It is not discovery or originality that marks off the Europeans from those who preceded them, it is energy — an almost demoniac energy to mould the world to its will. It was this which enabled Europe to arise out of darkness and enjoy its moment as the leader of the human race. This western idea of progress, this idea that 'what is not, can be', this acceptance of change as a part of a common process of thought, has been taken over by many Americans, Asians, and Africans and now dominates in the United States and Soviet Russia, the most powerful nations in the world.

So great has been the dynamism of the West during the European Age, so enormous and rapid the material changes it has brought about, that there are some who fear that it has caused a shift in emphasis in the world from quality to quantity. It might just as reasonably be argued that western productiveness diffused to the world offers the hope of great qualitative as well as quantitative changes. Yet no other civilization has placed so much emphasis upon precision, upon numbers and counting, upon production and output, upon time and speed, upon individual rights and acquisitiveness, and upon the all-eclipsing standard of living.

Europe's influence in the world grew out of both a scientific and a Christian background. When Europe's influence was growing, these two forces were closely aligned. There was an essential unity between them. In contrast, science and Christianity are thought of today, when the European age perhaps draws to its close, as forces opposed to each other, or at least they are thought of as separate forces. Science and religion now draw

[1] Erich Trunz (ed.), *Goethes Faust* (Hamburg, 1959), p. 44.

apart as, two centuries ago, science and philosophy drew apart. The conflict between science and religion in the West was foreshadowed in the work of several European writers. Among them were Francis Bacon, essayist and writer on scientific method. Also important were René Descartes, whose teaching earned for him the condemnation of many of the most influential of his countrymen, Thomas Hobbes who, in his *Leviathan*, raised the sovereign state as a 'mortall God', and Richard Overton, practical materialist and revolutionary, whose treatise *Man is mortal in all respects* was published in 1643. Simon de Laplace found it unnecessary, much to the consternation of Napoleon Bonaparte, to include any hypothesis of deity in his *System of the World*. Auguste Comte, John Stuart Mill, and Herbert Spencer contributed to a philosophy of evolution based on natural laws and reason. Yet the conflict between science and religion became explicit only in the nineteenth-century work of Charles Darwin, whose *Origin of Species* presented the concept of spontaneous evolution by natural selection. Darwin's laws of organic nature were quantitative and mechanical. They expressed a determinism alien to the Christian mind. His conclusion that 'as natural selection works solely by and for the good of each being, all corporeal and mental endowments will tend to progress towards perfection'[1] strengthened western man's belief in progress — but this was man-made, nature-made progress, without supernatural assumptions or aid. The conflict between the spirit of man and his material environment was further aggravated by Marx who claimed scientific authority for his discovery of an economic law of motion, as Darwin had previously discovered the laws of biological evolution. To Marx, drawing upon Hegel, the process of history is fundamentally a dialectic (a conflict of opposites producing progress); history is the history of the economic process, not of the working out of God's Divine Will; all is derived from the material conditions of life; all values are man-made. Yet even Marx never shook himself free of the Judaic and the Christian past. The eventual and inexorable destruction of the bourgeoisie by the proletariat was simply another way of restoring the chosen people (in this case) in an earthly rather than a heavenly kingdom.

Under these and other nineteenth-century secular influences — the effect of which has only been felt in recent decades — western ideas about man's ability to determine material progress were strengthened still further and given to the world.

* * *

The application of the western idea of progress can be seen through the impact of certain particular ideas. Not least important has been the

[1] Charles Darwin, *The Origin of Species* (Everyman's Library, 1951), p. 462.

introduction of European ideas concerning property rights and land ownership. Ignoring the numerous forms which property had assumed in the world — even within a community — the European administrator introduced his own crude ideas and rigid rules, with a subsequent loss to non-European societies of social cohesion and social stability. In contrast to the more predominant and often changing forms of land tenure, based on craft, creed, village, tribal, feudal, and monarchic custom, the European administrator, often ignoring the social and historic circumstances of the territory over which he ruled, introduced the western concept of individual 'ownership' of an 'estate' which could be transferred, bought, sold, and mortgaged by individual contract. The introduction of something resembling the English landlord system into India is a case in point. What had been the concern of the village community gradually became the private property of a newly created landowner. Land, like labour and capital, became a factor of production. Having its price like other factors it was put to the best economic use. This was an attitude totally alien to many parts of the world. Even where land was alienable before white intrusion, its transfer was strictly controlled by tradition and social custom. Sometimes the moving frontier of an imperial domain, as in India, enabled the European to learn from his experience. Yet so varied were the conditions, so disparate and loosely connected the regions, that the experience gained in one province of India was of little value in the administration of another province. In assuming uniformity where it often did not exist, in divorcing economic motives from the social environment, in emphasizing the individual against the group and the social character of ownership, in ignoring native traditions, the European administrator produced the same conditions of social turmoil which had afflicted European society in earlier centuries. These conditions have still to appear in many parts of Asia and Africa. Over most parts of Africa, despite the intrusion of western nations, the indigenous customs and laws which govern the division, ownership, and use of land and natural resources remain. Over most of the non-white world these indigenous customs provide a bar to modern enterprise.

From Europe also came the idea of a self-regulating open market for individual wage-labour. The West could never hope to mould the world to its will unless the derogatory implications traditionally attached to work and labour were removed, and an improved system of labour control was devised. The traditional forms of labour organization based on tribal authority, craft, slavery, and serfdom could not meet capitalist Europe's needs as efficiently as a wage system in which labour was increasingly bought and sold by money payments like any other commodity or service. The path that leads from tribal customs to the western wage system is neither short nor direct, but wherever European influence has been felt in the world it has resulted in a weakening of traditional and environmental factors in favour of a rationally ordered, time-keeping, money-wage, work system in which output is all-important. In this respect, the origins of the Industrial Revolution are more likely to be found in the changing forms of labour organization and employment than in the changing forms of motive power. First came changes in factory organization and labour control, and only then was it thought necessary to introduce and develop in general manufacture the power of steam. It is the West which first divorced work from other communal activities; it is the West which first placed such enormous importance on human employment. The so-called 'labour movement' did not exist until the West created it.

Although the older forms of labour organization existing in other continents were looked upon by some Europeans as uncivilized and degrading, as well as inefficient, they often proved to be less repressive than the European system of wage-labour; they were certainly more personal and often more humane than the European system came to be. The history of Asia and Africa shows that when sufficient numbers of free labourers were not forthcoming the European was prepared to resort to forms of compulsion — often to the pecuniary benefit of native labour contractors — difficult to distinguish from the slavery European governments had formally abolished.

Economically, the introduction of the European system of wage payments was probably more efficient; the loss was felt socially and culturally. The distress experienced by the peasantry and the labouring classes of north-west Europe in earlier times was felt in many parts of the world as European expansion and European dynamism brought great changes to all human life. The expropriation of land in Europe in the eighteenth and nineteenth centuries was repeated in Africa and Asia in the late nineteenth and the early part of the twentieth century. In the name of economic efficiency, by fair means or foul, the peasant and the tribesman were dispossessed of their individual, family, or tribal ownership of land. In capitalist (and increasingly today in socialist) countries the dispossessed peasant has one alternative open to him: to work for money wages in one form or another. Only by transferring labour from the land to the factory, so the argument goes, can the maximum use of human factors be made. The rural economic revolution taking place in the world today is an exceptionally rapid and ruthless application of a similar rural economic revolution that was spread over three centuries of western European history. Yet one should not exaggerate the changes that have taken place; the self-subsisting peasant is still the norm, not the exception. The vast mass of mankind still know nothing of the western wage system.

Writing at the time when European ideas were actively changing the world, Marx and Engels, in 'The Communist Manifesto' of 1848, rightly appealed to the 'workers of the world'. They emphasized the world rather than the nation because they saw all too clearly that the spread of European capitalism and European systems of production were creating social problems of a world-wide nature. Capitalism was the mainspring of western effort. The world was being transfigured by the West because it was the West which first developed a market-orientated, capitalist economy. Later in the century (1869) was formed the first Workers Internationale. No society has made the transfer from a pre-industrial economy to a capitalist industrial economy without great hardship and suffering. And the process continues. Even today, in the newly developing regions of Africa and Asia, one is struck by the similarity between the attitudes of certain native leaders, especially the intellectuals in government, and the most heartless, ambition-steeped factory masters and overseers of England a century and a half ago. Seemingly, some men must always pay the price of other men's ambitions. Yet in the nineteenth century, when the 'manifesto' was being written, little was done to lessen the evils of transition. Marx and Engels (and many Christian social thinkers, among them the German Catholic pioneer, Wilhelm Emmanuel von Ketteler) protested against the lamentable social abuses of European liberal-capitalism, with its emphasis upon individual initiative and its system of individual wage contract. In their belief nineteenth-century capitalism merely exchanged one form of slavery and serfdom for another. In 'Erewhon' Samuel Butler provided a remedy for the slavery of wage labour: destroy the machine, forbid its use.

As well as introducing great changes in land ownership and labour organization, the Europeans also introduced great changes in the use of money. Indeed, these changes are part of each other. Money had never had the dominant role in the world which the Europeans gave it. It had always existed in one form or another but, in place of several scales of value within a society, the Europeans substituted one monetary scale — an all-purpose money. The use of money — and, incidentally, the need to work for money wages — was encouraged by the direct systems of taxation (such as the head, hut, and gun taxes) imposed by western man in an effort to get the native to contribute towards the expenses of administration. As transactions were gradually turned into monetary transactions, and money was increasingly used as credit and capital, pre-monetary societies — societies where money had only been of incidental importance — were drawn into the orbit of a money economy. Exchange economies replaced subsistence economies, and the growth and distribution of wealth in monetary terms in non-European societies was radically altered. In a hundred different ways, that which had been held rigid by tradition and custom was dissolved by the European idea of an all-purpose money, which could buy and sell anything.[1] The more stress placed upon monetary wealth the more the absence of it came to be identified with what western economists, with extraordinary historical naïvety, called 'backwardness'. Where tribes were reluctant to become involved with the European idea of cash crops and market economies, laws were enacted obliging each tribal community to grow cash crops where produce could be marketed.

The increasing use of money also led the Europeans to form huge fictitious bodies called corporations with vast capital resources drawn from many parts of society. Powerful as this European idea has been in assisting the economic development of the world, the social implications, in all lands, of mobilizing great quantities of impersonal capital (the major concern being the dividend it can earn) are only now coming to be recognized. So huge have some of these corporations become that they represent a state within a state.

Whether dealing with the distribution and employment of land or labour, or the functions of money and wealth, an increasing number of western Europeans in the nineteenth century believed that their own and other people's economic needs would best be met by the unhindered forces of supply and demand. The rallying cry of this movement was 'Laissez faire, laissez passez!' — freedom to manufacture, freedom to trade. Especially important in England was the ideal of 'Free Trade'. 'Free Trade' was identified with civilization; out of greater international co-ordination would come the economic cosmos of the world; 'Free Trade' was peace and progress; 'Free Trade' would provide a natural harmony and order in human affairs. It was remarked above that much of the nineteenth-century European attitude towards commerce was enlightened self-interest. Britain in its trade policy was by no means altruistic; it was not regard for great economic truths or high moral purpose that led Britain to abandon the protection of its agriculture, industry, and shipping; it was the hope of economic gain. Yet some of the noblest and ablest minds in Britain believed in the dream of 'Free Trade' as they believed in Europe's civilizing mission to the world — and not for pecuniary reasons alone. In England at this time there was no conflict between the struggle for freedom of the intellect and the freedom of trade.

'Free Trade' proved to be an illusion. Its fault was the overwhelming importance it gave to economics; especially its attempt to apply to the world something that was built up on premises specifically English. But it was never a mean illusion, and it helped to strengthen the commercial ties binding nation to nation. Its influence extended far beyond Britain and the West. The impress of English liberal thinkers, such as Hume,

[1] Paul Bohannan, 'The Impact of Money on an African Subsistence Economy', *The Journal of Economic History*, vol. xix, Dec. 1959, no. 4, pp. 491–503.

Smith, Mill, and Bentham, is not only to be found on England's commercial policy in the nineteenth century; it is clearly marked on the post-reconstruction period (after 1868) of Japanese history.

Of particular importance in assessing the impact of European ideas in the world has been the introduction to other lands of European systems of administration. It is the West that over the past century has imparted to other societies (or revived) the art of government at local, regional, and national levels, the art of economic planning for an entire society, the art of public accounting and treasury control, the art of central administration and decision-making. The systematic development of administrative procedures in the European colonial empires is one of the most recent, and perhaps one of the most worthwhile contributions made by the Europeans to the welfare of their dependent peoples. It contrasts sharply with the arbitrariness of earlier periods of European expansion. Even in early Spanish America, where efforts were made to keep power under central state control, the isolation of the various regions meant inevitably that administrative decisions depended on the wilfulness of local officials. Of all the European nations perhaps Britain knew best how to produce a race of colonial administrators, most of whom were not only efficient but, even more strangely, against the backcloth of the past, remarkably dedicated to the people whom they governed, self-effacing and incorruptible. The administrative systems introduced from the West reflected the extension of the European idea of a centralized state authority in place of that of the clan, tribe, and religion, the substitution of written for verbal arrangements, the desire for uniformity, and the growth of secularization. The establishment of powerful European-controlled central governments enabled European administrators to establish — in place of haphazard tribal arrangements — certain fixed tribal boundaries. Under European administration some countries were set down on paper for the first time. In parts of Africa, Asia, and America the first written records of land ownership and tenure were prepared. Boundary disputes which had formerly been settled by age-old customs of oath-taking and curse-making, the direct use of force, or prolonged discussion leading to compromise, were now settled by western methods of administrative justice. Frontiers were laid down for the new countries which appeared in the nineteenth and twentieth centuries; political and administrative machinery was devised. An efficient machinery of revenue-collection was evolved. Uniform and certain law, one of the foundation stones of the western way of life, took the place of time-honoured custom, often based on land ownership. The introduction of the European idea of the impersonal rule-of-law, coupled with the increased power of the new European-controlled governments to enforce it, put an end to much mutually destructive inter-tribal warfare.

Out of western administration sprang nation-wide political organizations and, for many countries in Asia and Africa, eventually national political independence. Nationalism — the idol of the twentieth century — is far older than the European Age, but it was powerfully stimulated by European systems of administration; nationalism is probably stronger today than it has ever been. For instance, it was the introduction of a uniform rule-of-law into India (though no Briton should delude himself into thinking that the Pax Britannica brought peace and order for the first time to India), together with the introduction of the English language and western liberal thought, which enabled that country to achieve administrative unity and eventually political independence. This despite the efforts of many British officials in India to resist change. Among the earliest champions of the freedom of the press in India were Englishmen; the first newspaper was started by an Englishman in Calcutta in 1780; the first Indian-owned and -edited newspaper was published (in English) in 1818. The Congress Party, which eventually succeeded in its struggle for independence, was greatly assisted at its outset by Englishmen. It is not possible to understand the history of India in modern times without taking account of the tremendous impact of western liberal ideas, especially those which sprang from eighteenth-century European Enlightenment.

The secularizing influence of western administration and western legal institutions is widespread in the world. Japan's dependence on western systems of law is well-known. In China the impact of western legal ideas served to undermine the ethical basis of the Confucian state without successfully establishing western legal institutions and principles. Perhaps the secularizing influence of the West can best be seen in the experience of Islamic countries. Before these countries were subjected to western influence, law, like everything else, was part of religion. Human beings were believed to be living under the rule of Allah, as divinely revealed through the prophet Mohammed in the Koran. The Moslem religion entered into the practical day-to-day details of living. The Islamic code was the guide to proper conduct in both private and public fields of activity. Under western influence this was gradually changed. As in Europe in earlier centuries, a division appeared between the powers of Church and State, and the religious was eventually subordinated to the temporal power. While these European secular influences were largely imposed upon non-European peoples, there are examples where western secular ideas have been willingly accepted. During the 1920's and the 1930's Moslem Turkey was so eager to westernize itself under Mustafa Kemal Atatürk that it openly declared itself a secular state of western type. In 1928, the Ottoman Turks, losing faith in the traditions of their own civilization, abandoned the Arabic alphabet in favour of the Latin alphabet. The same willingness to westernize is evident in Moslem Egypt and Pakistan today.

And the questioning of ancient traditions in favour of western forms extends far beyond the Islamic world. Even Communist China is being forced to romanize Chinese writing in the interests of efficiency.

* * *

The impact of Europe in the world has pervaded the economic and social conditions of the whole human race. It has affected every branch of human behaviour, including other people's art, religions, politics, methods of government, the organization of labour and capital, languages, literature, dress, marriage customs, and the civil and penal codes of law. Too often we forget that international law is a western device. In many countries of the world a stroke of the western administrator's pen has created new rights, new crimes. Western judicial ideas in landholding, labour contracts, taxation, forgery, native magic and witchcraft — to take several examples — were often imposed on an alien consciousness. This movement has changed the conditions of those living in countries where the European system of capital and industry prevails, as well as those living outside its ambit. The impact made by the migration of large numbers of Europeans to the temperate areas of America, Africa, Australasia, and Siberia during the nineteenth and twentieth centuries, should not be allowed to overshadow that made by much smaller numbers of Europeans whose influence has been felt during the past five hundred years in many parts of the non-white world. In great and ancient countries such as China and India, in the short span of several lifetimes, a handful of white men caused the disintegration of traditional social and ideological structures which had served enormous groups of the human race for thousands of years. It would, indeed, be vain of the white race to think that their fleeting impact has been sufficient to blot out the great and rich heritage of these ancient civilizations. Far from it. But the fusing of Asia's heritage with the new western ways has created a different Asia and a different world.

It is the purpose of the chapters that follow to show how Europe's impact was made. In doing so there will always be the danger of over-emphasizing Europe's contribution to world development. We shall always be in danger of ascribing to this imprecise thing we have chosen to call European 'impact' a distinct and separate effect that in the real world it could never have had. The development of the modern world is far too complex a process to yield itself to such simple analysis. For this reason it is worth repeating the thought expressed in the preface to this book that great as the achievements of the European Age have been they should not be allowed to blind us to the cumulative developments of earlier epochs. Civilization was old long before the Europeans appeared. Those who would exaggerate Europe's contribution to mankind should dwell upon the richness and the enduring qualities of far older civilizations. Europe's achievements are not to be explained in terms of intellectual, material, or spiritual superiority. Europeans have transformed the material conditions of living in many parts of the world, but all the great revolutions of modern European history (French, Russian, Italian, and German) stand as a warning to anyone who thinks that Europeans have placed man in control of his destiny. All these revolutions have achieved results far different from those intended. Europeans like all men have stood upon the shoulders of others. No civilization has a monopoly of the noble things of life; no civilization carries the torch of humanity for long. In all things, even in many of the so-called Graeco-Roman-Hebraic characteristics which the Europeans identify exclusively with their own particular civilization, they have been men among men. Fixed concepts such as Orient and Occident cannot prevent the human family from being what it is: an organic whole.

The Europeans acted upon others and were themselves acted upon. The changes they introduced in the world sprang primarily from the shift in focus that they resolutely brought about. But these changes also sprang partly from the circumstances in which they found themselves. The Europeans were able to reach out from their small domains bordering upon the Asian land mass, and kindle a new flame of economic life in the world partly because it fell to them to play their part in the human drama at a time when epoch-making changes were about to take place. The moment had arrived in history when the scene was to shift from the nation to the world, when limited human and animal power was to give way to terrifying unlimited inanimate energy. All civilizations have transferred ideas about man, as well as ideas about art, science, and technology, but until the European Age no civilization had transferred them on a world-wide scale, with such speed, with such a degree of activity, or with such tremendous effect; in so many parts of the world Europe's intrusion shattered the traditional, static order of things. No civilization prior to the European had occasion to believe in the systematic material progress of the whole human race; no civilization placed such stress upon the quantity rather than the quality of life; no civilization drove itself so relentlessly to an ever-receding goal; no civilization was so passion-charged to replace what is with what could be; no civilization had striven as the West has done to direct the world according to its will; no civilization has known so few moments of peace and tranquillity. Even when the Europeans were most confident in putting abroad their idea that man is in charge of his earthly lot, history was mocking them. There have been imponderable forces at work in the European Age as in any other. But to say this will not lessen the attraction of the central western idea of progress one jot. It makes no difference to argue that much of the promised gold of progress has proved to be dust. Mankind is not drunk with this idea of progress because of what it has achieved in a material and physical sense, but because of what it promises. The idea that with western methods there might be removed from man the eternal haunting skeleton of want is so powerful that it might well, for a period, capture the imagination of the whole human race.

Today, European man is being driven back from parts of Africa and Asia; Europe's nineteenth-century civilizing mission to the world is passing into the hands of European man in North America; a Peace Corps has been formed to carry 'the white man's burden'. Yet western methods of creating wealth and power are sought after more eagerly than ever before. It is not only the Japanese people who have copied western ways. The tendency to imitate is deep in man, especially to imitate those who can show their superiority in wealth and power as the West has done. Non-European countries today show a far greater determination to impose upon themselves western egalitarianism and western systems of industry than Europe showed in its greatest moment of power. The key to improved material standards remains the accumulated scientific and industrial knowledge of the West. The curious fact is that while the world strives to obtain the western machine and western standards of living, formal western economic and religious beliefs are either despised or ignored. In great parts of the non-European world today western capitalism is condemned as irrational and unjust; the earlier excessively individualistic principles of western capitalism which wrought so much change in the world are unacceptable to the more collectively-minded communities of Asia and Africa; the universal validity claimed for European economic and social ideas in the eighteenth, nineteenth, and the early part of the twentieth centuries — particularly the central idea of laissez-faire or liberalism in the economic sphere — is now disputed by European and non-European alike.

Whether the promise of Christianity to all mankind was as unfounded as western individualism, is a problem upon which it would be difficult to obtain agreement. By and large, Asians and Africans have only been attracted to the practical, material things of the West. Christianity did not capture the Asian or the African soul. Its success as a world religion might have been greater had it not been so closely identified with the West. (It seems strange, looking back, that the Europeans should have equated Christianity with their own customs and even their own dress). In Christianity, as in the western liberal democracy, the West has had little success in spreading its ideas. We cannot blame Asian and African leaders if they express concern about the stability of a civilization whose religious message is brotherly love and self-abnegation, and whose economic policy in Asia and Africa has often been greed.

In the age that witnessed the rise and expansion of Europe in the world, the religious and temporal ideas of the Europeans were inextricably linked. Even today western methods of creating wealth cannot be introduced to non-western societies without affecting their culture and religion. Europe no longer thrusts Christianity upon non-European peoples, but it still affects their religious beliefs. The western machine makes its spiritual impact whether accompanied by formal Christianity or not. This, for instance, is the source of the conflict between European productive methods and the traditional Mohammedan religion in Pakistan today. The building up of a western secular state in Turkey under Mustafa Kemal Atatürk is an earlier version of the same story. And the example is repeated in other parts of the world. The impact of western science and technology cannot be divorced from the rest of life. It is impossible to introduce western productive methods and western standards of economic efficiency and at the same time exclude western cultural influences. Once the door is open to the West, Europeanization to a greater or a lesser degree follows. Even nineteenth-century Japanese leaders, whose only desire was to obtain western material power, were unable to exclude the cultural influences of the West. The Japanese have found, as other societies are finding today, that European standards of economic efficiency are accompanied by European ideas concerning the capacity and the needs of man. By their very nature these ideas must far exceed the economic data set down in this book.

Chapter II

THE COURSE OF EMPIRE

The drama of world colonization by European nations was well under way long before the period with which this book deals. More than two centuries earlier, by the Treaty of Tordesillas (1494), the Portuguese and the Spaniards in the first crusading age of discovery had, with astonishing presumption, divided the world between them. By the issue of a bull by Pope Alexander VI Spain received a title to North and South America. Tiny Portugal inherited Africa, India, and the Spice Islands of the East. The papal line of demarcation was subsequently moved further west, bringing Brazil within the Portuguese sphere. Within a generation Portugal had established a chain of forts reaching from the Persian Gulf via the west coast of India and Ceylon to Malacca in present-day Malaya and later to Macao in China; Portuguese adventurers, steadily supported by their government, had appeared along the whole coast of Africa. Meanwhile, the Spaniards were exploring their equally enormous, fortuitously acquired, American empire. It does not lessen the grandeur of Spanish might or the subsequent majesty of their American empire to say that, so far as territorial aggrandizement is concerned, Spain's acquisition of so much of the Americas must surely be one of the greatest accidents in history.

The grand design was not merely to enrich the Iberian Peninsula with the wealth of the two Indies, of Africa, Asia, and the Americas, but — especially on the part of the Portuguese — to extend the Kingdom of God. Since the eleventh century the tide of Islam had begun to turn. Now the process quickened. Cordoba, European centre of Arab culture and civilization, had fallen in 1236. Spanish Granada, outpost of the Arab world in Europe, also fell to the Christians in 1492. Fifty years later, in 1542, St. Francis Xavier (co-founder with Loyola of the Society of Jesus) arrived at Goa, in India, to begin the conversion of the whole of Asia. The influence of these soldiers of Christ, joined with that of western merchants, was soon to be felt throughout the East.

By 1600 the Spaniards and the Portuguese had laid claim to domains stretching across the entire world. Yet when the power of the Iberian Peninsula was apparently at its greatest (Spain temporarily annexed Portugal in 1580 and, in so doing, benefited from centuries of Portuguese exploration) its decline had already begun. With the destruction of Spanish sea power by the British in 1588 Spain forfeited her leading position in Europe. Throughout the seventeenth and eighteenth centuries Spanish and Portuguese power declined. In the seventeenth century English (1600), Dutch (1602), and French (1604) East India Companies were formed to wrest the monopoly of eastern trade from the Portuguese. British and French efforts were concentrated on the sub-continent of India. The Dutch set themselves to gain control of the entire Portuguese East Indies. In 1613 the Dutch broke the British hold on part of Timor. Portuguese forces were defeated by the Dutch at Amboyna in 1605, Jakarta in 1619 and Malacca in 1641. In 1658 they drove the Portuguese from Jaffna, last Portuguese stronghold in Ceylon; by 1667 their arms had triumphed in the Celebes. In the same year (1667) the Dutch secured a trading-port on the east coast of Sumatra. By 1700 all that was left of the Portuguese East Indian empire was part of Timor. Of the great string of forts which Portugal had built from the Persian Gulf to the East Indies there remained only Goa, Daman, Diu, and Macao. The wonder is not that the Portuguese were able to hold their East Indian empire together for little more than a hundred years, but that so small a nation, relatively inferior in manpower, economic resources, and sea power, should have managed to control such a precariously held, scattered complex of commitments for as long as they did.

At the same time Spanish and Portuguese power was also being contested in Africa and the Americas. The British entered the slave trade of West Africa in the mid-sixteenth century. In 1595 the Dutch appeared on the African Guinea coast; in 1652 the Netherlands began its colonization of the Cape Province. By the mid-seventeenth century the French had staked a claim to territory at the mouth of the Senegal and in Madagascar. Other groups of Europeans, including Prussians and Scandinavians, sought to gain a foothold on the west coast of Africa. However, until the 'scramble' for African territory in the second half of the nineteenth century, most European nations were content to maintain a number of coastal stations and uphold their claims to a share of the slave trade. The interior of Africa remained closed.

The commercial and territorial monopoly of Spain and Portugal was more persistently contested in the Americas than in Africa. Throughout the sixteenth, seventeenth, and eighteenth centuries the pressure of the other European nations was relentless, and the challenge grew as the sea and land power of the Iberian Peninsula declined. The inheriting by the king of Spain of the Crown of Portugal in 1580 helps to explain the subsequent invasion of Brazil by Dutch troops, as well as the systematic territorial expansion inland by the Portuguese 'Bandeirantes' (literally 'the flag-carriers'). The Dutch at one time (1635–44) invaded the northern half of Brazil, but were eventually defeated by a Luso-Brazilian force, led by Matias de Albuquerque a European, Henrique Dias a Negro, and

Filipe Camarão an Indian. It was an unusual experience for the Dutch to suffer defeat at the hands of such a polyglot force; but combined action of Europeans, Negroes and Indians forshadowed the future of the Brazilian nation. In any event, it was one thing for the contesting European powers to snatch coastal stations from each other in the east, and another thing for them to try to reduce the Spanish and Portuguese land empires in the Americas. Successful encroachments were made in the seventeenth century by Britain, France, and the Netherlands in the Guianas and in the West Indies. But these gains were not vital to either side. The western European nations never succeeded in breaking the imperial might of Spain and Portugal in the Americas. This was only done by Latin Americans of Spanish and Portuguese extraction in the revolutionary movements of the early nineteenth century. Indeed, there was a period in the second half of the eighteenth century, after the temporary elimination of France by the Seven Years' War, when it looked as if Spain, under the resolute leadership of Charles III (1759–88), might recover some of its old strength, but by then Spain did not even possess a navy strong enough to protect its shortest lines of communication with Central America. It was thanks to the rivalry existing between the other powers, rather than to its own might and consistency, that the Spanish empire lived on. The reign of Charles III proved to be only a temporary lull in the gradual decline of Spanish power.

For the Dutch to triumph in the eastern seas required more than the defeat of the Portuguese. No sooner had the Dutch gained ascendancy over the Portuguese than they were attacked by the other contestants for world supremacy, the French and the British. (Less influential in this struggle for world power were the Danes, the Swedes, and the Germans.) Three naval wars with the British (1652–74) and almost continuous fighting with the French (1672–1713) undermined Dutch strength. After the war of the Spanish Succession (1702–13) there was a marked and steady economic decline of Dutch power in India. Fearing that the Dutch might lend assistance to England's American colonists in their struggle for independence, England declared war on Holland in 1780. The outcome was the loss of some Dutch possessions in the West Indies, as well as the end of Dutch monopoly in the eastern seas. When the Dutch East India Company's charter expired in 1799 it was not renewed. The Company had probably reached its zenith a century earlier. With its dissolution a phase in Dutch history ended. Further setbacks came during the Napoleonic Wars. France occupied the Netherlands; out of fear of France, the British seized the Dutch Indies and the Cape. When the East Indies were restored to the Dutch at the Convention of London in 1814, Dutch power in the world had long since passed its peak. For more than a century the continuance of Dutch imperial rule had depended upon the protective shield of superior British sea power. Yet any efforts the British made to help the Dutch were more from fear of renewed French aggression than love of the Dutch. Unlike the Catholic Portuguese, the Protestant Dutch never tried to establish a universal empire of Christ. Nor, at the outset, were they hungry for power. Like the British, their central purpose was trade. Upon that basis, the small, hardy, resourceful Dutch nation, faced by incredible handicaps, had finally dominated the carrying trade of the world. Dutch pre-eminence rested upon commercial supremacy; with the loss of that supremacy the Dutch star began to fall.

The world-wide struggle between the European powers was now dominated by the British and the French. In this struggle, the campaigns of Wolfe in North America and Clive in India in the mid-eighteenth century laid the basis of British supremacy. The triumph of British arms over the Moghul Emperor at Buxar in Bengal was one of the decisive battles in establishing British rule in India. Yet India's fate was sealed by internal divisions and rivalries rather than by British fortitude or British military skill. By 1763, after seven years' far-flung struggle with the French, the British were triumphant in America and Asia. France ceded all claims to Canada. In India, French authority was recognized only in the tiny stations of Pondicherry and Chandernagore. The French Compagnie des Indes was formally dissolved in 1769. Neither the revolt of Britain's own American colonies, which in 1783 became the United States, nor the mischief-making of France, Holland, and Spain during the American War, weakened Britain in its position as the leading colonial and maritime power of the world. And five years after Britain was forced to concede defeat to the newly-founded United States and the colonists' European allies in 1783, it made good the territorial losses of the American colonies by sending the first white settlers to the enormous island continent of Australia. Secure in overwhelming strength accruing from its commercial and industrial development, Britain finally defeated France at sea at Trafalgar in 1805, and on land, at Waterloo, in 1815. Little more than a century before (May 1707) the English and the Scots, perhaps conscious of the greatness of their destiny, had decided to call their united countries 'Great Britain'. Little more than a century later British strength was undermined by the catastrophe of the First World War. The year 1914 marks the beginning of the end of British world supremacy.

While the other European nations were engaged in the conquest of an overseas empire, the march of Muscovy to the Pacific Ocean continued without pause. Since the sixteenth century the expansion of Russia, by military conquest, by peaceful annexation, and by pioneer settlements, never ceased. In the continuous expansion of their rule, in their ability to penetrate and to settle enormous and inhospitable areas of the earth, the

Russians played a remarkable if neglected role in European expansion. Like the Canadians and the Americans, the Russians were first drawn to the Pacific Ocean by the search for furs. In the sixteenth and seventeenth centuries fur was Russia's most important single item in its domestic and foreign trade. But the Russians not only sought furs, they also sought national aggrandizement.

The extension of Russian rule over non-Russian people began with the conquest of Kazan, capital of a Moslem Tatar Khanate on the middle Volga, in 1552. This was followed by the conquest in 1554–6 of a second Tatar Khanate, Astrakhan on the lower Volga, which gave the Russians access to the Caspian Sea and the Caucasus. Throughout the sixteenth and seventeenth centuries the Muscovite state extended and consolidated its holdings in Siberia. In 1587 the city of Tobolsk was established on the River Irtysh. Tomsk was built on the Tom in 1604; Yeniseisk on the Yenisei in 1619. The Lena River was reached in 1628, and Yakutsk established on its banks in 1632. By 1649 the continent had been crossed and Okhotsk founded on the Pacific seaboard. The Russian tide then swept southwards to the banks of the Amur. For two centuries the Russians were held by the Manchus. The Treaty of Nerchinsk, concluded in 1689, which demarcated the Russo-Chinese frontier and left the Amur region in Manchu control, was the first treaty concluded between China and the West. Contained in the south by the Manchus, the Russians turned their attention to the north. In 1707 the Kamchatka Peninsula, north of the Japanese Islands, was declared Russian territory. By 1741 the Russians had crossed the Bering Straits into Alaska.

After reaching the Pacific in the mid-seventeenth century the Russians extended their territories in Europe. By the early years of the nineteenth century Czarist power was supreme in the Ukraine, in the Baltic States, in Finland, and in Poland.

* * *

The high peak of European expansion was undoubtedly the nineteenth century. Yet when the century opened, the overseas empires of the various European powers were not altogether dissimilar from the scattered trading empires of earlier times. Only as the century wore on were the vast and relatively unoccupied grasslands of the northern and southern hemispheres penetrated and settled by the white man. Only in the second half of the century was the full impact of the European felt in the tropics of Africa and Asia. Only then was it possible to draw together administratively, through improved transport and communications, the far-flung parts of the European empires. While there was a consistent record of expansion throughout the first half of the nineteenth century, it was not until the later decades that the pace quickened and the enormous expansion of the

European powers took place. The 'scramble' for parts of Africa and Asia which began seriously in the 1870's was mostly completed by 1900.

The greatest influence upon the course of European empires in Asia in the nineteenth century was exercised by the British. Throughout the nineteenth century Britain extended its influence over the sub-continent of India. For the first time India became an appendage to another country thousands of miles away. The Indus Valley from Sind to Kashmir was occupied by the British between 1840 and 1850. In the 1850's Assam and Lower Burma were conquered; the closed door of Siam was opened. Baluchistan was added to the British Empire in 1876; Upper Burma was annexed in the 1880's. Tibet became a 'sphere of British influence' following the expedition under Younghusband in 1903–4. British influence had also been extended (in the 1820's) to Malacca and Singapore; in the 1840's, as a result of the First Opium War with China, Britain occupied the island of Hong Kong and gained access to a number of ports on the Chinese mainland. In the 1880's the Malay Protected States, Socotra, North Borneo Protectorate, Sarawak, and parts of New Guinea (Oceania) were added to the British Empire. From the 1880's until the end of the century Britain, together with France, Russia, Germany, the United States, and Japan, was busy marking out spheres of influence in China.

The only other power able to challenge Britain in Asia in the nineteenth century was Russia. Until, with supreme irony, fate threw them together as allies in the First and Second World Wars, Britain and Russia for a good part of the nineteenth century were deadly enemies. In the 1850's Britain had invaded the Crimea. In the 1870's the British had indulged in sword-rattling over Russian claims upon Turkey. Wherever the British and Russians met, there was friction. The real crisis in Anglo-Russian affairs came when the Russians, having penetrated Central Asia, reached the frontiers of Persia and Afghanistan. In Afghanistan Britain fought two disastrous wars (1839–42 and 1878–9) to block the Russian advance. Although almost 1,000 miles separated Russian and British troops stationed on the frontiers of Afghanistan, Britain was convinced that Russia intended to seize India.

There was also a clash of British and Russian interests in Persia. The Russians had defeated the Persians at Aslanduz in 1812 and at Ganja in 1826. Britain watched with growing anxiety as the Russians advanced through central Asia. The Khanate of Khiva fell to Russian arms in 1873; Bokhara fell in 1874, and Khokand in 1876. The occupation of the Merv oasis in southern Turkestan in 1884 brought Russia to the frontier of Persia. During the reign of Muzaffar Ud-Din (1896–1907) Anglo-Russian rivalry in Persia reached its most acute phase. Both countries would have driven the other out if they had had the strength to do so. The anarchy resulting from the Persian revolution of 1905, and the growing uncertainty regarding German intentions in south-west Asia forced them to come to terms with each other. In the agreement concluded between them in 1907, Persia was divided into British and Russian spheres of influence. The entire northern half of the country with approximately three-quarters of the population went to the Russians; Britain retained control of the Persian Gulf and the south-eastern part. The agreement also included recognition by Russia of Britain's predominant position in Afghanistan.

Held in central Asia by British power, the Russians extended their sway over eastern Asia. Ousted from the Amur Valley by the more powerful Manchus in the seventeenth century, the Russians returned in the nineteenth century. Urup, one of the Kurile Islands, was occupied in 1852. In 1853 Aleksandrovsk was founded on Castries Bay, and a post established on the western coast of Sakhalin, an island separated from the mainland by the narrow Tatar Strait. In 1858, when China was fighting both France and England, Russia extracted from China the Treaty of Aigun, whereby all the territory north of the Amur passed into Russian hands. China's attempts in the following year (1859) to dispute this treaty led to Russia's occupation of the whole of the maritime province of Manchuria. Russia now occupied all the sea coast north of Korea. In the 1870's northern Sakhalin was occupied. Only with their defeat by the Japanese in 1905 on land and sea was the Russian thrust in eastern Asia halted temporarily.

Most influential in determining French policy in Asia were the Catholic missionaries. It was due to the efforts of a great French missionary, Pierre Pigneau de Béhaine, that a treaty was signed in 1787 between the king of Cochin China and Louis XVI of France. French power in Asia in the nineteenth century extended throughout most of the territory later to be known as French Indo-China. By the middle of the nineteenth century, however, the missionaries had fallen out of favour with the Annamite Court. A number of executions, culminating in the death of the Spanish bishop of Tongking, resulted in Spanish and French armed intervention. Tourane on the Vietnamese coast was bombarded in 1858; Saigon was occupied in 1859. By the Treaty of Saigon in 1862 France obtained the three eastern provinces of Cochin China and greater freedom for western traders and Christian missionaries. Gradually, by the use of 'gun-boat diplomacy' common to the western powers at the time, France extended its control from Cochin China to Cambodia, Annam, and Tongking. In 1885, by the Treaty of Tientsin, a defeated China was compelled to recognize French control of Tongking. In 1887 the whole of this territory was administratively united as the Union Indo-Chinoise. Six years later, in 1893, France acquired a protectorate over Laos.

In the nineteenth century only the British could challenge French interests in Siam. In 1893, encouraged by the British, Siam began to use force in opposing French claims. Yet when it came to blows Britain was not prepared to fight for the nominal independence of Siam as it had fought for the nominal independence of those two other classic buffer states: Persia and Afghanistan. Siam was forced to yield to French claims. Three years later, in 1896, the French and the British tried to allay the growing suspicion they had of each other by formally guaranteeing the independence of Siam. By 1907, however, both powers thought it wise to be more specific. Siamese territory to the east of the Nam River was placed under French control, that west of the river, closer to Burma, was declared a British sphere of action.

Dutch imperial rule in the nineteenth century was largely confined to the islands of Sumatra and Java in the Malay Archipelago, restored to the Dutch at the close of the Napoleonic wars. In 1824 the British ceded Bencoolen (Sumatra) to the Dutch who reciprocated by giving up Malacca. From the 1820's until the 1880's native uprisings forced the Dutch to extend their control to the interior of both islands. The secession of Sarawak in northern Borneo to the British in the 1840's also encouraged them to extend their rule outside Java and Sumatra to southern Borneo, Bali, and Celebes. In 1859 they divided Timor and the neighbouring islands with the Portuguese. Until the Dutch East Indies were overrun by the Japanese in 1942, Dutch rule in the Netherlands Indies remained unchallenged.

* * *

Nineteenth-century European colonial history in Asia was especially significant for three great Asian nations: the Chinese, the Indians, and the Japanese. In particular, it is not possible to understand China's present antipathy to the West (including the U.S.S.R. and the U.S.A.) without knowing the history of western intrusion into China. If the story of western invasion into China has been told in some detail here, it is not only because of the size of China and the number of her people, but also because there is about the present situation much that is reminiscent of conditions prevailing a hundred years ago. Then, as now, China was conscious of the superiority of its age-old civilization and of its position as the centre of the universe. Then, as now, the Chinese Dragon breathed fire, and good men everywhere despaired of ever achieving a common understanding between East and West.

Western relations with China are far older than the nineteenth century. In the thirteenth century (in 1245) Pope Innocent IV had sent emissaries to Genghis Khan. Following closely came a Franciscan mission. But China was not prepared to tolerate 'barbarians from without'. With the fall of the Mongol dynasty and the succession of the native Ming dynasty in 1368, China severed her relations with the West. The next group of Europeans to penetrate the Chinese defences was led by the Jesuit Matteo Ricci. Coming by way of Canton and Nanking, Ricci eventually (in 1601) won toleration for the Jesuits at the Imperial Court at Peking. The Chinese were particularly impressed by the westerners' superiority in astronomy and mathematics, and it was largely because of the extraordinary scientific services rendered by the Jesuits to the Chinese Empire that European Catholics were tolerated. The missionaries outdid themselves in the success of their conversions and were bundled out of China in 1616. Gradually, however, they made their way back. There followed long periods of Christian toleration. Only in 1723, as a result of a bitter quarrel over Jesuit acceptance of Chinese rites towards Heaven, Confucius, and ancestor worship, as well as a growing conflict of imperial and papal authority, were Christian priests banished and the propagation of Christianity made illegal throughout the Chinese Empire. Now there was no slipping back into China. Only in the early years of the nineteenth century were Protestant missions (European and American) able to regain a foothold on the mainland. The pioneer was Robert Morrison (1782–1834) who reached Canton in 1807. Most of the missions, however, including the revived Catholic missions, had little opportunity to expand their evangelical and educational work until Britain's triumph over China in the Opium Wars of 1839–42. What had been foretold by those who had earlier opposed the introduction of Christianity into China had now come to pass. When, in the Uprising of 1900, the time came to pay off old scores it was the missionaries, whose influence in China had been felt over a longer period than that of the traders and concession hunters, upon whom the greatest blows fell.

The Opium Wars convinced China more than ever of the barbarian nature of western civilization. The Chinese had long been aware of the harmful moral and physical effects of opium: banned by the Emperor in 1729, opium was little known in China before British shipments from India (and smaller American shipments from Turkey) began arriving at the end of the eighteenth and the early part of the nineteenth centuries. Smuggling of opium was prohibited by Imperial Edict in 1808. The illegal trade in Indian opium had also reversed the age-long drain of bullion from the West. From the sixteenth until the late eighteenth century China's trade with the West in fine silks and porcelain, tea, and rhubarb had always been paid for by precious metals. In selling opium the West reversed the trend; China was now drained of silver. The real problem, however, was much more fundamental than the conditions of trade. For two hundred years since the Manchus had swept across the Great Wall in 1644, conquering all before them, China had followed a policy of deliberate isolationism. Its whole conduct was based upon the concept of the superiority of all things Chinese. China was the centre of the universe; all else was inferior and tributary. Unlike the Japanese, the Chinese did not have a tradition of borrowing from others. It wanted nothing of the upstart barbarian West except to be left alone. Seen in this light, the Opium Wars were an incident in the growing conflict between two entirely different civilizations. Opium was the pretext for western invasion of China.

In the humiliating Nanking Treaty of 1842, which followed the Opium Wars, China was forced to cede Hong Kong to Britain; the ports of Canton, Foochow, Amoy, Ningpo and Shanghai were opened to British trade and residence. The Chinese were required to pay a large indemnity (£21 million) for opium seized. In establishing a uniform maximum import tariff of about 5 per cent *ad valorem*, Britain ensured that its traders and manufacturers could enter the Chinese market at will. The other western powers were quick to exploit the bridgehead secured on the Chinese mainland. In 1844 the Americans and the French obtained the use of the same five 'treaty ports'. Belgium, Sweden, and Norway quickly obtained similar concessions. In 1851, a Russian trade mission was pressed upon the Chinese. Thanks largely to French efforts the persecution and intolerance shown by the Chinese to Catholic and Protestant groups was brought to an end. A new era opened in the history of the western religious missions in China. The principle of extra-territoriality, whereby foreigners in China could only be tried by their own courts and their own laws, was gradually extended to all western nations. The Opium Wars not only ensured the continuation of the opium trade — they legalized the commercial and religious penetration of China, and laid the foundations of much of the present misunderstanding between China and the West.

It was inevitable that hostilities would break out again, as they did at Canton in 1856, and that China would have to yield to even greater western demands. In 1858, by the Treaties of Tientsin concluded between China and Great Britain, France, the United States, and Russia, China was forced to agree to open eleven more ports to western traders, to establish foreign legations at Peking, and to permit the activity of foreign trade and Christian missions in the interior. The opium trade was legalized; western countries assumed control of all customs duties levied by China on foreign trade; a further large indemnity was demanded, as well as freedom for Chinese labourers to work in European colonial territories. The Chinese Court found these conditions unacceptable. In 1860, ostensibly as a result of the refusal of British demands for the admission of foreign diplomats to Peking, and the repulse of an attack upon the Taku forts before Tientsin, British and French troops marched upon Peking. The conduct of European troops in Peking only strengthened and deepened an already outraged Chinese sense of justice. Under the terms of the Treaty of Peking (1860) new commercial and religious concessions were extracted from the Chinese. As always, other western countries not directly engaged in the struggle were quick to exploit the situation. Russia pressed for the cession of the Chinese maritime province, and founded

Vladivostok. All too late, Chinese leaders began to study the sources of western superiority and to express a desire for western technology. For the next generation China was forced to yield to the claims of the western powers. There were further concessions in the seventies and eighties. Precipitating the unprecedented demands of the Great Powers upon Chinese territory in the nineties, was the Sino-Japanese War of 1894–5, resulting from more than a decade of rivalry between the Chinese and the Japanese in Korea.

Japan's gains under the Treaty of Shimonoseki of 1895 were considerable: China was forced to recognize the independence of Korea, which meant, in effect, that Korea passed under Japanese control, to cede to Japan the island of Formosa, the Pescadores Islands and the Liaotung Peninsula in southern Manchuria, and, following the example of the West, to grant to Japan a large indemnity ($180 million) and commercial privileges in four Chinese ports, as well as the use of Port Arthur. The Japanese victory over the Chinese not only aroused fear in the hearts of the Chinese but in the hearts of the European powers as well. Japan was therefore strongly 'advised' by Russia, Germany, and France (Britain chose to play a 'waiting game') to exchange her newly-won Liaotung Peninsula for a larger indemnity. Faced by such a show of power, and unable to secure Britain's support, Japan was compelled to yield to western pressure.

The 'scramble' for commercial concessions and Chinese territory was now accelerated. In return for intervention in the Sino-Japanese dispute Russia gained a defensive alliance with China (1896). China also granted Russia the right to build and operate the Chinese Eastern Railway as a link in the Russian Trans-Siberian line to Vladivostok. This line made possible the economic penetration of Manchuria. In 1898 Russia concluded a twenty-five years' lease of the southern half of the Liaotung Peninsula, including the ice-free naval base of Port Arthur and the commercial port of Dairen. As the Russian fleet was already in Port Arthur, the request for a lease of the territory amounted to a formality. Russia also obtained the right to construct a railway from Harbin in the north to the newly-leased ports.

France obtained a modification of the Sino-Annamese frontier and the opening of three new treaty ports. French engineers and manufacturers were to have prior rights in the event of exploitation of the mines in the Chinese provinces of Yunnan, Kwangsi, and Kwangtung. All railways built there were to be financed and built by French companies. The French also extended their influence to the island of Hainan in southern China close to their Tongking Protectorate. They also obtained an undertaking that China would never cede Hainan to any third power, nor the provinces which bordered French possessions in Indo-China.

Britain, the nation responsible for the first western imperialist war in

Asia (the Opium Wars of the 1830's and 1840's), had by the 1890's become reluctant to extend its dominions any further. The British expansionist phase of history had ended with the conquest of upper Burma a decade earlier. Britain's chief interests now were to extend British commerce and curtail Russian activity in eastern Asia. The arrival of the Russian fleet at Port Arthur prompted Britain to suggest to Russia that the whole of Asia should be divided into Russian and British spheres of influence. The northern sphere — north of a line running from Alexandretta in the eastern Mediterranean to Peking in China — to belong to Russia; the southern sphere to belong to Britain. Russia had no intention, however, of surrendering the better half of Asia to Britain. Russia's answer to the British note was to strengthen its forces in Port Arthur and Dairen. Advances to the Americans and the Japanese regarding possible collaboration in eastern Asia having proved abortive, Britain moved to safeguard its own interests. In 1897 it secured from the Chinese exclusive privileges in the Yangtze Valley; in 1898 Britain obtained a lease of Kowloon; also in 1898, five days after the Russians had occupied Port Arthur, Britain forced China to lease the neighbouring port of Wei-hai-wei.

The German seizure of the port of Kiaochow and the city of Tsingtao in southern Shantung in November, 1897, on the pretext of the murder of two missionaries, is usually looked upon as having precipitated the scramble of the western powers for Chinese territory. Germany had long sought a coaling station on the China coast, and felt that what it had taken was little enough payment for the assistance rendered with Russia and France to China against Japan. Germany had only recently joined the group of European nations seeking territorial aggrandizement overseas. Germany's actions in the Shantung Peninsula may have been ill-considered, but essentially they followed the pattern laid down by Britain and the other western powers.

The American 'Open Door'[1] policy of 1899, which provided equal commercial opportunity for the western powers (including the U.S.A.) in spheres of special interest in China, lessened the friction between the western nations, but it gave China no relief from western invasion. To the Chinese the American policy simply meant that America was able to reap the commercial and financial benefits of western invasion without having fought for them.

By 1900 the western nations had established claims in thirteen of the eighteen provinces of China; Russian influence was predominant in Manchuria. Even Japan had managed to extract something more from the Chinese, having claimed exclusive privileges in Fukien (opposite Formosa). Sovereignty still remained with the Manchu dynasty, but by the end of the nineteenth century the Manchus were largely puppets in the

[1] A misnomer. See G. F. Kennan 'Mr. Hippisley and the Open Door', ch. ii, *American Diplomacy, 1900-1950* (Chicago, 1951).

hands of the western nations. The structure of Chinese society was such that China managed to get the worst of both worlds, the old and the new. Its feudalism was enfeebled, its political and administrative organization prevented the rise of an aggressive, ambitious, capitalist class. China's dilemma was simple. Capital and skill from the West could only be obtained at the expense of further extension of foreign control within the Empire. Yet without foreign capital and skill China could not hope to resist foreign domination. In rejecting the Italian demand for the lease of the naval base of Sanmun Bay in Chekiang in 1899, China gave notice that her patience with the western invaders was exhausted. The hatred fostered among the Chinese against the aggressive foreign commercial and religious penetration eventually exploded in the Boxer uprising in 1900. The heaviest persecution fell upon the Christian missionaries and their converts; a fact which can only be understood in its historical context.

To meet the crisis the western powers combined with Japan to crush the rebellion. The legations in Peking were eventually relieved by an international expeditionary force from Japan, Russia, Britain, France, Germany, and the United States; a huge indemnity of $333,900,000, and further commercial and religious concessions were demanded. Yet with the exception of Russia the other European nations showed little interest in strengthening their hold upon Chinese territory. Russia, on the contrary, used the Boxer incident as a pretext to flood Manchuria with Russian troops. When in 1901 China appealed to the Great Powers for help to force the withdrawal of the Russian army from Manchuria, Britain tried to form an Anglo-German-Japanese bloc to bring pressure to bear on Russia. After much negotiation and intrigue the Anglo-Japanese military alliance of 1902 was formed, reflecting the degree of anxiety which Britain felt about Russian activity in eastern Asia. Its importance for Japan was psychological. A relative newcomer among Asian nations, Japan became an ally of the most powerful nation on earth. In effect, Britain gave notice that if Japan became involved in war with Russia it would go to Japan's assistance if any third party intervened. With this treaty Britain had strengthened Japan's hand against Russia enormously. The Japanese proposal that Manchuria should be considered a Russian and Korea a Japanese sphere of influence was rejected by the Russians. The Russians continued to penetrate both areas. And when Japan requested Russia to evacuate its troops from Manchuria, Russia treated the request with contempt. For this the Russians paid dearly. Unlike China, Japan had always recognized the superiority of western military techniques. For peaceful progress, Japan had modernized its economy at a pace unique in history. For war, it had incorporated in its army and navy all the best that French, Prussian, and British organization could offer. Without declaring war Japan attacked the Russian fleet at Chemulpo and Port Arthur.

Troops were landed on the Chinese mainland, and the Russian army was pursued and defeated a year later in February, 1905, at Mukden. In the naval battle of Tsushima Straits, in May 1905, the Japanese annihilated the Russian fleet of 32 vessels coming from European waters. For the first time a great European power had been completely defeated on land and sea by an Asian people. Europe no longer had a monopoly of sea power upon which European influence in the world depended.

As a result of Japan's victory over Russia, the Russians agreed to give up Port Arthur, to transfer to Japan the lease of the Liaotung Peninsula, and Russian mining and railway privileges there, to acknowledge Japan's paramount interest in Korea, to cede to Japan the southern half of the island of Sakhalin, and to evacuate Manchuria. Overnight Japan had become a Great Power. Japan's representations in the United States, Britain, France, Germany, and Austria were elevated to the rank of embassies. The axis formed between Britain and Japan in 1902 was renewed in 1905 for ten years and extended to cover India. Meanwhile, war clouds were gathering over Europe. England's fears of a Russian bogey had been replaced by fears of a German bogey. Germany, Britain's traditional ally, became its enemy; Russia, Britain's traditional enemy, became its ally in 1907. As Europe bent to the task of destroying itself, attention was diverted from eastern Asia. From time to time lip service was paid to Chinese national independence, but, except for Russia, European power had begun to decline in Asia. In 1910 Japan's annexation of Korea went unopposed by the West. In the same year (1910) the Japanese and the Russians tried to reach an understanding regarding their respective interests in Manchuria. The outbreak of the Chinese revolution in 1911 caused the Manchus to abdicate. There followed a struggle for power between the different political factions. Almost without pause Chinese fratricide continued until the victory of the communist armies in the 1940's.

The First World War marked the end of an epoch of European power in China and eastern Asia. When the war ended the future of the area no longer rested with western European nations but with Japan, Russia, China, and the United States.

* * *

The first links between the West and China had been overland; those with India were by sea. When the first European navigators, Vasco da Gama (1497), and Cabral (1500), appeared in the Indian Ocean, India had already had intimate contact with the Persians, the Egyptians, the Greeks, the Chinese, the Arabs, and the central Asians. In 1509 the Portuguese, Francisco de Almeida, had destroyed an Indian-Egyptian fleet in the battle of Diu, thus establishing European control in Indian waters. In that year began the governorship of Alfonso d'Albuquerque at

Goa. The direct commerce with India which the Portuguese had sought was thus achieved. And with European traders came European explorers, adventurers, and priests. The Portuguese Jesuits, Antonio Monserrate and Rudolfo Acquaviva, visited the Moghul Emperor Akbar in 1580; but neither they nor later missions had much success in converting the Moghul court to Christianity. Throughout the seventeenth century, as Portuguese power in India declined, that of the English increased. After the triumph of British arms in India in the eighteenth century the major impact on India was made by the British. It can be traced in every section of Indian life; in administration, politics, warfare, technology, trade, law, education, art, and religion. The unusual degree of tolerance shown by Hinduism to other religions helps to explain the inroads made by western culture. Not least was the impact of the British government. This undoubtedly was the source of much of the dynamic impulse behind nineteenth-century Indian economic advance. British law and administration having been established, British technical experts soon developed road and rail transport and communications, agriculture, and public health. Especially important was the construction of India's railways. These were built in anticipation of the country's needs, and continuously extended out of Indian taxes, but they opened up the interior of India, connected the main ports with important agricultural regions, stimulated the sale of British manufactured goods and the export of growing quantities of raw materials, combated famine, and helped to spread the knowledge and the application of engineering techniques.

Under British influence, Indians continued to play the dominant role in the internal trade of the country, but on the growing volume of foreign trade their influence was slight. Similarly, Indians played almost no part in providing the banking and insurance facilities necessary to support India's growing external commercial relations. Nor, before the First World War, did they contribute greatly to the development of the modern plantation, mining, and manufacturing industries. They did not do so partly because their efforts to develop native commercial and industrial institutions were often thwarted, discouraged, or dwarfed by the foreign government and foreign private business elements. More importantly, the whole social complex, consisting of the differing traditions and backgrounds, taboos and prohibitions of the various castes and communities, militated against it. The Indians themselves were too diverse, too bound by tradition, too divided in every respect among themselves, to take the initiative in these economic changes or even to desire them. Where the circumstances were favourable to the development of modern industry the Indian was able to make headway by himself. Thus, the Bombay textile industry, which became the nucleus of manufacturing industry in western India, was owned and operated from the beginning by the Indians themselves.

By and large, however, under the direction and influence of a relatively small number of nineteenth-century British officials, India became a classic type of modern colonial economy: the life of a mighty sub-continent was subordinated to that of a tiny group of British islands thousands of miles away; the native was given little voice in major economic decisions, he was taxed without adequate representation, and much of his traditional domestic industry was destroyed. Some authors believe that, at the time when the British gained power in India, India was on the threshold of great economic development. Colonialism, so the argument goes, stopped it.[1] The British government's determination to keep India as an agricultural hinterland of Britain — and this in the nineteenth century, the heyday of British economic liberalism — probably arrested India's growth. It is fortunate for India that the British government did not try to control the enterprise of the Europeans as it tried to control that of the Indians: the development of great industries such as jute, mining, engineering, tea, coffee, rubber, quinine, and foreign banking, insurance, and shipping facilities, was almost entirely the result of British private initiative.

Yet the general peace that India enjoyed after the Mutiny in 1857, the spread of western economic and political ideas, the contribution made in health and education, the growing unity of the Indian nation, the spread of western ways of doing things (in administration as in every other field of endeavour), all these influences should not be cast aside lightly. Ultimately, what carried India forward, or retarded its growth were Indian forces. Sometimes British rule allowed those forces to form and develop; the encouragement given by the government of India to the transfer of rubber-bearing plants from the Amazon basin is one of several examples. Sometimes they were stifled by a foreign hand. More often, in its attitude to the development of private business, the British government remained passive. Gradually, however, half a century before political independence was achieved in 1947, the Indians had extended their activities into fields that had hitherto been the preserve of the British. By the 1930's Indian industrial and commercial forces were widespread. In addition to the textile industry, Indians now controlled part or all of many industries, including jute, mining, plantations, iron and steel, cement, sugar, banking, insurance, and foreign trade and shipping. Yet India changes slowly; the main occupation of Indians remains what it has always been: the cultivation of the soil.

* * *

[1] The contention held by many Indian authors, including Jawaharlal Nehru in his *The Discovery of India* (London, Meridian Books Ltd., 1960). See also the *Note* by Pandit Madan Mohan Malaviya in the Report of the Indian Industrial Commission, 1916–18 (London, H.M.S.O., Cmd. 51, 1919, pp. 245–300).

Contact between Japan and the West began in 1542 or 1543 when a number of Portuguese landed from a Chinese ship on an island off the southern coast of Kyushu. With the introduction of the Portuguese musket Japanese warfare was greatly affected. Later in the sixteenth century, Japanese victories in Korea convinced the Chinese of the superiority of European arms. In 1549 the famous Jesuit missionary, St. Francis Xavier, introduced Christianity into Japan. The port of Nagasaki, opened to western trade in 1570, soon became Japan's greatest port for foreign commerce. In the early years of the seventeenth century there followed Spanish traders and missionaries, and, later, Dutch and British merchants. The scientific talents of the Christian missionaries helped them to gain a foothold on the Japanese islands. By the mid-century, however, as a result of growing Japanese xenophobia, European merchants had been banished from the mainland. Christianity had been stamped out, except for the merest spark, which was kept alive in some isolated rural communities of Kyushu. All that remained was a tiny peephole maintained by a group of Dutch traders in virtual imprisonment on the islet of Deshima in Nagasaki harbour. These and a few Chinese traders were Japan's only connection with the outside world. Thenceforth western intercourse with Japan almost ceased. In shutting the door to the West, Japan probably retarded its development of modern science by at least a century.

The Japanese islands had been one of the lodestars guiding and sustaining the Russians in their epic struggle across Siberia to the eastern seas. Since the early seventeenth century the Russians knew of Japan from the Chinese and Koreans; since 1736 there had been an Institute of Japanese Studies at St. Petersburg.[1] Yet when the Russians arrived in the Kamchatka Peninsula at the beginning of the eighteenth century, Europe's relations with Japan had long been terminated by the Japanese Edict of 1639, which severed diplomatic relations with Portugal. The Russian explorer, Adam Laxman, and the Englishman William Broughton visited Hokkaidō in the 1790's; American ships did a little trade with the Japanese on Dutch account during the years 1797–1809; in 1804 a Russian ambassador, Nicolai Petrovitch de Rezanov, made an unsuccessful attempt to open trade relations with Japan; but for all practical purposes the door to the West was closed. It took force to open the Japanese door — in the mid-nineteenth century the United States, Britain, Russia, Holland, and France extracted trade treaties — and the subsequent history of the foreign merchants who settled at Yokohama in 1859 shows that it took force to keep it open. In 1863, 1864, and 1865 the British, Dutch, French, and American governments backed up their arguments for trade by naval

[1] G. A. Lensen, *The Russian Push Toward Japan*: Russo-Japanese relations, 1697–1875 (Princeton U.P., 1959, p. 553). Also, an untranslated Russian work E. Y. Feinberg, *Russo-Japanese Relations, 1697–1875* (Moscow, 1960).

demonstrations at Kagoshima, Shimonoseki, and Osaka.

Japan was no more able to resist the western commercial treaties thrust upon it than China or India. But to a far greater extent than either of these countries — at least in the early period of renewed relations with the West — Japan was able to restrict the infiltration of European civilization to its techniques of gaining wealth and making war. The basic desire behind early Japanese industrialization was a more effective defence against the western powers. The Japanese government encouraged western technicians to lay the foundations of Japan's future navy and industry. Japanese students were sent to western Europe and to the United States for technical training. There were economic losses in this system of state intervention as well as gains. But Japan was not so much developing these industries as taking them over. And without the initiative shown by the state the transfer of western forms of manufacture would have been a slower process. Japan made its own forced march to industrialization; and having done so it was able to protect itself against later encroachment and exploitation by Europeans and Americans.

Western science also was adopted in many fields: in medicine, astronomy, biology, geology, geography, and, later on, in physics, chemistry, and mathematics. The influence of the West was extended rapidly; not a surprising fact if we consider the very small area covered by the Japanese islands. During the Meiji period (1868–1912) the borrowing from the West was comparable only to Japan's earlier imitation of China. By the end of the nineteenth century the impact of western civilization had not only been felt in the fields of science and technology, but also in education, philosophy, art, and literature. Western science and technology had proved inseparable from other aspects of western life.

We do not know what it was that enabled the Japanese to stand up to the western invader while the much more numerous Chinese were subjugated. Japanese initiative must have had something to do with it, for the Japanese were often doing what the Chinese were only talking about. It was probably a combination of many factors. One of the most decisive factors in Japan's progress was the way Japan absorbed its rapid population increase in non-agricultural activities. Between 1872 and 1940 Japanese total population grew approximately 35 million. Yet there was little change in the size of the rural population. Had there been a social stigma attached to the artisan and merchant classes (as there was until very recent times in China), the transfer of labour from the Samurai and the farming classes could never have taken place. Why the Japanese should have accorded an intrinsic dignity to all classes in society is a question whose answer can only be found in Japan's religious past.

It is easy to place too much stress upon a single factor; it is easy to exaggerate and antedate the more efficient use of Japan's agricultural resources. Undoubtedly, the proportion of the total working force employed in agriculture declined sharply in the years 1872–1940; undoubtedly, there was a rise in productivity which helped to strengthen the Japanese economy. But there is no marked increase in the productivity of particular crops before the 1890's; and the increases when they came were due to extra effort and a more effective use of existing resources rather than the result of improved western techniques. One factor we have tended to underrate was the impact of foreign trade relative to the growth of national income.

Japanese experience demonstrates the complex set of circumstances which help to determine a nation's destiny. If Japan had not put its own house in order with the political reformation of 1868, if the spread of clan warfare had robbed the nation of all leadership in national affairs, if any further serious provocation of the western powers had been made after the allied naval demonstration at Osaka in November, 1865, if Japan had been unable to alter its social structure; in any of these contingencies, and the 1860's were critical years when an issue might have gone either way, Japan might have suffered the same fate as China and India. Perhaps mutiny against the British in India in the fifties, civil war in the United States in the sixties, and the struggle between France and Prussia in the seventies, helped to deflect the attention of the West from Japan, and, in doing so, helped to preserve Japanese independence.

The essential point in explaining Japanese progress is that the fundamental human qualities were already there. The challenge of the western nations provided the necessary catalyst. Earlier periods of Japanese history reveal latent technological creativity in Japanese society. Industrialization of Japan was not the dramatic result of western impact, but a gradually accelerating process spread over many decades. Industrialization in Japan began not so much with the imitation of European technology, as with the mechanization of its own traditional industries. Japan was able to keep pace with European developments because industrialization in Europe itself was only in its early stages. The First World War provided Japanese industry and trade with unforeseen opportunities for further development.

The outcome of western intrusion in eastern Asia was the Japanese bid for supremacy over the western powers in December, 1941. The Pacific became one of the great theatres of the Second World War; the outposts of the western world were all but submerged as the irresistible tide of Japanese conquest surged on.

Most of the western outposts were of fairly recent nineteenth-century origin. As far as is known, with the exception of several hundred British convicts in Australia in 1788, and a score of British mutineers from the *Bounty*, who reached Pitcairn Island in 1790, there were no other European settlers in the south Pacific before the nineteenth century. Half a century later, however, in 1840, the British occupied New Zealand. As a result of French exploration, and the demands made by Australia and New Zealand, the British annexed Fiji in 1874. Papua, the south-east part of New Guinea, was added in 1884, and in 1887 (sharing control with France) the British added to their empire the New Hebrides. Protectorates were also established by the British over the Solomons (1893), and at the turn of the century over the Friendly (Tonga), the Savage, the Cook, and the Gilbert and Ellice Islands. The French initiated a policy of annexation in 1842 by taking the Marquesas and establishing a protectorate over the Society Islands, including Tahiti. Tahiti became a French colony in 1880. In 1853 New Caledonia, and in 1864 the Loyalty Islands were added to French possessions. In 1884 the Germans annexed the north-east part of New Guinea as well as the islands of the Bismarck Archipelago. New Guinea, the second largest island in the world, was now divided between the Dutch, who had held west New Guinea since 1828, the British, and the Germans. In 1885 the Germans also annexed the Marshall Islands and part of the Solomons. In 1899 they purchased from Spain the Marianne Islands and the Palau Islands. Also in 1899, England, Germany, and the United States agreed upon the division of Samoa. At the beginning of the twentieth century the Cook Islands (1901) were handed over for administration to New Zealand and British New Guinea (1906) to Australia. By then the United States had purchased Alaska and the Aleutian Islands (1867), acquired Midway (1867) and Wake (1890) Islands, annexed Hawaii (1898), occupied Guam (1898) and the Philippines (1898), and brought part of Samoa (1899) under United States protection.

The effect of western infiltration during the nineteenth century was also felt in many other parts of Asia and the Pacific, especially after the opening of the Suez Canal in 1869. To Ceylon, Burma, Thailand, Indo-China, Java, and Malaya the European brought with him improved techniques in agriculture, manufacture, public health, and administration, resulting in the support of larger populations and the rapid development of their trade with Europe. In all countries the introduction of European techniques, European capital and European business methods raised the level of economic development. Rarely did Europeans affect the religious beliefs of these people. In some countries, such as Malaya, the material influence of the European has been spectacular. But these achievements were often accompanied by the establishment of a characteristically 'colonial' economy as the interests of the native people were subordinated to those of the imperial power. The material influence of the West in some countries, such as Java, although among the first to feel the western impact, has been less spectacular; which only goes to emphasise the complexity of economic change.

European influence has also been felt in the East Indies, in the Philippines, and in the rich oil lands of south-west Asia. With few exceptions, however, the European has not settled in those countries and his influence has been limited to exploration, conquest, trade, administration, investment, the diffusion of technology (in transport and the oil industry), the establishing of new standards of health and education, and missionary work.

The rapid growth of Chinese and Indian populations in parts of south-east Asia today is directly linked with European exploration and penetration of these areas. While Asian migration is as old as recorded history, it was the expansion of European rule and the introduction of European technology — especially improved transport — which in the last decades of the nineteenth century enabled Asians to migrate to many parts of the world in growing numbers. Many of them followed in the wake of Europeans: to trade, to provide the labour to build roads and railways, to extract minerals, or to cultivate the plantations established by European enterprise. This explains the origin of Indian and Chinese communities in East Africa, parts of Latin America, south-east Asia and the islands of the Pacific.

* * *

Although Africa proved to be impenetrable to the European until very recent times, the 'Dark Continent' has always held the fascination of the white man. In the thirteenth century European merchants and missionaries were already established in Morocco. Under the leadership of Prince Henry of Portugal the west coast of Africa was gradually discovered and explored. The chief force driving the European onward was the search for souls, gold, and slaves, especially slaves. If the Portuguese were prepared to enter the 'Sea of Darkness' which was thought to lie beyond Cape Bojador, it was partly because only by braving the unknown could they hope to avoid the hard core of Arab resistance which blocked the path of European expansion in North Africa and the Mediterranean. In 1487 Bartolomeu Dias rounded the southern tip of Africa. In the same year (1487) the Portuguese reached Timbuktu overland from the coast. Shortly afterwards they were exploring the Niger and the Congo. While most details of missionary activity in the interior at this time have been lost to us, it is fairly certain that in Africa, as elsewhere, the Christian missions were the spearhead of European penetration. They went first and they stayed in the interior longer than any other group. By the 1600's Portuguese stations had been established on the east as well as the west coast of Africa, and Portuguese Jesuit missionaries had reached Ethiopia, which they thought was the legendary kingdom of Prester John. Systematic exploration by the Portuguese over a long period benefited all the other whites who followed them around Africa — especially the Spaniards, whose king ruled over Portugal between 1580 and 1640. In the seventeenth and eighteenth centuries, as the Portuguese were followed by the Spaniards, the Dutch, the British, and the French, the number of trading posts on the African coast grew. Even so, with the exception of the Dutch settlements in South Africa, European colonization was limited to the immediate neighbourhood of the coastal forts. The penetration of other parts of Africa had first to be preceded by a good deal of geographical exploration.

The exploits of James Bruce in Ethiopia in the 1760's, and the subsequent publication of the account of his journey, increased Europe's interest in Africa and helped to set the stage for further developments. In 1788 the British Africa Society was founded to promote exploration of Africa, as well as British trade and political authority. In 1793 Captain Maxwell, R.N., explored the estuary of the Niger as far as Boma. Mungo Park explored the upper Niger in the 1800's. Park established the fact that the great river flowed east. It was his reference to the 'mystery' city of 'Timbuctoo', north of the Niger, which set the scene for the journey in 1828 of René Caillié from Senegal to Timbuktu. Caillié then went by caravan across the Sahara to Fez in Morocco. In 1825 three Englishmen, Walter Oudney, Hugh Clapperton, and Dixon Denham, reached the Niger from Lake Chad. It had taken them three years to make the journey from Tripoli on the North African coast. They proved that the Niger had no connection with Lake Chad. In his explorations from Bussa to the Atlantic in the period 1830–4 Richard Lander finally settled the problems connected with the mouth of the Niger. In 1849 Heinrich Barth and Adolf Overweg crossed from Tripoli to the Niger. Barth's explorations in Africa extending over many years have caused authorities to rank his work with that of Livingstone. Another German, Georg Schweinfurth, between 1868 and 1871, proceeding from Khartoum, explored the central region south of the Sahara. Gradually the gaps on the maps of Africa were being filled in.

Of all those who helped in this work the contribution of David Livingstone stands out. From 1841, when he landed at Algoa Bay, until his death in 1873, Livingstone — known to the natives as Bula Matari, breaker of rocks — never ceased in his work as a missionary-explorer. He shared with others the hope that Africa might one day be free of the curse of slavery. Between 1853 and 1856 he crossed the continent from east to west and from west to east exploring the Zambesi. On this expedition he discovered the Victoria Falls. In 1859 he discovered Lake Nyasa. (The famous Portuguese explorer De Lacerda had narrowly missed both Lake Nyasa and Lake Bangweulu in 1798.) After his many African journeys, which exceeded 30,000 miles, Livingstone reached the southern end of Lake Tanganyika in the 1860's. It was in the vicinity, at Ujiji, that Henry Morton Stanley found him in 1871 — two years before Livingstone's death.

As a scientific explorer Livingstone's lasting fame is assured; what is not often appreciated is his contribution to the development of tropical medicine in Africa. The 'alleviation of human suffering' was the object to which Dr. Livingstone devoted his life. There are records of missionary hospitals from the sixteenth century onwards, but it was Livingstone perhaps more than anyone else who, by capturing the imagination of the western world, caused medical work to become widely established as a branch of missionary activity. The medical services of the Catholic and Protestant missions were expanded from the 1860's. The importance of western medicine to Africans (then and now) is far too important to bear summarizing here. As in the countries of western Europe, so in the African colonies medical services (and popular education) were gradually accepted as one of the functions of the Christian churches. Similar medical developments — sometimes as a means of promoting Christianity — were taking place at about the same time in China and other parts of Asia.

Stanley returned to Africa in 1874. Although he is best remembered as having found Livingstone three years earlier, he did, in fact, perform extraordinary feats of exploration. He sailed round Lake Victoria and Lake Tanganyika, confirming the work of earlier explorers; he then crossed to the Lualaba, which he descended to the Congo, finally making his way down the Congo to the Atlantic coast in 1877. Grimly determined to succeed, and ruthless as he was, this and later expeditions provide Stanley with a powerful claim to fame as an explorer. The fact that Stanley was equally proficient as a journalist helps to explain why so many people became aware of his activities, whereas the exploits of less literate men like Lieutenant Verney Lovett Cameron, who traversed the southern half of the Congo basin (also in an effort to find Livingstone) two years before Stanley, passed largely unnoticed and have long since been forgotten. In the 1880's Hermann von Wissmann carried out further exploration of the Congo basin.

Meanwhile, a great deal of geographical exploration had been done in the region of the Nile. A Swiss, Johann Ludwig Burckhardt, had journeyed up the Nile and crossed to the Red Sea in 1812–14. This was followed in 1827 by the expeditions of Linant de Bellefonds. Among other important journeys were those undertaken by Richard Burton, John Speke, James Grant, and Samuel Baker, during the 1850's and 1860's, who determined the source of the Blue and the White Niles and assisted in attracting attention to Africa.

In addition to stimulating interest in Africa, European exploration facilitated the hurried division of African territory by European nations in the last quarter of the nineteenth century. This phase of African history, which did not get under way much before the 1870's, was largely completed a generation later. In the 1870's the British possessed the Cape Province and the West African settlements of Sierra Leone, the Gold Coast, and Gambia. They had also secured possession of the Lagos Coast through treaties with the native chiefs. They then extended their control to the upper valley of the Nile. Protectorates were declared over British Somaliland at the mouth of the Red Sea (1884); Bechuanaland and the Rhodesias (1885); the hinterland of the Gold Coast, Ashanti (1886); Sierra Leone (1889); Zanzibar (1890); Nyasaland (1891); and Nigeria (1900). With the defeat of the Boers in 1902 the British had complete control of South Africa.

France's African empire in 1914 was even larger than that of the British. It was, in fact, larger than the whole of Europe. Whereas the British had spread north-westwards from the Cape, the French had moved southwards from Algeria (where in 1830 France began to establish a North African empire) and eastwards from the banks of the Senegal. To its possessions in North Africa (Algeria) and West Africa (Senegal and French Guinea) were added the Protectorates of the French Congo (1880); Tunis (1881); French Somaliland (1884); the Ivory Coast (1889); Dahomey (1890) (the colonies of the Ivory Coast and French Guinea were formally established in 1893; that of Dahomey in 1894). French power spread in Morocco from 1906 onwards and a French Protectorate was established there in 1912.

The Congo Free State, established as a neutral concession under international sanction in 1884, was annexed as a Belgian colony in 1908.

The Germans did not achieve political unity until the 1870's. Their active participation in the 'scramble for Africa' may be dated from 1884, when an international congress was held in Berlin to try to bring order to the struggle between the Europeans for African territory. The conference at least convinced Germany that possession was nine-tenths of any argument. In 1884–5 Germany took possession of Togoland and the Cameroons, obtained a block of coastland further south which became German South-West Africa, and acquired territory which was proclaimed the Protectorate of German East Africa in 1890.

Italy, like Germany, was a late-comer in the division of Africa. Its imperialism was short-lived. Italians established a colony at Massawah on the Red Sea in 1885. In 1889 the Italians took control of the territory which later became Italian Somaliland. In 1890 Italy's Red Sea possessions were organized as the colony of Eritrea. The Italians then overreached themselves. In trying to conquer the inland empire of Abyssinia (Ethiopia) they suffered overwhelming defeat at the battle of Adowa (1896). (Their hurt race-pride was avenged a generation later.) All Italian adventures in Africa, however, did not end in defeat. In the Turco-Italian war of 1911–12 the provinces of Tripoli and Cyrenaica were wrested from the Turks and re-named Italian Libya.

In the division of African territory in the nineteenth century, the Portuguese and the Spaniards, once foremost in exploring the continent, took little part. The Portuguese enlarged their earlier trading posts into the Protectorates of Angola and Mozambique. The Spaniards continued to hold, but did not enlarge, their small Guinea Protectorate, their possessions on the north-western coastline (the Ri'o de O'ro), and their part of Morocco opposite Gibraltar.

By 1914 there was no part of the African continent outside Liberia and Ethiopia that was not occupied or controlled by Europeans. Fifty years earlier European control in Africa had extended to no more than one-tenth of the total continent.

In the last quarter of the century, as European colonial rule was extended to great areas of Africa, it was the peculiar contribution of the European (especially the government official or colonial administrator) to put a country down on paper for the first time, to give it a name, to cause it to exist in the administrative and political sense, and to determine its specific boundaries. Under European guidance, and as a result of European initiative (in Liberia, American), the great agricultural export industries of tropical Africa (including oil seeds, cotton, coffee, tobacco, cocoa, sisal, maize, and rubber) were established. The impact of these developments has chiefly been felt in Nigeria, the Gold Coast, French West Africa, the Cameroons, Sierra Leone, Uganda, Kenya, Tanganyika, and Egypt. West Africa has never attracted European (or Asian) settlers as South, North, and East Africa have done. It is for this reason that relatively more of the economic development of West Africa has had to come from the Africans themselves. Where modern large-scale industrial enterprises have been established, as in the Belgian Congo, it is as a result of European enterprise. Mining is a very old African industry, but the enormous mining undertakings of present-day Africa have resulted from European capital and the initiative of small groups of European entrepreneurs and technicians. It is the highly trained and educated European whom the newly emerging countries of Africa can least afford to lose at this stage of their development. The hurried departure of European administrators from African countries in the 1960's has often resulted in a country being left at the mercy of unprincipled native pressure groups.

* * *

In 1914 the world was still a white man's world. Almost the whole of Africa and America, a large part of Asia, Australasia, and the islands of the Pacific Ocean were in European hands. At the end of the nineteenth century the German Emperor had sounded a warning note against the Yellow Peril that would one day shake European power to its foundations. Others spoke of the abyss into which European civilization would fall. But it was still high noon in the European Era. The world still danced to a

European tune; Europeans were still the leaders of the human race. No other people in the whole of history had benefited mankind as the Europeans had done, or at least so they thought. Yet this civilization which had reached the peaks of human effort — which had known one of the most brilliant periods of material and intellectual progress in history — had been quietly and meticulously plotting to destroy itself. So eager to do so in fact that military plans were completed almost a decade before they were used. The act of the young unknown Bosnian revolutionary, Gavrilo Princip, at Sarajevo, on 28th June, 1914, merely gave the signal for the European dance of death to begin. And, once begun, there seemed no end to Europe's inhumanity. It was a much changed Europe that emerged in 1919, and a much changed world. The European sun was still high in the heavens, but it was now long past high noon.

At the end of the First World War the whole structure of European civilization seemed to be on the point of collapse. The mighty empires of Russia, Germany, and Austria had fallen into dust; powerful nations had disappeared; the best that Europe had to offer lay dead on its battlefields; revolution was abroad. In many lands the middle class had been destroyed. Everywhere there was a growing sense of helplessness and remorse — a feeling that fate had taken a hand and the whole of Europe was hastening to its appointed doom. It was a time of little peace. To millions of Europeans it seemed that the war had never ended. Europe was never free of turmoil and torment. The desire to kill remained unsatisfied and brother continued to hunt brother. In a so-called time of peace there was slaughter in parts of Europe on a scale exceeding that of some of the worst battles of the Great War. For three years (1936–9) the Spaniards indulged in a veritable bloodbath in which every kind of horror was perpetrated. But this pales into insignificance when compared with the holocaust which descended upon Europe in the summer of 1939. For six years Europe was in darkness. Everything was submerged by the great wave of European insanity. No one, nothing was spared. Barbarity reigned. Had not Germany been beaten into submission before knowledge of atomic warfare had become widespread, the whole of Europe might have become a smoking hell. Behind the white man's back, the Japanese people had set out to conquer the whole of Europe's empire in south-east Asia.

The only European empire to extend its frontiers since the First World War had been the Russian. For a short period after the War the British had a vision of a new great empire stretching from Constantinople to Rangoon. But the vision quickly vanished in the realities of the postwar world. Out of the ashes of the Ottoman empire arose Turkey's saviour, Mustapha Kemal Atatürk. The seizing of German possessions in Africa and the Pacific provided Britain and France with a little more overseas territory, but the added responsibilities that went with it outweighed the gains. Italy's disastrous efforts to establish a new empire in Ethiopia in the late 1930's was a short-lived episode, at least a generation out of its time. Since the Second World War European imperialism has been a story of retreat and abdication. At a time when there is so much talk of 'imperialism' and 'colonialism' the dependent territorial empires of the European peoples, except for those of Russia, are smaller than they have been in almost half a millenium. In Africa the white man's power has disappeared almost overnight; in Asia only a few outposts remain. The Japanese, though eventually defeated themselves, helped to destroy white prestige throughout most of south-east Asia. Some European powers, like Britain, have had the wisdom or the good fortune to abdicate from their empires before they were driven out. Others have hung on bloodily. No European country has been able to resist the winds of change. Whether they have chosen to rationalize the surrender of power on moral grounds, as the British have done, or whether they have only yielded to superior force, contesting every yard of ground, as the French did in Indo-China and North Africa, the end result has been the same: the decline of Europe's imperial might. In one or two generation's time, if the present trend continues, the colonial overseas empires of the European powers will be mere historical remnants unworthy of effort or passion on the part of anyone. The short interlude of European colonization will be over. The age that began with Vasco da Gama and Columbus will have ended, and Europe will then seek her strength where it has always been — within herself.

* * *

The little that can be gleaned from history is that the imperialism of the European Age is not intrinsically different from that of ancient Egypt, Assyria, Babylon, Persia, Greece, or Rome. Nor does it differ from the Mongol, Chinese, Indian, and Arab Empires of Asia — unless it is in the fleeting nature of western imperialism. All empires have had subject peoples. White, black, brown, or yellow supremacy is nothing new in the world. The strong have always subjugated the weak. Extermination, eviction, enslavement, economic exploitation, racial discrimination, injustice, violence, and iniquity all existed before. Tyranny and despotism are not peculiar to the European Era. Excessive cruelty and ferocious barbarism can be found in all periods of history. There is nothing to distinguish the sacking of Melos by the Athenians almost half a millenium before the birth of Christ from the sacking of the towns and villages of the north-west plains of India by the dreaded White Huns a thousand years later. There is nothing to distinguish these acts from the thirteenth-century fate of the great central Asian cities of Bokhara, Samarkand, Herat, and Balkh, at the hands of the Asian Ghengis Khan. The twentieth-century fate of Hiroshima, Coventry, and Dresden is only another chapter in an endless story of human cupidity and madness. The evil that European man did (as well as the good) in the period of European imperialism and colonialism is part of a story as old as man.

'Imperialism' is neither uniquely European, nor is it uniquely capitalistic. Whether the concepts imperialism and capitalism should be regarded as inseparable or inherently opposed to one another depends largely on the place in history where one makes one's investigations. A century ago, it was thought by western Europeans that imperialism was opposed to capitalism. Today most people would take the opposite view. In any event, the relations between a colony and a metropolitan area have always been too complex to be described by either of these concepts. To explain the rise and expansion of Europe by the complicated development of the capitalist system moving inevitably to its doom, to say that the springboard of all European action was the search for wealth, means very largely that one had come to history ready to impose this interpretation upon it. There are examples where small groups of western capitalists brought pressure to bear upon their governments to engage in foreign adventures aimed at their own profit. The seizure of territories in South Africa and the African Congo are usually given as examples of this kind of economic determinism. Indeed, it is difficult not to recognize the overpowering personal ambition which drove Rhodes and other financiers on to seize the wealth of the South African Rand. Yet it is worth remembering that the Jameson Raid and the Boer War (1899–1902) which followed (and which Britain fought with overwhelming numbers and ruthless means until final victory was won) cost Britain dearly, not only in wealth but much more importantly in the moral prestige which Britain had enjoyed among the nations of the world. With the Boer War Britain forfeited its assumed role as the moral arbiter of the western world. It has never recovered it. Out of the whole affair Rhodes himself gained nothing. His was an emotional involvement rather than a financial one. Similarly, even allowing for the fact that the better side of Leopold II of the Belgians has perhaps gone by default, it is not difficult to detect the hunger for wealth and the overpowering personal ambitions which eventually drove so many Belgians to the heart of the Congo. Yet Leopold could no more raise enthusiasm among Belgian businessmen for tropical Africa than the British, French, or German leaders could do. Leopold only came into the picture after Stanley had failed to rouse his fellow Englishmen to the possibilities of opening up the Congo. Stanley's contemporary, Lieutenant Cameron, received even shorter shrift from the British government. When in 1874, after an heroic march across the southern Congo, he informed the Colonial Office that he had taken possession in the name of the Queen of the basins of the Congo and other African rivers, he received a very curt reply.

Early British traders found their government reluctant to make any move at all. Witness a memorandum[1] prepared by the British Foreign Office, dated 17 July 1886:

> It is said that the traditions of the Foreign Office and the Diplomatic Service are unfriendly or, at best, indifferent to the promotion of commercial interests; that there exists a certain disposition to snub British traders and to leave them without the countenance and support to which they were entitled . . .

To have felt it necessary to answer complaints of this kind hardly suggests that the British trading community had the government of the day in its pocket. When governments did intervene, as the British did in East Africa and the Upper Nile, they did so in areas least valuable to commerce. The anti-colonial spirit was epitomized by the British statesman Gladstone. Even when national prestige was at stake, Gladstone baulked at rescuing General Gordon in Khartoum. In fact, the first white men to explore Africa were neither businessmen nor government officials; they were men like Livingstone, De Brazza and Burton: missionaries, explorers, or agents of anti-slavery or philanthropic societies. Most business men are no different from men in other walks of life: reluctant to pioneer, to accept change, to face the unknown, to accept risk and hardship, to overcome practical difficulties. And, on this score, does the period in which we are making our study really make the difference?

As for the argument that nineteenth- and early twentieth-century businessmen and financiers were dictating a policy of colonial exploitation to their statesmen, the fact is that the business community rarely saw eye to eye with each other. The idea that economic gain must necessarily result from the use of force is not borne out by history. The scramble for Africa after 1880, and the race for concessions in China in the 1890's, were hastened as much by natural suspicion and fear among the European nations as by the hope of plunder. Britain's occupation of the Chinese port of Wei-hai-wei in the 1890's, for example, was a direct counter against the Russian occupation of Port Arthur five days earlier. And Britain's experience was repeated by all the other leading European nations in Asia and Africa. Indeed, there is some force in the argument that much of nineteenth-century European colonialism proves the primacy of politics rather than economics.[2]

[1] This memorandum suggesting conflict between the British government officials and British foreign business interests was thought sufficiently important to be circulated by the United States Department of State to all its consular officers. It can be found in vol. xx (Sept.–Dec. 1886) House Misc., Document no. 56, 2nd Session, 49th Congress, 1886–7, p. 5.

[2] D. K. Fieldhouse, 'Imperialism': An Historiographical Revision, *The Economic History Review*, 2nd series, vol. xiv, no. 2, Dec. 1961, p. 204.

Nor does the economic view do justice to the subtle and complicated relationships in which the colonial powers often found themselves enmeshed. The British in India would have been glad to follow the advice of Sir Thomas Roe, who arrived at the Moghul court in Agra in 1615 as ambassador for both the English East India Company and the English Monarch King James, when he urged his fellow-countrymen to seek their benefit '. . . in quiet trade' and 'avoid land wars in India'. But, like the other Great Powers, the British found themselves unable to limit their adventure. Strategic necessity or anarchy in neighbouring states compelled them — as it compelled the Dutch in Java and the French in Indo-China — to conquer wider and wider areas. Long after Plassey, the aim of the British was not political domination of India but trade. The idea of Britain seizing the whole of India would have appeared as ridiculous to a servant of Britain's East India Company in the eighteenth century as it would have been to the Indians themselves. The British acquired sufficient power to become serious contestants for the sovereignty of India only over a long period, and often unwillingly.

'You wish the red line of England on the map to advance no further', said General Jacob from India in 1858. 'But to enable this red line to retain its present position, . . . it is . . . absolutely necessary to occupy posts in advance of it.'[1]

Much imperialist action in the nineteenth century can be traced to the growth of an imperialist ideology, which eventually meant that unless a country obtained a share in the world's colonial possessions it could not rank as a Great Power. French action in Algeria in the 1830's, or German action in South-West Africa in the 1880's, sprang more from national pride than from the economic inadequacies of French or German capitalism. The German Chancellor, Bismarck, was never convinced that colonies were a necessity from the economic point of view. In fact, having decided to launch the nation on a colonial adventure, Bismarck and the German government found it difficult to obtain the support of the business community.

'. . . All great nations', the German historian Treitschke had written in 1887, 'in the fullness of their strength have desired to set their mark upon barbarian lands . . . Those who take no share in this great rivalry will play a pitiable part in time to come. The colonizing impulse has become a vital question for a great nation'.[2]

[1] *The Views and Opinions of Brigadier-General John Jacob, C.B.* (2nd Edition), London, 1858.
[2] Heinrich von Treitschke, *Politics*, trans. by Blanche Dugdale and Torben de Bille, 2 vols. (London, 1916), vol. i, pp. 115–16.

Half a century later when Adolf Hitler was demanding the return of the colonies lost by Germany during the First World War he did not rest his demands on the economic value of colonies but upon the fact that a Great Power, as Treitschke had said, had the right to set its mark upon barbarian lands: it was part of the purpose and the mission of the Germanic race. Italy's conquest of Ethiopia in the 1930's largely sprang from the same cause.

The growth of an imperialist ideology is, of course, closely linked with the European sense of a 'mission civilisatrice'. The idea that the white race was the 'chosen people', and all others were 'lesser breeds outside the law', was a most powerful idea prompting the actions of the white race in earlier times. From the fifteenth to the twentieth century the West has felt a psychological necessity to impose the goodness of its civilization upon others. Hear King Leopold, opening a Geographical Conference at Brussels in September 1876:

'To open up to civilization the sole portion of the globe to which it has not yet penetrated, to pierce the darkness which still envelops whole populations, is, I venture to say, a crusade worthy of this century of progress'[1].

Or Seton Kerr, Foreign Secretary to the government of India in 1883, stressing the Englishman's divinely appointed task in India: '. . . the cherished conviction which was shared by every Englishman in India, from the highest to the lowest . . . that he belongs to a race whom God has destined to govern and subdue'.[2] This idea helps to explain why the early European missionaries and the old-time colonial administrators stressed the need for religious change, western liberal education, a European life, and general European culture, as necessities at least for the ruling class of their colonial wards. It is plausible to argue that this idea set the European expansionist movement on its way, and that disillusionment with the idea meant the end of European supremacy in the world. Having for one reason or another become involved with the native people of other lands, the European felt he had incurred a moral responsibility for their welfare. The prevailing European belief in the superiority of the white race carried with it an obligation to the coloured peoples of the world. It was the duty of the western nations to disseminate their higher form of civilization and religion. There was a superb self-assurance on the part of the white people that their influence could only do good: a self-assurance which still characterizes the European. Was this self-assurance, which at times is indistinguishable from downright arrogance, the secret of Europe's

[1] George Martelli, *Léopold to Lumumba: A History of the Belgian Congo 1877–1960* (London, 1963), p. 19.

[2] Quoted in Edward Thompson and G. I. Garrett, *Rise and Fulfilment of British Rule in India* (London, 1935), p. 536.

success? Was it this which enabled a handful of European adventurers to impose their will upon far older, richer, and more enduring civilizations? At least these Europeans never questioned that their own maxims of law, ethics, politics, and economics might not be suitable to engraft upon other people's cultures. In all this they followed a long tradition in the life of mankind. They were not aware of the damage they would do. These lessons are very recent lessons. The West had a self-imposed task to raise other lands to the level of its own civilization. It undertook this task with tremendous energy and faith in its mission. To a greater or lesser degree all the European nations felt the same consciousness of destiny and duty to others. The degree of sympathy, of Christian humanitarianism, developed by the West for the whole of mankind, undoubtedly influenced its colonial development. Most French action in Indo-China, for instance, cannot be understood unless the significance of the Christian missionary movement in French colonial history is appreciated. It did not play a minor but a major role in determining French policy. There is a great deal of recent world history which cannot be understood without taking account of the Christian missions. With the benefit of hindsight it is not difficult to see that the ethics and the political ideology of the West would eventually be rejected by Africans and Asians. But the West was not to know this in the nineteenth century. Nor is it difficult to show how the 'missionary urge' and the 'civilizing mission' were often used to cloak less worthy aims. On the other hand, we shall never know what altruistic love of groups of Europeans for worse-off brethren in foreign lands has meant in helping to lighten the load (which often their own countrymen had made heavy) of what was for many non-Europeans a short-lived and wretched existence; nor shall we know what Christian charity has done to extend a sense of human pity in the world.

What caused Europe to puff itself up and extend its dominions all over the world will always remain something of a mystery. It is not enough to say that Europe had an urge to expand and possessed a sense of adventure. Unless one approaches history with a certain preconception in mind, it is impossible to say which of the many factors — economic, religious, political, and psychological — is the decisive one. Life is far too complex and ambiguous to lend itself to a simple overall explanation. Human motivation is too intimate to yield itself to the technical process of the historian. Only if we correlate the various factors at work can we glean a little knowledge of the past, and even then the knowledge we shall gain must be sought through an effort of imagination. The 'spirit' of Elizabethan England, the 'soul' of Castilian Spain, the 'mysticism' of the Portuguese, the 'counting house' mentality of the Dutch, or the sense of 'fair play' of the British do not yield themselves to scientific treatment. Scientifically, we shall never recreate the forces that led Europe to shed its inertia and gain its dominions. Only an artist's vision can hope to come close to describing the power of the human element when Europe was at its greatest. Whatever we do, the face of history will always remain partly concealed.

It is for these reasons that so little attention has been given in these pages to the many attempts to explain European imperial expansion — especially that of the years 1870–1914 — in economic terms alone. Nothing has been said of the non-Marxist economic explanation put forward by J. A. Hobson, whose book *Imperialism: A Study* appeared in 1902, or of the much more widely known Marxist work of the Russian leader Vladimir Lenin, *Imperialism, the Highest Stage of Capitalism* published in 1917. Yet these works are not without a hard core of truth. The search for privileged spheres of foreign trade and investment in the closing decades of the nineteenth century undoubtedly sprang from the changes taking place in the structure of the western industrial economies. There can be no denying the growing jostling and undercutting going on between the industrialized western powers. The causes of what has become known as the 'Great Depression', which started in Europe in 1873 and (broken by bursts of recovery in 1880 and 1888) continued into the middle 1890's, cannot be disassociated from what was happening to European foreign investment and European foreign trade during these years. Between the seventies and the nineties British exports, to take an example, had shrunk in value by 25 per cent compared with the peak of 1872. It was not until the turn of the century that Britain's peak trade figures of 1872–3 were surpassed. It is these conditions which helped to awaken in the West in the 1880's a new-found sense of the economic value of colonies — an awakening which occurred with remarkable simultaneity among the three leading industrial powers of Europe: Britain, Germany, and France. The most effective remedy for the enormous increase in European industrial production, it was thought, was to extend foreign trade and investment. Where else if not in the vast areas of the recently acquired empires?

Yet, contrary to what Hobson and Lenin thought, we know now that European investments played only a minor role in exploiting the colonial areas of Africa and Asia. A breakdown of British foreign investments in 1911, for instance, reveals the very small quantity of British capital invested in the dependent colonial empire.[1] The bulk of British investment at this time was in the United States (£688 million); South America (£587 million); Canada (£372 million); Australasia (£380 million); India and Ceylon (£365 million); and South Africa (£351 million). By contrast, there was only £29 million invested in West Africa; £22 million in the

[1] If India, Ceylon, and South Africa are included in the 'dependent colonial empire', then imperial investments are very much larger.

Straits Settlement and Malay States; and £33 million in the remaining British possessions. And, while there was a vast increase in European foreign investments after 1870, the bulk of these investments were made in independent sovereign states in the temperate zones rather than the newly-won colonial empires in Africa and Asia. Britain was the largest foreign investor in 1914 and 70 per cent of its investments were in politically independent lands where real wages were higher than in the United Kingdom. In 1913 Britain had only 12·7 per cent of its total foreign investments in its dependent colonial empire, including India; the vast majority of these funds — as with France and Germany — were not invested in private enterprise, but in foreign government bonds, especially in railways and other public utilities.

The same is largely true of the investment of other European countries. On the outbreak of the First World War France had only 4·5 per cent of its total foreign investments in its colonial empire. Proportionately, the German figure is even smaller. At this time German investments in British colonies — where it could hardly be argued that they exercised political control — exceeded those placed in its own colonial empire. The fact is that the vast majority of European investments were placed in politically independent lands — in self-governing sovereign territories in the temperate zone — where the European investor entered at his own risk and where standards of living were high rather than low. Whatever the finance capitalists did to encourage the 'scramble' for African and Asian territory, they were certainly reluctant to invest in colonies once the colonies had been obtained. And this despite the fact that the newer areas were normally compelled to offer higher rates of interest in order to attract the capital needed; although on the average, and taking defaults into account, the promise of higher yields on foreign investment was largely unfulfilled. There are many examples of private western capitalists forcing their countries to exercise political control over other lands. The extension of British control in Egypt in the eighties is cited by some authorities. There are examples, even in recent years, of western capitalists making enormous profits in countries where people are poorest, but one cannot draw from these examples an overall explanation of colonial rivalry and expansion. Quantitatively, at least, colonial investments were neither the malevolent force depicted by some authors, nor the civilizing medium depicted by others. They are part of the process of world development in which Europe has been engaged since the sixteenth century.

So far as the value of colonial trade is concerned, it is shown in Chapter VII, dealing with the development of world commerce, that the value of colonial commerce in the period 1870–1914 was an unimportant percentage of world trade, and it has remained so. Trade has not followed the flag. Exceptions have to be made in the case of French and Dutch colonial trade with the mother country in these years, but most European colonial areas — particularly those added in the late nineteenth century — were, and still are, relatively unimportant as markets or sources of raw materials. The capitalist European powers have always found the best markets among themselves as well as in the great white-settled areas of the Americas and Australasia. Whether, as Hobson argued, the economic imperialism of the late nineteenth century was an ill-judged attempt to increase the profitable fields of foreign investment and European trade, or, as Lenin had it, the 'scramble' for parts of Africa and Asia was the logical and inevitable outcome in the development of western capitalism trying to escape from its own inner dilemma, the facts that have come to light regarding investment and trade (or access to vital raw materials) do not support the theory.

The trouble with those who argue for or against an economic interpretation of European colonialism is that they are arguing about different things; so far as European colonialism is concerned, they are largely arguing about past things. Lenin's theory of imperialism cannot be explained simply in terms of economic theory, or disproved by what are called 'economic facts'. The Marxist-Leninist historical approach to 'colonialism' is not meant to 'fit the facts'; it is meant to help mankind through the jungle of historical happenings. It was Lenin's ability to see the story of life as a whole which gives his theory of imperialism power and significance. The power of Lenin's view does not lie in quantitative data, nor in its ability to score points, but in its vision. As long as Lenin's view fits in with the prevailing emotional attitude in the world no quantitative argument will have the slightest effect upon it. Scholars have shown — at least to their own satisfaction — that the economic interpretation of imperialism such as put forward by Hobson and Lenin is not supported by historical evidence. Other scholars have shown that the theoretical explanation of these writers is invalid; that the relation drawn between the expansion of capitalist Europe and the exploitation of non-capitalist economies is forced. So too is the link drawn between the supposed inherent economic instability of capitalism and overseas military adventure. These things were not and need not be causally linked. Yet the belief in an economic interpretation grows rather than declines. It does so not because the economic interpretation can be proved to be historically true or false, but because it provides a clue to the conflict and drama of life — a clue which happens to fit in very well with the prevailing emotional attitude towards the capitalist countries of the West. If Hobson and Lenin were to write today, instead of two generations ago, they would probably not change their position very much. It would depend more on their preconception of history rather than on the 'facts' dealing with investment and trade which have been unearthed during the past half-century. These so-called 'facts' have not succeeded in changing the views of those who today uphold Leninist doctrine. And why should they? A view of life is hardly likely to be affected by new sets of figures.

To the observer who comes to history without any firm preconceived notion or theory, however, the events of the years 1870–1914, upon which so much attention has been concentrated, seem to follow naturally from the events which preceded them. By and large, the frontiers that were being expanded after 1876 are the frontiers that were being expanded before. Similarly, without the aid of preconceived notions, it is difficult to believe that the colonial rivalry of these years was the chief cause of the First World War. Europe was bent on self-destruction in the early years of the twentieth century with or without the added complication of overseas empires. During the First World War the Austro-Hungarian Empire disappeared completely without overseas adventures. Russia was also deeply involved in the general conflagration, but Russia was not a maritime power with an overseas empire. Nor has the loss of European overseas empires since the end of the Second World War removed the threat of war in Europe. On the contrary, there is constant fear in Europe that one part will be overwhelmed and destroyed by another.

No matter how one looks at the term 'imperialism', it has been made to explain too much; and in trying to help us through the extraordinary expansionist phase of European history and the development of a world economy, most regrettably it explains far too little.

* * *

The complexity of European imperial history is not lessened when we try to explain Europe's decline; for we cannot deny that Europe has passed the period of its unchallenged supremacy in the world. Did imperial Europe overreach itself? Did Europe's power decline because of false pride, because of power that corrupted, because its sense of mission was lost? Was the critical factor human wickedness or human stupidity? Did the immeasurable vastness of its undertakings at last overwhelm it? Did it break down under its own weight? Was Europe's fate determined by the pendulum of time? Is the sudden collapse of Europe's power in Asia and Africa the judgement of God in history? Or is it, as the Marxist would have it, the inexorable working-out of the capitalist system: the fulfilment of Marx's general laws? Did the challenge and stimulus of the discovery of the 'New World' gradually wear off? For a civilization whose span has been relatively brief it can hardly be argued that the decline of Europe's foreign power is due to age alone; in any event, there is little to support the idea that the expansionist phase of any society has a predestined time-span determined by its very nature.

It will not satisfy mankind with its desire for complete answers to be told that we do not know. Mankind only listens to those who provide a simple, certain explanation for everything. At least it wants meaning, unity, and order in life. It will not bear with anyone who tries to tell the story of the past as it often was: overwhelmingly uncertain, complex, often irrational and accidental. When a tired, disillusioned Boris Pasternak caused his Dr. Zhivago to speak of mankind being 'hurled before the winds of fate', Pasternak's disgrace was certain. These were harsh words for those of his countrymen who since 1917 have struggled so hard, sacrificed so much to improve their worldly lot. To suggest that there is perhaps no ultimate meaning in anything is an idea equally unacceptable to Communist eastern and Christian western Europe.

Mankind does not hunger for truth; it hungers for certainty; in its worst moments it only asks that its dreams and illusions be confirmed. Yet on none of these matters can the historian speak with certainty; nor is he a purveyor of dreams. He can only say that almost all civilizations furnish examples of expansion and contraction, and that, as with most other civilizations, the seeds of Europe's decline were sown in Europe itself. Even before the decline of sea power, upon which Europe's initial predominance was based, Europe no longer believed in its imperial mission. The sense of adventure and the urge to expand gradually disappeared. The fires of its own beliefs burnt low. Unconsciously, unwittingly, Europe turned to itself. Imperceptibly, the genius, the magnificence, the majesty, the progressiveness of all that was Europe ceased to grow; the yeast that had caused Europe to rise was spent. Little Europe had come so far, done so much in the world; it needed to pause before going on to fresh adventures.

If Europe was undone then it was undone from within not from without. In the second half of the nineteenth century the Europeans never doubted their right and their duty to take charge of the world. They lost control of those forces only when they became sceptical of their ability to control them. Understandably, some of that scepticism was born on the battlefields of the Somme, Passchendaele, and Verdun; some of it arose out of the economic, political, and spiritual ruin which befell so much of Europe during the long dark night of fratricidal war; some of it sprang from Europe's growing obsession with its own future nemesis. And apart from the task of restoring shattered Europe at the end of the First World War, new ideas appeared aimed at internal European improvements — such as the application of the idea of a Welfare State — rather than the extension of European influence abroad.

No explanation of the rise or decline of Europe can afford to neglect the fact that Europe was a Christian civilization with a spiritual as well as a material standard of living. The influence of spiritual faith and power can never be neutral. The weakening of Christianity in the West was accompanied by the general European decline as the dominating force in the world. There was a time when the West was not filled with its present-day fundamental religious and ethical doubt and uncertainty — doubt and uncertainty that have bitten deep into the western sense of purpose.

Yet the decline of European power overseas has not come about because African and Asian nations wanted to return to a pre-European past. The impact of European ideas and beliefs has prompted and enabled many groups of Asians and Africans to find their nationhood and win their independence. It did not matter whether the West tried to delay or accelerate this process. The end result was the same. However well or badly the imperial power filled its role the final decline of western rule was inevitable from the moment the European impact was felt. A study of the lives of those who led the struggle for independence in many parts of Africa and Asia reveals that the fires they lit were kindled at a European flame. It is not the methods, or the economic goals of the West which are condemned, it is European tutelage which is resisted. From an economic point of view, the levels of agricultural and industrial production achieved by the new countries of Africa and Asia have depended on the extent to which these countries have been able to rid themselves of western political control while, at the same time, increasing the flow of western technical, financial, and administrative assistance. The need for the less economically developed parts of the world to draw upon the more advanced technology of the West increases rather than lessens when a country obtains its political independence. In the eyes of present-day Africans and Asians the evil of European 'colonialism' lies in white control of territories largely populated by Asians or Africans. This is the core of the problem facing the Republic of South Africa and the government of Southern Rhodesia today. The white people there can only hope to retain power over the much more numerous black inhabitants by resisting the present tide of change.

* * *

The prevailing ideas about European imperialism and colonialism are a mixture of truth and falsehood, objective reality and myth; witness the belief that expansion by annexing contiguous territory, as the United States, Russia, and China have done, was morally more justifiable than the sea empires of the countries of western Europe. How else could the small maritime nations of western Europe expand except across the seas? Domination across salt water is not the only or necessarily the worst kind of domination; the fate of indigenous peoples at the hands of an invader has largely been the same, whether the invader has come across land or sea, from the east or the west. European foreign rule is neither the basic evil force in the world, nor the greatest civilizing medium that the world has known. The mental image of imperialism and colonialism as seen by most men springs not only from what are known as 'historical facts' but also from men's imperfect vision, prejudice, irrationality, passion, enmity, and emotion. And myths and emotion are every bit as important in prompting action — especially for those just emerging from colonial rule — as objective reality. In its determination to impose its will on other races, Europe has followed a long tradition. Europeans were not the first people who wanted to impose their way of life upon others, and they will not be the last. European rule will pass, but imperialism will go on. To say that because Europe is in retreat imperialism is in its twilight hour is to ignore the lessons of history. The deliberations of Africans and Asians at the Bandung Conference in 1955, and of Africans at the Addis Ababa Conference in 1963, show that man is beginning to realize that imperialism is not something peculiarly European. It is universal. It is too simple to assume that the present division of the world into great and hostile camps is necessarily related to economic conditions. There is hardly a part of the world today that can seriously consider itself free from the threat of foreign domination. And that threat is not likely to disappear with the decline of European power. The collapse of western power in the world might mean greater enslavement not greater freedom for the emerging nations of Africa and Asia.

In all its splendour and squalor European rule has been much like the rule of other people. It was never our intention to create the impression that Europeans were somehow superior to all those who preceded them. False pride has always invited the wrath of the gods. In their conduct all men, all nations, within Europe or without, have been capable of reaching sublime heights as well as plunging to the deepest, foulest depths. It is difficult for those who bore arms in Europe's last great act of fratricide to believe aught else. It is just as foolish for Europeans to claim that they are ideologically and spiritually superior to Africans and Asians as it is for Africans and Asians to make the same claim against the 'materialistic' West. Nor has it been our purpose to catalogue the blood-stained pages of colonial history. The destruction by the British of the native people of

Tasmania, and by the Russians of the aboriginal people of eastern Siberia (even when judged in their historical context) are acts which cannot be pondered without feeling a sense of shame and despair at the enormity of human folly. Only a complete disregard for the sanctity of human life could have led the Europeans to act as they did; only false pride could have enabled them to show such a lack of understanding and such a contempt for native customs and traditions; only mental rigidity, stiff-necked self-assurance, and intellectual arrogance could have enabled them to assume universal validity for their way of life. It is this which is at the back of western misunderstandings with China and other Asian and African nations. Europeans could never understand why developments which were central to European life should have been only peripheral to the lives of other people. They first humiliated their subject peoples, and then, in Marxist-Leninism, provided a vehicle which could express the hatred felt by non-Europeans for western domination.

There are other chapters of the European story, however, dealing with altruistic service, and the extension by Europeans of human sympathy and compassion to the oppressed peoples of the world, which help to restore the balance. To study the life of mankind is to know the wisdom contained in the words 'Nolite condemnare et non condemna bimini'—'Judge not that ye be not judged'.

European imperialism does not differ so much from that of the past in its nature as in its consequences. Unlike all previous civilizations, it was the role of the European to colonize on a world scale. And the star that led millions of white people across the world was not simply the desire for conquest or booty; to an unparalleled extent the white man has sought to enrich and to transfigure the whole earth. In addition, this must be the first time that an imperial power has come to examine its past acts upon subject peoples in the light of moral laws; for there is in the West a widespread and extraordinary desire to atone for the misdeeds committed as an imperial power. Can our distress be partly explained by the fact that our actions fell so far short of our intentions? We are beginning to assess the impact of nineteenth-century economic forces in mid twentieth-century welfare terms; we are judging past actions by present standards. In a strange way Europeans have become retrospective. No early Briton expected the Romans to atone for their misdeeds; all subject peoples in the past have been only too glad to see their conquerors depart. Europe's desire to atone for past deeds is all the more extraordinary when it is remembered, as Lidice and Belsen more recently bear witness, that when the Europeans have wanted to strike the deepest terror or inflict unspeakable cruelty they have invariably done so upon themselves. This new guilt complex of the West has not only created a wish to make amends, it has also helped to create and strengthen — strange as it may seem — the anti-colonial movement of today. Out of European racial superiority and imperial arrogance has arisen the first community of interests of non-white peoples and the first racial division of the world.

Chapter III

EXODUS—THE DISPERSAL OF EUROPEANS SINCE THE EIGHTEENTH CENTURY

LONG before the eighteenth century, individual Europeans had left their impress upon many parts of the earth. Those Europeans who today probe the inner recesses of Antarctica, or are flung on voyages of discovery into outer space, follow a tradition established by Marco Polo, Alexander, Columbus, Vasco da Gama, Cabral, Magalhães (Magellan), De Soto, Xavier, Ricci, Livingstone, La Condamine, Cook, D'Urville, Burke, and Shackleton. To search for the mythical continent of Terra Australis, or the mythical East African kingdom of Prester John were as good reasons for exploration as any other. Accompanying the urge to explore and the love of adventure was the desire for conquest, the enthusiasm for trade, the search for treasure, the zeal to preach the Gospel. The European tide has flowed for almost half a millennium. Until a generation ago no physical or human barrier prevented its onward rush.

Yet, as we saw in a previous chapter, in Africa and Asia European explorers and colonizers were few in number until the nineteenth century; they rarely settled in the lands they discovered, conquered, and governed. Most of them lived a camp-like existence. Unlike earlier migrations of Asians, the Europeans seldom became absorbed into the country or the people whose life they shared; those Europeans who tarried in foreign parts were never happy until they had established a tiny outpost of western civilization — a European enclave in a foreign land. As late as 1800 more than half the land mass of the world was still untouched by the white race. And it would have remained so had not the Europeans multiplied and gone out in great numbers not so much to explore as to settle and colonize the world.

For more than a hundred and fifty years this tide of European settlers has swept onwards. In the Americas, Siberia, Australasia, as well as in the temperate parts of Africa, a new European world was established — a European world outside Europe, a greater Europe. In America, the mark of the Europeans is indelible. In Siberia and Oceania the European impress is less deep: the descendants of Europeans possess but have not yet had the time or the resources to develop and inhabit these vast regions. Elsewhere in the world many white people have been forced to retrace the steps their forbears took as European migrants more than a century ago. In Africa and Asia the high-water mark of European expansion is long past. Yet as the tide recedes it leaves behind it European ideas and European institutions which over the past two centuries have helped to change the destiny of the human race.

Between 1851 and 1960 (Table III/4) about sixty million Europeans left their homeland for areas overseas, or for Siberia. Reliable figures in the 1850's show that the largest group of migrants were the British and the Irish. They were soon joined by Germans and Scandinavians and from the 1880's onwards by Italians, Spaniards, Portuguese, Greeks, Austro-Hungarians, Turks (or, more accurately, minority groups living in Turkey), Poles, and Russians. By the early twentieth century the Latin and the Slav migrant outnumbered the Anglo-Saxon: they have continued to do so. The peak of the movement was reached in the first decade of the present century. The annual flow of 1·5 million emigrants who left Europe between 1909 and 1914 fell to about 700,000 in the 1920's, and to 130,000 in the 1930's.

Ever-increasing unfavourable world economic and political conditions were the greatest barrier to European mass migration after 1918. Few great fertile and readily accessible areas of the world remained unoccupied. The problems of assimilating migrants in countries such as the United States, Canada, and Australia, which hitherto had taken most immigrants, grew in the inter-war years. The United States, in particular, showed less ability to absorb labour than it had done in the nineteenth and the early part of the twentieth centuries. Growing less quickly and needing capital more than men, America's demand for labour was no longer unlimited. In addition, the supposed low level of social and political development of many of the immigrants created a widespread desire among native-born Americans to put an end to large-scale immigration. As a result, in 1921 the United States introduced the Quota System, which reduced the flow of immigrants to a fraction of its pre-First World War volume. Other forces tending to reduce the flow of migration were the economic depression of the 1920's, especially in the British Dominions, followed by the Great Depression of 1929–31. The repercussions of the Great Depression were world-wide; in particular, it put an end to schemes for British Empire settlement envisaged in the Empire Settlement Act of 1922. Russian emigration was stopped by the ban imposed by the revolutionary government after 1917. Not least important in drying up the stream of migration was the attitude of labour organizations in America and the British Dominions: faced with growing numbers of unemployed, the trade unions of these countries sought to restrict the number of immigrants. So influential were these various forces that for a short period during the 1930's Europe became an area of immigration rather than emigration. Since the Second World War the flow of migrants has been renewed. In the period 1946–60 about seven million emigrants left Europe. Of these, approximately half went to North America, one-sixth to Australia.

From whatever part of Europe the migrants came, they reflected the universally felt desire to improve their lot. Unlike many of the earlier migrations in history, the hallmark of the European exodus was individualism. Other migrations had been of a communal, warring, or tribal nature. The waves of Indian colonists, for instance, spreading throughout the countries of south-east Asia from the first to the ninth century after the birth of Christ were organized by the state. While there are examples of state-assisted migration, especially to parts of the British Empire, European emigration during the past two centuries was based largely on individual decision, individual courage, individual enterprise, individual hardship, and individual suffering. In the New World the migrant hoped to build a better and freer life than the one he had abandoned. The end of serfdom in Europe in the nineteenth century made it possible for some peasants to leave the land of their birth. The newly developed continents overseas offered an escape from crop failure and famine, religious and political persecution, compulsory military service and the upset of warfare. Others were induced to migrate by the colourful tales they were told of strange new lands, by the love of adventure and the urge 'to see beyond', the longing for high destiny, the power of individual genius, missionary zeal, the promise of gold, the urge to trade, curiosity, and the uncertainty surrounding what were until then largely unknown areas of the world. We can never hope to know all the material and spiritual factors compelling great numbers of people to cross the world. In intercontinental migration the propulsive factor has always been the greatest. A few men have always gone in search of the rainbow's end; most men, however, stay where they are unless driven to search for liberty or bread. Perhaps the primary stimulus, especially before 1900, was land hunger and the attraction of cheap land and better economic opportunities elsewhere. Although the proportion of artisans, factory and professional workers emigrating in the present century has increased, the majority of emigrants, at least until 1900, were land workers.

* * *

The migration of Europeans during the past two hundred years cannot be disassociated from the growth in their numbers during this period. The figures given in Table III/1 show that European population had increased more than fourfold since 1750; it grew at a faster rate than either Asian or

African population. If account is taken of the number of Europeans throughout the world (Table III/1) then the increase is approximately sevenfold. In 1750 Europe's share of world population was less than one-fifth; in 1900 it was more than one-quarter. It continued to rise, reaching its peak during the 1920's. While Europe's rate of growth, relative to the population of other continents, has slackened since then, Europeans still account for more than a fifth of world population and Europe remains as it was two hundred years ago — the most densely populated of all continents (Table III/8).

There is no single explanation for the rapid increase in European population in the period 1750–1960. It is doubtful if Europeans were more fertile than other races. Possibly one of the most important factors explaining the rapid increase in European population in the period 1750–1960 was the decline in the death rate. This resulted partly from the more efficient use of labour in industry and agriculture which made possible a rise in the general standard of living (or at least the avoidance of famine) partly from improvements — particularly during the past century — in cleanliness, public health, and medicine, and partly from the rapid conquest of distance, through the use of improved forms of transport and communications, which enabled Europe to draw upon the food and produce of other lands.

Not all European countries enjoyed these benefits. The Irish, for instance, were able to multiply in the second half of the eighteenth and the first half of the nineteenth century, not because of any improvement in agriculture or industrial techniques, or advances in public health or medicine, but because ever-greater quantities of Irish potatoes could easily be obtained to feed an ever-growing number of Irish mouths. It is life-creating rather than life-saving which explains the Irish figures. The rapid rise in Irish population was only reversed with the disastrous failure of the potato crop in the 1840's. Similarly, the growth of the Russian population during the nineteenth century can hardly have resulted from the factors mentioned. The Russians multiplied as they did because of a high fertility rate, assisted by the inner colonization within European Russia during the nineteenth century, as well as the formation of a trans-Ural society (Table III/2).

The decline in the rate of growth of Europe's population since the 1920's (despite the extraordinary success in conquering such illnesses as diphtheria and pneumonia) was largely due to a decline in the birth rate. In a very general way this decline followed the same course as the decline in the death rate had done earlier: beginning in north-western Europe and spreading gradually to the east and south. It is difficult to say what caused this fall in the European birth rate. Many factors, the most important of them impossible to assess quantitatively, determine the size of a family. Economics probably had some influence, but it is well-known that the fertility of the poor is higher than that of the rich. The growing inclination towards 'family planning', with the use of contraceptives, might be another cause for the fall in numbers, but, again, we have examples of Catholic countries such as Ireland, where presumably contraceptives are little used, whose birth rate followed the same downward course. The falling birth rate has also been explained by certain physiological and biological causes supposedly produced by the effects of modern, industrialized, urbanized western society. But the birth rates of rural France and Ireland followed the general trend. Some element of the mystery surrounding the will to reproduce, to live or die, will always elude the tangible explanation.

In most of Europe the decline in the birth rate appeared after 1870, and having once started to fall it fell more precipitously than the death rate. France diverged most from this pattern, having already experienced a steady decline in the birth rate since 1820. This is one of the reasons why French emigrants did not play as important a role in the migration of the years 1850–1914 as other European nations. For the rest of Europe, the fall in the birth rate after 1870 (Table III/3) could only have one result: a halt in rapid population growth. The decline in the death rate was less spectacular, as not even western medicine could lengthen the life-span beyond 'three score and ten' which for most men is its natural limit. One consequence of the decline in the rate of growth of European peoples was that the pressure on the land for employment became less acute. This, together with the spread of industrialization and social services, reduced the fear of unemployment and famine, which had always been strong motives for emigration.

* * *

During the past two centuries the United States of America has been the greatest field of European migration. By the Declaration of Independence on 4 July 1776, the English colonists severed their political ties with their home land. The first census taken in 1790 shows a white population of 3,930,000; the vast majority British. In 1800 the United States was still a small agricultural nation settled along the Atlantic seaboard. By the 1850's, by which time the American population had grown from 5 to 23 million, the frontier had spread from the Appalachians to the Mississippi Valley. Land-hungry and venturesome men had already pushed on ahead, crossing the Great Plains and the Rocky Mountains to reach California and Oregon; Brigham Young's handcart brigade of Mormons had marched from the banks of the Missouri to the arid land of Utah. By 1891, as a result of an increasing struggle to possess the land — a struggle fought out desperately between the French and the British in the eighteenth, and the European and the Indian in the nineteenth century — the frontier had reached the Pacific coast. The purchase of Alaska from the Russians in 1867 stimulated the American trade in furs and fish. The discovery of gold on the Klondike River in the 1890's caused an important influx of white population into that area.

The conquest of North America by the Europeans was not achieved without great distress being caused other races. The white man's success was the red man's undoing. European weapons, fire-water, and disease[1] had a disastrous effect upon the American Indian. His resistance was broken, his tribes scattered, his numbers reduced. In 1860 only about 45,000 Indians lived among the whites; the remainder, thought to be close to half a million, had been exiled on reservations, or driven beyond the frontiers of the United States. But the American Indian did not vanish. As with some other aboriginal groups in the world which have suffered white invasion, there has been a gradual recovery in numbers in the twentieth century. Much of the burden of the white man's conquest of North America also fell upon the shoulders of the black man. The combination of cheap, fertile land and the growing demand for cotton caused the slave population of the United States to increase from an estimated Negro population of 895,000 in 1800 to approximately 4 million in 1860.

Since 1850 almost forty million Europeans have sought a new life in the United States and, unlike migration to Canada, parts of Latin America and Australasia, the vast majority of immigrants entering the United States have stayed there. In terms of population growth, net immigration in the century before the Second World War contributed about 25 per cent. Until the 1880's, British, Irish, German, and Scandinavian immigrants predominated. Thenceforth, the flow of immigrants from the Austro-Hungarian Empire, Italy, Russia, and Poland grew until, by the first decade of the present century, it completely overshadowed that coming from north-western and central Europe. Foreign-born persons in the United States, according to the 1950 census, were almost 7 per cent of the total population.

The nineteenth- and twentieth-century European migrant provided much of the labour necessary to settle and develop the United States. A place was found for all kinds of Europeans — however illiterate, however alien, however unskilled, however poor. Although the Westward Movement is usually considered to be the work of that ambiguous creature known as the 'native American' (presumably those Europeans whose ancestors settled the eastern seaboard), a powerful stimulus was given by the waves of migrants reaching the American shore. Especially is this true of the Germans, Austrians, and Swiss who, in the nineteenth century,

[1] See especially Sir A. Grenfell Price 'The Importance of Disease in History', the George Adlington Syme oration, the Australasian College of Surgeons, Adelaide, 1964.

staked all they had in wealth, skill, and toil to settle the farming frontier of Wisconsin and Illinois; of the Swedes, Norwegians, and Danes whose lumbering wagon trains came to rest in the rolling prairies of Illinois, Iowa, Kansas, the Dakotas, and Minnesota; and of the Dutch who brought so much of the Netherlands to the Michigan peninsula. Allowing for exceptions such as the Scots-Irish migrants to Pennsylvania in the middle of the eighteenth century, there were other large groups of immigrants, among them the Irish, Poles, Russians, Greeks, and Italians, who helped to develop the urban areas of the east rather than the rural areas of the mid- and far west. Their reluctance to move westwards from the Appalachians arose partly from the desire to avoid a rural way of life which often was associated with famine and want, and partly from their ignorance of frontier life. Arriving in a period of rapid industrial development they found opportunities for work in the factories and mines as well as in building and public works of all kinds. Many of the newer immigrants from eastern and southern Europe followed the example set by the Irish in showing a natural proclivity for town life. They chose to remain with their own people and (for those who were Catholic) with their church in the great cities of the east and later of the mid-west. Individual Irishmen, Poles, Russians, and Italians are to be found in every part of the United States; as national groups they never felt the same need, the same urge, to settle the American frontier. Many arrived so destitute that they had no choice but to struggle to survive in the eastern cities. Most important, the majority of Latin and Slav immigrants (many of them peasant farmers) did not arrive in the United States until the late nineteenth or the early twentieth century (Tables III/4 and III/5), by which time the best land had been taken, and most employment was to be found in the towns. Even where land was available, immigrants often lacked the necessary capital and skill to settle it. After 1900, all immigrants, whatever their origin, found employment more readily in the industrial east rather than in the agricultural mid- and far west.

Many European immigrants brought highly developed industrial skills, and the history of certain American industries is linked with European national groups, such as the Germans in brewing and malting, or the Russians and Poles in the clothing industry, or the English and Welsh in a wide field of industrial effort including the textile and allied trades, the iron and steel industry, machine and manufacturing trades, and (with numbers of Scots) mining. Trained in the mines and factories of industrial Europe, many of the British moved directly into the more highly skilled American occupations; the English, Welsh, and Scots were also conspicuously successful in entering the professions. In the second half of the nineteenth century growing numbers of unskilled immigrants were absorbed by the American industrial system using mass production techniques. British highly skilled labour assisted in the establishment of the American tin-plate industry in the 1890's. Industries such as mining and quarrying, textiles, steel, and rubber found employment for the skilled and unskilled immigrants of all European nations. The fact that English was the official language often meant that the skilled occupations were more accessible to those commanding the use of English. But for the great numbers of immigrants who found a place as unskilled labourers language was no barrier.

Although the majority of European immigrants entering the United States after 1850 found employment outside agriculture, the development of sugar-beet and clover, the wine and wheat industries, to take several examples, are all indebted to valuable techniques of production introduced by European immigrants. The cattle ranges developed in the last quarter of the nineteenth century in Texas, New Mexico, and Wyoming were heavily indebted to British companies for stock and skilled immigrant labour. The major contribution of the European peasant was to help fill in the lands cleared by the earlier pioneers and frontiersmen. Among the immigrant peoples the Greeks were the least and the Scandinavians the most attracted to American agriculture. The Germans helped to develop the dairying industry; numbers of English and Welsh found employment as gardeners and nurserymen; Italian and Spanish immigrants provided a stimulus to the development of the market-gardening (truck-farming) industry of the eastern and later the western seaboard.

The impact of large-scale migration upon the American wage structure is extremely difficult to assess. The available data suggests that large-scale immigration was partly responsible for the fact that real wages rose relatively less in the United States in the period 1860–1913 than in Germany, France, Sweden, or the United Kingdom. In particular, the magnitude of immigration in the twenty years before the First World War was sufficient to affect the earnings of unskilled labour in several American manufacturing industries. Yet it is probably closer to the truth to say that immigration retarded rather than reversed the upward trend of American wages. Immigrant labour was more complementary than competitive. In agriculture and industry, and especially in public works, the immigrant took the work that many 'native Americans' did not want and for which they were not available in sufficient numbers. The arrival of the immigrant on the American farming frontier was often offset by the departure of the 'native American' to the areas further west. Similarly, in much of the rough labour needed in the building and construction industries, in coal mining, and iron manufacture, the immigrant started at the bottom and for much of his labour had no competitor. Far from depriving the American of his livelihood, the armies of workers who sought a new life in the United States, especially the armies of unskilled industrial workers, made possible the establishment of many skilled jobs for 'native Americans'. The fact that over a long period the demand for both skilled and unskilled labour exceeded supply makes it difficult to understand how migration could have seriously impaired the general standard of living, or could have been anything but an advantage to the economy as a whole. The same general conclusion might be drawn for other countries of large-scale migration, particularly those countries which have received enormous numbers of migrants over a relatively short period. In most cases the continuous influx from Europe of skilled and unskilled labour not only provided the reserves of labour necessary for rapid economic expansion, it also gave an important stimulus to the rate of population growth, which in turn, helped to provide an expanding working force and a high level of demand, particularly for housing and public utilities.[1]

The much more dynamic and socially fluid environment of the United States stimulated the immigrant's resourcefulness, initiative, ingenuity, and enterprise. Responding to the new challenge, some immigrant families quickly fought their way to the front of America's industrial, commercial, and financial life. But until the flood of American immigration was stemmed by the Quota Act of 1921, there were always other immigrants arriving, charged with the same ambitions and impelled by the same motives, eager to overtake those who had preceded them. Much of the fast tempo of present-day American life springs directly from these origins.

Since the end of the First World War the number of Europeans entering the United States has declined. Whereas in the nine years before 1914 nearly one million migrants on average entered the United States every year, this fell to an annual average of less than a quarter of a million during the inter-war years; and in the nine years 1946–54, the influx was only about 190,000 a year. The figure has not varied greatly since then. There has also been a change in the kind of immigrant. With the passing of the Immigration Bill on 26 May 1924 (which stipulated that the annual intake of 150,000 should be shared between the different European nations in proportion to their relative strength in the American population in 1920) Congress expressed a preference for the Anglo-Saxon rather than the Latin and Slav immigrant. However, the altered social and economic conditions of post-war Europe continued to draw people from the newer rather than the older countries of emigration. Between 1920 and 1950, as the percentage of north-western Europeans in the American foreign-born population decreased, that of southern Europeans, Canadians (other than French Canadians), and Latin Americans increased. Proportionately, the greatest

[1] The relation between population and economic growth during the past hundred years is discussed in 'Economic Growth: the Last Hundred Years', *National Institute Economic Review* (July 1961), pp. 24-49, N.I.E.S.R., New York.

fall was in the number of Irish, Scandinavian, and German immigrants; the greatest rise was in the number of Greeks and Italians. Since the 1920's an unusually large number of migrants have been refugees from racial and political persecution. Many of these refugees were drawn from strata of the European population that had previously contributed few migrants to the United States.

After the United States, the British Dominions of Canada, Australia, New Zealand, and South Africa, together with Argentina and Brazil, attracted the greatest number of Europeans. In the period 1815–1914, of the 20 million migrants leaving the United Kingdom, many of them in trans-shipment from the continent of Europe, approximately 4 million went to Canada. Gross immigration into Canada in the period 1920–58 amounts to approximately 3 million. (Table III/5.)

The rise in Canadian population since the middle of the eighteenth century from approximately 65,000 whites in 1763 to 16 million in 1960 is due more to the rapid rate of natural increase than to an increase resulting from net migration. This is especially true of the French, who throughout have had a consistently higher birth rate than the English-speaking Canadians. The 10,000 French people who began the settlement of Canada in the seventeenth century have largely provided Canada with its present-day French population of 5 million. Although gross immigration into Canada has been at a high level this has been offset by the continuous flow of migrants from Canada to the United States. Considerable numbers of so-called 'immigrants' chose the Canadian route to the United States in order to circumvent United States immigration regulations, or take advantage of an all-water route to the American mid-west. Between 1851 and 1950 unofficial statistics show (Table III/5 and 6) that Canadian emigration exceeded immigration in five of the ten decades. Over the period as a whole only about 10 per cent of the immigrants entering Canada stayed there permanently. (The figure for the United States is well over 70 per cent.) Net immigration into Canada furnished only 4 per cent of all population growth in the hundred years after 1850. In the period 1851–1900 it was a negative factor in Canada's population growth since the number of emigrants who left Canada was greater than the number of immigrants arriving there: 2·2 million as against 2·1. Whatever steps successive Canadian governments have taken to retain immigrants, they were able to do little before 1914 to offset the superior attractions of the United States with its surveyed land and settled towns and communities. Even in the inter-war years the gain in population, resulting from the increased flow of immigrants into Canada in certain years, was offset by heavy emigration to the United States.

Although France had ceded to England all claims to Canada in 1763, it was not until the end of the Napoleonic Wars in 1815 that large groups of Europeans — almost entirely British immigrants — began to make their way up the St. Lawrence to join earlier groups of Canadian settlers. Most of the immigrants were discharged British soldiers, farmers, agricultural labourers, and groups of artisans; some of them were assisted by the British government. Unlike the immigrants entering the United States, those entering Canada were drawn almost entirely, as they would continue to be until the 1880's, from the British Isles. Many of the English and Scots settled in homogeneous farming communities. The Irish immigrants, on the other hand, showed a preference for town life, or preferred to make their living in the fisheries, in forestry work, or as labourers working on the roads, canals, and railways.

The overwhelming majority of immigrants who went to Canada in the first half of the nineteenth century undoubtedly hoped to settle on the land. In Canada (unlike the United States) pioneering work has been left much more to the newcomer. The early nineteenth-century settlers made their way into Upper Canada because land was more plentiful there, and also because the hostility of French Canadians to the influx of Anglo-Saxon immigrants was less intense than in Lower Canada. It was also felt by the British authorities that the immigrants might help to keep the Americans out of Upper Canada. The stream of migrants changed the balance of population between British and French Canadians. By 1852 British immigrants in Upper Canada (centred on Toronto) out-numbered the much longer-established French population in Lower Canada (centred on Quebec).

Although the Confederation of the British colonies in North America in 1867 provided the political and economic framework upon which could be built a larger and more diversified economy, the rate of immigration slowed down between 1860 and 1890. This was because most of the free land of the more settled areas of Ontario was now occupied and also because the prairie lands to the west were inaccessible without rail communications. Moreover, the figures dealing with Canadian migration to the United States between 1870 and 1890 (in this period Canada received 1·5 million immigrants from Europe and lost 2 million emigrants, most of them Canadian-born, to the United States) illustrate the drain upon Canadian population. It also suggests that the United States was not as seriously affected as Canada by the economic fluctuations felt during the period 1873–96. The figures dealing with European emigration in the same twenty years to the United States, Australia, and Argentina show that Canada did not compete successfully for European immigrants. Yet by 1900 Canada had more than doubled her population since 1850, reaching about 5·3 million.

Since the beginning of the present century, Canadian population has increased to more than 17 million in 1960. Especially pronounced was the rise by over 1·8 million in the decade 1901–11, a rise exceeding that of the previous thirty years. A little more than half of this increase was due to immigration. (Included in this figure is a remarkable increase in the number of Canadian Indians, whose forbears had been decimated by European invasion.) Canada's ability to absorb people has continued to grow since the beginning of the present century. Arrivals of immigrants, which numbered 82,000 in 1891, had climbed to almost 190,000 in 1906, and by the eve of the First World War had reached a record number of almost half a million. As a result of this, a prairie population of little more than a quarter of a million in 1891, and less than half a million at the beginning of the present century, exceeded 1·3 million by 1911. In addition to the growing number of immigrants who were attracted by improved economic conditions, other factors encouraging the development of the western regions of Canada from the latter part of the nineteenth century were the government's policy of free land grants, the general adoption of an early-maturing variety of wheat that reduced the risk of frost damage, the adoption of dry-farming practices to conserve moisture, mining discoveries in British Columbia, favourable world markets for Canadian produce, an adequate capital supply, increased shipping from Pacific ports, and a growing railway network. Further important discoveries of mineral resources (in the vicinity of Great Bear Lake) and oil deposits (on the Mackenzie river) in the inter-war years have improved Canada's position with the rest of the world.

A great part of Canada's ability to attract and absorb immigrants during the inter-war years has come from diversified industrial expansion for the growing home market. Since the 1920's Canada has shown a preference for skilled industrial workers essential to the rapid expansion of manufacturing industry and construction works. More than anything else it is the growth of Canadian industry during the past forty years which explains the rise in Canada's net immigration figures. Whereas prior to the Second World War agriculture was Canada's major industry with 29 per cent of its labour force employed in farming, by 1962 less than 11 per cent of the labour force was employed in agriculture and less than 18 per cent of the population lived on the land. Between 1920 and 1938 Canada took 850,000 British immigrants (Australia took 700,000, and the United States 500,000). Since the Second World War Canadian immigration from Europe has increased, Canada taking 1·2 million in the decade 1946–55, a much higher proportion of immigrants to its population than the United States, but not as high as Australia or Israel. In 1957 more than a quarter of a million immigrants were admitted, a figure maintained during the next three years. It has been estimated that net immigration accounted for 22 per cent of the total increase in population over the period 1951–1961. An increasing number of Canadian immigrants entering the country since 1880 have been of Latin, Slavonic, and other non-Anglo-Saxon origin.

South and south-east of the United States — seven thousand miles from Mexico to Patagonia — stretch the countries of Latin America. The total area is almost equal to the whole of North America. These countries differ in size (Brazil is almost as large as the United States, Haiti is as small as Maryland); they differ also in history, race, population, wealth, topography, and climate (only Uruguay lies wholly outside the tropics or sub-tropical regions). They are equally diverse in language: the official language of Brazil is Portuguese, that of Haiti is French, that of Argentina, Spanish; in Paraguay the much changed native Guarani is still spoken. The pre-conquest peoples, upon whom the European imposed his civilization, ranged from the most savage tribes to the highly developed Aztec and Inca cultures. The racial composition of the people who inhabit this area of the world consists of Europeans, Africans, Americans, and Asians; it is so mixed that estimates of the ethnic composition of Latin Americans vary widely (Table III/7). The name 'Latin America' can hardly be expected to cover such a variety of conditions and such a conglomeration of peoples. Catholicism is perhaps one of the few firm ties between these diverse peoples.

The history of European influence in Latin America dates from Columbus's discovery of Santo Domingo in 1492. His purpose was to find a sea passage to the East, but most of the Spaniards and Portuguese who followed him preferred to plunder the riches of the Americas rather than continue to search for a western route that would lead them to the coveted trade of Asia. Performing incredible feats of exploration and warfare, Cortez conquered Mexico; Alvarado: Guatemala; Pizarro: Peru; Quesada: New Granada; Montejo: Yucatan. These men were individual adventurers typifying the freebooting phase of European expansion; the authority of the Castilian crown was extended to the lands they had conquered only when their individual conquests were completed. Portuguese colonization of Brazil (discovered by Cabral in 1500) proceeded at a more leisurely and a more peaceful pace. The Portuguese were not opposed by the Indian population as the Spanish 'Conquistadores' were. Perhaps with good reason when one reflects on the utter ruthlessness of a Pizarro.

By the time Balboa had reached the Pacific in 1513 the promise of great treasure had diverted attention from the Eastern to the Western Hemisphere. Less than a generation after Columbus's landfall, the whole eastern shore of Latin America had been explored. In two generations Spain and Portugal (in 1494 the reigning Pope had divided the world between them), possessed an empire in Latin America twice the size of Europe. Although the exploitation of gold and silver became the chief source of crown revenues in the New World, and the basis of much private wealth, countries such as Chile, Yucatan, and Rio de la Plata were developed from the beginning as agricultural and pastoral regions. The feudal estate has remained the basic farming unit of Latin America.

In the conquest of Latin America the role of the Catholic Church was all-important. With a handful of soldiers to protect them and to establish European rule, the missionaries were often the first to penetrate the interior of the continent. They helped to found and to maintain the political authority of their nation, and to transmit culture and education as well as the principles of their faith. They were a civilizing and unifying force. Where they could, the missionaries tried to protect the native from the cruelty and rapacity which inevitably accompanied white invasion. The Jesuits in particular tried to temper their countrymen's eager quest for wealth. True, the Peruvian Incas would curse the memory of Father Vicente de Valverde, who, as spiritual guardian of Pizarro and his men, sanctioned the perfidious slaying of the Inca leader Atahualpa. But there were other men of the cloth, such as Father Antonio Vieira, in the Maranhão province of Brazil, who did their best to protect the natives from the shock of western intrusion. Yet to stand between the native and those who would exploit him was often to earn the enmity of the temporal power, and in the mid-eighteenth century the interfering, intransigent Jesuits were shipped home to Spain. Western greed, aided by superior western weapons and the devastating sicknesses which the Europeans brought with them (including measles, smallpox, typhus, and influenza), accelerated the decline of the Aztec, the Maya, the Chibcha, and the Inca civilizations of the Americas.

By 1600 Spanish power extended from New Mexico and Florida in the North to Chile and the Rio de la Plata in the South. Spain and Portugal were not left in undisputed possession of the New World, but for a further two hundred years the wealth of the Americas was used to enrich the Iberian Peninsula. Then, in a matter of two decades (1810–30), as the cry of liberty resounded throughout Latin America, the richest and most majestic empires the world had known disappeared; their place was taken by thirteen independent states. All that remained of former imperial might were Cuba and Puerto Rico. The control which Spain and Portugal had exercised over the New World for three centuries was broken. The door of Latin America was now flung open to the trade and migration of the world.

The white population of Spanish America in 1574 was estimated at 160,000; that of Portuguese Brazil in 1583, 25,000. By the end of the colonial period (1820) Spanish America had 3,276,000 whites, 7,530,000 Indians, and 776,000 Negroes. Without women of his own race the European conqueror mixed his blood with the women of the indigenous Indian tribes as well as with the Negresses brought as slaves from Africa. The union of Europeans and Indians which had been going on since the beginning of the white invasion had by 1820 produced 5,328,000 mestizos. In Brazil, in 1818, there were 843,000 Europeans, 1,887,500 Negroes, 259,400 Indians and 628,000 mestizos. The comparative ease with which Negroes could be transferred from Africa and the West Indies to the Brazilian mainland, coupled with the demands of its semi-colonial plantation industry and the unsuitability of most Indian labour, explains why today so many Negroes are found in Brazil and in the islands of the Caribbean. Negro slavery had long had a place in Spain and Portugal. In the sixteenth century the black man became the white man's unwilling assistant in the agrarian colonization of the New World. The number of mulattos (resulting from the union of Europeans and Negroes) and the number of zambos (resulting from the union of Indians and Negroes) in Latin America is hard to assess.

As a result of this process, more than half the 200 million people of Latin America (Table III/7) in 1960 were of mixed blood, less than one-quarter were white, one-seventh Indian, and one-sixth Negro; exact racial analysis is impossible. The typical 'homo Americanus' has become a mixture of all races. The racial composition of the different Latin American nations today is dependent upon their history. Bolivia, Peru, Guatemala, and Ecuador have remained predominantly Indian; the Antilles, Costa Rica, Uruguay, and Argentina are predominantly white (the Indians of Argentina were either banished or exterminated). In Chile there has been a complete fusion of the white and the Indian elements. In Mexico, Colombia, continental Central America, Venezuela, and Paraguay the bulk of the population is mestizo, but there are in addition separate groups of Indians and Europeans which stand apart. Haiti is a Negro Republic; its neighbour, the Dominican Republic, claims to be white, but is in fact mostly Negro and mulatto. Cuba is extremely heterogeneous in its racial composition: its main strains are European and Negro. Portuguese Brazil has a racial pattern unlike the others; it is about half white, the remainder is made up of mestizos, Negroes and Indians. The Portuguese in Brazil showed a greater willingness to mix with the native Indian tribes than the Spaniards did in Argentina or the Anglo-Saxons in the northern half of America. The earlier Moorish domination of Portugal had created a tradition of tolerance and intermarriage.

In the century prior to the Second World War net immigration to Latin America amounted to about 8 million. In terms of population growth, net immigration contributed about 8 per cent of the total increment between 1840 and 1940. Most immigrants came from Europe, but the number included Negro slaves brought earlier from Africa as well as some Asiatic immigrants. Foreign-born persons living in Latin America in 1940 numbered approximately 9 per cent of the total population. During the Second World War immigration to Latin America almost ceased. The number of immigrants admitted to several Latin American countries has increased markedly since 1945. Italy, Spain, and Portugal have remained the principal sources of immigration. Between 1947 and 1951 almost 100,000 displaced persons were settled in Latin America (chiefly in Argentina and Brazil) by the International Refugee Organization. The majority of Europeans settled in Argentina (gross 6·4 million) and Brazil (gross 4·4 million). The only other Latin American countries to receive large numbers of Europeans in the period 1851–1960 were Cuba (629,000), Uruguay (642,000), and Mexico (287,000). The bulk of European immigrants were Spaniards, Italians, Portuguese and, to a much lesser extent, immigrants from north-western and central Europe. The Latin Europeans predominated because the rigid control of immigrants by the Spanish and Portuguese crowns during the colonial period had established a strong Latin tradition in the southern half of the American continent.

The modern period in the history of the development of the greatest of all the South American countries, Brazil, begins with the Treaty of Madrid in 1750. By this treaty, Portugal found itself in possession of half the land mass of South America. Portuguese interest in Brazil, especially in the exploitation of brazilwood and sugar, was evident from the sixteenth century onwards. However, the eighteenth-century discovery of gold and diamonds, iron, manganese, and other minerals, quickened Portuguese interest. In 1650 only about a quarter of an estimated population of 150,000 to 200,000 were Europeans. At the end of the colonial period in 1819 about one million of an estimated total population of 4·4 million were of European stock. In the mid-nineteenth century the Brazilian population was estimated to be 8 million, including 2·5 million slaves. At the census of 1936 the figure was 42,400,000; by 1960 this had increased to 71 million, about 40 per cent white.

The number of European migrants going to Brazil (Table III/5) was unimportant until the closing decades of the nineteenth century. The largest intake in any single year in the nineteenth century was in 1888, with 133,000 immigrants; the nineties saw the fastest flow. By the end of the century slavery had been finally abolished; the gradual decline of the slave trade from the 1830's onwards had stimulated the demand for free labour. The granting of complete freedom to slaves in 1888 undoubtedly stimulated immigration from Europe; it also helps to explain the sharp fall in the coffee harvests of the next three years, which had disastrous effects on Brazilian exports. Assisting the increase in numbers was the greater degree of political stability resulting from the long and stable rule of the Emperor Pedro II (1840–89). After the mid-century, agriculture, commerce, and industry were all expanded, and a network of roads and railways were built from the Brazilian seaboard to the interior of the states of São Paulo, Paraná, and Rio de Janeiro. (The river and lake systems of Latin America generally have not provided easy access to the interior except in the state of Rio Grande do Sul.) Following the all-time peak of the 1890's (gross immigration was 1,129,000), the number of immigrants was halved in the first decade of the twentieth century (gross immigration fell to 671,000). Yet the level of immigration in the period 1900–30 was high (Table III/5). Following a fall in the depressed 1930's and the war-torn 1940's, there has been a recovery in the 1950's and 1960's. An overall figure for immigrants entering Brazil in the period 1874 (when reliable data first became available) to 1949 has been set at 4·5 million, the majority, it is thought, having settled in the state of São Paulo and the southern regions of the country.

Most European immigrants into Brazil were Italians, Portuguese and Spaniards. Italy and Portugal provided about two-thirds of them. The number of Spaniards were about one-eighth. Figures for the period 1820–1940 show the Italians leading, followed closely by the Portuguese, Spaniards, and Germans. The peak of Italian immigration was reached in the 1890's (130,000 in 1891), coinciding with the peak in total immigration, but it was particularly strong between 1887 and 1920. In the decade 1888–98, 1·25 million Italians entered Brazil; between 1904–13 another million followed. The effect of the First World War and the depressed state of world agriculture from the mid-twenties until the late 1930's reduced Italian immigration; also some migrants were deflected by the Italian government to Italy's North African colonies. Between 1914 and 1925 the number of Italian immigrants never exceeded 16,000 in any one year; after 1925 the number never exceeded 10,000. The falling off in Italian migrants in the 1950's is partly to be explained by improved economic conditions in Italy, and partly by the better opportunities offered in Argentina and Australia. Although migration from Portugal and Spain has been going on since the sixteenth century, its peak was reached only in the decade 1911–20. Immigration from Portugal since the Second World War, in comparison with groups of other immigrants, has shown a marked upward trend.

Immigration of other Europeans into Brazil has been relatively unimportant. Between 1820 and 1940 a quarter of a million Germans settled in Brazil; the peak of German immigration was reached in the decade 1921–30 with 75,861 immigrants. In 1824 the first German settlements were established in Rio Grande do Sul. The more than one million Germans concentrated today in the southern state of Rio Grande do Sul, Santa Catarina, and Paraná is a result of the high rate of German immigration in recent decades as well as the large families which nineteenth-century German immigrants raised in Brazil. The only other important group of Europeans consists of Russians, Ukrainians, and Poles.

In the present century there has been a number of Japanese settlers; between 1908 and 1940, about 200,000. The peak of 86,414 immigrants was reached in the decade 1930–40. Thenceforth, as quota restrictions were imposed upon all Asian immigrants — chiefly by the government of the state of São Paulo — the flow of Japanese immigrants was reduced to the smallest trickle; it has now almost ceased.

More than half the population of Brazil is concentrated on its coastal strip and in the southern region of the country from Minas Gerais and Espirito Santo to Rio Grande do Sul. These states, comprising one-sixth of the land area of Brazil, have today more than half of Brazil's population, and the bulk of its agricultural industry, transport systems, and manufacturing potential. The greater part of Brazil's mid- and far west remain largely untouched. There has never been continuity of settlement — a moving frontier — in South America as there was in the North. Very little of the land area of Brazil is under cultivation; it is not likely to be increased unless large quantities of capital are forthcoming.

The Portuguese have contributed to every phase of Brazil's development. The early Portuguese exploited Brazilian dye woods, developed the pastoral industry and built up the trade in hides. With the help of African slaves they made cotton and sugar the two principal agricultural products of colonial Brazil. Until the development of sugar production on the islands of the Caribbean in the nineteenth century, the Brazilian sugar industry was the greatest in the world. It was the basis of the wealth of the Brazilian empire. Throughout the colonial period the value of sugar exports was greater than all other products combined, including gold and diamonds; in the mid-seventeenth century it exceeded the value of England's total exports. Similarly, for most of the eighteenth century Brazil was a leading exporter of cotton. In the nineteenth century, particularly since slavery was abolished in 1888, Brazil's agricultural development was furthered by Italians, Germans, Spaniards, and more recently by the Japanese. Able to acquire good land cheaply, numbers of Germans and other central Europeans helped to settle the prosperous agricultural cattle areas in southern Brazil. In the state of Santa Caterina the Germans retained their national identity until the Second World War.

The enormous influx of Italian labourers (unlike the early Germans who were chiefly peasant farmers) in the second half of the nineteenth century found employment on the coffee plantations of São Paulo, Minas Gerais, and Espirito Santo. Without them the spectacular growth of the coffee industry at the end of the century could not have taken place. But the Italian contribution extends far beyond the development of the coffee industry. It is especially marked in the agricultural and industrial history of the state of São Paulo. In 1891, 130,000 Italian immigrants arrived; half a million more followed between 1894 and 1903. They made São Paulo and Santos the chief Italian cities of Brazil. Between 1908 and 1935 most Italians went to the state of São Paulo. Conditions proved equally hard as those they had left behind in Italy and Sicily and many were unable to sink their roots in the land; encouraged by cheap ocean transport, about half of them returned to Europe. Other Italians found employment in developing the rubber industry of the Amazon valley, but the history of Brazilian rubber, like the history of so many other Brazilian products, is the story of boom and collapse. In the different phases of the country's history Brazil's fortunes have been linked with sugar and tobacco, gold and diamonds, cotton and hides, rubber, and especially coffee. Brazil's peak in coffee production was reached in 1925, when it supplied four-fifths of the world's needs. In these circumstances, it is hardly surprising that the Brazilian economy should have known so much general instability.

In 1960 agriculture constituted approximately 30 per cent of the total national income. The increases in yields in recent years have come more from the expansion of the cultivated area for the principal crops, than from general increases in productivity. In 1960 exports of food, drink, and agricultural raw materials provided Brazil with most of its foreign earnings. Coffee accounted for only 15 per cent of farm income, but for about half the value of total exports. Brazil continues to be the leading coffee producer in the world, as well as one of the world's foremost producers of cocoa, sugar, cotton, and livestock.

Except for the great gold rush to Minas Gerais at the end of the seventeenth and the beginning of the eighteenth centuries, which later spread into the Mato Grosso and Goiás, minerals have never been a major cause of immigration into Brazil. The country's vast mineral resources — particularly of high-grade iron ore and manganese ore — are only just beginning to be developed.

The industrialization of Brazil did not get under way before the twentieth century. Until then many of the chief prerequisites for industrialization — labour, skill, capital, markets, and power resources — were absent. Perhaps more importantly, Brazil, like many other parts of Latin America, lacked innovational drive to change. The original Portuguese settlers had become a landed class. Many of the immigrants who came later, especially those coming from parts of Europe unaffected by rapid industrial change, were happy to accept the existing order of things. Steam power had been employed in sugar milling since the second decade of the nineteenth century. There had also been an expansion of cotton, wool, and jute manufacture, flour and saw milling, and a certain amount of metal- and leather-working had been done. Further development, however, awaited the impetus provided by the intervention of the Federal Government in 1906, and especially the outbreak of the First World War.

The First World War, by curtailing Brazilian imports of manufactures, provided the initial stimulus for industrialization. The rising level of occupational skill of the immigrants entering Brazil in the inter-war years reflects Brazil's gradual transition from intense specialization in coffee production to the development of a more diversified economy. The fact that Brazil (like Argentina and Uruguay) has not had to face the same formidable social and economic barriers provided by crafts and craft occupations in certain other Latin American countries has facilitated the transition. A start was made with heavy chemicals, machine and metal-working of various kinds, cement manufacture, electrical goods, auto-assembly, rubber tyre manufacture, and the production of rayon and other textile polymers. The 1920's saw the introduction of the first integrated iron and steel operation. Progress, however, was uneven. There were many setbacks, especially as a result of over-expansion of the textile industry in the 1920's, but by 1938 the value of industrial production had outstripped the value of agricultural production; light industry, aimed at meeting the needs of domestic consumers, still predominated.

The Second World War provided a further stimulus to the industrial sector. The establishment of the Volta Redonda Steel plant in the state of Rio de Janeiro in 1941–2 is a landmark in Brazil's efforts to lessen its dependence on what in the past has been a most unstable system of mono-culture. While the greatest contribution in this effort has been made by the Brazilians themselves — chiefly the descendants of the Portuguese and the Italians — considerable help has also been given by many other groups of Europeans and (with the Syrians and Lebanese) Levantines. Since 1912 much industrial knowledge has been diffused by United States and Canadian firms operating branch factories in Brazil.

In 1960 Brazil's output of steel was two million ingot tons (small for such a large country, but rising fast). In the 1950's major expansions took place in the chemical and pharmaceutical industries (including petrol refining), in the manufacture of automobiles, paper and pulp, heavy mechanical and electrical equipment, machine tools, and agricultural tractors. Brazil has not been able to keep pace with its electrical power and transport needs, but since 1945 facilities have been expanded rapidly. Measured by the rate of economic growth in recent years, Brazil qualifies as one of the leaders of the western world. Measured by income per head, however, the economic levels enjoyed by Brazilians are still far below those prevailing in western European and North American countries.

While the growth of industry in recent decades is of the greatest significance to the Brazilian economy, two-thirds of Brazil's population remain rural, and industrial development is heavily concentrated in the São Paulo, Bello Horizonte, and the Rio de Janeiro areas.

Discovered by Spanish explorers, headed by Juan Diaz de Solis, Argentina remained under Spanish domination until the revolt of 1810. Its population, which grew from less than a third of a million in 1800 to approximately two million by the first national census in 1869 and twenty million in 1960, has remained almost entirely white. There are few Indians and mestizos. The invasion of the European with his firearms and diseases resulted in the extermination of most of the Indian population. The plains Indians were not, however, subdued before the 1880's, and there are still remnants of Indian tribes in the Gran Chaco and in Patagonia.

Immigrants have come overwhelmingly from Latin Europe, mainly Spaniards and Italians. Small British and German agricultural colonies were, however, established in the vicinity of Buenos Aires in the 1820's. Immigration remained unimportant until greater political stability was achieved in the second half of the nineteenth century (a federal constitution was adopted in 1853), and until railroads were extended to the growing agricultural and pastoral regions. The sharp rise in immigration in the late 1880's (219,000 in 1889) was followed by a fall in the depressed years of the 1890's, which in turn was followed by the more prosperous conditions and an increase in the flow of migrants during the decade preceding the First World War (1912 was the peak year with 323,000). The increase in Argentina's total population resulting from immigration in the decade before 1914 exceeded the natural increase of the population (Table III/6). In 1914 one in three of the inhabitants of Argentina was foreign-born. The disruptive effects of the First World War reduced the stream of immigration. Since the 1920's (Table III/5) the flow has continued to rise and fall according to world economic and political conditions. The peaks of 1889–1912 were never reached again after the First World War, and the catastrophic fall in agricultural prices and land values during the 1920's reduced the flow of immigrants and encouraged the introduction of restrictions on immigration by the Argentine government. Between 1857, when the first rough statistics were compiled, until 1930 it has been estimated that six million Europeans entered Argentina, but we do not know how many settled permanently. Net immigration for the period 1857–1940 was about three and a half million. At this time (1940) one in five of Argentina's population was foreign-born. Since the end of the Second World War, net immigration has amounted to approximately 600,000. The proportion of Argentina's population that was foreign-born in 1958 was about one in seven.

Although Argentina was colonized by Spain, more than half of its immigrants have come from Italy. In the nineteenth century there were more Italian immigrants than all the rest of Europeans combined, including Spaniards. Between 1857 and 1940 about three million Italians went to Argentina. Spain provided about two million immigrants in the same period. The rest were German and German-Russian, Polish, French, British, Turkish, and Austro-Hungarian immigrants. A long and friendly history between the British and the Argentinians (based partly on British willingness to trade and invest in Argentina) has given the relatively small British colony in Argentina's major cities almost a special position among immigrant groups. There have been few slaves from Africa because the development by the European of one of the world's greatest pastoral industries did not encourage the wholesale importation of slave labour.

The foundations of the Argentine economy were laid during the period of Spanish colonial domination. The economic progress of the past two centuries has consisted of the astonishing transformation of the Argentine pampas from a poor sheep-raising territory to a wealthy cattle-raising, wheat- and flax-growing region. This transformation is fundamentally the work of the Spanish colonizers and immigrants, but during the past century it has depended more on the Italians and other Europeans, who accepted the need for change more readily than did the longer settled Spaniards. The Italian contribution has been made in every walk of life; the northern Italians went on the land assisting in its transformation, the southern Italians flocked to the cities of Argentina making Buenos Aires one of the greatest Italian cities. The early German settlers were peasant farmers who established their settlements at Esperanza in the Santa Fé province in the 1850's. The German immigrants who have entered Argentina since the First World War belong primarily to the professional, commercial (they are particularly strong in banking and shipping), and to the artisan classes.

The expansion and improvement of Argentine agriculture, which has made Argentina one of the great granaries of the world and the world's greatest meat producer, depended upon the continued influence of the European immigrant and European capital. It also required the introduction of a modern system of refrigeration, improved transport and, as on the great plains on the northern half of the American continent, barbed wire. Yet it was not until 1875 that Argentina became a net grain-exporting country (wheat, corn, barley, rye, linseed, and oats are the principal crops) and only at the end of the nineteenth century did the value of other branches of agriculture exceed the pastoral. The introduction in the eighties of refrigeration ships greatly assisted Argentina to become the world's greatest meat exporter. Yet only in 1905 did the shipments of Argentine beef reaching England exceed those from the United States. Beyond the pampas, in the western provinces, the European, Latin and non-Latin alike, has pioneered and developed the cultivation of sugar-cane, tobacco, vines, and fruits.

The industrialization of Argentina is in its infancy. A number of the early industries are identified with European national groups, such as the

Italians with footwear, the Spaniards with clothing, the Germans with brewing and glass manufacture, and the British with textiles. Much recent development in Argentine industry is concerned with the processing of its primary produce; some of these developments have depended upon imported European (and American) skills and techniques (but, as in agriculture and commerce, the leading role is played by Argentine-born Spaniards and Italians). Argentine industrialization, however, did not get under way before the 1930's, and major developments have been impeded by the absence of significant quantities of coal and iron, and by an inadequate or remote power supply. Forty per cent of the population are urban dwellers. Buenos Aires, with about a fifth of the total population, illustrates Argentina's problem of excessive urbanization.

Other Latin American countries receiving large numbers of European immigrants since the end of the colonial period were Cuba, Uruguay, and Mexico. The impact of the European has been felt in Cuba since shortly after Columbus's first voyage. Cuba's present population of approximately seven million is made up of half white, mostly of Spanish origin, a quarter Negro, and the remainder of mixed white, Indian, Negro, and oriental stock. The only figures available for European migration to Cuba in the nineteenth and twentieth centuries are for the period 1820–1930 when 857,000 Spanish migrants entered Cuba. The people of the United States have exercised a dominating influence upon Cuban economic and political life during the past century.

European influence in Uruguay (present population approximately three million) is much more concentrated than in Cuba. Nine out of ten Uruguayans are of European descent; the majority are Spanish followed by Italians and smaller numbers of Brazilian Germans and Portuguese. The other one-tenth of the population is made up of Negroes, Indians, and mestizos. Uruguay is a neighbour of Argentina and like Argentina is a complete projection of European life into the American hemisphere. The state is generally acknowledged to be one of the most vigorous and dynamic of the Latin American republics. In the period 1820–1930 the gross immigration figure was well over a million, chiefly Italians, Spaniards, and Portuguese (Table III/5).

Mexico, like Cuba, is a product of the extensive intermingling of blood brought about over a long period by white invasion. Of Mexico's present population of 35 million, nine-tenths are mestizos and Indians. There are also a few pure whites and Negroes. The typical Mexicans are descendants of the Spaniards who mixed with the aboriginal Indians. The number of Europeans migrating to Mexico chiefly from Spain in the period 1820–1930 was approximately 200,000.

The influence of the few Europeans entering other parts of Latin

America far exceeds their numerical importance. In Chile the present population of 7 million is composed chiefly of whites and mestizos. The cross of the Spaniard and the Araucanian native — one of the few primitive groups to resist successfully the white invasion — has produced a new kind of person called a Chilean. The number of European immigrants entering Chile during the past century has been small — perhaps 100,000 in a hundred years — and they, like most other white and black forerunners, have been assimilated. The exception is the German immigrant who has retained his language and customs. Small groups of German farmers played a distinctive part between 1846 and 1861 in colonizing Valdivia and, in the 1880's, the frontier region south of the Bio-Bio. In southern Patagonia a small German colony has striven to cultivate Chile's last undeveloped territory. Between 1937 and 1941 Chile gave refuge to several thousand German Jews. In the twentieth century a number of migrants have come from other parts of Europe, but none of them have played the same dominant role as the Germans have done in Valdivia.

In Peru and Bolivia the Europeans, the vast majority of them the descendants of the Spanish invaders, comprise a small section of the community: in Peru about 10 per cent and in Bolivia about 15 per cent. Yet in both countries the impact of this white minority has had a marked influence in commerce and finance. In the inter-war years a handful of Germans controlled the business life of great sections of the Bolivian economy. The British have given considerable assistance in the development of Peruvian public utilities and transport systems. British and American influence has also been felt in the development of the petroleum industry of Mexico, Colombia, Peru, and Venezuela.

The demographic diversity of Latin America is great enough to invalidate most generalizations. It is fairly certain, for instance, that the present rapid growth in the number of Latin Americans is the result of a rapidly declining death rate, combined with a high or a slowly declining birth rate and a large population. But the extent to which mortality rates have fallen in the different countries of Latin America is very uneven. In 1960 the death rate for Guatemala was 50 per thousand; in Uruguay it was 8 per thousand. Similarly, with movements in the birth rates, there are widely different levels. Corresponding figures for the birth rate in Guatemala and Uruguay in 1960 were 21 and 50 per thousand. Yet certain general trends are fairly clear: one is the extent to which, within Latin America, the most rapid increase in numbers is found in the tropical rather than the temperate zone; the other, the more rapid overall rate of natural increase of Latin Americans than of North Americans.

* * *

Whereas Europeans have made their way to the American continent since the sixteenth century, their influence in Australia has only been felt since the first British settlers arrived in 1788. In sharpest contrast to the ethnic composition of the population of Latin America, almost all Australians are of European descent. There has been little mixing of European blood with that of the indigenous natives. There never has been a great influx of non-whites. Until very recently, the Australian aborigine and the half-castes were largely excluded from the white society.

First discovered and explored by the Dutch and later by James Cook during his first voyage (1768–71), little was known about this enormous island continent before the mid-nineteenth century. Several considerations drew the British to Australia, not least the growing need to establish a naval base in the Southern Hemisphere, as well as the possibility of augmenting the supply of naval stores (especially flax and main-mast timber). In the event, Australia was used until the 1840's largely as a place of exile for the inmates of Britain's overcrowded prisons. Australia has remained until recent years a remote British dominion. Yet the economic and racial ties binding Australia to Britain are strong; seen through the eyes of the non-Australian they are surprisingly strong. The Battles of Gallipoli and the Kokoda Trail loom large in Australian history, as indeed they should — but there is no Gettysburg, no battle of Carabobo (Bolívar's liberation of Venezuela), no event of such magnitude to force Australians to find themselves. The ordeals out of which an Australian identity will emerge have still to be endured.

From the arrival of the first convicts in 1788 until 1821 the colony remained a penal settlement engaged in subsistence agriculture in the Sydney area. Mounting transport costs, not insuperable mountains, confined the early colony to the fairly adequate agricultural resources of the coastal plain. However, the growth in numbers, coupled with the setbacks occasioned by drought and insect plague encouraged the early settlers to extend Australia's first frontier to the rich pasture land beyond the Blue Mountains. The exploits of Gregory Blaxland, William Lawson, and W. C. Wentworth (who in 1813 had succeeded in piercing the Blue Mountains west of Sydney), and John Oxley (who in 1817–18 had explored the Lachlan and the Macquarie rivers) encouraged the gradual move inland. However, in 1821 out of an estimated population of thirty-six thousand only one-fifth were free settlers — the first of whom had arrived in 1793. Only after 1820 was the original Port Jackson colony extended into the pasture lands beyond the Blue Mountains. Meanwhile, in the mid-eighteen thirties, colonies for free settlers, many of them assisted by state and private charitable organizations, were founded in Victoria and South Australia. The population then — as now — was almost entirely British. In 1837 a British parliamentary committee reported unfavourably on the system of transportation; the 'last' shipment of convicts to New

South Wales arrived in 1840. Alas, governments and officials being what they are, nine years later, in 1849, the piteous *Harkaway* tried to disembark a further 212 male convicts at Sydney. Only the most hostile demonstrations persuaded the home government to inform the colonists that no more convicts would be sent to New South Wales.

From the 1820's to the 1850's, while the early settlements were growing, a good deal of exploration was taking place. Hamilton Hume and William Hovell in 1824–5 had crossed the south-east corner of the continent from Sydney to the site of the present city of Geelong. Between 1827 and 1830 Charles Sturt had discovered the Darling River, and had descended the Murray to its mouth. Allan Cunningham had reached rich pastures in the hinterland of Brisbane which subsequently became known as the Darling Downs. A trickle of white settlers followed. Perth in Western Australia was founded in 1829. The colony of South Australia was established in 1834–6. In 1841 Edward J. Eyre had journeyed from Adelaide in South Australia across the great desert to Albany in West Australia. In the 1840's Ludwig Leichhardt had also made a remarkable journey of 3,000 miles from Brisbane to the Gulf of Carpentaria. Leichhardt later disappeared when trying to cross from east to west the great 'dead heart' of Australia.

In 1861 Robert O. Burke and William J. Wills succeeded in crossing Australia from Melbourne to the Gregory River on the Gulf of Carpentaria, but lost their lives on the return journey. McDouall Stuart's expedition from Adelaide to Darwin the following year (1862) is considered the first successful crossing of the continent from south to north.

Stimulated by gold discoveries Australia's population almost trebled to more than a million between 1851 and 1861 (438,000 to 1,168,000). The flow of migrants was further encouraged by the development of pasture and arable farming, gold, silver, lead, copper, and coal mining, and the growth of the urban settlements of Melbourne, Sydney, and Adelaide. In 1850 Port Philip, now named Victoria, was founded as a separate colony; Queensland followed in 1859 with Brisbane as its capital.

During the years of depressed conditions in Europe between 1876 and 1890 the number of British immigrants increased rapidly. The rate of Australian population growth in the twelve years after 1876 (exceeding 3 per cent) is probably one of the highest for any similar period in the nation's history; though not as high as the 1850's. The number of immigrants fell in the early 1890's as European conditions improved. By 1901, when the Commonwealth was formed, Australia had a population of approximately four million. Encouraged by the development of industrialization in the present century, by a unified immigration policy, and by the provisions of the Empire Settlement Act of 1922 (which in the 1920's assisted almost a third of a million British migrants), the number continued to rise until halted by the depression of the late 1920's, and early 1930's. So marked has been the cyclical nature of Australian immigration that there were years at the end of the nineteenth century and in the depressed conditions of the years 1931–5 when more people returned to Europe than entered Australia. Since 1945, in proportion to its population, Australia has received more immigrants than any other country with the exception of Israel. The one million immigrants arriving in Australia between 1945 and 1955 represent the greatest number received in any decade in the nation's history. Between January 1947 and March 1956, Australia's total population increased by nearly two million, from 7,500,000 to 9,400,000. The net gain from immigration was over 800,000 people — about 43 per cent. The figure is higher still if we take account of the children born to immigrants arriving in Australia in this period. Australia's population at the end of 1960 was almost ten and a half million. The recovery in the rate of natural increase from approximately 8 per thousand in 1933 to 13 or 14 per thousand since the end of the Second World War has disproved many pre-war forecasts. Population growth resulting from net immigration has not only added to Australia's productive capacity by adding to its labour force; it has also added to the number of consumers and their demands for goods and services. On the other hand there has been a heavy and sudden demand for the social capital needed to provide shelter and public services of all kinds for this large number of immigrants. (Tables III/5 and III/6).

Although a number of Germans had arrived in South Australia as early as the 1830's, the overwhelming majority of immigrants before 1939 were British. In contrast, more than half of those arriving in the decade 1945–55 were non-British — most of them Italian, Dutch, German, Polish, Greek, and Baltic. The economic and cultural impact of these people has far outweighed their importance in numbers. Coloured immigrants have been deliberately excluded under the 'White Australia' policy evolved during the past century.

Except in the beef-cattle industry of Northern Australia, the aborigine has not contributed to Australia's economic development. Overwhelmed from the beginning by the white invaders' sicknesses, as well as by their aggressiveness and brutality, the aborigine has found it difficult, if not impossible, to adapt to the white man's ways. The inevitable clash between the aboriginal people of the world and the white invaders produced one of history's saddest tragedies; perhaps in terms of human misery that tragedy reached its deepest depth in Australia. Until a more humane attitude to the aborigines was developed in the twentieth century, only remoteness from European settlement saved them from complete extinction. We do not know how many aborigines there are in Australia: they have never been counted. We do suspect, however, that there has been a dramatic dwindling of their numbers since the white man came to their land. The rough guesses of 20,000 to 30,000 for 1960 are thought to be about one-eighth to one-tenth of the eighteenth-century figure. In contrast to parts of Africa and America, where Negro and native aboriginal labour is employed on the land, tropical Australia has had to rely for most of its development on the supply of white labour. The system (introduced in the 1860's) of importing native labourers from the Solomons and other islands to work on the Queensland sugar plantations, quickly degenerated into something similar to slavery and was abandoned. The nineteenth-century colonies of Chinese gold miners have gone. Queensland is the only place in the world where tropical crops are worked entirely by Europeans — many of them coming from southern Europe.

The scarcity of skilled agricultural workers made an extensive and casual agriculture inevitable. This was the experience of several other countries poor in population but rich in land. Vital to the enormous expansion of the sheep-raising industry was a growing British demand for Australia's pastoral products. The development of the wheat (which covered 60 per cent of the total cultivated area in 1960), wine, dried fruits, and dairying industries came later and was materially assisted by German and Scandinavian immigrants.

The effects of the discovery of gold in the 1850's were felt throughout Australia. An important impetus was given to the expansion of road and rail construction, manufacturing, urban development and, some years later, coal mining. More than anything else it was the discovery of gold which brought a tremendous increase in immigration. The gold output of the 1850's and the 1860's exceeded the value of wool. Yet the importance of wool in the development of Australia has been much more fundamental and much more continuous.

Both Australia and New Zealand are concerned about the competition provided by synthetic fibres, but on the whole the primary products they have sold have found an ever-growing market. Like all primary-producing countries, there is a marked tendency in both economies for instability in income and employment. But not as much, let it be said, as certain other primary-producing countries whose fate has depended upon the unusual price-instability of rubber, tin, coffee, etc. Yet the trend over the past fifty years has been towards industrialization; woollen manufacture, meat processing, sugar refining, brewing, and dairy manufactures were established about a century ago. Many farm implements, mining-machines, and certain railway construction materials were being manufactured in Australia before the end of the nineteenth century. In the first twenty years of the present century, encouraged by a joint policy of protection among the states and the development of a larger home market, the proportion of workers engaged in secondary industry increased almost twofold. The First World War gave a further stimulus to the development of Australian industries.

Since the Second World War the process has continued at such a pace that Australia today is regarded as a modern industrialized state. In 1961 13 per cent of Australia's labour force were in primary industry, providing Australia with the bulk of its foreign earnings; 38 per cent were in secondary industry, largely engaged in supplying the home market with consumer goods. With an income per head in 1961 of $1,210, Australia's standard of living ranks higher than the United Kingdom. It is exceeded only by New Zealand: $1,327; Canada: $1,496; and the United States: $2,714. However, there are some economists who feel misgivings at Australia's (and New Zealand's) continued dependence on the export of primary products and their seeming reluctance to diversify and strengthen the export section of these countries. Few countries are as blessed as Australia with the rich and accessible deposits of iron ore (greater than the known deposits of North America), coal, and limestone necessary for further industrial expansion.

Without the European immigrant — particularly without the tremendous number of Europeans of working age who have arrived since 1945 — Australia's industrial and commercial progress would have been delayed. The immigrant's influence is widespread throughout the steel, cement, sugar, mining, building, automobile, transport, and catering industries. Continental European immigrants such as Poles, Balts, Hungarians, and Italians have taken up the more arduous labouring jobs. In recent years the huge public works aimed at increasing Australia's power supply, such as the Snowy Mountains and Kiewa schemes, as well as the project in the Latrobe Valley for the gasification of brown coal, have been undertaken with a majority of technicians and labourers recruited from recently arrived Europeans. Considerable technical assistance has been given by American and German companies. The rapid development of the Australian economy in the public and private sectors has caused many American and European organizations to establish branches in Australia, bringing with them much new and improved technology.

The future settlement of Australia cannot be considered without taking account of its proximity to overcrowded Asia. The Australian nation is the only nation in the world with a continent to itself. The present population density in Australia of three to the square mile, compared with over nine hundred for neighbouring Java, has led the world to look upon Australia as an empty island continent. Australia's total population in 1962, 10·8 million, is roughly the same as the population of Greater London. Over two-fifths of Australia's population live in the cities of Sydney and Melbourne, in the urbanized south-eastern corner of the continent; over half the total population live in cities with 100,000 or more inhabitants, making Australia the most urbanized nation in the world.[1] Figures such as these cause many people to question the present 'White Australia' policy. However, while the pressure on the possible areas of settlement in Australia is low by world standards, there are great tracts of Australia (as there are of Siberia and Canada) which, except for small groups of nomadic aborigines, are not fit for permanent occupation — at least not in the immediate future (Table III/8).

New Zealand, re-discovered by Cook in 1769 (Tasman had sailed along its western coast in 1642), has also been until recently a remote British Dominion in the South Seas. The first white men to go there were seal and whale hunters; New Zealand also attracted some of the human flotsam and jetsam of the Pacific area. The first permanent settlements were Christian missions. Chiefly responsible for sending the first free British agricultural settlers (who landed at Port Nicholson in Cook Strait in 1840) was a private British organization — the New Zealand Company; land was the great incentive. One of the Company's leaders, Edward Gibbon Wakefield, had earlier helped to found the colony of South Australia. Both the Christian missions and the British government were lukewarm to white invasion of New Zealand. The missionaries were well aware what white invasion would mean to the natives; the British government was reluctant to take up further commitments in the South Seas. Yet precipitated by Wakefield's action, British sovereignty was extended to these islands in 1840, a few weeks before the arrival of a group of French settlers.

The white invasion of New Zealand was bitterly contested by the warlike Maori. Disputes about land caused the First Maori War of 1843–8 in the North Island. Similar disputes over land were the basis of the series of outbreaks called the Second Maori War 1860–70. In their battles with the Maori the British never won a decisive victory; the tribes fought on until they had obtained equal status from the white community. However, by changes in the indigenous system of landholding (chiefly by allowing free trade in land and by introducing individual land ownership in contrast to tribal ownership) most of the good land was in the hands of the whites by the 1890's. The entry of other coloured peoples into New Zealand was restricted by the legislation introduced in 1881 and 1889. In 1907 New Zealand became a Dominion within the British Empire.

The gold discoveries in Otago in 1861 and in Westland in 1865, caused an enormous influx of European immigrants and a doubling of the population in five years. These discoveries made the South Island the more populous and the richer of the two islands — as it was to remain for the next forty years. The improvement of steamship communications in the 1870's and the successful introduction of refrigeration in the 1880's made

[1] United Nations' *Demographic Yearbook*, 1960, Tables 1 and 8.

possible the development of a great meat and dairy industry for the British market. In 1960 wool accounted for 34 per cent of exports, dairy produce for 26 per cent, and meat for 27 per cent. Taken together, these three groups accounted for approximately 87 per cent of total exports. In 1961 the pastoral industry, employing a small part of New Zealand's labour force, earned the bulk of foreign earnings. New Zealand's reluctance to change its role as a supplier of wool and food comes partly from its small population relative to land, partly from the fact that the present arrangement provides a good income, and also partly from the fact that it finds it difficult to shake off mental attitudes acquired as a former colony of Britain. The white population of about 100,000 in 1860 had risen to 250,000 in 1870, 489,000 in 1890, 770,000 in 1900, and about 2·5 million today (including about 150,000 Maoris whose numbers are now increasing).

Although assisted immigration for selected British settlers has been government policy since the 1870's, New Zealand now realizes that it cannot rely upon British immigrants to assist in the development of the country to the same extent as in the past, especially for the highly skilled immigrants who can assist its industrialization. New Zealand possesses the necessary reserves of water power to enable it to develop considerable industry; its most serious deficiency is skilled labour. (Table III/5.)

* * *

Earlier in this book, when tracing the course of European colonial empires in Africa, we saw how for hundreds of years Europeans had voyaged there in search of slaves and precious metals, and in order to control the sea route to India. Yet it is only since the closing decades of the nineteenth century that the European migrant has felt attracted to the more temperate regions of that continent.

The greatest area of European settlement within Africa, the present Republic of South Africa, is, of course, far older than the past two or three generations. The history of European migration there began in 1652 when the Dutch East India Company landed a number of soldiers at the Cape of Good Hope. The purpose was to create a staging post on the long voyage to Batavia. Gradually other Dutchmen and women followed. Little resistance was offered by the native people. There grew among the Dutch the same spirit to create a New World as the Pilgrim Fathers had taken to America. In 1689 several hundred French Huguenot families sought refuge at the Cape. By 1800 there were about 27,000 Europeans. Then came annexation by the British in 1806 during the Napoleonic Wars and the number of British migrants settling in the Cape Province increased steadily. By the Treaty of Paris in 1814 the British had obtained definitive possession of the Cape Colony. This encouraged the British government to assist about 4,000 British colonists to settle in the eastern coastal region. In the 1830's, as a result of growing friction between the British and the Dutch settlers, the Boers commenced their great and historic trek to the interior. Native resistance in Natal was strong. The Boers were able to settle there only after much bloodshed.

A century ago the European population of South Africa was about 300,000. It was still a poor community depending largely on the proceeds of an extensive and casual agriculture. Then, in 1866, came the momentous discovery of diamonds at Kimberley, and of gold on the Rand twenty years later. Both discoveries were in the northern areas colonized by the Dutch. They provided what hitherto South Africa had lacked: a great staple export industry and, indirectly, the capital necessary for economic development. This transformed South Africa's economic and political future, setting the scene for a growing struggle between the British and the Dutch settlers culminating in the Boer War in 1899.

The discovery of diamonds and gold encouraged the influx of European migrants. Accurate figures of white immigrants entering the Cape Province between 1865 and 1910, when the Union of South Africa was formed, are not available. The European population of Cape Colony, however, increased from approximately 181,000 in 1865 to 1,276,242 at the time of the first census in 1911. Most of the white population in the Cape in 1911 were African-born. Between 1910 and 1960 the number of whites increased from 1·3 million to 3·1 million. The number of Africans increased in the same period from 4·0 million to 9·9 million. Contrary to common belief, the proportion of Africans to Europeans remains today roughly what it was half a century ago. In 1963 the European community in the Republic of South Africa numbered about 3,250,000 (mostly of English and Dutch extraction); the number of non-Europeans was over 13,815,000, including native Bantus, people of mixed racial origin and Asiatics. South Africa's inability to attract European migrants in the present century — in no decade since 1900 have there been more than 120,000 — is explained by the traditional reluctance of Europeans to live in black Africa and by the better economic and cultural opportunities offered elsewhere. Surprisingly enough, the recent racial disturbances in the Republic of South Africa have not put an end to white immigration. During the three years 1960–3 more whites have migrated to South Africa than have left. By one inducement or another the present white South African government is determined to increase the flow of European immigrants. Net immigration in 1963 reached an estimated 26,000 — the highest total in the last fifteen years. Almost half of these have come from Britain; the remainder from Holland, West Germany, Italy, Portugal, Greece, and Scandinavia. The Republic of South Africa is also a refuge for many whites fleeing other African territories. (Table III/5.)

During the past generation, while mining remains of vital significance to the South African economy, there has been a gradual shift in emphasis from pasture and agriculture to manufacturing and the service industries. To the original diamond and gold mining industries (South Africa is the richest gold and diamond country in the world) have been added platinum, asbestos, uranium, iron, coal, copper, manganese, lead, chrome, and tin. Events that have enriched South Africa were the abandonment of the gold standard by western nations in 1932 (which caused the price of gold to rise), the powerful stimulus of the Second World War, and the discovery of new gold fields and uranium in the post-war period. Other major industries established by European immigrants have been in foodstuffs, footwear, cement, chemicals, hardware, tools, and electrical equipment. In agriculture progress has been made in improving the quality of cattle and wool (in 1960 merino wool had a larger export value than diamonds), pigs, horses, sugar, wheat, tobacco, cotton, and wines. In mining, agriculture, industry (including a highly developed steel and engineering industry), commerce, and finance the Republic presents a picture of a most diversified and advanced economy. The Republic's economic standard may be low by international comparison, but it still emerges, whatever the economic criteria chosen, as the most advanced nation in the whole of what is a most economically backward continent. No other African country can equal the Republic's *per capita* income.

North-west Africa (Algeria, Tunisia, and Morocco) is the other major area of white settlement; its importance has declined with the recent exodus of white people from Algeria. Since 1830 the French have poured men and money into the area. In 1835 some 11,000 Europeans were in Algeria, the vast majority of them Frenchmen. The number of Europeans increased to 95,000 in 1845, and 200,000 in 1860. What proportion of this number were recent immigrants is not known. A century later (1960) there were one million whites. North-west Africa today has a population of about 20 million people, one-tenth of them of European origin. Unlike the British African colonies, where the administrator followed upon the heels of the explorer, trader, and the missionary, France's North African empire has been a soldier's and an administrator's empire from the beginning; a century ago military colonists were settled in many parts of Algeria. France opened up the African coast to other Latins as well. Notwithstanding the rivalry between Italy and France, the French conquest of Tunisia in 1881 provided a new outlet for Italian migrants. The Italians became active in railway and general construction, in mining, and in the development of the Tunisian vineyards. By the First World War Italians in Tunisia far outnumbered the French. Similarly, the majority of Latin European settlers in Algeria today do not come from metropolitan France but from all parts of Latin Europe. Yet it was French ambition, capital, and skill which Europeanized North Africa, which built the railways across the North African plains and created the great olive groves, wheat fields, and vineyards. As a result of French enterprise, the modern cities of Algiers, Tunis, and Casablanca have risen on the sites of old Arab ports. Although Spanish and French influences have been present in Morocco since the first half of the nineteenth century, it was not until 1904 that the French and Spaniards agreed on their respective zones of influence and the other Great Powers gave them a free hand to penetrate Morocco. French Morocco was annexed in 1912. Morocco and Tunis gained their independence in 1956. In Algeria in 1962 an intensely bloody struggle ended between the French colonists, the native population, and the government of metropolitan France; the outcome was a victory for Moslem demands for self-government — a victory achieved only by bringing the country close to total anarchy. Of the million French settlers in Algeria in 1960 only about 100,000 remain. The European proportion of Tunisia's 4 million at this time was about 280,000; in Morocco in 1960 there were about half a million Europeans out of a population of approximately 10·5 million.

Until French power was broken in North Africa, the French had succeeded in introducing an economic organization dependent on and subservient to the interests of metropolitan France. Central features of this organization were a wage economy, capitalist farming, modern mining (in 1963 the French were still active developing the oil industry in southern Algeria), improved communications, and European standards of administration, health, and education.

Europeanization is also evident in many fields of activity in Central and East Africa. In the early 1960's Europeans played a predominant role in trade, industry, finance, public works, and the civil service. Yet the small native peasant farmer is still the most important figure in the East African economy. In contrast to North and especially South Africa, nearly all the present white inhabitants of East Africa were born in Europe; the economic development of East Africa has also been markedly assisted by the contribution of Indians and Arabs. Excluding the much earlier Portuguese settlements in Mozambique, East Africa had few Europeans at the beginning of the present century. In 1926 Southern Rhodesia had a white population of 39,000. Southern Rhodesia's European population increased in the period 1921–51 by 100,000; net immigration accounts for 67,000; three-quarters since the Second World War. One of the primary causes for this influx has been the spectacular expansion of tobacco growing, and to a lesser extent, building and manufacturing. In 1961 the population of Southern Rhodesia of approximately 2·5 million included almost a quarter of a million whites. Of the white immigration to Southern Rhodesia about one-half is British, less than one-half South African.

The European population of Northern Rhodesia is much smaller and has been influenced to a great extent by the changing fortunes of the northern copper-mining industry — one of few known major mineral deposits in the whole of East Africa. In 1920 there were only about 3,000 Europeans in Northern Rhodesia. In 1925 enormous deposits of easily-worked sulphide ores were discovered (the presence of copper had been known since 1899), giving a stimulus to white immigration. In 1961 the total population exceeded two and a quarter million. The number of whites had risen to about 74,000; most of whom were immigrants from South Africa. About one-third were employed in the mining industry. The combined white population of Nyasaland and the two Rhodesias in 1961 was about a third of a million. The federation of the two Rhodesias and Nyasaland had a short-lived existence from 1953–63. In 1964 Nyasaland became the independent state of Malawi; Northern Rhodesia became Zambia; in 1965 the white-controlled government of Southern Rhodesia broke its political ties with Britain and the Commonwealth. In the early 1960's growing political uncertainty and racial disharmony in the Rhodesias caused a flight of capital and a sharp fall in net white immigration.

In Kenya and Nyasaland farming conditions have been particularly attractive to European settlers. In Kenya, which in 1963 achieved inpendence, the largest export crop is coffee. The largest export crop in Nyasaland is tea. The economic history of these countries has been determined by the rise and fall of plantation industries under European control, all of them dependent on cheap native labour. In 1900 there were virtually no white settlers in Kenya. White migration into the upland region of British East Africa was initiated by a British land grant of five hundred square miles in 1902. By 1911 the European population (chiefly British) numbered 3,175. At the census of 1948 the figure was 29,660. The total population of Kenya in mid-1961 was about 6·5 million, including approximately 66,000 Europeans and 174,000 Asiatics. In Uganda as in Nyasaland, there are few Europeans. The extent to which native producers of cotton and coffee dominate the export sector of Uganda is in sharp contrast to the European-dominated economy of Kenya. European producers in Uganda have developed the sugar, tea, rubber, and part of the coffee industry, but their income is very much smaller than that of native producers. Until the First World War the white population in Tanganyika (until 1918 part of German East Africa) was largely German. In 1961 there were about 23,000 whites in Tanganyika, mostly British. The total population in 1961 was approximately 9 million. Although European estates occupy only about one per cent of the land, they account for almost half of the total agricultural exports. The chief plantation crops are sisal and tea; the chief native crops are cotton and coffee. The European planter in Tanganyika is much more important than in Uganda but not as important as in Kenya. In 1964 Tanganyika and Zanzibar joined to become Tanzania.

A study of European migration to Africa reveals its smallness relative to total European emigration, to the size of the African continent, and to the low density of African population (Table III/8). The European population of Africa has remained during the past sixty years roughly what it was in 1900 — 10 million — whereas the European population living on the American continent and in Oceania has more than doubled since 1900. Of those Europeans seeking a new life overseas in the period 1886 to 1929 only about 6 per cent went to Africa. In America the European immigrant and his offspring are now firmly established. In Oceania, especially in Australia, which is on the rim of overcrowded Asia, the European foothold is still precariously placed along the coastal regions of an almost empty island continent. In Africa, however, over two hundred million non-Europeans face ten million Europeans, and the course of events is such that the power and initiative which white Africa has held for so long is being quickly wrested from them, with momentous consequences for Africa, Europe, and the world. White men in Africa have always been a tiny minority in an overwhelmingly large black community. The ominous difference between past and present situations is that the Europeans no longer have dominant economic or political power.

* * *

Europeans moved not only westwards but also eastwards across the Urals. Starting at the Ural Mountains during the reign of Ivan the Terrible, in the sixteenth century, the Russian advance swept across the continent following the river systems of the Ob, the Irtysh, the Yenisei, the Lena and the Amur. By the mid-century the Russians had reached the Eastern Ocean Sea, the Sea of Okhotsk. Meanwhile, the English were at the other side of the American continent, founding New England. The Russians then forced their way across the Aleutian Islands until in the mid-eighteenth century they reached the Alaskan Peninsula. By 1812, urged on by the greed for furs, by Russian ambitions in the North Pacific, and by the insatiable European quest 'to know what lay beyond', a Russian colony had been established in California. This was the further-most point of Russian expansion. By the 1840's the Russian tide had receded from the American mainland. In 1867 Russia sold Alaska to the United States for $7 million. If the Russians had followed a curious course in their march to the Pacific — tending sharply northwards away from the classic routes of the Mongols who had migrated westward centuries earlier, rather than thrusting directly to the east — it was because the open steppe and desert regions were dominated by the warlike peoples of

Central Asia, and also because the best fur regions lay within the northern forest belt.

Throughout the eighteenth and nineteenth centuries Moscow consolidated its hold on the area east of the Urals (Siberia alone contains 4,729,450 square miles). It was the individual trapper, trader, hunter, priest, fugitive, nomad, soldier, adventurer, and scout who first forced his way into the unknown, but in the settling and developing of the vast regions east of the Urals, once they had been opened, the Russian government played an unusually powerful part. The state alone in Russia had the necessary finance and impetus to sustain large-scale colonization. Moscow's eagerness to consolidate and especially to tax its new dominions in the east strengthened the tide of Russian invasion. It was not the nomadic yearnings of the Russian soul that caused so many peasants to push on still further, across Siberia, but the search for sustenance and, by remaining beyond the reach of the forces of the state, the desire to escape the process of enslavement which (more than anywhere else in eastern Europe) in the eighteenth and nineteenth centuries had reduced the Russian peasant to a chattel or commodity.[1]

As Russian ambitions in Siberia grew, the roles of the Asian and the European peoples were reversed. The Russians now penetrated the east as earlier the Mongols and Ottoman Turks had penetrated the west. Throughout the eighteenth and nineteenth centuries western power increased and eastern power declined. As it did, the Russians emerged from the forests in the north and challenged the more warlike peoples who inhabited the regions south and south-east of the Urals. Gradually, during the second half of the nineteenth century, the great cities of Khiva, Bokhara, Samarkand, and Kashgar were invaded and the native peoples subjugated. North of the Amur vast tracts of Chinese territory were occupied and have been held to this day.

By the end of the nineteenth century the Russian settlers had pierced the inner fastness of Siberia and a new trans-Ural society had been created. In 1891, confident of their power in the east, the Russians began to build the Trans-Siberian railway. In 1905 the work was completed and St. Petersburg on the Baltic was linked with Vladivostok on the Pacific more than six thousand miles away. Reducing the journey from European Russia to the Soviet Far East from years to weeks, this railway helped to open up Siberia. In 1709, according to Russian estimates, the total population of Siberia (aboriginals and Europeans) had been approximately a quarter of a million. A century later (in 1809) the population was estimated at one and a half million; in 1860 at three million; on the eve of the First World

[1] See L. L. Adolphe, Marquis de Custine, *Russia in 1839*, abridged from the French, London, 1854. Also Marquis de Custine, *Lettres de Russie*, Éditions de la Nouvelle France (Paris, 1946).

War it stood at nine million. The figure today is about twenty-five million. If we include the population of Soviet Central Asia and Kazakhstan, the population of Asiatic Russia increased from about thirty-four million in 1939 to about forty-seven million in 1959. Conflicting accounts exist concerning the fate of the indigenous peoples of Siberia subsequent to European invasion; it was probably similar to that of other indigenous peoples under European impact: decline or extinction.

Available estimates dealing with European migration into Siberia show that during the century prior to the First World War (from the early 1800's) approximately seven million European Russians moved from Europe into Asia — the eastward movement of Russians into Asia often exceeding the westward movement from European Russia to America and elsewhere. Of the seven million roughly three-quarters were peasant settlers (most of them fleeing oppression and poverty), the remainder were prisoners and exiles.[1] These migrants settled predominantly in Siberia, others went southwards into the steppe country, others to eastern Asia and Turkestan. While the First World War, and the disruption that followed it, decreased the outward flow to Asiatic Russia, the return of more settled conditions in the late 1920's, and the provision of additional railways, gave a new impetus to the eastward movement and the continuous agricultural and industrial expansion of those areas. With the German invasion of Russia in 1941 Siberia became 'the inner bastion of Soviet defence'. The tendency has been to exaggerate the shift of industry into Siberia; however, a Russian estimate of new migration of European Russians to the whole of Asiatic Russia in the period 1939–59 places the figure at 9·2 million. (Table III/5.)

The tangible results of Russian expansion eastwards are evident in agriculture and in industry. Great new areas have been brought into cultivation, new towns have been established, and two enormous industrial areas — those of Magnitogorsk, the great iron and steel centre of the Urals, and the Kuznetsk river basin (located in the north-western foothills of the Altai Mountains, roughly 1,400 miles east of the Urals) which has the largest coal reserves in the world — are being developed. Still further east, between Krasnoyarsk and the Angara river, new huge hydro-electric power stations have been installed at Bratsk and near Irkutsk. The intention is that they should serve the industrial developments of central Siberia. Roughly a thousand miles beyond Irkutsk is the industrial and mining centre of Yakutsk. The development of the Soviet Far East has proceeded at a much slower pace than that of other parts of Siberia. Yet the last generation has witnessed remarkable growth in industry and urban development in centres such as Vladivostok, Komsomolsk, Khabarovsk,

[1] See *Siberia and the Exile System*, G. F. Kennan (abridged from the first edition of 1891) (Chicago Univ. Press, 1958).

and Birobidzhan.

Despite the immensity of the regions, their inhospitable climate and relative inaccessibility, Russian expansion into Siberia since 1945 has grown. Military and economic strategy have stimulated the process. The Asian parts of Russia have doubled their population since 1913 and, as far as numbers are concerned, are growing at a faster rate than Russia west of the Urals.

* * *

The indelible impress of European religion and culture, politics, science, and technology is now on every continent. The economic impact of European migrants in the world has been enormous. Labour has gone to areas where it was scarce. New and higher orders of skill, and new sets of values conducive to economic development and expansion, have been diffused. The Indians, the Chinese, the Japanese, and the Africans have all migrated in large numbers during the past two centuries. None of them has had as great an impact as the European migrant.

The major influence prompting the movement of great numbers of Europeans overseas, and across Siberia, was the scarcity of land. As the New World was settled, and as industrialism progressed, the number of skilled industrial migrants increased. But until the First World War, European large-scale migration was essentially a transfer of agricultural workers from one part of the world to another: from areas where land was scarce to areas where land was plentiful. The predominant motive was the quest for wealth for oneself and one's family. In the early colonization of the Cape Colony in Africa, Upper Canada, Siberia, Australia, and parts of Latin America the state was the consolidating force, but, on balance, European migration during the past two hundred years has been more the expansion of peoples than the expansion of states.

While the motive of economic gain was probably all-important in prompting large-scale migration from Europe, it is doubtful if there is any one completely satisfactory explanation. Being a human story it is naturally complex and ambiguous. What prompted the Europeans, singly, in families, or in multitudes, to cross the great oceans and the continents of the world, enduring incredible hardship and privations, cannot be found in a single explanation. There are few major European ventures that did not require a willingness 'to leap into the dark'; the tidier an account of these things. the more likely the account is false. The actions of the 'handcart brigade' of Mormons, who forged their way westwards from the banks of the Missouri to found the State of Utah, or the early Dutch settlers at the Cape of South Africa, who with their oxen-carts eventually pierced the seemingly impassable Drakensberge, cannot be swept up into a general pattern of behaviour. Each of these events was an epic in itself. How can we recreate the atmosphere felt aboard the first caravelles to cross the oceans of the world? Do we know what it was that caused men to search for their pot of gold in the diggings in California, Australia, Alaska, and South Africa? How shall we recapture the spirit of the great nineteenth- and twentieth-century railway and timber camps of the world; how shall we know the feelings of Europe's huddled masses, 'the refuse of your teeming shores', as, tempest-tossed, they sought a new life in the cities and factory towns, or on the prairies or the pampas of the rising parts of the world? It is not impersonal forces that have changed the world. The principal factor in Europe's economic expansion is not physical or institutional — it is human. We cannot hope to bring home the importance of a human life. Much of man's story goes with him to the grave. For the rest there is often doubt, silence, and much conjecture.

Moreover, as we tried to indicate in the previous chapter, many Europeans (especially the missionaries and those others whose professional pride and humanitarian instincts enabled them to set aside thoughts of personal gain and ambition) had the highest sense of duty and vocation to peoples whose destiny they controlled. They willingly took up 'the white man's burden'; their purpose was to civilize, to succour, to lift up. If little is said in this book about the work of the religious missions it is not because their impact was unimportant. On the contrary, in human terms, it is doubtful if any other group of westerners ever got as close to other peoples as did these men of the Word. We do not know a great deal about the missionary story from the side of those receiving the missionary impact, but we know enough to recognize the missions as one of the most influential channels of western influence.[1]

Disinterested philanthopy and religious zeal were not, however, the hallmarks of European expansion. The springboard of European action during the past two centuries was the quest for wealth and power. It was this quest, backed as it often was by vastly superior weapons and devastating European sicknesses, which disturbed the roots of traditional social life of many non-European peoples and opened the door to the acquisitive instincts not only of the white man but also the brown, the yellow, and the black.

Europe's rapid increase in numbers during the past two hundred years set in motion an international migratory movement of the greatest significance. As the force of death was weakened and the average length of life was raised, Europeans grew in numbers and influence. Pressed by want they sought better conditions elsewhere. The continuous advance

[1] A full outline of the history of missions and extensive bibliography will be found in the work of K. S. Latourette, *A History of the Expansion of Christianity*, 7 Vols. (1937–1945).

made by European (and American) medical science during the past century, especially in the more recently developed methods of malarial control, coupled with the existing high birth rates of Asian and Latin American countries, has given to many people the opportunity to multiply and has resulted in a rate of population growth of unprecedented speed, especially in the poverty-stricken parts of the world. Significantly, the fall in mortality rates in Europe during the past two hundred years, which was partly responsible for the expansion of Europe in the world, was a long-run phenomenon, whereas the fall in mortality rates today, particularly in parts of Asia, where European influence has been felt most, is remarkably sudden and abrupt. The population densities of European-held lands outside Europe — including Australia, Brazil, and Siberia — stand today in the sharpest contrast with many of the overcrowded countries of Asia. Anyone who thinks over these matters, especially if they contrast what is happening in Asia today with what happened in Europe at an earlier point in history, must be impressed by the fact that when Europe sought a solution to population pressure there was a vast New World waiting to be developed. It was lightly held by native tribes, and in its conquest Europe had overwhelming superiority of weapons and organization. The difference between Europe's position then and Asia's position now is that Europe could find immediate relief in one of the greatest migrations of all time.

TABLES

III/1 to III/8

Table III/1

Estimates of World Population by Continents, 1750–1960[1]

Year	*World*	*Europe and Asiatic U.S.S.R.*		*North America*		*Latin America*		*Africa*		*Asia*		*Oceania*		*Area of European settlement*[2]	
	millions	*millions*	%	*millions*	%	*millions*	%	*millions*	%	*millions*	%	*millions*	%	*millions*	%
1750	728	144	19·8	1	0·1	11	1·5	95	13·0	475	65·3	2	0·3	158	21·8
1800	906	192	21·2	6	0·7	19	2·1	90	9·9	597	65·9	2	0·2	219	24·2
1850	1,171	274	23·4	26	2·2	33	2·8	95	8·1	741	63·3	2	0·2	335	28·6
1900	1,608	423	26·4	81	5·0	63	3·9	120	7·5	915	57·0	6	0·4	573[3]	35·8
1920	1,811	486	26·9	117	6·9	91	5·0	141	7·8	966	53·5	9	0·5	703	38·9
1930	2,015	532	26·5	135	6·7	109	5·5	157	7·8	1,072	53·5	10	0·5	786	39·1
1940	2,247	573	25·5	146	6·5	131	5·9	176	7·9	1,212	54·0	11	0·5	861	38·4
1950	2,510	576	23·0	167	6·7	162	6·5	206	8·2	1,386	55·0	13	0·5	918[4]	36·6
1955	2,691	606	22·5	183	6·8	183	6·8	223	8·3	1,481	55·0	15	0·6	987[5]	36·7
1960	2,995	641	21·4	199	6·7	206	6·9	254	8·5	1,679	56·0	16	0·55	1,062	35·5

Notes:

[1] Figures for years up to 1900 from Carr-Saunders; after 1900 from U.N. sources.

[2] Includes North America, Latin America, Europe and Asiatic U.S.S.R., and Oceania.

[3] Ladame's estimate of number of Europeans in the world for 1900 is 540 million.

[4] Woytinsky's estimate of the number of Europeans for 1950 is 854 million.

[5] Ladame's estimate of number of Europeans in the world for 1955 is 800 million.

Sources:

Carr-Saunders, A. M., *World Population: Past Growth and Present Trends* (Oxford, 1936).

Ladame, P. A., *Le Rôle des Migrations dans le Monde Libre* (Genève, 1958).

United Nations, *The Determinants and Consequences of Population Trends* (New York, 1953).

Demographic Year Book (1956, 1961).

Population and Vital Statistics (1960).

Woytinsky, W. S. and E. S., *World Population and Production* (New York, 1953).

TABLE III/2

Estimates of European Population in Selected European Countries, 1750–1960

Year	Europe (incl. Russia)	United Kingdom		France		Germany		Russia		Italy		Sweden		Poland[1]		Netherlands		Spain	
		millions	%	millions	%	millions	%	millions	%	millions	%	millions	%	millions	%	millions	%	millions	%
1750[2]	144	10	7·0	22	15·2	n.a.		20	13·9	n.a.		1·5	1·0	n.a.		n.a.		8	5·5
1800	192	16	8·3	27	14·1	25	13·0	37	19·2	18	9·4	2	1·0	n.a.		n.a.		11	5·7
1850	274	28	10·2	36	13·1	36	13·1	60	22·0	24	8·8	4	1·4	n.a.		3	1·1	16	5·8
1880	335	35	10·4	38	11·3	45	13·4	88	26·2	29	8·7	5	1·5	8	2·4	4	1·2	17	5·1
1900	423	42	9·9	39	9·2	56	13·2	111	26·0	33	7·8	5	1·2	9	2·1	5	1·2	17	4·0
1910	456	45	9·9	40	8·8	65	14·2	140	30·7	35	7·7	6	1·3	10	2·2	6	1·3	19	4·2
1920	486	44	9·0	39	8·0	62	12·7	158	32·4	37	7·6	6	1·2	27	5·5	7	1·4	21	4·3
1930	531	46	8·7	41	7·7	65	12·2	176	33·3	40	7·5	6	1·1	31	5·8	8	1·5	23	4·3
1940	572	48	8·4	40	7·0	70	12·2	192	33·6	44	7·7	6	1·0	33	5·8	9	1·6	26	4·5
1950	574	50	8·7	42	7·3	68	11·6	181[3]	31·6	47	8·2	7	1·2	25	4·3	10	1·7	28	4·9
1955	606	51	8·4	43	7·1	70	11·5	197[3]	33·5	48	7·9	7	1·1	27	4·4	11	1·8	29	4·8
1960	641	53	8·3	46	7·1	73	11·4	214	33·4	49	7·7	7	1·1	30	4·7	11	1·7	30	4·7

n.a. = not available.

Notes:

[1] Poland 1880–1910: pre-First World War boundaries.
1920–40: inter-war boundaries.
1950–60: post-Second World War boundaries.

[2] 1750: estimates based on Mulhall.

[3] 1950, 1955, Russia: United Nations estimates. Compare with estimates of H. Schwarz in *Russia's Soviet Economy* of 200 million for 1950, and 210 million for 1955.

Sources:

Carr-Saunders, A. M., *World Population: Past Growth and Present Trends* (Oxford, 1936).

Mulhall, M. G., *Dictionary of Stastics* (London, 1899).

Svenillson, I., *Growth and Stagnation in the European Economy* (Geneva, 1954).

United Nations, *Demographic Yearbook* (New York, 1956, 1961).

Woytinsky, W. S. and E. S., *World Population and Production* (New York, 1953).

Table III/3

Crude Rates of Natural Increase of Selected European Countries, 1871–1960[1]

(Average annual rate per thousand of population)

Country	1871–80	1881–90	1891–1900	1901–10	1911–19	1920–30	1931–38	1941–50	1951–60
England and Wales	14·0	13·1	11·7	11·8	7·5	6·6	3·0	4·4	4·1
Ireland	8·1	5·4	4·8	5·9	4·0	6·1	5·5	7·7	9·0
Norway	14·0	13·9	14·1	13·3	11·3	9·2	4·9	9·9	9·7
Sweden	12·2	12·2	10·7	10·9	9·0	5·8	2·6	7·9	5·0
France	1·7	1·8	0·7	1·2	−3·4	2·0	0·1	2·4	6·6
Netherlands	11·9	13·2	14·1	15·3	13·6	14·4	11·9	14·6	14·0
Germany	11·9	11·7	13·9	14·3	8·6	7·9	6·3	3·5[2]	5·6[2]
Austria	7·5	8·4	10·5	11·4	12·3	−0·4	1·0	0·6	3·7
Italy	7·0	10·7	10·7	11·1	7·1	11·6	9·4	7·6	8·3
Spain	7·1	4·5	5·3	9·2	7·0	7·0	10·7[3]	7·9	12·0
Russia	n.a.	n.a.	15·1	16·8	n.a.	21·1	n.a.	n.a.	17·0[4]

n.a. = not available.

Notes:

[1] Crude rate of natural increase is equal to crude birth rate less crude death-rate.

[2] Federal Republic of Germany only.

[3] Based on incomplete data.

[4] 1952–60.

Sources:

Calculated from W. S. and E. S. Woytinsky, *World Population and Production* (New York, 1953).

Ladame, P. A., *Le Rôle des Migrations dans le Monde Libre* (Genève, 1958).

Calculated from *U.N. Demographic Year Book* (New York, 1954, 1961).

TABLE III/4

Emigration from Europe, 1851–1960
(thousands)

Origin	*1851-1960*	%	*1851-60*[1]	*1861-70*[1]	*1871-80*[1]	*1881-90*[1]	*1891-1900*[1]	*1901-10*[1]	*1911-20*[1]	*1921-30*	*1931-40*	*1941-50*	*1951-60*
British Isles	20,501	33·6	1,313[2]	1,572[2]	1,849[2]	3,259	2,149	3,150	2,587	2,151	262	755[3]	1,454[4]
Sweden	1,265	2·1	17	122	103	327	205	224	86	107	8	23[5]	43[6]
Norway	882	1·4	36	98	85	187	95	191	62	87	6	10[7]	25[8]
Finland	426	·7	n.a.	n.a.	n.a.	26	59	159	67	73	3	7[9]	32[9]
Denmark	575	·9	n.a.	8	39	82	51	73	52	64	100	38[10]	68[11]
France	548	·9	27	36	66	119	51	53	32	4	5	n.a.	155[12]
Belgium	284[13]	·5	1	2	2	21	16	30	21[14]	33	20[15]	29[16]	109
Netherlands	631[17]	1·0	16	20	17	52	24	28	22	32	4[18]	75[19]	341[20]
Germany	6,485[21]	10·6	671[22]	779[22]	626[22]	1,342[22]	527[22]	274[22]	91[22]	564[23]	121[21 23]	618[24]	872[24]
Austria	4,241[25]	6·9	31	40	46	248	440	1,111	418[26]	61	11[27]	n.a.	53[28]
Switzerland	383	·6	6	15	36	85	35	37	31	50	47	18[29]	23[30]
Spain	5,184	8·5	3	7	13	572	791	1,091	1,306	560	132	166[31]	543[31]
Portugal	2,950	4·8	45	79	131	185	266	324	402	995	108	69[32]	346[33]
Italy	11,511	18·8	5	27	168	992	1,580	3,615	2,194	1,370	235	467[34]	858[35]
Russia[36]	2,238	3·7			58	288	481	911	420	80[37]			
Poland	3,048[38]	4·9								634[39]	164[40]		
TOTAL	61,152		2,171	2,805	3,239	7,785	6,770	11,271	7,791	6,865	1,226	2,275	4,922

n.a. = not available.

Notes:

[1] Unless otherwise indicated, figures from 1851–1920 are taken from Ferenczi and Willcox. The term 'total emigration' in the notes is used to denote intra-continental and inter-continental migration combined.

[2] Figures are not available for 1851 and 1852, nor for emigrants from Irish ports before 1880.

Source: Austrian Statistical Office, *Monthly Statistical Bulletin* (1913), p. 65. Figures after 1910 include all overseas emigrants and are estimates published in the Austrian Statistical Handbooks.

[26] 1911–13 only.

[27] 1931–7 only.

[28] 1954–60 only.

U.N., *Demographic Year Books.*

[6] *Statisk Arsbok for Sverige* (1961).

[7] 1946–50 only; other years not available. U.N., *Demographic Year Books.*

[8] U.N., *Demographic Year Books*, and *Europa Year Book* (1961).

[9] U.N., *Demographic Year Books* and *Finnish Year Books.*

[10] Figures include 'Total Emigration' from Denmark 1941–4. U.N., *Demographic Year Books.*

[11] U.N., *Demographic Year Books*, and *Statistick Arbog* (1961).

[12] Reliable French emigration figures are not available. This estimate for 1946–59 is given on page 177 of *The I.L.O. Report No. 54* (1959). This does not include emigration to French overseas territories.

[13] Figures provided by Director-General of the National Statistics Institute, Belgium.

[14] 1913–18 excluded.

[15] 1940 excluded.

[16] 1941–7 excluded.

[17] Until 1940, estimate only.

[18] Figures for 1937–40 are not available.

[19] 1946–50 only. Excluding emigration to Dutch territories overseas.

[20] Emigration to Dutch overseas territories excluded. Source for 15, 16, 17, 18: Deputy Director-General of Statistics, Netherlands Central Bureau of Statistics, The Hague.

[21] Figures for 1937–40 are not available.

[22] *Statistik des Deutschen Reiches*, vol. 360, pp. 227, 229.

[23] *Statistisches Jahrbuch für das Deutsche Reich*, 1939–40, 58, p. 72.

[24] Figures provided by the Statistical Bureau of the Federal Republic of Germany.

[25] All figures prior to 1913 refer to the whole of the Austrian Empire, while figures from 1921 onwards refer to the post-First World War Republic of Austria. The total figure for 1851–1960 includes all overseas emigrants, but the figures given by decade until 1910 refer only to Austrian emigrants.

U.N., *Demographic Year Books*, and *Europa Year Book* (1961).

[32] 'Total Emigration' for 1941–9. *Source:* I.L.O., *Year Book of Labour Statistics* (various).

[33] U.N., *Demographic Year Books*, and *Europa Year Book* (1961).

[34] U.N., *Demographic Year Books.*

[35] *Abstract of Italian Statistics* (various).

[36] These figures are taken from Woytinsky, p. 75, Table 34. It is thought that they underestimate overseas emigration from Russia (U.S.S.R.) considerably.

[37] Estonia and Lithuania.

[38] Before the First World War there was no official registration of emigrants from the Polish lands. An estimate, however, gives the figure of about 2,250,000 emigrants for the period 1871 to 1913. *Source:* Director, Central Bureau of Statistics, Warsaw. No records are available for years during the two World Wars.

[39] 1919–30 (incomplete data). *Source:* Director, Central Bureau of Statistics, Warsaw.

[40] 1931–38. After the Second World War there has not been any significant overseas emigration from Poland. *Source:* Director, Central Bureau of Statistics, Warsaw.

Sources:

Ferenczi, I. and Willcox, W. F. (eds.), *International Migrations*, vol. i (New York, 1929).

Woytinsky, W. S. and E. S., *World Population and Production* (New York, 1953).

Ladame, P. A., *Le Rôle des Migrations dans le Monde Libre* (Genève, 1958).

United Nations, *Demographic Yearbook* (various).

I.L.O., *Report No. 54* (1959).

I.L.O., *Yearbook of Labour Statistics.*

Europa Yearbook (1961).

Statistical Year Books of the following countries: Sweden, Netherlands, Federal Republic of Germany, Switzerland, Italy, United Kingdom, Ireland, Finland, Denmark.

Statesman's Year-book (various).

TABLE III/5

Intercontinental Immigration into Selected Areas, 1851–1960
(thousands)

		1851–1960	1851–60[1]	1861–70[1]	1871–80[1]	1881–90[1]	1891–1900[1]	1901–10[1]	1911–20[1]	1921–30	1931–40	1941–50	1951–60
U.S.A.[2]	*gross*	34,711	2,536	2,160	2,433	4,852	3,684	8,666	4,775	2,723	443	804	1,635
Canada[3]	*gross*	6,156	n.a.	290	220	359	231	947	1,154	987	82	419	1,467
Argentina[4]	*gross*	7,602	20[5]	160	261	841	648	1,764	1,205	1,397	310	461	535
	net	4,109	+11	+77	+85	+638	+320	+1,120	+269	+878	+73	+385	+253
Brazil	*gross*	5,413	122	98	219	525	1,129	671	798	840[6]	239[6]	131[6]	591[6,7]
	net	2,477				570[8]		940[9]		860[10]		107[11]	
British West Indies	*gross*	1,030	75	101	98	66	61	170	459	n.a.	n.a.	n.a.	n.a.
Cuba	*gross*	629	6	13	n.a.	n.a.	n.a.	243	367	n.a.	n.a.	n.a.	n.a.
Mexico	*gross*	287	n.a.	n.a.	n.a.	n.a.	n.a.	n.a.	107[12]	113[13]	37[13]	16[14]	14[14]
	net	14									4[15]	10[15]	
Uruguay	*gross*	642	n.a.	85	112	140	90	21	57	21[16]	57[17]		59[18]
Australia[19]	*gross*	4,592						652	1,172	949	143	491	1,185
	net	2,541		167	192	383	25	40	208	313	32	362	819
New Zealand[20]	*gross*	961	33	69	145	65	35	89	91	116	32	58	228
	net	240	n.a.	n.a.	n.a.	n.a.	n.a.	n.a.	n.a.	90	−2	18	134
South Africa[21]	*gross*	439	n.a.	n.a.	n.a.	n.a.	n.a.	n.a.	71	100	53	97	118
	net	212									42	83	87
Asiatic Russia[22]	*gross*	15,220	191	254	248	419	1,208	2,282	918	500			9,200[23]

n.a. = not available.

Notes:

One of the difficulties in interpreting migration statistics lies in the widely differing definitions of immigration employed by different countries. In many cases, no official statistics on migration exist and the estimates given must be treated with caution. The following notes are designed to indicate the sources of the figures and to assist interpretation by pointing out significant variations in the methods of compiling the statistics.

[1] Unless otherwise indicated, figures from 1851 to 1920 are taken from Ferenczi and Willcox, vol. i.

[2] Figures before 1921 adapted from Ferenczi by Davie. Figures for 1921–60 from U.S., *Abstract of Statistics* (1961). No official net immigration figures have been collected by the United States Department of Justice, Immigration and Naturalization Series.

[3] Immigration figures from Official Canadian Year Books. Figures before 1939 are regarded as unreliable. (See comment on page 186 of *The Canada Year Book* (1950).) Official Canadian emigration figures have never been collected, and any net migration figures must, therefore, be estimates.

The following figures supplied by the Dominion Statistician, relating to Continental and Intercontinental immigration into Canada are of interest:

(Thousands)

	1851–60	1861–70	1871–80	1881–90	1891–1900	1901–10	1911–20	1921–30	1931–40	1941–50	1951–60
Gross	209	187	353	903	326	1,759	1,612	1,203	150	548	1,539
Net	123	−190	−86	−207	−179	682	282	111	−91	169	898

On the controversy about Canadian migration figures refer to the following articles:

[illegible] 'The Growth of Canadian Population', *Population Studies*, Vol. IV, No. 1. (June 1950).

Census, Buenos Aires.

[5] 1857–60 only.

[6] The figures for periods after 1921 are classified as 'First permanent establishment in the country'. *Source: Anuario Estatistico do Brasil* (various), also from figures provided by the National Director of Statistics, 28 August 1963.

[7] 1951–9 only.

[8] Estimate for 1871–1900.

[9] Estimate for 1901–20.

[10] Estimate for 1921–40.

[11] Estimate for 1941–50. No official emigration figures for Brazil have been collected. Estimates (9), (10), (11), (12) are taken from *O Brasil em numeros* supplement to *Anuario Estatistico do Brasil* (1960).

[12] Figures to 1924 are from Ferenczi; since then from I.L.O., *Year Book of Labour Statistics* (various).

[13] 1941–9 only.

[14] Total permanent immigrants from Europe only. Under the Mexican Migration Act, permanent immigrants are defined as those foreigners who fulfil the necessary requirements to be allowed to reside in Mexico permanently. *Source:* Mexican Director-General of Statistics.

[15] Net figures from I.L.O., *Year Book of Labour Statistics* (various).

[16] 1920–9 only; U.N., *Latin America, Seminar on Population* (1958).

[17] I.L.O., *Year Book of Labour Statistics* (various).

[18] 1951–8 only; I.L.O., *Industry and Labour* (1960), and I.L.O., *Report No. 54* (1959).

[19] Gross immigration figures before 1931 refer to total arrivals. The figures since 1931 have been calculated 'Intended permanent arrivals and departures'. *Source:* Commonwealth Bureau of Census and Statistics, *Yearbook of the Commonwealth of Australia* (various). Net immigration figures before 1941 are from Borrie; since 1941 from the *Yearbook of the Commonwealth of Australia* (various).

[20] Total immigration figures are based on 'Intended permanent residence and departures'. *Source: New Zealand Official Year Book* (various).

[22] From 1851 to 1930 supplied by U.S.S.R. Academy of Science (Institute of Historical Studies).

[23] 1939–59. Net immigration into Western Siberia, Urals, Eastern Siberia, Kazakhstan and Soviet Far East from European Russia. Estimates only. *Source:* P. G. Pdyachikh, *Population of the U.S.S.R.*, Moscow (1961).

Sources:

United States Department of Commerce, *Statistical Abstracts* (various).

Thomas, B. (ed.), *Economics of International Migration* (London, 1958).

Davie, M. R., *World Immigration* (New York, 1936).

I.L.O., *Year Book of Labour Statistics* (various).

Industry and Labour (various).

Report No. 54 (1959).

Woytinsky, W. S. and E. S., *World Population and Production* (New York, 1953).

Ferenczi, I. and Willcox, W. F. (eds.), *International Migrations*, vol. i (New York, 1929).

Treadgold, D. W., *The Great Siberian Migration* (Princeton, 1957).

U.N., *Demographic Year Book* (various).

Ladame, P. A., *Le Rôle des Migrations dans le Monde Libre* (Genève, 1958).

Europa Year Book (1961).

Statesman's Year-book (various).

Dominion of Canada, *Official Year Book* (various).

Union of South Africa, Bureau of Census and Statistics, *Union Statistics for 50 Years* (1960).

New Zealand Official Year Book (various).

Brazil, *Anuario Estatistico do Brasil* (various).

Commonwealth Bureau of Census and Statistics, *Year Book of the Commonwealth of Australia* (various).

Pdyachikh, P. G., *Population of U.S.S.R.* (Moscow, 1961).

Borrie, W. D., *Immigration: Australia's Problems and Prospects* (Sydney, 1949).

TABLE

Approximate Population Growth and Net Immigration

Year	*U.S.A.*[1]			*Canada*[4]		
	Population (in thousands)	*Approximate decennial % increase in population*	*Gross immigration as approximate % of total decennial increase*[3]	*Population (in thousands)*	*Approximate decennial % increase in population*	*Net immig as approxi of total de increa*
1850	23,261	..	..	2,483[5]	..	..
1860	31,513	36	31	3,263	31	15
1870	39,905	27	26	3,689[5]	13	-44
1880	50,262	26	23	4,325[5]	17	-12
1890	63,056	24	38	4,833[5]	12	-41
1900	76,094	21	28	5,371[5]	11	-33
1910	92,407	21	55	7,207[5]	34	37
1920	106,466	15	34	8,788[5]	22	18
1930	123,188	16	16	10,208	16	7
1940	132,122	7	5	11,381	11	-8
1950	151,683	15	4	13,712[7]	20[6]	7
1960	179,323[2]	18	6	17,814	30	22

Notes:

[1] United States Department of Commerce, Bureau of the Census, *Historical Statistics of the United States, Colonial Times to 1957* (1960), p. 7.

[2] United States Department of Commerce, Bureau of the Census, *Statistical Abstracts of the United States, 1901* (1961), p. 5.

[3] Because no reliable net immigration figures are available for the period 1850–1960, gross intercontinental immigration figures have been used.

[4] National Industrial Conference Board, *The Economic Almanac, 1962* (1962), pp. 523 ff.

[5] 1851, 1871, etc.

[6] Newfoundland became a Canadian province on 31 March, 1949.

[7] Excluding Newfoundland.

[8] Commonwealth Bureau of Census and Statistics, *Official Year Book of the Commonwealth of Australia* (various volumes).

[9] 1851 and 1861.

[10] Argentine figures have been provided by the Argentine Director-General for Statistics and Census.

[11] Estimate by De la Fuente, 1849; the figure does not include unassimilated aborigines.

[12] Estimate by De la Fuente for 1859; on the basis of data obtained for the 1869 census.

[13] Population according to the 1869 census; the figure does not include the members of the Armed Forces then engaged in military operations outside national territory; nor does it include the aboriginal population estimated at 93,000.

[14] Population estimated by geometrical growth, according to the 1869, 1895, and 1914 census; published in vol. 4, 1914 Census Returns.

ited States, Canada, Australia, and Argentina, 1850–1960

Australia[8]			Argentina[10]		
Population (in thousands)	Approximate decennial % increase in population	Net immigration as approximate % of total decennial increase	Population (in thousands)	Approximate decennial % increase in population	Net immigration as approximate % of total decennial increase[17]
405[9]	..	..	935[11]	..	..
1,146[9]	183	77	1,304[12]	39·5	..
1,648	45	33	1,737[13]	33·2	..
2,232	35	33	2,493[14]	43·5	36·5
3,154	41	41	3,378[14]	35·5	96·6
3,765	19	4	4,152[14]	22·9	51·2
4,425	18	6	6,024[14]	45·1	62·9
5,411	22	21	8,861[15]	47·1	15·8
6,501	20	29	11,896[15]	34·3	32·2
7,078	9	6	14,169[15]	19·1	8·1
8,307	17	29	17,119[15]	20·8	18·9
10,398	25	39	20,724[15] [16]	21·1[16]	15·7[16]

[15] Population estimate based on both natural growth and net migration.
[16] Provisional figures.
[17] Until 1913 inclusively migration figures referred only to the movement of passengers entering and leaving the country by ship in 2nd and 3rd classes; from 1914 onwards they have included all persons leaving and entering the country by any means and class of transportation.

Sources:

United States Department of Commerce, *Statistical Abstracts* (various).
Thomas, B. (ed.), *Economics of International Migration* (London, 1958).
Commonwealth Bureau of Census and Statistics, *Yearbook of the Commonwealth of Australia* (various).
Woytinsky, W. S. and E. S., *World Population and Production* (New York, 1953).
The Statesman's Year-book (various).
United Nations Economic Commission for Latin America, *Economic Survey of Latin America* (1949).
United Nations Department of Social Affairs, *Demographic Year Book* (various).
National Industrial Conference Board, *The Economic Almanac* (1962).

Table III/7

Ethnic Composition of the Population of Latin America, 1955[1]

Country	*Total*[2] (*thousands*)	*White*[3] (%)	*Indian*[4] (%)	*Negro*[5] (%)	*Mixed*[6] (%)	*Other*[7] (%)
Argentina	19,111	99	n.	n.	1	n.
Bolivia	3,198	3	94	n.	3	n.
Brazil	58,456	42	8	15	34	1
Chile	6,761	46	4	n.	50	n.
Colombia	12,657	17	7	16	60	n.
Costa Rica[8]	951					
Cuba[W]	5,829[9]	63	n.	28	n.	9
Dominican Republic[W] [10]	2,404					
Ecuador	3,675	3	84	n.	13	n.
El Salvador[W]	2,193	10	40	n.	50	n.
Guatemala[W]	3,258	5	60	5	30	n.
Haiti[11]	3,305					
Honduras[W]	1,660	3	4	2	90	1
Mexico[W]	29,679	15	28	n.	55	2
Nicaragua[W]	1,245	5	5	7	83	n.
Panama[W]	910	17	9	15	53	6
Paraguay	1,565	6	6	n.	88	n.
Peru	9,396	2	94	n.	4	n.
Uruguay	2,615	96	n.	n.	4	n.
Venezuela	5,774	8	3	n.	88	1

n. = negligible

Notes:

[1] Percentages given in this table are calculated from Ladame, with the exception of those related to countries marked with (W) in the first column. These percentages are based on Woytinsky. Estimates of ethnic composition vary widely. Some of them are based on little more than conjecture.

[2] Estimates given by the United Nations.

[3] Persons of pure European descent.

[4] Indigenous natives. (In the case of Paraguay this group includes mixtures with Spanish stock.)

[5] Persons of pure African Negro blood. (In the cases of Cuba, Colombia, and Guatemala this group includes mixtures with other stock.)

[6] Mainly Indian-white, Negro-white and Indian-Negro mixture.

[7] Mainly Orientals (Chinese and Japanese).

[8] No detailed data available, but the population here is 'overwhelmingly white'.

[9] *De jure* population.

[10] No detailed data available, but the mixed-blooded form the 'mass of population'.

[11] The majority of the population here consists of Negroes, with a 'great number' of 'mixed-blooded' and very few whites.

Sources:

Ladame, P. A., *Le Rôle des Migrations dans le Monde Libre* (Genève, 1958).

United Nations, Department of Economics and Social Affairs, *Demographic Year Book 1956* (New York, 1956).

Woytinsky, W. S. and E. S., *World Population and Production* (New York, 1953).

Angel Rosenblat, *La población indigena y el mestizaje en América* (Buenos Aires, 1954).

TABLE III/8

Area and Population of the World, by Continent and Region, 1960

Continent and Region	*Area*[1] (*Thousands of square kilometres*)	*Population* *Adjusted*[2] *estimates at mid-year 1960 (millions)*	*Density (per square kilo-metre) 1960.*	*Annual rate of increase 1950–60 (%)*
World				
Total	135,175	2,995	22	1·8
Europe[3]				
Total	4,953	427	86	0·8
Northern and Western Europe	2,254	142	63	0·7
Central Europe	1,015	139	137	0·8
Southern Europe	1,684	146	86	0·9[4]
U.S.S.R.	22,402	214	10	1·7
America[5]				
Total	42,040	405	10	2·1
Northern America	21,499	199	9	1·8[4]
Central America	2,746	66	24	2·7
Southern America	17,795	140	8	2·3
Oceania[5]				
Total	8,559	16·5	2	2·4[4]
Asia[6]				
Total	26,930	1,679	62	1·9
South West Asia	5,595	77	14	2·6
South Central Asia	5,120	559	109	1·7
South East Asia	4,489	214	48	2·0
Eastern Asia	11,726	829	71	2·0
Africa				
Total	30,291	254	8	2·2
Northern Africa	10,327	88	9	2·2
Tropical and Southern Africa	19,964	166	8	2·1

Notes:

[1] Comprising land area and inland waters, but excluding uninhabited polar regions and some uninhabited islands.

[2] Adjusted for under-enumeration and errors in estimation.

[3] Excluding U.S.S.R., including European Turkey.

[4] Rate reflects combined effects of natural increase and migration.

[5] Hawaii is included in Oceania.

[6] Excluding U.S.S.R., including Asiatic Turkey.

Source:

United Nations, Department of Economic and Social Affairs, *Demographic Yearbook, 1961* (New York, 1961).

Chapter IV

EUROPE—BANKER TO THE WORLD A STUDY OF EUROPEAN FOREIGN INVESTMENT[1]

ACCOMPANYING the movement of European peoples was the outpouring of European wealth. With its help vast agricultural and mineral resources in the Northern and Southern Hemispheres were developed, towns were built, industry and trade encouraged; new forms of transport and communication were introduced which drew the world together. By the First World War Europe's network of world finance, upon which depended the growth of world transport, trade and migration, had caused a shift in emphasis from the nation to the world.

At the beginning of the eighteenth century European foreign investment was largely in the hands of closely restricted and privileged foreign-trading companies, whose concern was to obtain maximum profits from Europe's far-flung trade in luxuries, precious metals, and slaves. Portugal, Spain, Holland, France, and Britain had all sunk money in the conquest and subsequent exploitation of their colonial empires since the sixteenth century; but, with the exception of investments made in European plantations overseas, these earlier ventures did not contribute much to the productive enterprise of other lands. Europe's earlier aim was trade with coastal settlements rather than the development and colonization of vast continents.

The nineteenth century saw a general democratization of the European capital market. The sums amassed for foreign investment grew throughout the century as capital was drawn from a growing middle class. The control of foreign investment, which in earlier centuries had rested in the hands of a privileged group of merchant princes, passed to a number of highly specialized foreign-banking and investment houses, able to dispose of vast amounts of capital. Equally important was Europe's development of credit money which contrasted to the earlier forms of money often valued according to weight (i.e. pound, livre, drachma, etc.). By means of a book

[1] The main emphasis in this chapter will be placed on investment of a 'long-term' nature, i.e. capital loaned for more than one year.

entry, or the use of a bill, cheque, or bank-note, European capital (most of it increasingly removed from the control and responsibility of the individual investor) was transferred to any country willing to meet Europe's terms. The importance of the use of credit money in this way lay not in its novelty but in the manner in which it facilitated an enormous increase in international commerce and investment. Few countries outside Europe advanced economically without first increasing their borrowings and subsequently their trade with Europe. For many nations which have emerged during the last century and a half, Europe's foreign investments were the fundamental basis of their economic development. With the help of European loans many countries were settled and developed at a faster rate and with less sacrifice than if they had had to rely on their own resources.

In the European parts of the world, such as the United States, the former British Dominions, and certain Latin American countries, ideas regarding the employment of wealth have generally been the same as those accepted in Europe. The different attitudes towards wealth in the non-European parts of the world, however, often limited the use of European funds; before undertaking large-scale investments in these areas Europe had first to promote effective government, education, and competent administration; much more importantly, it had to change the outlook of whole sections of African and Asian communities towards wealth and economic progress. In the nineteenth and the twentieth centuries, western concepts concerning saving, investment, and production were introduced to foreign communities for the first time. In this period, static, self-subsisting economies, hitherto dominated by religious and social values, were subjected increasingly to dynamic European commercial ideas. Much of the impact of European foreign investments lay in the extent to which they transformed the economic ideas and social values of non-European peoples. Some societies quickly adapted themselves; others, such as the Chinese, were peculiarly resistant to western ways.

In the two or three decades before the First World War, as the economic and political rivalry of the European powers increased, vast new areas of Africa and Asia were seized and spheres of trade and investment were established along the lines of earlier mercantilism. With the exception of Italy's conquest of Abyssinia in the 1930's the First World War marked the end of this last phase of European expansion. By the late 1920's, partly as a result of the sale of European foreign assets during the war — more importantly because of the changing general economic positions of Europe and North America — the United States had become the chief source of international funds. Continental Europe, especially Germany, had become a substantial debtor. Britain (with foreign investments roughly equivalent in nominal value to its 1913 holdings) had lost financial leadership to the

United States. British holdings (Table IV/1) were still larger than those of the United States, but Britain had ceased to be the prime lender in the world.

The passing of financial leadership from the United Kingdom to the United States is possibly one of the factors contributing to the onset of a world commercial depression in 1929–30. The trading relations of the two economies with the world were dissimilar, and leadership passed to the Americans before they had had the time to build up the necessary financial traditions and institutions. With the depression, the flow of long-term foreign investment was halted. The gold standard was abandoned and the free convertibility of currencies replaced by exchange controls of many kinds. As will be shown in Chapter VII, the volume of international trade declined rapidly. Since the 1930's Europe's overriding concern has been to preserve its own economic stability rather than to further the economic development of other continents. The changing international investment pattern between the wars is revealed in Tables IV/3 and IV/4.

The war of 1939–45, and the political turmoil in Asia, Africa, and Latin America that followed it, have strengthened the inward turn of European economic and financial interests. Today, international investment is dominated by the United States. Since the Second World War there has been a remarkable resurgence in international capital movements. The major changes have been the increasing role of the United States foreign investment (especially direct private investment) and the changing media of international lending. Official loans or donations transacted directly between states have grown rapidly during the past decade and a half. In particular, a vast system of American and Russian economic and military aid exists. (Tables IV/6, IV/7, and IV/8.) Unlike the international investment position prior to 1914 (when the purchase by individual investors of foreign government or municipal bonds was the normal procedure of transferring capital) the transfer of funds is now dominated by three agencies: 'bilateral' intergovernment loans and gifts, private and official loans transacted by international financial agencies, such as the World Bank, and private direct business investment.

* * *

The period 1850–1914 was the great age of European foreign investment. The economic and political environment of the time was propitious. Foreign investment provided an outlet for Europe's growing wealth; it also supplied the rising parts of the world with badly needed funds for development. The movement was encouraged by the prevailing economic liberalism, by the growing volume of migration and trade, and by the relative political stability of the times. The gold standard provided a reliable international monetary yardstick. In terms of volume, range, and impact, the capital movements of the leading creditor countries — Britain, France, and Germany — were infinitely more important during these years than they had been earlier. These years were also important for the major borrowing countries: the Dominions of the British Commonwealth, the United States, China, and several Latin American republics (Tables IV/1, IV/2, and IV/3). In absolute monetary terms, international indebtedness was higher in the inter-war years, and higher still after the Second World War, but, in relation to general price levels and total capital formation, it was never as great as in the early years of the present century.

British influence in international investment was supreme throughout the nineteenth century. Britain inherited financial leadership from the Dutch during the Napoleonic Wars; by the 1820's it had won the struggle for world mastery between the European powers. For most of the nineteenth century Britain enjoyed peace, and, provided with a favourable social and political environment, it was able to amass sufficient wealth to develop the institutions and trade connections conducive to financial success. London became the centre of a financial empire. Many types of highly specialized institutions appeared: commercial banks, issue houses, private banks, accepting houses, issuing brokers, and financial land and investment companies. There was a multitude of these specialized agencies. Not many men who came to the London capital market with a reasonable request for funds were turned away empty-handed. All of which stimulated foreign development.

The financial mechanism of continental European countries was never orientated towards foreign investment as that of Britain. By 1915 British foreign investments equalled or even exceeded the combined total of the rest of Europe, amounting to twice those of the French and almost three times those of the Germans. In the period 1850–1914 Britain's foreign investments dominated those of the rest of the world. A hundred years ago the United Kingdom was lending half its savings abroad. To a greater extent than any other nation, British investments were world-wide. On the outbreak of the First World War about 65 per cent of British foreign investments were concentrated in the Americas and Australasia; 17 to 18 per cent was in central and eastern Asia; less than 6 per cent was in continental Europe. In contrast, French and German investments were largely concentrated in Europe or in the Mediterranean area (Table IV/3). Germany's limited resources were needed for its own industrial development. French money was made to serve French national ambitions; France helped Russia in order that Russia might one day stem the German thrust towards European domination. The traditional preference shown by French investors for the security offered by low-interest-yielding Government bonds enabled French governments to mobilize French finance. Holland, Switzerland, and Belgium also had investments placed abroad (chiefly in North America, the Belgian Congo, and the Dutch East Indies) but they were relatively small. Britain had the greatest incentive to place its money in the developing areas of the world. Rapid industrialization had not only created the necessary surplus wealth but also the need for new sources of food and industrial raw materials. More than any other European nation, it needed the foodstuffs and the raw materials which its investments made available. To a greater extent than is true of other European nations, and especially so of the United States, Britain's overseas investments cheapened the things it wished to buy. Like most other European nations, Britain's foreign portfolio investment in 1913 was in railways and other undertakings of a public nature. In contrast, three-quarters of United States foreign assets in 1913 were direct business investments.

* * *

We are so accustomed to think of the United States as the richest country of all that it is difficult to imagine it as the world's greatest debtor nation before the First World War. For almost two centuries before 1914 there was hardly a year when European funds were not invested in North America. In 1789 the United States owed Europe about $60 million; by the late 1830's this figure had more than quadrupled; by 1900 it had grown forty-five times; and by the start of the First World War over one hundred times. French loans had helped the Americans to secure victory in the Revolutionary Wars; by 1793 France had provided $6–7 million. In the same year the Holland Land Company paid cash for five million acres in the States of New York and Pennsylvania. A decade later, in 1803, the Americans purchased the Louisiana territory from Napoleon with funds ($11 million) largely obtained from the London, Amsterdam, and Paris money markets. Constant help was given to American merchants engaged in foreign trade. In 1793 the United States held a position next to England in the value of its foreign trade. When account is taken of its small population at this time relative to Britain, the United States was probably the first commercial nation in the world — a position it could never have achieved without the aid of foreign, particularly British, capital. In the 1830's about one-half of America's cotton exports were supported by London funds. The amount of British commercial credit outstanding in 1837 was estimated at $100 million. The influence of British credit was felt by the most remote storekeeper, planter, and farmer as well as by the great commercial houses of the American Atlantic seaboard.

In the early part of the nineteenth century, European loans of any magnitude went almost entirely into the ambitious public-works programmes (state-financed turnpikes, canals, and, later, railways) of the newly created states and into speculative purchases of land. As the westward movement gained momentum, and the lands beyond the Alleghenies were explored and settled, the flow of European funds increased rapidly. In 1825 $7 million worth of bonds were taken up by British investors to finance the strategically important Erie Canal which went westwards through New York to Lake Erie. In providing communication between the coast and the interior of the United States the canal put an end to food shortages on the Atlantic seaboard. In the late 1830's the over-extension of British commercial credit resulted in a financial crisis; the boom in public works collapsed, nine American states defaulted on their interest payments, several defaulted altogether and for roughly a decade the flow of funds to the United States came to a halt. There was a point in the 1840's when the level of American credit-worthiness could not have been lower. The discovery of gold in California in 1848, however, gave a new impetus to expansion, and capital again flowed from Europe in ever-increasing quantities to the benefit of trade, banking, public works (especially railways), and manufacture. In 1860 the United States Treasury estimated the total foreign investment in the United States at $400 million. When the Civil War ended in 1865 Europeans held almost one-half of the entire war debt of the Northern Government; meanwhile they continued to invest large sums in almost every branch of the American economy. British land companies assisted further settlement; their cattle and equipment were particularly important at the end of the nineteenth century in helping to develop the cattle ranges of Texas, New Mexico, and Wyoming. Between 1879 and 1900 British financial interests promoted thirty-seven cattle companies with capital exceeding $34 million. In the late 1880's there was a flurry of British investment in American manufacturing industry. But the popularity of this kind of investment quickly died away. State and municipal borrowing grew from the 1870's onwards. Cities like Boston in Massachusetts and Providence in Rhode Island used considerable amounts of foreign capital to finance municipal development. In the period 1907–14 no year passed without New York City borrowing from Europe.

The most important single item of European investment before 1914 was the financing of American railways, especially the dramatic transcontinental lines. In 1853 Europeans held one-quarter of the nominal value of American railroad securities and by 1890 perhaps one-third. Britain was the principal market for American railway securities for three-quarters of a century, providing the finance needed to double the United States railway mileage between 1866 and 1873. Even as late as 1914 railway bonds accounted for more than one-half of all outstanding foreign investments in the United States. The increase in railway investments was largely responsible for the doubling in the value of European investments in the United States between 1870 and 1900. But even when the majority of American railways were built, European investments continued to grow at a rapid rate. They spread into every field of economic activity, including agriculture, mining, iron and steel production, and many other branches of manufacture and commerce. By 1914 the value of European investments in the United States had reached $6·5 billion,[1] representing no less than 14 per cent of international indebtedness at that time, 22 per cent of European foreign investments, and about 91 per cent of total foreign investments in the United States.

The First World War brought a marked change to this situation. During the war the fighting nations of Europe sold many of their investments to pay for arms and provisions purchased from the United States. By 1918 European investments were less than one-half of their 1914 values. In the inter-war years European holdings in the United States fluctuated considerably, and since 1945 there have been some new investments in American industry and commerce by European companies and a marked increase in European holdings of American stocks. European investments, however, have declined to a fraction of their 1914 value. Since the Second World War Britain has not only lost its position as the world's leading creditor nation to the United States (in 1960 United States foreign direct investments alone amounted to roughly $33 billion), it has itself become a net debtor to that country. (Tables IV/4 and IV/5.)

Relative to its population, foreign investments in Canada in the nineteenth and twentieth centuries have been unequalled by those of any other nation. Between 1850 and 1914 Canada was a consistent net importer of capital. Without foreign aid the country could not have developed its natural resources, or created the extensive transport facilities needed to bind the scattered British North American colonies together to form a national market; at least if Canada had depended upon its own low rate of domestic capital accumulation, it could not have been done so quickly. In 1913 nine-tenths of British investments were in public utilities aimed at developing the country.

In the early stages of the country's growth investments were made primarily by the French, whose influence extended from the St. Lawrence to the Mississippi. By the nineteenth century the promotion of Canadian trade and industry was dependent upon the flow of funds from London. These funds, marshalled by the financial houses of Europe, helped to build Canada's railways, waterways, and cities, and to develop the land, the mining industry, and the banking system. The Grand Trunk Railway, begun in the early 1850's, was heavily indebted to Britain for financial and technical assistance. Often thrust across territory lightly settled or largely

[1] U.S. billion throughout this book.

unexplored, it is hardly surprising that the Grand Trunk had a particularly stormy financial career. The Canadian Pacific Railway, one of the most vital links in Canadian development, was unusually slow to attract British investors (after its charter was granted in 1881) but by 1915 63 per cent of its stockholders were located in England; railways in fact remained the largest single field of investment in Canada until the Second World War. However, the heavy British investments of the 1850's brought over-expansion to the Canadian economy which resulted in the collapse of 1857. The end of the Crimean War, which had interfered with supplies of timber from the Baltic and wheat from the Ukraine, further depressed the Canadian market. There was a loss of confidence and much foreign capital went elsewhere. The recovery of capital imports in the 1860's was again offset by the fears aroused by the Vienna and New York financial crisis of 1873, and many Canadian projects had to be curtailed or postponed until domestic and foreign capital became more abundant at the end of the century.

The value of foreign investments in Canada about doubled between 1900 and 1914, and again increased by over 70 per cent between 1914 and 1938. (Tables IV/2, IV/3, and IV/4.) There were strong grounds for supposing that very great investment opportunities were already present in Canada in the decade before British investments recovered in 1904; and that the great influx of capital in the decade after 1904 served to stimulate the expansionary forces already at work. Improvements had been made in the last two decades of the nineteenth century in transport and agriculture and mining technology, which now made it possible to open and settle the Canadian West. Stimulated by these forces Canadian economic growth in the period 1900–14 was greater than at any time since the Act of Confederation in 1867. After 1914 Canada was by far the largest *per capita* debtor in the world. The first period (1900–14) coincided with the rapid influx of migrants and an expansion of population towards the western seaboard. With the aid of foreign capital and technology Ontario became a great mining state, the fishing and timber industries were developed, and the railway mileage was doubled — to the benefit of the undeveloped central and western areas. Between 1900 and 1914 Canada absorbed more funds from the United Kingdom and from the United States than any other country. During the 1920's investments in Canada expanded at only a slightly lower rate than those of the previous decade; until 1930 Canada's dependence upon foreign capital probably increased. The new foreign investments, however, were made almost entirely by the United States; and the emphasis had shifted from public works — favourite field of the British investor — to direct private United States investment in agriculture and industry. Between the two World Wars British foreign investments increased only slightly, and Europe's share as a whole declined from nearly 80 to less than 40 per cent. During the inter-war years and particularly after 1930 domestic investments became progressively more important, and by 1960 accounted for nearly 85 per cent of total private investments; the United States accounted for about 70 per cent of the remainder. Since the 1930's Canada has lent considerable amounts of money abroad (some of it of United States rather than Canadian origin). (Table IV/1.) But in 1960 Canada remained, overall, a 'net debtor' on a large scale.

European investments in Latin America have never been as important quantitatively as those in North America. Their traditional role has been to stimulate the exploitation of one or two staple commodities as well as provide transport and other public utilities. Only in the past generation have they helped to diversify the Latin American economies. However, as the average level of income (and hence the level of domestic investment) has always been very much lower in Latin America, European investments have had considerable effect in stimulating the economic growth and development of the southern half of the American continent.

Spaniards and Portuguese had begun to exploit Latin America in the sixteenth century. Plantations were established by the British, the French, and the Dutch. Important investments, however, were not made until the early decades of the nineteenth century. The first boom, which occurred shortly before and immediately after the recognition of Argentine independence, in 1824, ended in widespread default. As political stability grew from the mid-century, increasing supplies of capital entered the continent. By 1870 British investments alone in South America were estimated at $425 million, of which the greater part was in Argentina and Brazil. The most rapid increase in investments occurred in the decade before 1914. In 1914 the total value of foreign holdings in Latin America stood at $8·9 billion, of which British investments accounted for 42 per cent, United States 19 per cent, French 18 per cent, German 10 per cent, and those of other countries (primarily from Belgium, Holland, Portugal, Spain, and Sweden) 11 per cent. Of this total, one-third was located in Argentina, one-quarter in Brazil, one-quarter in Mexico, and the remainder chiefly in Cuba, Chile, Uruguay, and Peru. (Table IV/3.)

The First World War was a turning point in the history of foreign investment in Latin America; it halted the flow of European and increased the flow of United States funds. Most of the United States investments, which had increased from $1·7 billion in 1914 to $4·2 billion in 1938 (Table IV/4), were placed in North American-controlled enterprises. In 1930 British and United States investments in Latin America were roughly equal. With the onset of the world depression in the 1930's and the widespread default of Latin American governments both European and United States investments in Latin America declined sharply. The flow of capital to Latin America ceased. Many countries had already taken on obligations far exceeding their capacity to pay. Heavily dependent upon one or two export staples they were particularly hard hit by the collapse of world trade. Between 1929 and 1933 the prices of their principal exports fell in value by two-thirds. The thirties was a period of sad reappraisal. Those Europeans who had invested heavily in government bonds learned to regret it. On the eve of the Second World War, however, United States holdings stood at two and a half times their 1914 values; United Kingdom investments in the same period had increased by about a third; French and German holdings had declined — French investments falling to one-quarter of their 1914 value and German investments to one-sixth. (Tables IV/3 and IV/4.) The important qualitative change that had taken place since the commercial depression of 1929–33 was the shift, on the part of domestic as well as foreign investors, towards productive enterprises aimed at satisfying the growing home market of Latin American countries.

The reluctance to invest in Latin America which characterized the 1930's persisted during the Second World War and the post-war period. The inflow of private capital since 1945 has consisted largely of direct investments by United States enterprises, and official loans from the United States Export-Import Bank and the International Bank for Reconstruction and Development. The establishment of the Volta Redonda steel plant in Brazil in 1941–2, for instance, was supported by a United States Export-Import Bank loan. As of 1962 the World Bank had loaned Brazil $267 million to help purchase electrical power and transport equipment from abroad. Bank of England figures show a drop in outstanding foreign investments of the United Kingdom in Latin America from about £774 million ($3,870 million) in 1938 to about £630 million ($2,500 million) in 1945 and to £170 million ($475 million) in 1955. These figures are quoted at nominal value and exclude a substantial part of United Kingdom oil interests. The overall decline is partly due to the redemption of external public debts by many States, partly to the repurchase of a substantial amount of foreign-owned securities in Argentine public and private business enterprises. Foreign-owned petroleum properties in Mexico and Bolivia were expropriated in the 1930's; British railway properties in Argentina were subjected to forced sale during the 1940's. During the past twenty-five years wage rises (without corresponding increases in prices to meet the extra costs of production) have been forced upon foreign private interests controlling Brazilian railways, shipping, oil extraction, steel, and alkali production. Devices of all kinds have been introduced by Latin American governments to restrict the activities of foreign capitalists. Yet, in contrast to the downward trend of European holdings, United

States direct investments in commercial enterprises, which had declined from \$3·5 billion in 1930 to \$2·8 billion in 1940, reached the record level of \$8·4 billion in 1960. (Table IV/5.) The United States also provided in the period 1945–59 economic aid to Latin American countries totalling three and a half billion dollars. (Table IV/6.)

European funds in Latin America have been used primarily to develop public utilities such as transport and communications, ports, harbours, wharves, power and water supply; in 1914 these accounted for two-thirds of all foreign investments. Railways absorbed perhaps half of this amount. An estimate made in 1949 showed that three-quarters of Argentina's railway tracks were built with British and French capital, and the remaining quarter, although government owned, was largely financed by Europeans. Europe's contribution to transport and communications was not, however, restricted to railways; the origins and development of the tramways and subways of Buenos Aires, the air transport of Brazil, Bolivia, and Ecuador, and shipping, telephone, and cable companies throughout Latin America, are heavily indebted to the European investor and technician. There are few major public works in Latin America today which do not owe their nineteenth- or early twentieth-century origins to a decision made by one of the financial houses of London, Paris, Berlin, Madrid, or Lisbon.

These public works usually depended upon the actual or potential development of large-scale exports of agricultural and mining produce. European money was used to exploit the mineral resources of Mexico, Chile, Bolivia, Peru, and Colombia, countries poor in other natural resources. Both directly and indirectly (through induced expansion of railways and other public utilities and the increase of wealth and foreign currency reserves) the investments in the mining industry have contributed immeasurably to general economic development. More recently, the emphasis in mining has shifted to petroleum: a branch of the mining industry in which the investments of the European have been dwarfed by those of the United States' investor. Foreign investments in petroleum have gone primarily to Venezuela.

In areas with few or undeveloped mineral resources, European capital has gone primarily into agriculture and land development. The investments in the vast virgin grasslands of Argentina in the second half of the nineteenth century reaped a harvest of cheap grains which (together with the produce of the other newly developed grasslands of the Northern and Southern hemispheres) drove many a European farmer into bankruptcy. Argentine wheat exports more than tripled during the 1890's. In addition to grain production, considerable investments, mainly British, were made in Argentine livestock and timber. In Brazil, where foreign investments in agriculture and extractive industries were relatively small, European interests, again mainly British, were concentrated in the processing of agricultural products, such as coffee, cotton, and flour. European finance also provided the banking, insurance, transport, and marketing facilities for these and other agricultural industries. The tropical fruit industry of Colombia, Costa Rica, Guatemala, Honduras, and Nicaragua is, however, in the hands of American investors.

In the development of the manufacturing industry of Latin America the influence of certain European countries has been most pronounced. The Spaniards developed the cotton textile industry of Mexico, the Germans the chemical and plastics industry of Brazil, and the French and Belgians the South American steel production. Sometimes a group of Europeans controlled complete sectors of an economy, as in Argentina prior to the First World War, where the majority of industrial establishments were European owned; sometimes a European nation dominated the manufacturing life of a whole country, as the Germans did in Bolivia in the interwar years.

European capital was first invested in Asia to develop trade with the West. The amount has always been relatively small, but in providing a vehicle for western economic ideas and attitudes its influence was considerable. The economic penetration of Asia by the western powers provided the first serious challenge to civilizations strongly conservative and isolationist in spirit; for many Asians western economic progress provided the first serious challenge to Asian poverty.

India was one of the first Asian countries to experience the impact of European investment. Traditionally, the division between trade and finance was never sharp in India, and Portuguese merchants were the first Europeans to invest in Indian commerce. In the early years of the seventeenth century English, French, and Dutch East Indies Companies were formed. The triumph of British arms at Buxar and at Plassey in Bengal in the middle of the eighteenth century established British supremacy; and for another century, until the Mutiny of 1857, the British East India Company controlled the foreign trade and much of the economic development of the Indian sub-continent. It has been estimated that between 1845 and 1875, when India was experiencing one of the most rapid phases of British economic penetration, nearly $500 million were invested by the British in Indian guaranteed railway loans. The guarantee was clearly necessary if sufficient capital was to be obtained. In the period 1854–69 about $750 million of British capital were invested in railways, shipping, tea plantations, jute mills, banking and other mercantile houses; and once the process of investment had been established in the first half of the nineteenth century it continued for more than fifty years. The unusual amount of direct business investments in India at this time is partly explained by the development there of a managing agency system which facilitated and encouraged direct British investments.

Before the First World War the Indians themselves provided very little capital for the expansion of these modern enterprises. Tradition prevented them from doing so. Most castes had a background unfavourable to the new developments. The idea of using money to improve the economy was largely alien to the Indian mind.[1] In comparison with traditional investments in property, money-lending, trade, and jewellery, money spent in improving agriculture and industry bore a lower yield. Even where they bore a higher yield, ignorance and apathy had to be overcome. It took some time before the native investor developed the economic outlook of the European. And when a class of Indian investors emerged it was usually content to follow in the path marked out by the British. Yet Indians financed and controlled the early cotton textile mills, and in 1913 they founded what has become the vast Tata Iron and Steel Corporation. On the outbreak of the First World War, about 70 to 75 per cent of the recorded outstanding investments in India ($1,100 million) had come from foreign capitalists and entrepreneurs. Of this total no less than two-thirds was invested in railways. Next in order of importance were irrigation works, representing 7 per cent of total investments; tea plantations and port facilities each took up 4 per cent; municipal loans, 3 per cent.

The proportion of domestic investment increased during and after the First World War. By the early 1920's, encouraged by the success of the British investor and entrepreneur, Indians had begun to provide much of the new capital required for the expansion of trade and industry. In 1934 they owned practically all the cotton mill shares, over half the jute shares, nearly all the iron and steel interests, and over half the national debt. A study[2] made by the Reserve Bank of India reveals that, at their book-values, foreign business (non-banking) investments in India were worth nearly $1,200 million in 1958, of which the United Kingdom owned more than $800 million and the United States $120 million. The figure given by the Bank of England for United Kingdom investments (Table IV/5), which includes only stock-exchange securities at nominal value, is much lower. About 39 per cent of these investments was located in manufacturing, 21 per cent in petroleum, 17 per cent in plantations, 8 per cent in utilities and transport, and 5 per cent in trading. Offsetting

[1] This generalization needs careful qualification, for there is much evidence to the contrary. See, for instance, the part played by native capital in the financing of early British capitalist enterprise in N. C. Sinha, *Studies in Indo-British Economy* [*A*] *Hundred Years Ago* (Calcutta, 1946), especially Chapter II of Part I.

[2] Reserve Bank of India, Bombay, Research and Statistics Department, Division of International Finance, Report on the Survey of India's Foreign Liabilities and Assets as on 31st December, 1955 (Bombay, 1957).

the decline in foreign-owned business investment ($1,200 million in 1958 against $2,400 to $2,600 million in 1939) was a tremendous growth of investments by Indians; it is doubtful if in the post-war years foreign capital has provided more than about 5 per cent of total new investments. However, it would be wrong to conclude from this that Indian domestic investments are widely held or that they are adequate; they are in fact confined to a relatively small rentier and business class. At the current rate of about 8 to 9 per cent of the national income, Indian domestic investments are only about half the amount required if India is to become an advanced industrial country.

One of the most interesting developments during the past decade has been the degree of economic aid given to India by the Soviet Union and the United States. In 1955 India was granted a credit of 500 million roubles ($125 million) for the construction of the Bhilai Metallurgical Plant. Another long-term credit of 500 million roubles was granted to India to pay for the equipment, technical aid, and other outlays needed for the construction of India's heavy machine-building and other capital goods industries. For the construction of industrial plants during India's third Five-Year Plan (1961–5), the Indian government was again granted a credit of 1·5 billion roubles ($375 million). The total of Soviet credits to India (as at 1961) exceeds 720 million new roubles or roughly $800 million. (Table IV/8.) Much greater has been the economic aid given by the United States. This exceeded $800 million in one year alone (1962) and for the period 1945–62 approached 4 billion dollars.

The economic and political penetration of China by the West came later than that of India and reached its height only in the closing years of the nineteenth and the opening years of the twentieth centuries. The inroads made into Chinese life by foreign investment and enterprise before the last quarter of the nineteenth century were imperceptible, and Chinese governments were content that they should remain so. China was never drawn into world commerce to the same extent as India.

China's defeat in Korea by Japan in the mid-1890's, and the subsequent opening up of the country to western and Japanese influence, was a turning point in western penetration. To pay the indemnity imposed on China by Japan the Manchu Government between 1894 and 1899 had to obtain foreign loans totalling £51 million ($255 million). Between the suppression of the Boxer Rebellion in 1900 and the outbreak of the First World War the value of foreign investments in China more than doubled. (Table IV/3.) By 1931 they had more than doubled again, and China was now one of the five great debtor nations; though even at this time China's foreign debts per head of population were amongst the lowest in the world.

The share of total investments held by the major investors in China in

1914 was as follows: Britain, 37 per cent, Russia and Germany, each 16 per cent, Japan, 14 per cent, France, 9 per cent, and the United States 3 per cent. (Table IV/3.) During the period 1900–30, when investments in China were expanding most rapidly, Britain was the leading investor with more than one-third of the total ($1,200 million in 1931). Most of this capital, particularly after the First World War, was invested in British-owned business enterprises in the Shanghai area. Chief among these were trading companies, followed by investments in real estate and manufacturing. Transport absorbed only 14 per cent of British capital and most of this was in shipping. Russian investments, like those of Japan, were determined by political and military events in Manchuria; by far the largest part was invested at the turn of the century in the construction of the Chinese Eastern Railway across Manchuria. (The Trans-Siberian Railway was not completed until 1905.) Banks, real estate, and trade, the favourite fields of the British investor, were left almost entirely alone. Germans invested in railways in the Shantung province. French investments were spread more widely and their political and military motives were not as apparent as those of Russia, Germany, and Japan. Yet a great deal of French capital was spent in extending the railways from French Indo-China into China proper.

On the outbreak of the First World War two-thirds of foreign investments in China were in the form of direct business investments. Transport was the largest single field, absorbing about one-third of all foreign capital. European nations as a whole supplied more than four-fifths of the funds invested. Between 1914 and 1931 foreign investments more than doubled, but this was mostly due to the development of Manchurian industry by Japanese companies and the increase in American investment. By 1938 Japan had replaced Britain as the largest foreign investor, and by the end of the Second World War Japanese investments in China dominated the rest. Today China has liquidated every foreign direct investment including Russian ownership and control of the Chungchang Railway across Manchuria which was returned to China at the end of 1952. China's bonded debt, although in total default, has not so far been denounced. (Table IV/4.)

The old pattern of foreign economic intervention in China has gone for good. With the Japanese driven from the mainland and European commercial and financial interests confiscated or expelled, economic development now depends on the efforts and privations demanded of the Chinese by the State. The capital goods and technical assistance received by China from the Soviet Union since 1950, relative to China's needs and to the assistance given by the Soviet Union to the East European satellites or to India, Indonesia, and Egypt, are surprisingly unimportant. It is true that since 1900 the Chinese have increasingly developed their own trade and industry, but their network of railways, their modern shipping industry, the public works of their principal cities, and the manufacturing centre of Shanghai are largely European creations. These, along with industrial Manchuria, which virtually owes its existence to Japan, are today among China's most valuable assets.

This broad picture of capital formation and distribution in India and China holds good for Indonesia, Malaya, Siam, Indo-China, the Philippines, Burma, Ceylon, and what today is Pakistan. The great majority of domestic investors in these countries have preferred to put their money into small-scale trading ventures with limited turnover and high profits or into money-lending at high rates of interest. Hence, almost all the fixed and working capital required for large-scale industrial ventures, public works, and development projects has had to come from foreign investors and foreign entrepreneurs.

Foreign investment *per capita* in Malaya has been by far the highest in any Asian country. Yet when Singapore was founded by the British in 1819, the Malayan Peninsula supported the smallest of populations. Today Singapore is one of the great maritime market-places of the world. The national income per head of the Malay States is 70 per cent of that of Japan, the only other highly westernized economy in Asia. The whole apparatus of British technical and commercial skill, as well as the bulk of British investments in Malaya, have been employed in developing Malaya's commercial and transport facilities, and the tin and rubber industries. (The mid-nineteenth-century discovery and development of the rich tin deposits of western Malaya, however, depended largely upon the capital and labour provided by Malayan Chinese.) Investments in government bonds have accounted for only one-fifth of total foreign holdings because most of Malaya's extensive public works have been financed out of the current revenue of a wealthy state. A good deal of Malaya's progress since the First World War has resulted from the expansion of domestic Chinese and American as well as European investments. Approximately 40 per cent of the present population of Malaya and more than 70 per cent of that of Singapore are Chinese.

In Indonesia more than two-thirds of the foreign capital invested has come from the Netherlands and the greatest proportion has always been in the form of direct business investments. Since the Dutch wrested control of the East Indies from the Portuguese in the seventeenth century Dutch capital has helped to develop these islands. Loans have financed the construction of railways, irrigation projects, and other public works. Direct business investments have created the great export industries in sugar, coffee, and tobacco. In addition to Dutch capital, British and American money is invested in rubber, oil, and tobacco; investments by the overseas as well as Indonesian Chinese in Indonesia are widespread. Since the

1930's (until the expulsion of the Dutch in the late 1950's) foreign capital has flowed steadily to Indonesia, mainly to finance further government projects and to expand the oil and manufacturing industries. The effect of European capital in Indonesia was not as great, in terms of investment per head of population, to affect directly, as in Malaya, the majority of the people. Nor did it encourage, as in India, the rise of a native business class or the growth of domestic savings. Paradoxically enough, many of the benefits of foreign capital have been offset by the tremendous increase in population which Dutch rule has helped to bring about. Java's population increased from an estimated four to five million inhabitants in 1800 to sixty-three million in the early 1960's. (Tables IV/3, IV/4, and IV/5.)

In contrast to the sharp decline in recent years in private overseas investment in Indonesia, there has been a considerable increase in foreign official aid. Since the 1950's Indonesia has received credit from the Soviet Union and the United States. In 1956 the U.S.S.R. granted Indonesia $100 million for the payment of Soviet industrial equipment and machinery. In 1960 an agreement was signed between the U.S.S.R. and Indonesia, providing the latter with a long-term credit of 225 million new roubles (about $250 million) to be used in the construction of aluminium and metallurgical plants, a hydro-power plant in Sumatra and other projects. Since 1945 the Americans have made available financial assistance for similar purposes exceeding $600 million. (Tables IV/6, IV/8.)

Japan is an example of what a poor country can do with a moderate amount of foreign assistance. In the half century after the Meiji Restoration in 1868 Japan transformed itself into one of the world's most progressive industrial nations. By 1941 Japan was sufficiently powerful to challenge in war the combined strength of the western allied powers. The Japanese did not fail because they lacked the will to win or the ability to make sacrifices — the rise of modern Japan can surely leave us with no doubt on those scores — but rather because Japan could not hope to match the vast natural resources and the productive power of the western nations.

Much of what the Japanese were able to achieve during the past hundred years can only be understood in the light of Japan's historical and geographic background. More particularly, the economic development of Japan was achieved by a high rate of domestic savings rather than by the investment of foreign capital or by reinvesting the profits of an extensive foreign commerce. The financing of Japanese early industrialization was done through the taxing and borrowing policies of a strongly organized state, conscious of the growing threat of the western powers. To a degree equalled only by Russia and China in the present century, the Japanese plan of economic development was inspired by strategic motives. Internal decisions and needs decided what would be done. The land-tax reforms of the 1870's enabled the central government to tap the savings of the agricultural sector of the economy. More importantly, they introduced national uniformity in land taxation and registration. What capital resources Japan was able to amass were used most effectively; it is this, and the intensity of the labour effort in agriculture and industry, which explains Japan's economic success. The Japanese were encouraged in their efforts by their victory over the Chinese in 1895 and by the Anglo-Japanese Alliance of 1902.

Before 1900 European investments in Japan were negligible. Between 1900 and the outbreak of the First World War Japanese governments resorted frequently to the London and Paris money markets. However, by 1914 only about $1,000 million (perhaps half coming from Britain, most of the remainder from France) had been invested in Japan — considerably less than the amount invested in China. More than 90 per cent was in the form of government or municipal bonds, used principally to finance the wars with China and Russia, and the building of public utilities, particularly railways; the remainder was mostly invested in shipping and the foreign exchange business.

The tremendous stimulus given by the First World War to Japanese trade and industry helped Japan to exchange its role as an international debtor for that of an international creditor. During the inter-war years Japan raised foreign loans to assist reconstruction after the earthquake of 1923, as well as to finance the large-scale development of electrical power, which facilitated the industrial expansion of the 1930's. By then, Japan had become the only non-western net creditor nation, with large investments in Manchuria and other parts of Asia. Yet as European investments in Japan declined relative to Japanese domestic resources, their nature became more varied. There were more direct business investments and a number of joint European and Japanese enterprises were established to utilize European (and American) patents and skills. In 1938 Japan's debt to the West was smaller than it had been in 1914 (Tables IV/3 and IV/4); *per capita*, it was the lowest in the world next to China. With the exception of Turkey, Japan was the only important Asian country to reduce its indebtedness to the West between 1914 and 1938. On the eve of the Second World War the United Kingdom owned over half the foreign investments in Japan; today the leading position is held by the United States. The American government has also made available since 1945 economic aid exceeding $2,600 million. (Table IV/6.)

Of the remaining countries of Asia only Turkey absorbed appreciable amounts of European capital before 1914. The first loan to the Ottoman government was made by France in 1854. Thenceforth, influenced by political and strategic motives, France, Britain, and Germany made loans to the Turkish government. French investments have been uniformly important throughout the past century; German investments grew after 1888 with the building of the Berlin–Baghdad railway. By 1914 Europe had invested almost 6 billion francs; of these France held 60 per cent, Germany 25 per cent, and Britain 14 per cent. After the collapse of the Ottoman Empire at the end of the First World War the value of European holdings in Turkey declined and new investments came to a halt. However, the Russian–Turkish treaties of 1925 and 1929, and the final arrangement with European creditors for the payment of the Ottoman debts in 1933, helped to restore confidence and by 1939 foreign capital amounted to almost 15 billion francs, most of it French and British. Since the Second World War Germany and France have made direct investments in commerce and industry. Considerable financial assistance has also been given by the United States government (especially for military rearmament) and the International Bank for Reconstruction and Development.

European capital invested in Iraq, Lebanon, Iran, Syria, and Palestine has done little to change the traditional way of life of the people of these countries. French and British capital provided railways as well as other public works and assisted the commerce of the area, but until the 1920's European influence had hardly affected what are still largely traditional agricultural economies. The most important development since the twenties has been the growing amount of European and American capital invested in oil production. The earliest mining concessions in this area were given by Iran in the 1890's to the British and the Germans. In 1909 the Anglo-Iranian Oil Company was formed. A few years later oil concessions were taken up in Iraq by Americans, British, Dutch, and French, who later financed large-scale oil production and the building of pipelines from Kirkuk to Tripoli and Haifa on the Mediterranean coast. In 1934 British oil companies financed the laying of the pipe-line from Mosul to Haifa. In recent years there has been substantial investment by European and American oil companies in the Persian Gulf States. Investments in Saudi-Arabia are entirely American. Several pipelines have been built, including that from Dhahran to Saida.

The oil revenues, together with the financial and technical assistance provided by the United States, and international agencies such as the World Bank, have enabled these countries through the development of improved systems of transport, power supply, flood control, and irrigation to take the first steps towards creating a modern economy along western lines. While nineteenth- and twentieth-century European investments have undoubtedly stimulated the economic development of the countries of south-west Asia, the actual progress made, with the exception of Israel and Lebanon, has been extremely small. To develop progressive economic communities along western lines out of what are in many cases ancient feudal kingdoms is an enormous task which above all else requires time.

Even where constant and large supplies of capital are available, as in Saudi-Arabia, economic and social change is slow.

In comparison with European foreign investments in the Americas, Asia's dependence upon European capital, relative to its needs and its population, has been small and restricted to a brief period of time. With the exception of India, there was no major flow of capital into Asia before the 1890's. Most investments have been made since the turn of the century and a great deal of these have been used to discover and exploit the oil resources of south-west Asia. Not only has Asia's financial dependence on the West been remarkably small, and in the case of oil highly localized, but in the past fifteen years or so Asia has more completely rid itself of private foreign capital obligations than any other continent. On the other hand, United States government economic aid to Korea, Japan, and Formosa, as well as to Turkey, India, and Pakistan, has increased enormously in the same period.

European investments in Africa before the second half of the nineteenth century did not extend beyond the financing of trade in slaves, precious metals, ivory, and ostrich feathers. The simple needs of the African natives could be met from their own resources. Long after the commerce of other continents had been developed most of Africa remained isolated and self-sufficient. The traditional systems of agriculture practised in Africa before the coming of the white man were extremely crude, yet they sufficed to maintain a relatively stable standard of subsistence.

The one great force which helped to change this situation was the discovery of important deposits of gold and diamonds in South Africa almost a hundred years ago. The mining of precious minerals (as well as the vast deposits of copper in Northern Rhodesia) provided a comparatively high yield per unit of capital invested by the Europeans. Of the foreign capital invested between 1870 and 1930 south of the Sahara, about two-thirds was absorbed by the highly mineralized territories of South Africa, the Rhodesias, and the Belgian Congo. European mining ventures provided the stimulus for the building of many of Africa's railways, ports, and towns, and laid the foundations of the present-day European communities. The impact of the great capital resources, which the mineral wealth of Africa has attracted, has, however, been limited to the European mining areas.

In those parts of West, Central, and East Africa where mining is of little importance, European capital has been used primarily to establish commercial agriculture. Since the sixteenth century, when the Portuguese brought groundnuts, cassava, and maize from America, Europeans have introduced many new plants and crops. In the nineteenth and twentieth centuries many of these have been developed on a commercial scale in response to the ever-increasing needs of the world's industrial centres. Thus, European enterprise and investment have created the agricultural export industries of Africa: cotton and coffee in Uganda, cotton, sisal, and tobacco in East Africa, cocoa in the Gold Coast, groundnuts and palm oil in Nigeria, vegetable oils and fats in the Belgian Congo. Increasingly, the native has been induced to look upon agriculture as an industry of cash crops rather than a means of subsistence. The introduction of new plants and new methods of cultivation has brought benefits to native farmers and communities throughout the central, western, and eastern parts of Africa, though on the whole the economic progress resulting from the introduction of European systems of cultivation has been restricted to European plantations and a small part of the African community. The benefits conferred by the Europeans in the development of tropical agriculture have also brought serious disadvantages in their train. In the black man's Africa the native has struggled with problems to which he was accustomed, such as those connected with shifting cultivation, pestilence, famine, slave-raiding, and tribal warfare. In the white man's Africa — quite apart from the human sicknesses and plant pests and diseases introduced by the European invaders — the native was detribalized, his traditions were undermined, and he was beset by commercial problems of a world-wide nature.

Considerable investment in Central and East Africa has been made since the Second World War, especially in development projects such as the Owen Falls Hydro-Electric Scheme in Uganda and the Kariba Hydro-Electric Scheme in the Rhodesias. For the Kariba Scheme the International Bank, the Colonial Development Corporation and other organizations contributed £45·6 million. Of the total loans made to African countries by the International Bank up to 1962, the Rhodesias received 36 per cent; in the same period they received 41 per cent of the total financial assistance given to African countries by the Colonial Development Corporation. In the early 1960's much of the Owen Falls power generating capacity was still unused.

North of the Sahara, European investments have been more varied in character and have probably had a more widespread effect in introducing western civilization. From Alexandria in Egypt to Casablanca in Morocco, there is hardly an important city, industry, transport or irrigation system, port or harbour that is not the result of European (particularly French) enterprise and capital. The Suez Canal, one of the greatest and most influential contributions to world commerce, is the result of French engineering and French money. The establishment of the Gezira cotton-growing scheme in the Egyptian Sudan and the building of railways and other valuable public utilities throughout North Africa were inspired and financed by Europeans. Much European capital, however, was obtained at a high price, and the problems connected with its repayment often led to armed intervention and annexation by the European powers; this was Egypt's experience in the second half of the nineteenth century.

Before the French occupied Tunisia in 1881 its finances were governed by an International Commission established in 1869 in which the French, British, and Italians had equal interests. Under French direction the main road system of Tunisia has been almost entirely rebuilt; a network of railways has been established with a total length of 1,300 miles; the production and export of valuable and varied minerals (particularly the natural phosphates and iron ore) have been developed on a large scale; Tunisian exports of wine, olive oil, wheat, and barley have become one of the main sources of Tunisian wealth; thermal power stations, established by the French in the inter-war years, have helped to improve Tunisia's inadequate power resources.

The French have been in Algeria since the 1830's and since then have done much to encourage Algeria's economic development. Until Algeria gained its independence in 1962 it was considered to be part of metropolitan France. Mostly at the direct expense of France, modern ports were built at Algiers, Oran, and Bône, dams and reservoirs constructed, and an excellent network of roads and railways built. The railway network begun in 1857 today exceeds three thousand miles. It links the Atlantic ports with those of the Mediterranean and connects the whole of French North Africa. Public and private French capital has also been invested in the mining industry (particularly iron-ore, natural phosphates and, more recently, oil); the main sources of Algeria's power have been developed; the production of cotton, tobacco, flax, and silk has been encouraged; and large quantities of cereals, fruits, olives, and wines, which still provide the basis of Algeria's wealth, have been produced for export and home consumption. The French-financed Bank of Algeria, founded in 1851, and the Land Loan Bank of Algeria and Tunisia, founded in 1881, have provided further assistance in financing the country's development. Between 1945 and 1960 French public investments in Algeria amounted to $1·6 billion. During 1962, however, there was a dramatic withdrawal of French public and private investments from war-torn Algeria.

It is only in the twentieth century that the French and the Spaniards have helped to develop Morocco. Roads, railways, and ports have been built, minerals exploited and agricultural production improved and extended. Financial assistance was first given in 1904 by a French syndicate on the security of customs duties. In 1910 another important French loan was issued by the State Bank of Morocco. In 1912 French Morocco was declared a protectorate. Since then, investment has generally followed along the lines of that made in Algeria and Tunisia.

Both in absolute terms and in relation to the population and domestic capital formation, European investments in Africa reached a peak in 1914 with approximately \$4·5 billion. At that point they reflected strongly the success of the various powers in 'the scramble for Africa' of the previous forty years, each nation retaining virtually a monopoly of investment within its own colonies. Britain accounted for more than half of all foreign investments; the Union of South Africa and the Rhodesias absorbing three-quarters of British capital, West Africa, East Africa, and Egypt sharing the rest. France was the second greatest investor with about two-thirds of the remaining capital, invested mostly in Egypt and in the French North African territories. Germany and Belgium had considerable — if smaller — investments principally in German East Africa, South Africa, and the Belgian Congo.

Between 1914 and 1938 the value of foreign investments remained fairly constant at about \$4·0 billion (Tables IV/3 and IV/4), making Africa the only continent outside Europe in which foreign investments did not show any increase in absolute terms during this period. Per head of population their value dropped by nearly a quarter; this resulted partly from the liquidation of German assets, as well as from the repayment of loans, and purchase of foreign holdings by domestic investors in the Union of South Africa and Egypt. However, in French North Africa, the Belgian Congo, and the newly created Italian territory in East Africa, investment increased considerably.

Since the Second World War there have been substantial changes in Africa's position in the world economy. War-time shortages in agricultural produce and minerals encouraged the return of an earlier belief that Africa was a continent of limitless resources awaiting an adequate supply of capital. The high prices obtained for produce in the years immediately following the war confirmed this view and further encouraged African development. Accompanying this was a change in the outlook of white and black Africans towards Europe, and of the European powers towards their African dependencies. The war had given white and black Africans the desire for greater political independence; it had also fostered in Europe a greater sense of social responsibility towards Africa. In the economic and social spheres the outcome of this has been the emergence of special forms of European government agencies whose task it has been to promote the economic and social development of native peoples.

The chief source of financial assistance to African countries in the period 1953–4 to 1958–9 has been bilateral assistance rendered by the governments of France and Britain to their former colonial territories. France was, by far, the largest contributor to the external financing of African economic development. Total net public direct expenditures, grants, and loans in the overseas franc area between 1956 and 1959 averaged 700 million to 800 million dollars annually. Traditionally, Britain has never given as much government assistance to its colonial territories as France has done; most British funds have come from the London capital market. In the changed conditions of the post-war period, however, Britain has developed an extensive institutional framework for public assistance to Commonwealth countries. While the framework was built on earlier foundations (the British Colonial Development and Welfare Act of 1929) it is only since 1945 that a special stimulus has been given to colonial development. British public bilateral assistance to all areas combined rose from an average of an equivalent of $140 million in 1952–3 to an estimated $330 million in 1959–60. As with French government assistance, most of these funds have been spent in public works, agriculture, health, education and other social services. Other European non-Communist countries rendering assistance to African development since the Second World War are Belgium, Portugal, Italy, and, much more recently, West Germany. The amount of assistance given by these countries, when compared with that coming from France and Britain, is modest and has been invested chiefly in the Congo, Angola, Mozambique, and Italian Somaliland.

It is not only European governments which have revised their attitudes towards Africa in the post-Second World War period. The United States has also provided direct and indirect financial aid, particularly to Egypt, Morocco, Tunisia, Libya, Ghana, Liberia, and Ethiopia. The total amount of public economic assistance given by the United States Government to African countries has risen from a total of about $96 million for the years 1945–54, to about $669 million in the six years ending 30 June, 1960. Soviet and Chinese interest in financing the development of African countries is much more recent than that of western European countries and the United States. Bilateral assistance between African countries is not unknown: loans were made in the early 1960's by the U.A.R. and Ghana to Mali. Unlike most financial assistance given by Moslem countries, the Arab loan to Mali carries with it an interest charge. (Tables IV/6 and IV/8.)

In addition to the bilateral assistance between governments, aid has also been given since the Second World War by multilateral agencies and international organizations; the most important of these is the World Bank. Most investments have been made in public utilities, but manufacturing, mining, and agricultural development have also been financed. The largest loans made by the World Bank went to Rhodesia and Nyasaland and the Belgian Congo. The largest single loan was made to the Rhodesian Federation in 1956 to finance the building of the Kariba Hydro-Electric project mentioned earlier.

A distinctive feature of recent African development is the low level of industrialization. The only modern large-scale industrial enterprises in Central Africa today exist alongside the large copper and diamond mining industries of the Belgian Congo and in the Republic of South Africa. In all other continents a considerable amount of foreign investment has gone into manufacturing industry. In Africa, the basic facilities, potential demand, knowledge, and skills essential for successful industrialization are largely absent. Foreign investment, public and private, still concentrates on public works and primary production. Yet some of the investments made since the end of the Second World War in the development of hydro-electricity have quickened the pace of commercial and industrial activity; and there are other major public works at present under construction. Encouraging as these changes are, they are small, however, when set against the task remaining to be done. Africa has arrived late in the process of world economic development and without many of the advantages to which western countries owe their success; Africa's lateness, its relative poverty, its physical inaccessibility, its social and cultural systems, its appalling illiteracy, its ecological conditions, its economic and political uncertainty are today the major deterrents to the investment of foreign capital. Especially important is Africa's present political uncertainty. The lack of confidence in Africa's immediate future has caused many European and American private investors and entrepreneurs to lose interest in African developments. Yet no emerging nation of Africa can be indifferent to the foreign private investor; for some of them upon their ability to attract foreign private funds depends economic progress. Even in an economically advanced country such as the Republic of South Africa, where most capital requirements are provided from domestic savings, the flight of foreign capital, and the cessation of capital imports, beginning seriously in 1960 has caused the loss to the Republic of much of the risk capital (and the new technological knowledge which has invariably accompanied it) needed for new mining and industrial ventures. Elsewhere in Africa (in the Belgian Congo, Morocco, Algeria, etc.) the financial position in the early 1960's was much more difficult than it was in the Republic of South Africa. With a few exceptions such as Nigeria and Liberia, which in 1963 were still attracting increasing quantities of foreign private capital, many new nations of Africa could only obtain foreign capital at a relatively high cost. The situation could hardly right itself without improved political and racial conditions. (Table IV/5.)

Australia and New Zealand are outstanding examples of the stimulus given by foreign borrowing to economic development. All the major public works built in New Zealand in the second half of the nineteenth century were financed in London. From the gold rush of 1863 to the collapse of the land boom in 1879 borrowing abroad by New Zealand increased rapidly. A much needed railway and harbour system was built, though the debts incurred for these developments weighed heavily in the lean times of the 1880's and the early 1890's. The coming of the refrigeration ship and the subsequent development of the meat and dairy industry in the 1890's, however, gave a new stimulus to foreign borrowing, which grew rapidly in the decade before the First World War. In the inter-war years New Zealand's experience was somewhat parallel to that of Australia. New Zealand still borrows heavily on London to cover the deficit in the balance of trade. Sterling loans to the New Zealand Government outstanding at the end of 1962 totalled some £137 million ($380 million) and, according to the United Kingdom Board of Trade, the value of United Kingdom direct investments in New Zealand at the same date was some £76 million ($210 million). There is also considerable British and American investment through subsidiary corporations.

The flow of capital to Australia began in the 1780's with the establishment of a penal settlement, and, until the late 1820's, consisted primarily of grants from the government in London to the colonial administration in Sydney. Bills drawn on the British Treasury in London were used to settle Australia's external payments. To finance the great pastoral expansion in New South Wales and Victoria during the 1830's, new sources of foreign and domestic capital had to be developed. The most important of these were the British banks and mortgage companies, established to do business in the Australian colonies. Later in the century Australian-founded banks and land companies recruited in London an impressive array of 'lords, baronets and other personages' whose appointment as directors served to encourage a gullible investing public.

British investments in Australia reached a peak at the end of the 1830's. There followed the slump of the forties which was relieved by discoveries of copper in South Australia in 1844 and gold in New South Wales and Victoria in the early fifties. The lure of gold caused a great increase in population during the fifties and sixties, which in turn created a most urgent need for urban development and for additional transport facilities and public works of all kinds. Colonial government borrowing in London (begun by New South Wales in 1842) entered a new phase. From the mid-fifties to the late eighties there was almost continuous public and private borrowing overseas. With the help of British capital Australia underwent a period of rapid economic growth. The pastoral industry spread into western New South Wales and Queensland. The wheat and sugar industries were developed, new roads and railways were built, and manufacturing was encouraged. There was considerable and, in the opinion of some writers, extravagant urban development, especially in Melbourne in the period 1884–91. Accompanying all this was the need to finance many kinds of public works. There were also large sums invested in mining. In the eighties, silver (and later lead and zinc) was discovered at Broken Hill, copper at Mount Lyell, gold in Queensland and Western Australia. For a period, metals outstripped wool as the leading export.

The eagerness of British investors to supply Australia with increasing quantities of capital at high rates of interest helps to explain Australia's rapid rate of growth in the second half of the nineteenth century. Two-thirds of the new capital invested between 1860 and 1890 came from Britain. Public borrowing rose throughout the period until it exceeded private borrowing in the nineties. The major use of foreign capital was to finance public works (particularly railway building during the eighties) and town development. Agricultural and pastoral development were also important fields of investment at this time but in these industries private domestic capital played the leading role.

Public capital expenditure in Australia in the half century before the First World War is thought to have had a stabilizing influence on the entire expanding economy. On the other hand, Australia's public and private borrowings overseas created a financial dependence on Britain, and a serious drain on Australia's balance of payments to service its external debt. This was felt most acutely when the fluctuations in the investments of the different Australian colonies in the eighties led to a temporary cessation of Australia's growth in the down-swing of 1891–4. The boom in gold production in Western Australia in the nineties, however, coupled with the diversification and expansion of Australian exports, did much to relieve the depression of those years. The economic collapse of the 1890's, which had resulted partly from the extravagant use of British capital, put an end to the rapid inflow of foreign money until the 1920's, when federal, state, and municipal borrowing from London carried foreign investment in 1930 to a record level of $3·8 billion, three-quarters of which were public loans. By the thirties, however, a substantial decline in the relative importance of foreign compared with the domestic supply of capital had occurred; a trend which has continued as Australia's domestic savings have grown.

During the world depression of the 1930's there was little new foreign investment in Australia. Since the Second World War there has been a continuous and heavy flow of capital into Australia. However, whereas nineteenth-century and inter-war capital imports were predominantly public investments, mainly government borrowing through overseas loan issues, capital imports today are mostly in the form of private direct investment in branches or subsidiaries of overseas companies; during the 1950's less than 2 per cent of the expenditure on public works came from public borrowing abroad. And whereas private investments before 1914 were primarily intended to finance the development and export of agricultural and mining produce, which provided the money needed to effect dividend payments and debt redemption, the greater part of direct investments since the Second World War have gone into manufacturing industries and oil prospecting for the Australian market. The import-saving effects of some of these investments are making a useful contribution to Australia's balance of payments problem. The situation is complicated in the case of American companies, such as the motor-car manufacturers, General Motors-Holden, whose stock ownership is restricted to stock-holders in the parent company in the United States. Another important change since the Second World War is the fact that the United Kingdom no longer retains the virtual monopoly (over 90 per cent in the 1930's) of foreign investment in Australia. After the Second World War the United Kingdom's share fell to about two-thirds, while that of North America has increased from less than one-fifth in the late 1940's to about a third in the early 1960's. In 1961 United States and Canadian new private investment in Australia exceeded that of the United Kingdom for the first time in the history of the Australian Commonwealth. The Australian Federal Government also borrowed large sums from the World Bank and small amounts in New York, Montreal, and Zürich. Assisted by the development of oil and manufacturing, United States investments in Australia increased more than fourfold between 1950 and 1960 from $200 million to $860 million. An Australian estimate of the amount of overseas funds received for private investment (including reinvested profits) during the fifties sets the figure at almost £1,000 million.

Australians (as are the Canadians for that matter) are conscious of the many benefits, including the introduction of improved technology, accompanying the rapid growth of American private direct investment in their country. Recent discussions, however, reveal a growing concern in Australia with the economic and political disadvantages attending large foreign private investments of this kind, not least the control exercised by American corporations over the export trade of their subsidiary companies in Australia. (A similar concern was felt regarding the growing role of British investors in America at the end of the last century.) Many Australians — and the argument can be extended to include Canada, Latin America, and other developing areas — wonder whether the price they have to pay to the foreign investors is not unjustifiably high, even allowing for payments for the risk-bearing enterprise, technical knowledge, and entrepreneurial skill invariably accompanying foreign investments. The most promising sign for Australia is that the current proportion of the gross national product devoted to capital formation is 50 per cent higher than for the United Kingdom and the United States, and that Australia's investment programme in the 1960's was overwhelmingly based not on foreign but on domestic resources. Only a fraction of the total expenditure on public works is provided by borrowing abroad; of the private capital for new developments four-fifths are raised in Australia. (Tables IV/3, IV/4, and IV/5.)

* * *

To conclude from this chapter that European foreign investment is the sole cause of economic growth and development would be quite false. Economic development is too complex a process to exaggerate the role of any one economic agency. Economic progress requires much more than investment and the borrowing of European skills; it is also dependent on a country's stage of development, the terms on which it trades with others, its natural potential, its human resources and their social and cultural heritage, its technology, government, and administration, its political autonomy, and its sense of national purpose. Ultimately, the strength of a great people must be found within itself. European overseas investment in the century before 1914, in terms of its contribution to productive enterprise and world development, was undoubtedly of greater magnitude (especially if allowance is made for the depreciation of world currency) than that which preceded it in the eighteenth century, and that which has followed during the past two or three decades; but it was not the only or the most important factor in the development of a country or of a world economy.

Economic development was often the cause as well as the effect of European investments. Indeed, on a world scale, very little is known about the causes of the ebb and flow of European foreign investments in the century before 1914. Even at their height in the early years of the present century they accounted for only a limited fraction of world gross capital formation. Much depended on the innovating and creative role of foreign investment as well as its magnitude. Some investments, such as those made in railways, initiated a series of changes which eventually altered the social and economic structure of a society; others actually discouraged native development. Where the circumstances were favourable, as in the United States, the British Dominions, Japan, and certain Latin-American countries, the effect of European foreign investment was considerable. These are the areas which before 1914 received most financial assistance from Europe. In the economically less developed (largely non-European) regions of the world, including China, India, most of Africa and Latin America, its visible impact was limited to those sectors of the economy in which European influence was greatest. Its most important (if less apparent) effect was to break down the traditional static views of non-European societies and to introduce them to the dynamic ideas underlying western economic progress.

While much change has been wrought in the world by people who largely sought to invest their money at a profit, it would be wrong to regard European expansion as the result of Europe's quest for wealth. To do so would be to over-simplify a highly complex process in which many factors were at work. To assume that the European investor always gained at the non-European's expense is to miss the importance of the movement altogether. It was to the benefit of the whole world that European capital was used to develop the world's resources. Whether Christian Europe should have charged the price it did is a theological rather than an economic question. Even in narrow economic terms the history of British private investments in Latin America shows that the borrowing country often got the best of the bargain; defaulters usually kept equipment. The higher yields of most foreign investments were often offset by the greater speculative nature of foreign ventures. In the European colonial areas, where by common agreement the possibility of economic exploitation was greatest, many different situations were met with. During the scramble for parts of Africa and Asia in the last quarter of the nineteenth century the interests of the native people were often lost sight of altogether. On the other hand, in the more recent phases of European colonial investment the interests of the native people have occupied a central position. This kind of investment is rooted in a sense of obligation towards colonial people; it has been made, not for profit, but at the bidding of national conscience. Thus, out of the excesses and abuses of nineteenth-century colonialism there has also arisen an international conscience, which is beginning to make itself felt in the investment policy of the World Bank and in the other mutual-aid policies adopted by the western world. (Table IV/7.)

Whether Europe's role as the world's banker was beneficial or malevolent will always be disputed. It depends on the point of view of those who judge it. Hitherto, it stood condemned by the Moslem world because the European took interest for his money; but there are signs as in the recent United Arab Republic loan to Mali that the Moslem attitude to interest is changing. To the Marxist, foreign investment was an exploitive aspect of capitalism, although the present government of the U.S.S.R. prefers interest-bearing loans to outright gifts as a form of foreign aid. However judged, its effects cannot be undone. For the bulk of European foreign loans in the century before the First World War went into critically important public utilities — especially transport and communication — which have helped to open up the entire world. They provided the economic foundations upon which others have built. To a greater or lesser degree all countries have been affected. And although in recent decades private foreign lending has been given a tremendous stimulus by the Americans it is doubtful if private foreign investment today has the same overall stimulating effect as similar earlier European investments. Much American money since the First World War has gone into war and reconstruction loans and direct and localized investment in mining (particularly oil) and manufacturing industries; and, with the exception of agricultural investments in Latin America and the money spent in the development of oil supplies in the countries of south-west Asia, American private money has been invested in Europe instead of those areas of Africa and Asia which now await development. The most extraordinary development since the Second World War has been the economic and military aid given by the governments of the United States and (to a very much lesser extent) the U.S.S.R., and China. It would be difficult to assess the total impact of the approximately one hundred billion dollars which the American government has provided for foreign countries all over the world during the two post-war decades. Without this kind of financial assistance western Europe's economic recovery could never have been as rapid as it was. (Tables IV/6 and IV/8.)

Whatever the future of international investment, it is fairly certain that a new pattern is emerging. Africans and Asians today are unlikely to accept nineteenth-century European capitalistic principles. Many of these people not only want their newly-won political independence but economic independence also. Everyone recognizes the need for a rapid expansion of foreign private investment. But on what terms? In the past Africans and Asians have resented the control exercised over their economies by the West. Even among Europeans at home and overseas new criteria are being applied. International investment is no longer as private profit-dominated as it was in the nineteenth century. In the conduct of foreign investment economic liberalism is giving way to social welfare and international security. In fact, there exists today a network of international lending agencies and government-controlled foreign investments in which the economic values and implications are inseparable from the social, the political, and the military. A recent study of world investment in the period 1956–9, however, shows that private foreign investment in the economically less advanced parts of the world did not fall much below the amount ($12 billion against $15 billion) contributed by official grants and loans.

What the new pattern of investment will be it is difficult to foretell. Perhaps the world will return to an idea mooted in England in the seventeenth century and establish global private corporations in which the people of all lands may join; perhaps we shall see a great increase in the importance of internationally controlled organizations such as the World Bank. Even with the loosening of political ties between the West and dependent colonial empires the signs are that western nations are likely to increase their bilateral aid. Certainly, without the support of international organizations and foreign governments, the outlook for private investors in what are today called the 'underdeveloped' parts of the world is most unattractive.

Fundamentally the problem is a human problem; it concerns changes in human attitudes as well as changes in financial institutions; it concerns the ability to allocate very scarce resources to their most productive use; it concerns the willingness of a people to put off till tomorrow the facilities and the conveniences it cannot afford today. The overwhelming fault of western nations in their relations with the less developed parts of the world is the emphasis they have placed on western capital and western technology. We are so engrossed with the power of the western machine that we have forgotten that for a nation to advance rapidly it must not only possess the necessary natural resources and skills; it must also possess what western society used to refer to as virtues: diligence, thrift, dynamism, perseverance, and a stable and honest administration. In the last resort, widespread and rapid economic development must spring from within a nation rather than from without. Taken alone, money does not change man or nature; the social inertia or social vigour of a country cannot be explained in monetary terms alone; capital accumulation, whether viewed nationally or internationally, is not automatic; the desire to consume is stronger than the desire to save. It will be a long time before the western idea of forgoing the present in order to invest intelligently in an uncertain future gains world-wide acceptance. Historically speaking, people have worried more about their ancestors or their own spiritual salvation than about how the next generation was to be fed. Moreover the loans made by international organizations today to countries needing capital will achieve little if the funds provided merely prove to be a substitute for domestic saving. They will achieve even less if the loans (as is true of some European investments in the past) encourage an increase in population far outstripping the gradual increase in production. Whatever the outcome of present trends, it will certainly be a poorer world unless some means can be found to enable those who have great wealth to assist those who have little.

TABLES

IV/1 to IV/8

EUROPEAN FOREIGN INVESTMENTS

General Notes on the Tables

The main object of these tables is to show Europe's role as a source of capital to the world. The growing impact of American (and more recently of Russian) investments is also shown.

The definition of foreign investments in the tables is the total of outstanding investments in other countries, public and private, made on a long-term basis, converted into U.S. dollars at the current rates of exchange. ('Long-term' denotes a period exceeding one year.) Short-term investments have generally been excluded. The growing role of loans from international agencies and government grants are dealt with in Tables IV/6, IV/7 and IV/8. Methods of valuation vary according to the sources, but, in general, government and other public bonds are taken at their nominal value, other portfolio investments at their market value, and direct investments at their book value.

'Direct' investments are investments in the private business enterprises of another country. The term 'direct' is usually restricted to investments which have considerable influence in the management of foreign enterprises. Other private or 'portfolio' investments consist of the holdings of miscellaneous foreign securities which do not involve any control of the foreign business by the investor.

Foreign investments are estimated to the nearest $50 million or $100 million. The figures given are approximate, compiled from a variety of sources, frequently conflicting, employing different methods of calculation, and often incomplete. Preference has been given to the most recent figures, and to official sources. Widely diverging estimates from different sources are indicated in the footnotes, and more obviously incomplete figures are put in brackets. Due to rounding off, figures in the tables do not in all cases add up exactly to the totals shown.

Bank of England figures used in the tables are probably too low. They include only investments in stock exchange securities; the capital is represented by the nominal value of these holdings. As overseas assets of U.K. companies operating partly abroad but mainly at home are not covered, an important part of U.K. direct investments overseas is omitted. Assets of U.K. oil companies are not fully included in the figures for individual countries.

The depreciation of many currencies in terms of the dollar during and after the Second World War may exaggerate the declining importance of European overseas investments when converted into dollars (e.g. Bank of England figures show a fall in the value of British overseas investments between 1938 and 1955 of about two-fifths when measured in sterling, compared with a fall of about two-thirds in dollar terms. Much the same applies to other European countries).

Table IV/1

Growth of Foreign Investments of Selected Leading Capital-exporting Countries since the Nineteenth Century (in millions of U.S. dollars to the nearest $100 million)

Country	*1825*	*1840*	*1855*	*1870*	*1885*	*1900*	*1915*[1]	*1930*	*1945*	*1960*
United Kingdom .	500	700[2]	2,300[3]	4,900[4]	7,800[5]	12,100[6]	19,500[7]	18,200	14,200	26,400
France . . .	100	(300)	1,000[8]	2,500	3,300	5,200	8,600[9]	3,500[10]		
Germany . .	..	..	..	..	1,900[11]	4,800[12]	6,700[13]	1,100		1,200
Netherlands[14] . .	300[15]	200	300	500	1,000	1,100	1,200[16]	2,300	3,700[17]	
Sweden . . .	..	..	..	..	..	..	100	500[18]		
United States . .	n.	n.	n.	n.[19]	n.[20]	500[21]	2,500[22]	14,700[23]	15,300	63,600
Canada . . .	..	..	..	n.	n.	100	200	1,300	2,000	5,900

n. = negligible.

Notes:

General: Figures for the period 1855–1930 used in this table are generally based on Staley. Widely diverging estimates are given in the notes.

[1] Figures for 1914.

[2] Figure for 1843.

[3] $1,000 million (Royal Institute of International Affairs); $2,900 million (Syed, quoted by Staley).

[4] $3,700 million (Cairncross).

[5] $6,200 million (R.I.I.A.).

[6] $7,600 million for 1895, and $9,600 million for 1905 (R.I.I.A.).

[7] $20,000 million (as estimated in Table IV/3).

[8] $500 million (Cameron).

[9] $9,000 million (as estimated in Table IV/3).

[10] $2,500 million (Dunning).

[11] $1,200 million (Feis for 1883).

[12] $2,400 million to $3,100 million for 1893; $3,600 million to $4,300 million for 1905 (Feis).

[13] $5,800 million (as estimated in Table IV/3).

[14] Figures for the Netherlands (excluding the figure for 1930, which is Staley's) were provided by the Nederlandsche Economische Hoogeschool, Centrum voor Onderzoekingswerk, or taken from the Netherlands' C.B.S. source.

[15] $600 million (Luzac/Alting Boesken).

[16] Staley's estimate is $2,000 million.

[17] Figure for 1948.

[18] $400 million (Lindahl).

[19] $100 million (U.S. Department of Commerce).
[20] Estimated at $400 million.
[21] $700 million (U.S. Department of Commerce).
[22] $3,500 million (as estimated in Table IV/3).
[23] $15,200 million (U.S. Department of Commerce).

Sources:

Alting Boesken, J. A., *Over Geldleeningen Hier te Lande Door Vreemde Mogendheden Aangegaan* (Amsterdam, 1864).

Bank of Canada, *Statistical Summary* (various).

Cairncross, A. K., *Home and Foreign Investment 1870–1913* (Cambridge, 1953).

Cameron, R. E., *France and the Economic Development of Europe 1800–1914* (Princeton, 1961).

Conan, A. R., *The Rationale of the Sterling Area* (London, 1961).

Dunning, J. H., 'Capital Movements in the Twentieth Century', in *Lloyd's Bank Review* (April 1964), No. 72, pp. 17–42.

Dominion Bureau of Statistics, *The Canadian Balance of International Payments, 1960* (1962).

Feis, H., *Europe the World's Banker 1870–1914* (New Haven, 1930).

Fisk, H. E., *Inter-Ally Debts* (New York, 1924).

Fleetwood, E. E., *Sweden's Capital Imports and Exports* (Stockholm, 1947).

Hobson, C. K., *The Export of Capital* (London, 1914).

Jenks, L. H., *The Migration of British Capital to 1875* (London, 1927).

Lewis, C., *America's Stake in International Investments* (Washington, 1938).

Lindahl, E., Dahlgren, E., and Kock, K., *The National Income of Sweden, 1861–1930*, parts 1 and 2 (Stockholm, 1937).

Luzac, E., *Hollands Rijkdom*, vol. iv (1780–3), (Leyden, 1801).

Mackay, R. A., and Rogers, E. B., *Canada Looks Abroad* (London, 1938).

Royal Institute of International Affairs, *The Problem of International Investment* (Oxford, 1937).

Staley, E., *War and the Private Investor* (New York, 1935).

The Economist, 15 February and 15 March 1913, London.

United States, Department of Commerce, *Historical Statistics of the United States 1789–1945* (1949).

Statistical Abstract of the United States 1962.

West Germany, Bundesminister für Wirtschaft, *Tages-Nachrichten*, no. 4416 (March 1963).

Table IV/2

Geographical Distribution of Foreign Investments of the United Kingdom, France, Germany, and the United States at the Beginning of the Twentieth Century (in millions of U.S. dollars to the nearest $50 million)

To	From	*U.K.*[1]	*France*[2]	*Germany*[3]	*U.S.A.*[4]
Europe	*Total*	1,250	4,100	..	50
		(10·4%)	(70·6%)	..	(10·0%)
North America					
U.S.A.		1,550	100	..	..
Canada		700	50	..	150
	Total	2,250	150	..	150
		(18·8%)	(2·6%)	..	(30·0%)
Latin America					
Mexico		150	50	..	200
Cuba		n.	n.[5]	..	50
Argentina		550	200	..	50[6] (Argentina, Brazil, Chile, Peru)
Brazil		200	150	..	
Chile		150	50	..	
Peru		100	n.[5]	..	
Uruguay		100	50	..	
	Total	1,250	650	..	300
		(10·4%)	(11·2%)	..	(60·0%)
Oceania					
Australia		1,550	n.	..	..
New Zealand		50	..	..	..
	Total	1,600	n.	..	..
		(13·3%)			
Asia					
Turkey		n.a.[7]	50	..	..
India		1,450[8]	..	..	..
China		150	150[9]	..	n.
Japan		100	..	..	..
	Total	1,700	200	..	n.
		(14·2%)	(3·4%)	..	..
Africa					
British Africa		1,650	..	..	..
Egypt		250	300	..	..
Tunisia		..	100	..	..
South Africa		..	300[10]	..	..
	Total	1,900	700	..	..
		(15·8%)	(12·1%)	..	..
Rest of World and other investments[11]		2,050	..	..	..
		(17·1%)			
World Total		12,000	5,800	4,800[3]	500
		(100%)	(100%)	(100%)	(100%)

n.a. = not available.
n. = negligible.

Notes:

General: The following exchange rates have been used in this table:

Sterling £1 = $4·87
French Franc 1 = $0·19
German Mark 1 = $0·24

[1] Figures for 1896.

[2] Figures for 1902.

[3] Statistical data on the distribution of Germany's foreign investments at this time are incomplete.

Most of them were in Europe itself. Investments of importance outside Europe were in:

North America (chiefly in U.S. and Canadian railways);

Latin America (mainly in Argentina but to a lesser extent also in Brazil, Chile, Venezuela, and Mexico);

Asia (mostly in Turkey and the remainder mainly in China);

Africa (Johannesburg received about $120 million in 1896).

[4] Estimate for 1900.

[5] Nearly $50 million was invested in Cuba and Peru, each country receiving about half the amount.

[6] Total amount invested in the remainder of Latin America.

[7] Individual country data not available. (Figure, if any, included in 'Rest of World'.)

[8] Including Ceylon.

[9] Figures include some $30 million invested in the rest of Asia, mainly in the French colonies and the Philippines.

[10] Transvaal.

[11] About 80 per cent of the sum represents an allowance for shipping, banking, insurance, etc., companies; private investments of British subjects in land and buildings, etc.; and sums employed by finance and mercantile houses in financing foreign trade, etc.

Sources:

Aitken, H. G. J., *et al.*, *The American Economic Impact on Canada* (Duke, N.C., 1959).

Brecher, I., and Reisman, S. S., *Canada — United States Economic Relations* (Ottawa, 1957).

Clapham, J. H., *The Economic Development of France and Germany 1815–1914* (Cambridge, England, 1961).

Crammond, E., in *Quarterly Review of Economics No. 428* (July 1911).

Dunn, R. W., *American Foreign Investments* (New York, 1926).

Feis, H., *Europe the World's Banker 1870–1914* (New Haven, 1930).

Henderson, W. O., *Studies in German Colonial History* (London, 1962).

Lewis, C., *America's Stake in International Investment* (Washington, 1938).

Mackenzie, J. A. P., 'Investments of French Capital Abroad' in *Journal of the Royal Statistical Society*, vol. lxvi (Dec. 1903), pp. 729–31.

Moulton, H. G., and McGuire, C. E., *Germany's Capacity to Pay* (New York, 1923).

Royal Institute of International Affairs, *The Problem of International Investment* (Oxford, 1937).

Staley, E., *War and the Private Investor* (New York, 1935).

Wilson, R., *Capital Imports and the Terms of Trade* (Melbourne, 1931).

Table IV/3

Geographical Distribution of Foreign Investments of the United Kingdom, France, Germany, and the United States on the Outbreak of the First World War (in millions of U.S. dollars to the nearest $50 million)

To / *From*	*U.K.*	*France*	*Germany*	*U.S.A.*[1]	*World*
Europe . . . *Total*	1,050	4,700	2,550	700[2]	12,000
	(8·75%)	(39·2%)	(21·25%)	(5·8%)	(100%)
North America					
U.S.A.	4,250[3]	400[3]	950[3]	..	7,100[3]
Canada	2,800	(100)[4]	200[4]	900	3,850
Total	7,050[5]	500	1,150	900	11,100
	(63·5%)	(4·5%)	(10·4%)	(8·1%)	(100%)
Latin America					
Mexico	500	400	n.a.	850	2,200[6]
Cuba	150	..	..	350[7]	(500)
Argentina	1,550	400	(200)	}	2,950[6]
Brazil	700	700	(500)	}	2,200[6]
Chile	300	50	n.a.	} 450[8]	}
Peru	150	..	(100)	}	} 1,000[6]
Uruguay	200	50	n.	}	}
Rest	100	n.	n.	..	100
Total	3,700	1,600	900	1,650	8,900
	(41·8%)	(18·1%)	(10·2%)	(18·5%)	(100%)
Oceania					
Australia	1,700	(100)	..	..	1,800
New Zealand	300	..	..	..	300
Rest	(200)	..	..	..	(200)
Total	2,200	(100)	..	..	2,300
	(95·7%)	(4·3%)	..	..	(100%)
Asia					
Turkey	100	650[9]	450[9]	..	1,200
India and Ceylon	1,850	..	..	..	1,850
Indo-China	..	(200)	..	..	(200)
Straits Settlements	150	n.	n.	n.	200
Dutch East Indies	200[10]	n.	n.	n.	750
China	600	150	250	50	1,600[11]
Japan	500	(200)	n.	50	1,000[12]
Rest	(150)	n.	n.	150[13]	300
Total	3,550	1,250	700	250	7,100
	(50·0%)	(17·6%)	(9·9%)	(3·5%)	(100%)
Africa					
Egypt	(200)	(500)	..	..	(700)
British West Africa	200	..	..	..	200
South Africa	1,550	(100)	..	..	1,650
Rhodesia	250	..	..	..	250
British East and Central Africa .	150	..	..	..	150
Anglo-Egyptian Sudan . .					
Rest of British Africa . . .					
French North Africa	..	(200)	..	..	(200)
French Africa (South of Sahara) .	..	100	..	..	100
German Colonies	..	..	400	..	400
Belgian Congo	..	..	(100)	..	300
Rest	100[14]	..	..	..	100
Total	2,450	900	500	..	4,050
	(60·5%)	(22·2%)	(12·3%)	..	(100%)
World					
Grand Total	20,000	9,050	5,800	3,500	45,450[15]
	(44·0%)	(19·9%)	(12·8%)	(7·8%)	(100%)

n.a.=not available. n.=negligible.

Notes:

[1] In 1914 the U.S.A. was a net debtor country with $3,500 million in foreign assets and $6,800 million in foreign liabilities.

[2] The balance of U.S.A.'s foreign assets after deduction of its investments in the rest of the world.

[3] Lewis's par-value estimates, which diverge from the market-value estimates by approximately 10 per cent. Included in the world total are the following investments:

$650 million from the Netherlands,
$250 million from Canada,
$150 million from Austro-Hungary, Turkey, and Bulgaria.

[4] Woytinsky's rough estimates, which are probably high.

[5] Feis's total of $6,200 million is made up of:

$3,700 million for the United States, and
$2,500 million for Canada.

[6] Based on U.N. calculations. These figures include investments of other countries.

[7] Including other West Indies.

[8] Including other Latin American countries.

[9] Including Turkey in Europe.

[10] Rough estimates, based on the assumption that 70 per cent of total foreign investment came from the Netherlands and the remainder from the U.K.

[11] Including $250 million from Russia and $200 million from Japan.

[12] Principally European.

[13] Largely invested in the Philippines.

[14] Grants-in-aid to the British territories in Africa.

[15] The figure of $44,000 million given by the U.N. includes investments made by:

U.K.	$18,000 million	Belgium, Netherlands, Switzerland	$5,500 million
France	$ 9,000 million		
Germany	$ 5,800 million		
United States	$ 3,500 million	Other countries (Japan, Russia, Portugal, and Sweden)	$2,200 million

Sources:

Aitken, H. G. J., *et al.*, *The American Economic Impact on Canada* (Duke, N.C., 1959).

Allen, G. C., and Donnithorne, A. G., *Western Enterprise in Far-Eastern Economic Development, China and Japan* (London, 1954).

Western Enterprise in Indonesia and Malaya (London, 1957).

Feis, H., *Europe the World's Banker 1870–1914* (New Haven, 1930).

Frankel, S. H., *Capital Investment in Africa* (London, 1938).

Hanson, S. G., *Economic Development in Latin America* (Washington, 1951).

Lewis, C., *America's Stake in International Investment* (Washington, 1938).

Moulton, H. G., *Japan, an Economic and Financial Appraisal* (Washington, 1932).

Moulton, H. G., and Lewis, C., *The French Debt Problem* (London, 1925).

Organization for European Economic Co-operation, *Report on International Investment* (Paris, 1950).

Remer, C. F., *Foreign Investment in China* (New York, 1933).

Rippy, J. F., *British Investments in Latin America, 1822–1949* (Minn., 1959).

Royal Institute of International Affairs, *The Problem of International Investment* (Oxford, 1937).

Staley, E., *War and the Private Investor* (New York, 1935).

United Nations, Department of Economic and Social Affairs, *International Capital Movements during the Inter-War Period* (New York, 1949).

Foreign Capital in Latin America (1955).

Wilson, R., *Capital Imports and the Terms of Trade* (Melbourne, 1931).

Wood, G., *Borrowing and Business in Australia* (London, 1930).

Woytinsky, W. S. and E. S., *World Commerce and Governments* (New York, 1955).

Table IV/4

Geographical Distribution of Foreign Investment of Selected Leading Capital-exporting Countries on the Eve of the Second World War (1938)

(in millions of U.S. dollars to the nearest $50 million)

To \ From	U.K.	France	Germany[1]	Netherlands	Belgium and Luxemburg	Switzerland	Sweden	U.S.A.	Others	World
Europe										
Total	1,750	1,050	250	1,650	300	800	350	2,550	1,600[2]	10,300
	(17·0%)	(10·2%)	(2·4%)	(16·0%)	(2·9%)	(7·8%)	(3·4%)	(24·8%)	(15·5%)	(100%)
North America										
U.S.A.	2,750	400	100	950	150	750	50	..	1,800[3]	7,000
Canada	2,700	50	..	..	..	..	..	3,800	100[4]	6,650
Total	5,450	450	100	950	150	750	50	3,800	1,900	13,650
	(39·9%)	(3·3%)	(0·7%)	(7·0%)	(1·1%)	(5·5%)	(0·4%)	(27·8%)	(13·9%)	(100%)
Latin America										
Mexico	900	100	n.	50	..	n.	..	650	100[5]	1,800
Cuba	150	n.a.	n.	n.	..	n.	..	650	..	800
Argentina	1,950	150	n.	n.	350	50	..	600	100[6]	3,200
Brazil	800	50	50	n.	..	n.a.	..	550	500[7]	2,000
Chile	400	n.	n.	n.	n.	n.	n.	600	200[8]	1,300
Colombia	50	n.	n.	n.	n.	n.	n.	250	..	300
Peru	100	n.	n.	..	..	..	n.	150	50[9]	350
Uruguay	150	n.	n.	..	..	..	..	50	..	250
Rest	400[10]	50	50	150[11]	..	..	..	650[12]	n.	1,300
Total	4,900	400	150	200	350	50	n.	4,150	1,000	11,300
	(43·4%)	(3·5%)	(1·3%)	(1·8%)	(3·1%)	(0·4%)		(36·7%)	(8·8%)	(100%)
Asia and Oceania										
Australia	2,650	n.a.	n.a.	n.a.	n.a.	n.a.	n.a.	200	900[13]	3,750
New Zealand	700	n.a.	n.a.	n.a.	n.a.	n.a.	n.a.	n.	n.	700
Turkey	200	300	n.a.	n.a.	n.a.	n.	n.	n.	100[14]	600
Iran	100	..	..	50	..	..	..	50	..	200
India[15]	3,050	..	..	..	..	..	..	50	n.	3,100
Siam	100	..	..	..	..	..	..	n.a.	100[16]	200
Indo-China (including New Caledonia)	..	400	..	..	..	..	..	n.	100[17]	500
Malaya	400	n.	..	n.	..	..	..	n.	250[18]	700
Netherlands East Indies	200	50	n.	1,900	..	..	..	50	150[19]	2,400
Philippines	50	..	..	..	..	..	..	150	150[19]	300
China	850	100	150	50	100	..	n.	250	1,100[20]	2,550
Japan	250	n.	..	n.a.	..	..	..	150	100[21]	550
Rest	50	50	..	n.	..	..	..	50	n.	150
Total	8,600	900	150	2,000	100	n.	n.	1,000	2,900	15,650
	(55·0%)	(5·8%)	(1·0%)	(12·8%)	(0·6%)			(6·4%)	(18·5%)	(100%)
Africa										
Egypt	200	300	..	n.	..	n.a.	..	n.	n.a.	500
Algeria and Tunisia	..	200	..	..	..	..	..	n.	..	200
Morocco	..	250	..	n.	..	..	..	n.a.	..	300
French West and Equatorial Africa		150								

Belgian Congo . . .	50	..	..	..	350	..	..	n.	..	[illegible]
British East Africa[25] . . .	150	..	..	..	..	..	..	..	..	150
British West Africa[26] . . .	200	..	..	..	..	..	..	..	..	200
South Africa and Rhodesia[27] .	1,250	50	..	..	..	..	..	50	..	1,400
Rest of British Africa . .	150	..	..	..	..	..	..	n.[28]	..	150
Portuguese Africa . . .	100[29]	..	..	..	..	..	..	..	100[30]	200
Spanish Africa[31] . . .										
Rest[32]	..	..	..	..	..	..	..	50	..	50
Total	2,150 (53·1%)	1,050 (25·9%)	.. ..	n. ..	350 (8·6%)	n.a.	..	150 (3·72%)	300 (7·4%)	4,050 (100%)
World *Grand Total*	22,900[33] (41·7%)	3,850[34] (7·0%)	700 (1·3%)	4,800 (8·7%)	1,250 (2·3%)	1,600 (2·9%)	400 (0·7%)	11,650[35] (21·2%)	7,700 (14·0%)	54,950[35] (100%)

n.a. = not available.

n. = negligible.

Notes:

[1] In 1938 Germany's obligations abroad exceeded its foreign investments by more than $2,000 million.

[2] Including $350 million from European countries not listed; $350 million from Asia and Oceania and $100 million from Africa. The remainder from countries not identified.

[3] Including $1,200 million from Canada,
$50 million from China,
$50 million from Japan,
and $100 million from countries not identified.

[4] Unspecified.

[5] 30 per cent from Canada and the remainder from countries not identified.

[6] Mainly from Spain and Italy.

[7] $300 million from Portugal and $200 million in sterling securities held outside the U.K.

[8] Chiefly sterling securities held outside the U.K.

[9] Half in sterling securities held outside the U.K.; the remainder from Italy and China.

[10] Including $200 million in British West Indies,
$50 million in Venezuela,
$50 million in Bolivia.

[11] $50 million in Venezuela and the rest in the Netherlands West Indies.

[12] Including $250 million in Venezuela and $50 million in each of the following countries: Guatemala, Dominican Republic, Netherlands West Indies, Panama, Honduras and British Honduras and Costa Rica.

[13] From countries not identified.

[14] Mostly from countries not identified.

[15] Including Ceylon and Burma.

[16] From China.

[17] Includes $80 million of Chinese investments.

[18] $200 million from China.

[19] Mainly from China; lesser amounts from Japan.

[20] Almost all from Japan; only $50 million from the U.S.S.R.

[21] From countries not identified.

[22] Including Cameroon, Madagascar, Somaliland, Reunion, and Togo.

[23] 70 per cent in Madagascar and Somaliland; the remainder mainly in Cameroon.

[24] From Italy.

[25] Including Anglo-Egyptian Sudan, Somaliland, Kenya, Uganda, Tanganyika, Zanzibar, and Nyasaland.

[26] Including Nigeria, Gold Coast, Sierra Leone, and Gambia.

[27] Including Basutoland, Swaziland, South West Africa, and Bechuanaland.

[28] In British West, East, and the rest of British Africa.

[29] 80 per cent in Angola and the rest in Mozambique.

[30] Portuguese investments: 55 per cent in Angola, 35 per cent in Mozambique and the remainder in Cape Verde and Guinea.

[31] No record available.

[32] Including Liberia.

[33] Bank of England's estimates covering the nominal capital value of U.K.'s overseas investments through the medium of securities quoted on, unofficially dealt in, or otherwise known to the London Stock Exchange, give the total of $17,750 million. Widely diverging estimates concerned the following areas:

Debtor area:	*Lewis:*	*Bank of England:*
Europe	$1,750 million	$1,200 million
U.S.A.	$2,750 million	$1,350 million
Canada	$2,700 million	$2,100 million
Mexico	$900 million	$300 million
India, including Burma and Ceylon	$3,050 million	$2,200 million
China	$850 million	$200 million

[34] Gold francs converted at 4c. (U.S.), the average value for the franc in 1937.

[35] A higher figure than that given by Lewis. The divergence arises from the different estimates given by debtor and creditor nations.

Sources:

Bank of England, *United Kingdom Overseas Investments 1938 to 1948* (1950).

Lewis, C., *The United States and Foreign Investment Problems* (Washington, 1948).
Debtor and Creditor Countries: 1938, 1944 (Washington, 1945).

Woytinsky, W. S. and E. S., *World Commerce and Governments* (New York, 1955).

Table IV/5

Geographical Distribution of Foreign Investments of the United Kingdom, Western Germany, and the United States in the late 1950's and early 1960's
(in millions of U.S. dollars to the nearest $10 million)

To	From	U.K. (end 1957)	W. Germany (1962)	U.S.A. (1960)[1]
Europe	*Total*	460	490	6,680
North America				
U.S.A.		480	90	..
Canada		570	160	11,200
	Total	1,040	250	11,200
Latin America				
Mexico		60	10	800
Cuba			n.	960
Argentina		100	60	470
Brazil		80	190	950
Chile		70	10	740
Peru		20	10	450
Venezuela			10	2,570
Rest		150[2]	60[3]	1,460[4]
	Total	480	340	8,390
Oceania				
Australia		920	30	860
New Zealand		260	n.	50
Rest			n.	80
	Total	1,180	30	990
Asia				
South-West Asia			10	1,140
India		310[5]	20[6]	160
Malaya[7]		190	n.	
Indonesia		40	n.	180
China (Taiwan)		100	n.	
Japan		60	10	250
Rest			n.	560[8]
	Total	710	50	2,290
Africa				
North Africa				200
Egypt		30	n.	
Sudan		10	n.	
Algeria			10	
Morocco			n.	
West Africa		130		290
East Africa		190[9]		50
South Africa				
Rhodesia and Nyasaland		380	n.	80
Union of South Africa		410	20	300
Rest			50[10]	10
	Total	1,150	80	930
World				
Rest of world		870[11]	..	2,300[12]
	Grand Total	5,890[13]	1,240[13]	32,780[14]

n. = negligible.

Notes:

[1] Revised figures for 1960.

[2] About half the amount invested in the British West Indies.

[3] Including: $20 million in the Netherlands' Antilles;
$20 million in Colombia;
$10 million in Nicaragua.

[4] Including: $880 million in the rest of Central America and the West Indies, and $430 million in Colombia.

[5] Including Pakistan, Ceylon, and Burma.

[6] Including Pakistan and Ceylon.

[7] Including Singapore.

[8] Mainly in the Philippines.

[9] British East Africa.

[10] Including $20 million in Liberia and $10 million in Guinea Republic.

[11] Including $760 million 'not classifiable'.

[12] Including $1,420 million 'International' investments, i.e. investments in shipping enterprises and in Western Hemisphere dependencies.

[13] Total of all foreign investments.

[14] Total of foreign direct investments only.

Sources:

Bank of England, *United Kingdom Overseas Investments 1957*.

United States, Department of Commerce, *Survey of Current Business* (August 1962).

Western Germany, Bundesminister für Wirtschaft, *Tages-Nachrichten*, no. 4416 (25 March 1963).

Table IV/6

Geographical Distribution of Foreign Assistance from Selected Countries to Latin America, Asia, and Africa, 1945–59
(in millions of U.S. dollars to the nearest $50 million)

To / From	U.S.A.	U.K.	France	West Germany, Netherlands, Belgium[1]	International Agencies[2]	Western World[3]
Latin America						
Mexico	450	..	..	..	200	650
Cuba	50	..	..	..	..	50
Argentina	550	50	n.[4]	50[5]	..	600
Brazil	1,200	..	..	..	300	1,500
Chile	300	..	..	..	100	400
Colombia	200	..	..	..	150	300
Peru	250	..	..	..	50	300
Uruguay	n.	..	..	..	50	50
Rest (including global aid)	500[6]	250[7]	250[8]	50[9]	150	1,150
Total	3,500	300	250	50	1,000	5,000
Asia (Including Oceania)						
Turkey	950	..	..	..	50	1,000
Iran	500	..	..	..	150	550
Israel	600	..	..	..	..	600
India	1,350	100	..	50[10]	550	2,100[11]
Pakistan	800	50	..	..	150	1,000[12]
Ceylon and Burma	150	n.	..	..	50	200
Thailand	250	..	..	..	100	350
Indo-China	850	..	..	..	..	850
Cambodia	200	..	n.a.	..	..	200
Laos	200	..	n.a.	..	..	200
Vietnam	1,200	..	n.a.	..	..	1,200
Malaya[13]	n.	150	..	..	50	200
Indonesia	300	..	..	..	..	500[14]
Philippines	450	n.	..	..	n.	450
China (Formosa)	1,100	..	..	..	..	1,100
North Korea	1,750	..	..	..	..	1,750
Japan	900	..	..	..	250	1,150
Rest (including global aid)	500[15]	400[16]	n.a.	50[17]	50[18]	1,100
Total	11,850	700	n.a.	100	1,450	14,400
Africa						
Algeria	n.	..	1,600[19]	..	n.	1,600
Morocco and Tunisia	200	..	700[20]	..	..	900

Union of South Africa	100	n.	..	..	200	300
Madagascar	..	..	250[23]	..	n.	250
Rhodesia, Nyasaland	50	50	..	..	150	250
Congo (and Ruanda-Urundi)	..	..	..	100[25]	100	200
Somalia	n.	50[26]	n.[23]	..	n.	150[27]
Kenya	n.	150	..	..	n.	150
Tanganyika and Uganda	..	50	..	..	n.	100
Ethiopia	50	..	..	..	n.	100
Sudan	50	..	..	..	50	50
Rest (including global aid)	50[28]	250[29]	200[30]	..	n.	500
Total	750	750	4,250	100	600	6,700
All Continents						
Grand Total	16,100	1,750	4,500	300[31]	2,900	26,100

n.a. = not available. n. = negligible.

Notes:

General: The figures given represent grants and medium- and long-term loans assigned as financial aid. Medium- and long-term loans are defined as those for which there is a schedule of repayments extending beyond the period of one year from the date on which the loan becomes effective. (The U.N. figures used do not include medium-term loans.)

1 Data from the German Federal Republic and from the Netherlands only for the period 1956/7 to 1959.

2 Comprising I.B.R.D., I.F.C., and the Overseas Countries and Territories Development Fund of the E.E.C.

3 Excluding the Soviet-Communist Bloc.

4 Slightly over $5 million in 1958/9.

5 From the German Federal Republic.

6 Including $160 million to Bolivia, $60 million to Guatemala, $60 million to Haiti, $50 million to Ecuador, $30 million to Panama, Costa Rica, and Paraguay (each).

7 Including $140 million to the West Indies Federation, $50 million to British Guiana and $20 million to British Honduras.

8 To French Guiana, Martinique, and Guadeloupe.

9 From the Netherlands, chiefly to its Latin American territories.

10 From the German Federal Republic.

11 Including about $90 million from Canada and $30 million from Australia and New Zealand.

12 Including about $70 million from Canada and $30 million from Australia and New Zealand.

13 Including Singapore.

14 $180 million from Japan.

15 Including $160 million to Jordan, $130 million to Afghanistan, $60 million to Lebanon, $50 million to Saudi Arabia.

16 Including $100 million to Palestine, $60 million to British North Borneo, $60 million to Cyprus, $50 million to Aden, $20 million to Hong Kong.

17 From the Netherlands to Netherlands New Guinea.

18 To British North Borneo and Nepal.

19 Including a French grant of $350 million to Algeria and the Sahara in 1959.

20 Including $30 million granted in 1959.

21 Including a $30 million loan from Italy.

22 About $20 million.

23 Excluding a possible share of $320 million to 'Overseas Departments' and 'States of the Community and Overseas Territories' granted in 1959.

24 U.S. aid to Liberia.

25 From Belgium, chiefly to Ruanda-Urundi.

26 To British Somaliland.

27 Including $100 million from Italy to Italian Somaliland.

28 About half to Portuguese Africa.

29 A little more than half the amount was for global aid, while the remainder was divided chiefly between the Mauritius Islands, Sierra Leone, Ghana, Swaziland, and Bechuanaland.

30 Including $100 million to Togo.

31 Includes about $50 million German and Dutch aid, for which no distribution data are available.

Sources:

International Bank for Reconstruction and Development, *Annual Report* (various), Washington.

International Finance Corporation, *Annual Report* (various), Washington.

L'Economie (Paris), no. 10 (1959).

Organization for European Economic Co-operation, *The Flow of Financial Resources to Countries in course of Economic Development 1956–1959* (Paris, 1961).

United Kingdom Information Services, Australia, *Britain's Contribution to Economic Development Overseas* (1960).

United Nations, Department of Economic and Social Affairs, *Statistical Yearbook* (various).

United States, Department of Commerce, *Foreign Grants and Credits by the United States Government, Quarterly Report* (various).

Zaneletti, R., *Public Financial Aid to Developing Countries*, published by the General Confederation of Italian Industries, Research Department (Rome, 1961).

TABLE IV/7

International Economic Aid to Underdeveloped Countries from Selected Contributing Countries and International Agencies
(Fiscal years 1954 through 1959)
(in millions of U.S. dollars to the nearest $10 million)

Contributing country or agency		*Amount*
U.S.A.		7,440
Canada		180
U.K.		900
France		4,250
Western Germany		80
Netherlands		100
Belgium		70
Switzerland		n.[1]
Sweden		n.[2]
Japan		180
Other Countries		360
	Total	13,570
UNTA[3], UNICEF, UNKRA, UNRWA, IBRD, IFC, OAS	*Total*	1,550
	GRAND TOTAL	15,120

n. = negligible.

Sources: United Nations, *Statistical Yearbooks* (various).

Notes:

General:

Bulgaria, China (mainland), Czechoslovakia, Eastern Germany, Hungary, Poland, Rumania, and the U.S.S.R. are not included, since official information on economic assistance extended by these countries to underdeveloped countries has not been obtained by the U.N. in comparable form.

[1] Less than $1 million.

[2] Less than $5 million, but exceeding $1 million.

[3] UNTA: United Nations Technical Assistance (Regular) Programme.
UNICEF: United Nations Children's Fund.
UNKRA: United Nations Korean Reconstruction Agency.
UNRWA: United Nations Relief and Works Agency, for Palestine Refugees in the Near East.
IBRD: International Bank for Reconstruction and Development.
IFC: International Finance Corporation.
OAS: Organization of American States.

TABLE IV/8

Major Foreign Assistance from the Communist Bloc by Country,[1] 1954–60

(in millions of U.S. dollars to the nearest $10 million)

To / From	U.S.S.R.	China	Others	Total
Europe				
Poland	180	..	..	180
Rumania	70	..	..	70
German Democratic Republic	30	..	..	30
Bulgaria	30	..	..	30
Hungary, Czechoslovakia, Albania[2]	n.a.	..	..	n.a.
Total[3]	310	..	..	310
Latin America				
Argentina	100	..	20	120
Brazil	..	..	n.	n.
Cuba	100	60	90	250[4]
Total	200	60	110	370
Asia				
Syria	n.a.	n.a.	n.a.	320
Iraq	n.a.	n.a.	50	250
Yemen	30	20	..	50
China	2,100[5]	..	..	2,100
Mongolia	180	..	..	180
North Korea	..	320	..	320
Nepal	20	10	..	30
Afghanistan	180	..	n.[6]	180
India	800	50	..	850
Ceylon	50	..	20	70
Burma	40	..	..	40
North Vietnam	..	320	..	320
Cambodia	30	10	..	40
Indonesia	350	60	50	460
Total	3,780	790	120	5,210
Africa				
U.A.R. (Egypt)	500	n.a.	n.a.	620[7]
Sudan	n.a.	n.a.	n.a.	n.[6]
Tunisia	n.a.	n.a.	n.a.	10
Ethiopia	100	..	10	110
Guinea	..	20	..	20
French West Africa	40	..	n.	40
Total	640	20	10	800
World				
Total	4,930	870	240	6,690

n.a. = not available.
n. = negligible.

Notes:

[1] Figures used in this table are possibly too high or in some cases even exaggerated.
[2] Recipient countries listed by Bystrov. Amounts not given.
[3] Excluding Hungary, Czechoslovakia, and Albania.
[4] According to a statement by the Foreign Trade Minister of Cuba, Alberto Mora, quoted by Bystrov.
[5] Quoted by the Chinese Minister of Finance in July 1957.
[6] $5 million.
[7] Figure given by Benham.

Sources:

Benham, F., *Economic Aid to Underdeveloped Countries* (New York, 1961).
Berliner, J. S., *Soviet Economic Aid* (New York, 1958).
Bystrov, F., 'Soviet International Credit Relations', *Problems of Economics*, vol. v, no. 4 (New York, August 1962).
Zaneletti, R., *Public Financial Aid to Developing Countries*, published by the General Confederation of Italian Industries, Research Department (Rome, 1961).

Chapter V

THE DIFFUSION OF EUROPEAN TECHNOLOGY[1]

CLOSELY linked with European migration and European investment has been the diffusion of European technology. Many techniques which are today universally employed in agriculture, industry, and commerce, are fundamentally European. While the interaction between the three economic forces of people, money, and techniques has been a constant feature of Europe's impact in the world, the spread of European technology since the eighteenth century has had a much greater and much more fundamental effect than either the movement of European peoples or the investment of European wealth. Whereas many parts of the world have proved unsuitable for large-scale European settlement and the effect of European investment has often been of a marginal nature, there are few parts of the world today that have not been affected — some of them have been transformed — by the diffusion of European technology.

The foundations of modern technology were laid long before the eighteenth century. For western Europe the Middle Ages are probably the crucial period.[2] The spinning-wheel and the clock are essential stages in the development of mechanical devices. The impact of steam was preceded by the extraordinary impact of the windmill and the geared water mill. Mechanical power was used for milling grain, sawing timber, and hammering wrought iron long before it was used for spinning and weaving, pumping mines, or driving locomotives. Whether concerned with inventive capacity, with the role of applied science in industry, with the degree of sophistication in the early crafts, with the concentration of labour in factories for the production of goods in large quantities — in all these and other matters dealing with the emergence of modern industry — there is no sudden transition in the West from darkness to light. The Industrial Revolution in western Europe in the eighteenth and nineteenth centuries sprang not from novelty in machines or power, but from new

[1] Derived from the Greek word 'techne' meaning 'art' or 'skill'. I am using the word broadly to describe changes taking place in machines and processes devised by man to meet his material needs. Where I use the word 'science' I mean 'knowledge' (from the Latin word *scientia*) related preponderantly to the natural sciences.

[2] A. Rupert Hall, 'The Changing Technical Act', *Technology and Culture*, vol. iii, no. 4 (Autumn, 1962), p. 508.

magnitudes in what was (in principle) already known.

Yet apart from progress in the utilization of metals, in military engineering, in navigation, and in printing, the general state of technical knowledge in Europe at the beginning of the eighteenth century differed little from that of the later Middle Ages. Similarly, the enormous strides made since the fifteenth century in the study of natural science, by great and original thinkers such as the Pole Nicolas Copernicus, the Italian Galileo Galilei, the German Johannes Kepler, the Englishman Isaac Newton, and the Frenchman Pierre Simon de Laplace, had affected the life of mankind only slightly. Agriculture, the most important branch of economic activity, was technically speaking the most backward. The main sources of power available in the eighteenth century were human and animal, though power was also obtained from wind and water, especially for navigation and milling. The age of inanimate energy from coal, oil, and nuclear fission, with all its potential for world destruction as well as world development, lay in the future. Manufacturing was largely carried on in the home or in small workshops using simple and traditional methods. Some branches of industrial activity such as metallurgical engineering and heavy chemicals hardly existed. Financial and commercial techniques had benefited from earlier European expansion, but their application was limited. Even the forms of transport were essentially what they had been since the discovery of the sail, the wheel, the stirrup, and modern harness.

Not only might the general level of technical knowledge be called low in the early part of the eighteenth century, but some of the techniques adopted by Europe before then had been introduced from Asia. The contribution of Asian technology is only now becoming known. It is possible that some of the major technical advances, especially in manufacturing and transport, between the fall of the Roman Empire and the seventeenth century, came from the East rather than the West.[1] In the history of science the sixteenth century is the transition period. Recent studies have shown that between the third and the fifteenth centuries Chinese and Indian science and technology were more advanced than those of Europe; the standard of Chinese agriculture, in spite of its lack of technical apparatus, compared favourably with most parts of Europe until well into the nineteenth century. We are also coming to have a better appreciation of the highly organized earlier civilizations of Africa and America. When Cortez reached the Aztec city of Tenochtitlan (Mexico City) in 1519 he was astonished at the artistic, industrial, and administrative achievements of its inhabitants. Certainly what we have learned of the contributions of Asia to the scientific and technical development of the

[1] See N. J. T. M. Needham, *Science and Civilisation in China* (Cambridge University Press, 1954–62), vols. i–iv.

world suggests that we should not call it 'undeveloped', save in the nineteenth century. It is perhaps only to be expected that the spread of nationalism during the past century and a half should have led many people to overlook the interdependence of mankind — an interdependence that grows daily with the conquest of distance — and to make exaggerated claims for their own nation's contribution to the development of science and technology.

Europe's relative retardation in the industrial arts underwent marked change from the eighteenth century onwards: Europeans became inventors and innovators on a scale previously unequalled. Whatever the cause of Europe's advance, it was especially true of the hundred years after 1770, when technical changes in Europe were marked as much by their variety as by their fundamental nature. In that century the ancient skills of the craftsmen gradually gave way to a European technology dependent upon metal, machines, inventors, and trained engineers. These changes represent a major landmark in world history. Especially significant was Europe's development of sources of inanimate energy (Table V/5). These changes did not take place in the industrial arts without a price being paid for them. Western Europe's growing emphasis upon the scale of production — evident since the fourteenth century — meant that much beauty would eventually be sacrificed to utility.

Europe's ability to play a decisive role in technological developments sprang most of all from its social and cultural conditions. For instance, the growing obsession of Europeans with precise measurement, since the late Middle Ages, cannot be restricted to matters such as time or distance: it also manifests itself in law, philosophy, and theology. Some writers have stressed the factors of religion, geography, climate, diet, race, or the methods of warfare, and the influence of economic factors such as the availability of capital, obtaining dominance in world commerce, or a stronger desire for economic gain. Earlier on we examined the role of Christianity in Europe's rise to power and greatness. Climate is another attractive explanation. It can hardly be a coincidence that the great seats of western technology and the factory system are to be found in those parts of the world which have mean annual temperatures of about 50°F., (10°C.) and have moderate extremes and frequent cold fronts.[1] The best climatic conditions for the age of the factory system are to be found in north-west Europe, east of the American Great Lakes region, the south-east corner of Australia, and parts of South America and Japan.[2] There

[1] See S. C. Gilfillan, 'The Coldward Course of Progress', *Political Science Quarterly*, vol. 35, pp. 393–410. Also by the same author, 'The Inventive Lag in Classical Mediterranean Society', *Technology and Culture*, vol. iii (1962), pp. 85–87.

[2] The Californian coast is one of the few areas in the world which lacks cold fronts and yet has a high standard of what is referred to in the world as western civilization. The

is a best climate for all civilizations, so it would be argued. What was suitable for the Sumerian civilization is not suitable for the western civilization. What is suitable for the western civilization might not — if history is a guide — be suitable for the civilization of tomorrow.

Whatever the origins of Europe's power there can be no doubt about its effect. To an extent without parallel Europeans set themselves not to enjoy but to transform the whole earth. The western interest was in a working, productive earth. More than earlier cultures, the central feature of European life came to be its practicality and materialism. Temporarily, it was far more acquisitive, progressive, dynamic, and expansive than other civilizations. It was this which enabled Europeans to become world explorers, world traders, and colonists as well as world leaders in technology.

The emphasis upon practical ends was supported further by Europe's achievements in science. In eighteenth-century Europe a new spirit of objective inquiry was born. Europe's science, like its technology, became increasingly an active, dynamic, progressive process. Interaction grew between science and technology, each evoking the other. Science was stimulated and conditioned by the growing problems surrounding the rapid development of western forms of production. Patent laws were introduced throughout the western world, to protect inventors' rights, and, it was hoped, stimulate invention. Without the extraordinary degree of scientific dogmatism shown by some nineteenth-century European scientists, progress might have been even greater than it was. The remarkable thing is that, unlike earlier civilizations, Europe experienced simultaneous progress in both science and technology. For part of the eighteenth and nineteenth centuries the French led in science, the British in technology. For a period in the late nineteenth and the early part of the twentieth centuries the Germans excelled both in theory and in practice. In some fields the pacemaker in technological development at the turn of the twentieth century was the United States. Some of us used to think we knew why Britain in particular came to be the home of the 'Industrial Revolution', but the more work done in recent periods of history the more sceptical we are becoming about past explanations. Part of the answer at least is more remote from technology and economics than we have been inclined to believe. The heart of this change was qualitative rather than quantitative. A completely satisfactory explanation must be sought along an immensely broad front of many sciences and of eighteenth- and nineteenth-century scientific, technological, and social change.

The essential distinction between European technology of the past century and the preceding one, is the extent to which progress in

concentration of factory production in the warmer, more humid Auckland, New Zealand, rather than in the more temperate Christchurch and Dunedin, is perhaps another exception to the general rule.

technology has come to depend upon progress in the sciences. Empiricism gradually gave way to exact science. Developments in industrial chemistry created many modern industries. Each discovery in natural science opened new possibilities of industrial development. The scientific discoveries of Michael Faraday, for instance, provided a tremendous stimulus to the use of electric energy. It was largely the scientific advances made by Europeans in physics, chemistry, biology, and geology, and the growing desire to put science to practical use, that enabled Europe to develop industrialization before other continents and to maintain technical leadership on a broad front. Indeed, the challenge made by other continents to European technical leadership in more recent years has often rested on European speculative thought and European scientific progress. The nineteenth-century contribution, to take one of many examples, of the English physicist J. P. Joule, who established a precise relationship between heat and work, is just as fundamental now as it was when Joule published his findings in 1847.

* * *

One result of Europe's expansion since the eighteenth century was the development of the great primary-producing areas of the world. Europe's demand for food and raw materials, its outflow of migrants and capital, and the construction of a world-wide network of transport and communications, opened up vast areas in temperate and tropical zones for primary production. An essential prerequisite was the diffusion of European technology in the primary and extractive industries. All basic foods and all economically useful animals had been introduced long before the European era began, except in Africa and Oceania. The significance of Europe's contribution was to diffuse and improve upon the knowledge it had inherited.

Yet the agricultural methods introduced to the large temperate zones of the world settled and inhabited by Europeans were not a replica of those used in Europe. Often, as in North America, there was a blending of the practices and the crops of the Old World with those of the New. For instance, there was no crop so important to the early European settlers of North America as indigenous corn (maize) — more valuable there than the wheat of the European. Moreover, European techniques of intense cultivation — using much labour and little land — were not applicable to European settlements overseas where rich, virgin land was plentiful and labour scarce. The techniques of summer fallow and dry farming, necessary for successful wheat cultivation in the American prairies, had to be developed by the Europeans who went there. In these circumstances, many of the agricultural techniques carried by Europeans to other parts of the world such as crop rotation, methods of preserving soil fertility with animal or artificial fertilizers, and scientific plant and animal breeding, were at first found to be unnecessary or impractical in the vast continental expanses of the Americas, South Africa, and Australasia. The illusion of unlimited regions of fertile soil encouraged soil mining rather than soil cultivation. It was only as agricultural yields declined, the European demand for food grew, and science came into vogue in the second half of the nineteenth century, that some of these older European techniques gained widespread acceptance.

This reluctance to adopt European practices did not apply to the use of European agricultural tools, implements, and machinery. Stimulated by a shortage of labour these were quickly adopted and improved overseas. The North Americans improved the European axe — a symbol of America's frontier — and the mattock. The European plough and the harrow were lightened and strengthened to meet America's needs. The cradle was developed from the European hand-scythe. As early as the 1830's improved threshing-machines and reapers were being constructed and used by the Americans. A similar eagerness to employ agricultural machinery, whether manufactured locally by Europeans or imported directly from Europe, marked the agricultural development of Australasia. In New Zealand reapers were in use in the 1850's and mowing-machines and self-binders in the 1870's. During the second half of the nineteenth century European agricultural machinery, particularly harvesting and mowing equipment, came to be used extensively in the farmlands of Argentina and the Union of South Africa. In most temperate areas of the world the manufacture of agricultural machinery constituted one of the earliest forms of industrialization, and became one of the first branches of industry to achieve independence and self-reliance outside Europe.

Not only did the Europeans in the New World adapt and improve European machinery, they also devised many new forms of agricultural equipment, especially labour-saving and cost-reducing implements. In 1843 Australians developed the wheat-stripper, and in the 1870's the stump-jump plough. Americans developed a satisfactory mowing-machine in the 1830's, a chilled-steel plough capable of turning the prairie sod in the 1840's, and a twine-binder (the Appleby Knotter) in the 1870's. Attached to the wheat-reaper, the knotter provided a mechanical binder. A modified threshing-machine was then combined with the reaper and binder. In the present century the thresher, reaper, binder, and tractor were built as one unit to form the completely automatic combination-harvester. During the past hundred years most of the credit for the mechanization of agriculture goes to the Europeans who settled the temperate areas outside Europe, especially to the North Americans. United States Consul Reports[1] show that by the 1860's American manufacturers

[1] U.S. Dept. of State, *Reports from the Consuls of the U.S., on Agricultural Machinery in their several districts in answer to a circular from the Department of State.* U. S. Congress, 48th Congress, 2nd Session, 1884–5, H. R. Misc. Documents, vol. 10, no. 48 (Dec. 1884). Also 49th Congress, 2nd Session, 1886–7, H. R. Misc. Documents, vol. 4, no. 66 (Aug. 1886).

had already begun to invade the European market for agricultural machinery. Before the end of the nineteenth century United States machinery manufacturers had established branch factories in Europe, Canada, and Latin America.[1]

Perhaps Europe's greatest, if less evident, contribution to world agriculture was the gradual introduction of scientific methods. Europeans penetrated into the organic processes of the vegetable and animal kingdoms in the nineteenth century. Europe's earlier contribution had been to diffuse to the Americas the crops, animals, and practices Europe already possessed. Europe had given the New World cereals such as wheat, rice, barley, rye, oats; fruits such as bananas, oranges, limes, peaches, apricots, and pears, better apples and grapes, and sugar; beverages such as tea and coffee; draft animals such as the horse, mule, and oxen (the only draft animals before European impact were the llama and alpaca of Peru and the dog of the North American Indian); and animals for food, such as fowls, hogs, sheep, goats, and cattle. The traffic was not one-way, and the European species were mostly Asian in ultimate origin. Europe's navigation and discoveries throughout the world enabled it to transfer to the other continents many American plants, including corn, cacao, certain beans, yams, manioc, potatoes, peanuts, pineapples, tomatoes, and tobacco. From Peru were transferred two plants, the source of two great drugs: quinine and cocaine. The sweet potato first carried by European monks from South America is still known in the Philippines by its Aztec name: 'Camote'. Whatever knowledge Europe diffused before the nineteenth century concerning the breeding of plants and animals, systems of cultivation, the use of fertilizers and irrigation, was largely of an empirical kind. A number of improving landlords were active in western Europe in the eighteenth century. The best known is the English group led by Charles Townshend and Jethro Tull. In the nineteenth century, however, important theoretical work was done by the French in plant physiology and microbiology. The study of soil bacteriology begun in France by J. J. Schlösing became a science with the work of the Russian S. N. Vinogradsky. German agricultural research, which grew rapidly after 1870, was particularly strong in the development of synthetic nitrogenous compounds. Research in dairying was made notably in Denmark. The Russians, whose work in the colonization of the areas east of the Urals in the nineteenth and twentieth centuries has gradually become known, helped to advance the science of soil morphology and plant breeding.

An example of the diffusion of a European agricultural technique based upon European scientific progress is the spread of knowledge concerning artificial fertilizers. These had been used on a small scale by earlier

[1] Agricultural machinery in Australasia is dealt with in the U.S. Reports for 1884–5 cited above, pp. 749–51.

American civilizations, but it was in Europe that the science of soil chemistry and the systematic use of chemical fertilizers was first developed. Landmarks were the publication in Britain of Humphry Davy's *Elements of Agricultural Chemistry* in 1813, and Justus von Liebig's *Organic Chemistry* in Germany in 1840.[1] Liebig added to the work of the gifted French agricultural scientist Jean Baptiste Boussingault. Another landmark was the foundation of the Rothamsted Experimental Station in England in 1842. By the 1840's most of the important fertilizers, such as bone-dust, guano (sea-bird droppings), nitrates, and superphosphate (made by treating bones or mineral phosphate with sulphuric acid), were being used in Europe. Within the next half-century use of these fertilizers spread gradually to other temperate areas of the world. Guano was exported from Peru to the United States, Australia, and other areas from the 1840's. Superphosphates were introduced into the United States and Canada from the 1850's, and into Australia and New Zealand from the 1880's. By the end of the nineteenth century farmers in other temperate regions of the world, including the Union of South Africa and parts of South America, had begun to realize the value of fertilizers. In these areas, as elsewhere, methods of crop rotation were used extensively in conjunction with both animal and artificial fertilizers. Much more dramatic was the widespread adoption since the First World War of the German Haber-Bosch process for the fixation of atmospheric nitrogen. This process revolutionized the supply of nitrate fertilizers and caused the collapse of the Chilean nitrate mining industry.

In stressing the scientific side of Europe's contribution to the improvement of world agriculture, we should not lose sight of the extent to which, until close to the end of the nineteenth century, so much of Europe's work was of an empirical nature; it was largely a matter of using eyes, instincts and experience. The same is true of techniques being diffused from other continents. The 'ring-barking' introduced into Australia from the United States, about the time of the gold discoveries in the 1850's, did not require profound scientific knowledge, but it helped to clear the land for livestock and people and put new heart into the pastoral industry. (To a lesser extent the same might also be said of developments in nineteenth-century industry. Developments in the textile and metal industries were not the result of the application of modern science, but the result of empirical discoveries.) When scientific laws were discovered and formulated it took a considerable time before they were generally accepted and applied. The work of the Austrian monk, Johann Gregor Mendel, for instance, whose experiments during the 1850's and the 1860's led to the discovery of the basic principles of heredity and subsequently to the science of genetics, was passed over for a generation. Independently, and almost simultaneously,

[1] *Die organ. Chemie in ihrer Anwendung auf Agrikulturchemie und Physiologie.*

three men discovered and saw the significance of Mendel's paper published thirty-four years before. When, in the early years of the present century, R. H. Biffen at Cambridge, England, used Mendel's principles to conquer yellow rust in wheat his efforts were greeted with a great deal of scepticism by his fellow-scientists. Yet it is due to the work of the pioneering geneticists that varieties of plants have been developed resistant to particular diseases.

It required much practice, over long periods of time, before Europe was able to give to the world many improved breeds of plants and animals. But from Europe came further cultivated plants, such as clover and the sugar beet. Improved breeds of British cattle and pigs, German, Spanish, and British sheep, and horses from Belgium, stocked the herds and flocks of pastoral America, Australasia, and Africa. The story of the rapid development of the sheep flocks of the world is one of the most extraordinary aspects of European impact. Knowledge of genetics was not a factor in plant and animal breeding until the beginning of the twentieth century. In recent decades, however, it has been responsible for many important contributions — North America's development of hybrid corn is one of these. A growing knowledge of genetics has also encouraged the introduction of artificial insemination in animal breeding.

Assisting the spread of European improved methods of agriculture were the research institutions and experimental farms established in many new countries on European lines towards the end of the nineteenth century. From Canada's Ontario Agricultural College, founded at Guelph in 1873, and the Dominion's Experimental Farm System, established at Ottawa in 1886, came many new varieties of wheat, oats, and barley, including in 1903 the famous Marquis wheat, the first hybrid strain of wheat with early maturing qualities. Shortly after the turn of the century Australia produced a strain of wheat with rust-resistant qualities; later improved strains have come from Argentina. In Australia, important research on arable farming was carried out at Lambrigg, New South Wales, and at the Waite Agricultural Research Institute at Adelaide. Since 1925 much help has come from the Commonwealth Scientific and Industrial Research Organization. The privately endowed Cawthron Agricultural Institute of New Zealand has made many contributions to agricultural development, especially in the cultivation of grasses and clover with high feeding value. Major contributions have also been made by the research stations of the Department of Agriculture, of which the animal research station at Rua Rura is probably the most famous. The introduction of improved agricultural methods from Europe to the United States has a long history. When, in the summer of 1862, the first United States Commissioner of Agriculture despatched a botanist and an entomologist to Europe and Asia to study foreign plants and agricultural methods, he was merely strengthening the links already forged. It was America's willingness to learn from Europe, coupled with its own scientific spirit towards agriculture, which enabled it to develop one of the most advanced agricultural systems.

Other parts of the world have benefited from developments within Europe. Major contributions also have been made by white settlers overseas. Since the introduction into Australia and New Zealand in the early decades of the nineteenth century of prize merino sheep, the Australian and New Zealand yields of wool have been increased several times. Europeans in South Africa have contributed greatly to the breeding of horses and goats. The Veterinary Research Station of Onderstepoort became one of the leading veterinary centres in the world, but it was, until recently, the only veterinary college in Africa south of the Sahara. A common feature of animal husbandry outside Europe has been the interbreeding of the local hardy stock with the less hardy but higher-yielding imported animals. In many parts of North and South America the semi-wild long-horn cattle of Spanish origin were interbred successfully with cattle imported from Britain and other parts of Europe. Parts of Brazil are dominated by Zebu and Brahmin humped cattle introduced and cross-bred by Europeans. Indian Nelore cattle have also been introduced recently into Brazil, chiefly in the southern state of Paraná. In South Africa and Uruguay there has been similar successful interbreeding of imported merinos and other fine-woolled sheep with existing native flocks.

During the past two hundred years, especially during the past few decades, European enterprise and technical assistance have also brought great changes to the tropical and sub-tropical regions of the world. Europe's interest in the tropics began in the sixteenth century when settlements and plantations were established by the Dutch, the Spaniards, and the Portuguese in the West Indies and South and Central America. In the seventeenth and eighteenth centuries similar settlements were made in these areas by the British and the French. Only during the past century, however, have considerable developments occurred in the vast tropical territories of Africa, Asia, the western Pacific Islands, and the Australian continent. The Christian missions were probably the first to introduce improved European methods and ideas to native agriculture in the tropics.

Progress in tropical agriculture has relied to a great extent upon new techniques developed either by Europeans within Europe, with the intention of applying them overseas, or by Europeans in the tropical areas themselves. Perhaps the most important single way in which European influence was felt was through the establishment in Europe, as well as overseas, of botanical gardens, laboratories, experimental stations, and departments of agriculture. These agencies experimented in plant and animal breeding, combated insect and fungoid pests, studied faunas and floras, and stimulated agricultural education. They were the pace-setters in agricultural experiment and change; they occupied in the tropics and semi-tropics the place held in Europe by enterprising individual farmers. Most important was the founding of the Royal Botanic Gardens at Kew, London, in 1759. Fourteen years earlier the French had inaugurated an experimental plantation at Pamplemousse in Mauritius which was subsequently expanded to become the Poivre Gardens. An event of almost equal importance was the establishment by the Dutch in 1817 of the gardens at Buitenzorg in Java. Throughout the nineteenth century other botanical gardens were established by Europeans in many other lands, culminating in the establishment by the British during the 1890's of botanical gardens on the west coast of Africa. The most important of these was that at Aburi on the Gold Coast, established in 1890. From these, as from agricultural schools in Europe, such as the school at Wageningen in Holland, came a stream of scientific information, many plants and seeds and often highly-trained personnel, which in time were to transform the economies of many parts of the tropics. In the Netherlands Indies (Indonesia) Dutch agricultural scientists pioneered in many branches of agriculture, especially in plant pathology and soil chemistry.

In the present century European influence upon tropical agriculture has grown enormously, especially in Africa. Since the First World War many research stations have been founded. In 1922 the Imperial College of Agriculture was opened at Trinidad. In 1927 members of the British Empire (now the British Commonwealth) undertook to finance the establishment and further maintenance of research centres throughout Britain, whose purpose it was to obtain and disseminate information on research in selected branches of agriculture. Also important in the inter-war years was the re-opening and expanding of the Agricultural Research Institute originally founded by the Germans at Amani in Tanganyika. At the Agricultural Stations at Gezira and Madani in the Anglo-Egyptian Sudan important work was done on cotton and other crops. Specialized agricultural research organizations established in the inter-war years include the Rubber Research Institute in Malaya, as well as research institutes for tea, rubber, and coconuts in Ceylon, sugar-cane in Mauritius, the West Indies, and South Africa, cotton, coffee, and sisal in East Africa, and cotton in North Africa. In the Belgian Congo and Portuguese Angola extensive provisions for agricultural research were made from the early 1930's. The Belgian government agricultural service in the Congo was instituted in 1910 'to study soil and climate and conduct experiments on crops and methods of cultivation'. In tropical Australia some of this work is just beginning.

Until recently, agricultural progress in the tropics was more limited than in the temperate zones and was centred overwhelmingly around the development of the European plantation system. Ignorance of the natural environment, disease, the scarcity of capital relative to labour, and the nature of crops grown have all impeded progress. On balance, difficulties arising from ecological conditions — particularly the lack of an adequate rainfall — have been greater in tropical Africa than in tropical Asia. Environmental factors made the introduction of European techniques in animal breeding in many parts of tropical Africa almost impossible. It has been one thing to transfer scientific principles from the West; it has been another thing to transfer the technologies developed from them.

Throughout the tropics European research institutes probably exerted their greatest influence on crop cultivation. Few of the crops upon which great tropical areas now depend were indigenous. The introduction of new crops to these areas was a task calling for much botanical knowledge, and it was due to European guidance and skilled management that many plants, among them rubber, cacao, cinchona, coffee, sugar-cane, tea, cotton, tobacco, and bananas, were transferred from one part of the world to another. This is particularly true of the introduction by Europeans of many new crops to tropical Africa. The European is also responsible for the widespread cultivation of coffee in Ceylon, tea and jute in India, rubber in the Federated Malay States and what was formerly the Dutch East Indies, sugar in Queensland, and cacao in Northern New Britain. Europeans not only transferred plants from one side of the world to the other; they also converted some wild into cultivated plants.

Whereas most of the commercial crops in tropical Asia had been introduced before the end of the nineteenth century, it was not until the turn of the twentieth century that they were introduced to tropical Africa. Coffee, tobacco, tea, and sisal began to be cultivated in East and Central Africa, cacao, rubber, and cotton in West Africa, and cotton in the Sudan. Earlier intensive experiments in cotton-growing (both native and foreign kinds) had been carried out by the Germans at their experimental station at Tove in Togoland and by the British at Aburi on the Gold Coast. (Palm-oil from West Africa, however, began to reach Britain in the last quarter of the eighteenth century.) During the past two generations many tropical plants have been transferred from one tropical area to another, including the growing of cotton in Jamaica, rice in British Guiana, and tropical fruits, rice, and sugar-cane in Northern Australia. Europeans were not only transferring plants and animals from one part of the world to another — the Spanish and Portuguese had done this in the sixteenth century — they also improved indigenous crops by introducing better varieties, such as the Otaheite sugar-cane, which the British carried to the Americas from Tahiti in the South Pacific. In addition, European practices of plant breeding assisted the cultivation of many tropical and sub-tropical plants, including cassava, sugar-cane (which was greatly improved by the British and the Dutch), and cotton. During the 1920's the Dutch began a series of experiments in Java and Sumatra with the breeding of selected strains of the rubber tree, much increasing its yield. In the transfer and improvement of varieties of plants much has been done. Yet much more remains to be done. Efforts to meet Africa's pressing need to develop a variety of sweet potato resistant to virus disease have so far failed.

Although soil chemistry in Africa has just begun, investigations have already been made on the application of manures and fertilizers for tropical crops, such as on oil palms and groundnuts in West Africa, tobacco and coffee in East Africa, and cotton in the Sudan. In certain areas of tropical Asia and America the application of manures and fertilizers has become a well-established practice. The use of nitrates and phosphates is now fairly widespread on the sugar plantations of south-east Asia and the West Indies, and various fertilizers have been applied to the rubber plantations of Malaya, to cotton fields and coffee plantations of Brazil, and banana plantations in the Caribbean.

In the control of tropical animal and plant diseases and pests the veterinary research laboratories established by Europeans in various parts of Africa, in conjunction with research centres within Europe, have played an important role. International organizations for the control of locusts were encouraged by the British in the 1930's, and are now directed by several international organizations. Advances have also been made on the biological methods of control devised by the Chinese and Arabs in earlier times: the natural enemy of the insect pest is introduced or encouraged. More significant during the past generation has been the development of chemical methods of control, such as synthetic and systemic insecticides. Many plant diseases have been brought under control through the use of chemical sprays, dusts, or soil disinfectants, and the introduction of a system of quarantine. The ravages of rinderpest and numerous fly- and tick-borne diseases have been reduced. The control of such diseases as swollen shoot in cacao, and leafcurl in cotton, has depended upon strong local government action. There has also been a growing use of selective weed-killers since their discovery by European and American research workers in the 1930's. The chemical compounds which drastically changed the concept of insect control are D.D.T. (Dichlor-diphenyl Trichlor-ethane) and benzene hexachloride.

A study of Europe's impact in the tropics might give the impression that European scientific and technical assistance was restricted to European plantations. Although directed primarily to this end, many of the more important research stations, notably the Rubber Research Institute of Malaya and the Tea Research Institute of Ceylon, have helped to improve the standards of the small peasant cultivator. Others, including the British

Empire Cotton Growing Corporation and the Coconut Research Institute in Ceylon and India, are concerned primarily with improvements of crops produced on small holdings. The University of Louvain in Belgium has devoted much attention to this particular aspect of tropical agriculture, and in 1931 organized its own research centre in the Belgian Congo with the special object of improving peasant agriculture. Similar aims explain the establishment in Nigeria in 1938 of an experimental station for research on peasant palm-oil production, and a cacao research station in Ghana to serve the peasant cacao industry of West Africa. The large exports by African peasant producers of cacao, cotton, nuts, palm-oil, and kernels, tobacco, hides, coffee, and rubber indicate that the technical information Europe has brought to the tropical areas has not been confined to European plantations. (Table V/1.)

Although minerals have attracted the attention of mankind from the earliest times it was not until the end of the eighteenth and the beginning of the nineteenth centuries that any real advance was made in the science of mineralogy. Measured by volume, almost 90 per cent of the world's mining activity has come into existence during the past century and a half. And in the nineteenth century it was lucky chance rather than systematic prospecting that enabled man to discover vast quantities of gold, diamonds, copper, lead, and zinc.

Europe's contribution to the development of the science of mineralogy (concerning the form, content and nature of minerals), metallography (concerning the structure of metals and their alloys examined microscopically) and metallurgy (concerning the extraction and preparation of metals), lay along the broad front of natural history, chemistry, physics, crystallography, geology and geography. Only in recent decades, however, has science had an important effect on world mining activity. (Tables V/2 and V/4.)

Europe's special contribution to the spread of mining technology lies in the improvement of certain mechanical and chemical processes. From the early eighteenth century the Europeans developed steam-driven machinery for draining, cutting, boring, hauling, winding, and ventilating, without which deep mining would have been impracticable. Outstanding contributions came from the mining areas of Cornwall, north-eastern England, and Scotland. British miners, particularly from Cornwall and Scotland, carried the new technology all over the world. The early experiments to harness inanimate energy for use in Europe's mines eventually resulted in the development of inanimate power (wood, water, coal, oil, gas, and atomic) on a scale sufficient to effect the greatest change in the life of mankind. While other forms of energy capture the popular imagination today, it remains true that the improvement and introduction of steam power by the western nations in the nineteenth century is one of the most significant events in modern history. (Tables V/5 and V/7.)

Early types of excavators and dredges had been designed by the French and employed in canal and railway building in Europe, as well as in the digging of the Suez Canal. With certain exceptions, however, German lignite being one, the techniques of open-cut mining have evolved in America, Africa and Australasia. From these countries the improvements spread to alluvial and surface workings all over the world. American improvements on late eighteenth-century European steam-driven excavators and elevator dredges have had a most marked influence. The principal technical advances of the Malayan tin-mining industry, for example, as of those of Indonesia and other areas of south-east Asia, came from America and Australasia. More important than the steam engine and the centrifugal pump, introduced into Malaya from Europe in the 1870's for draining the mines, was the introduction of hydraulic sluicing and gravel pumping from the United States and Australia in the late nineteenth century. Similarly, important contributions were made by the New Zealand dredge brought to Malaya shortly before the First World War, and by other improved types of dredges developed in America. It was the application of these techniques which turned relatively small-scale Chinese placer workings into a large-scale mechanized industry dominated by European, American, and Australian companies.[1]

The rapid growth of coal and copper mining in the world was based to a great extent upon large-scale mechanized techniques devised initially in Europe, and assisted by the export of European equipment, skilled engineers, miners, and capital. The same is true of the mining of many base metals, as well as precious minerals. The first areas to exploit coal deposits on any considerable scale outside Europe in the early nineteenth century were the United States, Canada, and Australia. In the United States large-scale coal mining began about 1820. A century later the United States possessed the world's greatest coal-mining industry, with an output of approximately six hundred million tons. Large-scale production and modern methods in coal mining were introduced to Canada in the 1820's with the formation of the General Mining Association in Nova Scotia, and to Australia from the 1840's with the development of deposits in the Hunter River area. Similar developments assisted by European and American techniques were under way in Asia in the 1860's and 1870's. From an output of about half a million tons in the 1860's India's production in 1913 was approximately fifteen million tons. Extensive

[1] Reference to Australian developments in mining will be found in U.S. Dept. of State, *Reports of the U.S. Commissioners to the Centennial International Exhibition at Melbourne 1888*, U.S. Congress, 51st Congress, 1st Session, 1889–90, Senate, Executive Documents, vol. 4, no. 18, Washington (Govt. Printing Office, 1890).

mechanization was introduced after the First World War, when the first coal-cutting machines were used, and electrification of mines was begun. In China, the modernization of traditional small-scale coal mines began in the 1870's with the introduction of the first mining pumps from Europe. However, it was only with the increase after 1900 of the influence of the Japanese and certain western nations that the industry became of any consequence. The Japanese industry developed rapidly from the 1870's with the assistance of British technicians and equipment. In the last quarter of the nineteenth century the Japanese government took the initiative in bringing to Japan mining engineers and geologists from England, America, France, and Germany. By 1900 Japan had acquired the necessary techniques from the West. In Manchuria, under Russian and Japanese enterprise, coal mining became an important industry from the 1890's. New Zealand produced significant quantities of coal from the 1860's, South Africa and Mexico from the 1880's and Indo-China from the 1890's. Since then many other countries, including Brazil, Chile, Turkey, and Southern Rhodesia, have begun to produce coal on a large scale by modern methods of production, often from Europe. A powerful stimulus to progress in large-scale extraction and handling of coal and other minerals, phosphate mining in particular benefiting from large-scale equipment, was given by the First and Second World Wars.

From a small-scale industry in a few areas at the beginning of the nineteenth century, the mining of copper has become a highly mechanized industry found today in many parts of the world. During the second half of the nineteenth century, stimulated by the development of electricity, world output of copper increased at least ten times. Between 1900 and 1950 this increase was approximately fivefold. Until the development of the Lake Superior mines in the 1840's the output of copper in the United States was negligible. By the First World War it had risen to about 60 per cent of the world's output. While the application of machinery and modern methods to copper mining was largely pioneered in the United States, this work was greatly assisted by European invention and workers, especially those from the Cornish mines. European mining machinery was first used in Latin America in the second and third quarters of the nineteenth century when the British, with steam-operated pumps, hoists, and crushing machines, began to develop and modernize the mining industry. Later the exploitation of copper resources, particularly in Chile and Mexico, came to be dominated by American companies with immense technical resources. During the last quarter of the nineteenth century Europeans were responsible for introducing large-scale, mechanized copper mining in Japan, in Canada (with the discovery of the Sudbury and British Columbian fields), and in Australia (with the working of the Tasmanian deposits). In the present century, especially during the past thirty years,

Europeans have developed the copper resources of Central Africa. Today Northern Rhodesia and the Congo rank as the third and fifth greatest copper producers in the world. In the Congo British and Belgian engineers and technicians have played a leading part in the transfer of technology from the West. Until 1910–11 the development of the important Katanga deposits depended upon British technicians. Responsibility then passed to Belgians led by an American engineer.

Because most minerals are found in close association with others (a few such as gold and platinum occur in the uncombined form), a number of separating and concentrating processes were developed in Europe. Especially important are the cyanide and the flotation processes. Early efforts to provide a cyanide process for the extraction of gold were made in Scotland in 1887. Dissolving the gold by a well-aerated dilute solution of potassium cyanide, this process made it economically possible to exploit ores with only a fraction of the gold content of those worked previously. In doing so it revolutionized gold production and was quickly adopted by all the gold-producing countries. Cyanide plants were established in the British Dominions, the United States, and Mexico during the 1890's. More important than the cyanide process, especially for the treatment of sulphide ores of copper, lead, and zinc, was the development toward the end of the nineteenth century of flotation techniques, which made vast deposits not only of low-content ores usable, but also complex ores containing several metals. Much of the world-wide industrial expansion of the past sixty years owes its development to the introduction of these flotation techniques which separate the metal from the ground-up gangue, as well as the separation of one metal from another. The first steps in the development of this process were taken by a group of Europeans in the 1870's. However, it required much more work before it was possible to demonstrate the technical practicability of flotation in the 1890's. The first commercially successful flotation plant resulted from the work of the Australians at the beginning of the present century. Later progress, particularly in techniques of selective flotation, came from the North Americans.

These various flotation techniques developed by Europeans at home and overseas about the turn of the century were adopted rapidly and extensively. The American continent was one of the first areas to take up the process on a wide scale. In Canada an early form of flotation reached British Columbia in the early 1900's, and by the end of the First World War various forms of it had been adopted to exploit deposits of low-grade ores and compound ores, particularly the zinc-copper, lead-silver ores of the Sudbury region. In the United States the Minerals Separation Company, formed in 1901, obtained a virtual monopoly of American patents for flotation techniques, and was largely responsible for their development and distribution. By the 1920's flotation techniques were applied to a wide variety of ores, including copper, lead, zinc, silver, molybdenum, and graphite. These techniques were especially important in the exploitation of copper deposits in Montana, Utah, and Arizona. In Australia, flotation techniques were used by the Broken Hill Proprietary Company Ltd. as early as the 1900's for the concentration of zinc ore waste. By 1904 there were no less than six million tons of zinc at Broken Hill awaiting the development of an effective separating process. A major step was taken in 1912 when it was discovered that lead sulphide could be separated from zinc sulphide by adding eucalyptus oil or another organic substance to the pulp and then aerating. These developments at Broken Hill influenced metallurgical work on base metal concentration in many parts of the world. In Mexico, the introduction by European and American companies of selective flotation in the 1920's enabled the working of important deposits of compound ores and the extraction of zinc from ore dumps accumulated over centuries at silver-lead mines. The discovery of traces of uranium has also given new value to the waste accumulated from gold mines. In Chile, the exploitation of low-grade copper ores became economical with the introduction of flotation techniques by American companies about the First World War, since when Chile's copper output has expanded more than twentyfold, making it today the second largest producer in the world. In other parts of Latin America, in eastern Asia, India, and southern and central Africa, European and American flotation techniques were introduced mostly during and since the First World War. (Table V/4.)

In contrast to the hydro-metallurgical (the wet way) flotation processes discussed above, European and American extraction processes have been introduced which treat the ores in electrolytic furnaces. Such a process enabled bauxite to become an economically suitable raw material for aluminium extraction. More recently techniques have been developed for the recovery and utilization of uranium, titanium, beryllium, zirconium, and vanadium, used in nuclear reactors, etc. The changing value of materials is illustrated by radium and uranium, which occur together. Before the Second World War radium was the prize, uranium was of little value. After the discovery of nuclear reactors the situation was reversed: uranium became the prize, the radium mattered little.

Of tremendous importance in world development has been the exploitation of petroleum during the past century. Although F. Selligue had produced shale oil in France in 1838, James Young had refined crude petroleum at the Riddings Colliery in Derbyshire in 1848, and Rumania produced its first crude petroleum in 1857, it was only with the drilling of the Drake oil well in Pennsylvania, United States in 1859, that petroleum for illumination was produced on a commercial scale. Oil was obtained in

Italy in 1860, in Canada in 1862, and in Russia in 1863. The growth of the Russian oil industry in the Baku area of the Caucasus between 1873 and the end of the nineteenth century was most rapid. At the beginning of the twentieth century Russian output of crude oil exceeded American production. Between 1860 and 1914, when the demand was chiefly for lamp and lubrication liquids, the annual world crude oil production increased from approximately half a million to four hundred million barrels. In 1902 the United States regained, and still holds, the leading place among the world's oil producers. Shortly before the First World War the demands for fuel oil for land, sea, and air transport began to make themselves felt. Oil became one of the world's greatest sources of energy. By 1962, world crude-oil production exceeded a billion tons.

Despite the overwhelming importance of the United States in the growth of this industry (in 1962 the United States still accounted for 29·7 per cent of world production), the origins of petroleum science and of many of the techniques employed today were widespread. Stimulated by the decrease of whale sperm oil in the mid-nineteenth century, increasing attention was given by western geologists to 'the source, accumulation and occurrence' of other kinds of oils, especially petroleum. Some of the most important work was done in the 1860's in the United States and Austria. Although American geologists during the 1880's put many of the earlier scientific generalizations to the test, it was another generation before they were applied. The industry was able to obtain all the oil it needed from hit or miss methods of prospecting. The only important sustained efforts to organize geological work as an aid to prospecting in the early part of the present century were probably those of the Dutch in the East Indies and the British in Mexico. Since the First World War, however, with the sharp increase in demand for fuel oil, empiricism has given place to applied science. The considerable general progress made in the western world in geophysics and geochemistry since the 1920's has considerably reduced the costs involved in preliminary investigation of oil and other mineral-bearing geological structure. Oil is now sought (in Central Africa, on the continental shelves and margins under the oceans, and in the far north of America) where previously it was considered wellnigh impossible to investigate.

Europe made important contributions to the development of scientific methods in oil mining. These include the introduction of a rapid-drilling machine in Germany in 1895; and a diamond drill as an exploratory tool in Holland in 1905–15, first used in the United States in 1910. The torsion balance devised by a Hungarian in 1890 was gradually taken up in the present century by other Europeans and Americans. It was employed by the British in one of the first surveys in Egypt in 1921–22. Also important in oil surveying was the seismograph, developed by a German in 1919. In the present century increasing use has been made of the rotary or hydraulic system of drilling, which, for certain purposes, has largely replaced percussion drilling (inherited from the much older brine-wells industry). First used in 1846 in drilling a well at Perpignan in France, it was improved between 1910–20, by providing a double-core barrel for the rotary drill, and by the introduction, in 1928, of electrical coring. Strictly speaking, this is not a method of drilling but an important geophysical method of recording. New steels and hard-cutting alloys have vastly improved the drilling bits used by the industry. (Table V/2.)

With the appearance at the end of the nineteenth century of a commercially successful internal-combustion engine, the importance of petroleum and its derivatives has increased enormously. Simple refining methods had been developed from the 1850's, principally by the Russians and the Germans, but it is only during the present century that the complex techniques of modern oil refining have been perfected. Especially important was the work on oil 'cracking' (which by heat and pressure breaks down the oil to the lighter consistencies required), done by two British chemists, Boverton Redwood and James Dewar, who obtained a patent in 1889. The Americans William M. Burton and Robert E. Humphreys, however, working for the Standard Oil Company of Indiana, United States, were the first to produce a high-temperature, high-pressure cracking still in 1913. Since then the most important technical developments have been fathered by both American and European scientists. During the 1920's six American inventors developed a thermal cracking process which was considered superior to the Burton process, in yield of motor gasoline. Also during the 1920's the Frenchman, Eugène J. Houdry, developed the first practical catalytic cracking process which improved the quality of the gasoline.

The European and American companies responsible for opening up the world's oil fields and developing drilling and refining techniques have also created the world's oil-refining industry. In the late nineteenth and early twentieth centuries a number of small refineries were set up at or near the oil fields in Mexico and Cuba by British American companies, in Burma by the British Burmah Oil Company, parent of the Anglo-Iranian Oil Company, in Indonesia by the Royal Dutch Company, and in Japan by the American Standard Oil and the British Shell Companies. Among the foreign companies Americans have dominated oil refining in Latin America. In south-west Asia the exploitation of oil resources from the 1920's led to the establishment of a number of refineries by European and American interests. In 1913 the Anglo-Iranian Oil Company constructed a refinery at Abadan in Persia, and at the same time a Shell subsidiary established the first plant in Egypt. During the inter-war years oil refineries were established in Bahrein and Saudi-Arabia by American companies, and in Iraq and Lebanon by British and joint European enterprises. Since the Second World War oil refining in Arabia has been extended by the Anglo-Iranian Oil Company to Aden, and by a joint British-American enterprise to Kuwait. In many other parts of the world refineries have been established either to process the oil of nearby oil fields, as in Persia and Arabia, or to supply the domestic market, as in Australia, where large-scale refining has been developed since the Second World War by two European and two American companies.

Until the Second World War the Caucasian region was the major source of Soviet oil, but by 1962 it supplied only 17 per cent of it. The Soviet's main increase since the 1940's has come from newly discovered oilfields in the Ural–Volga region, which now accounts for more than 70 per cent of their oil. Using the latest geological, geophysical, and drilling techniques the Soviets have now begun to tap the oil resources of Siberia and Soviet East Asia, including the Pacific island of Sakhalin, long known for oil.

* * *

The most obvious aspect of Europe's impact on the world has been the diffusion of its industrial technology. Agriculture and mining pre-date the European era, but the scale of industrialization which Europe set going is modern. World employment in manufacturing in 1960 was no more than about 10 per cent of the world's employed labour force; and this was heavily concentrated in western Europe, and in North America from the Great Lakes eastward. The acceptance of the factory by European and non-European societies alike has only been achieved by overcoming formidable cultural and social barriers. There could be no progress until *change* became an acceptable social process. The barriers to change have fallen as the industrial nations' burgeoning power and wealth have come to be identified with industrialism. In industrialization the Europeans provided a new goal for the whole human race.

Europe and the United States not only encouraged the world to accept the idea of industrialization, but also helped to put the idea into effect. Pioneering the process of industrialization along a broad front, where one stage of progress depended on another, Europe made it possible for other countries to be much more selective in their choice of industries. Once the embargo on the export of European machinery, and the restrictions on migration of skilled artisans, were lifted in the early decades of the nineteenth century, the countries of the world could pick and choose their technology, benefiting from Europe's experience and mistakes.

The extent to which other parts of the world have drawn upon European industrial technology has depended upon their mental outlook, and on their cultural environment; European communities overseas usually industrialized at a faster rate than non-European folk. Certain African and Asian communities have found the gap between their own and the European way of doing things too great to bridge by a drastic change of technology, though this is less true of Asians, with their own long technological traditions, than of Africans. Japan is an example of an Asian country industrializing fast, primarily on its own initiative. It created a factory system in little more than half a century because it already possessed a domestic manufacturing system, and because the pioneering of the factory system had already been done in the West. Before the United Kingdom could use textile machinery it had to build it; Japan in the early stages of its industrialization imported it. It did not have to pass through each stage of industrial evolution. But Japan not only borrowed western technology and western capital, it also accepted change along western lines as a desirable social process. In many parts of Africa the mental leap from tribal methods has not yet been made, save by a tiny minority of the producers.

Where certain European techniques were imposed on colonial areas in an attempt to increase the flow of food, minerals, and other raw materials to Europe, the technological impress was highly localized. General industrialization of these areas has only been encouraged as they have emerged from colonial rule. The important change which has occurred in the newly created nations of Africa and Asia since the Second World War lies not so much in the nature of the technological assistance given as in the motives of the country or agency rendering assistance. Nineteenth-century colonialism, whatever the arguments made for it, was based on private commercial exploitation of native resources, often for the benefit of European investors and consumers. Many of the present generation of technical experts who go out to Africa and Asia are sent there as government workers or as representatives of international agencies. Their aim is to accomplish a specific task. And the important thing is that they do so at the request of the native people and with their full co-operation. In the twentieth century political expediency has lent a new urgency to the transfer of western industrial technology. Hence the present-day flow of Russian technical assistance to China, Cuba, Ghana, and Egypt, for instance, and western European and American assistance to other parts of the world. Present-day economic and technical assistance is greatly dependent on political rather than economic considerations.

The course of diffusion of European technology during the past one hundred and fifty years is too complicated to allow us to trace it, save through major groups of industries within specific periods. A parallel cannot be drawn between the diffusion of agricultural and industrial techniques, as they arose out of different experiences. As for the diffusion of industrial techniques, broad and general categories such as light manufacturing, processing and refining, heavy and modern industries, can be suggested to illustrate the course of diffusion. But no great reliance can be placed here. European technology has been diffused over the years through a much steadier flow of minor and seemingly unrelated improvements in techniques. Tracing the diffusion of European technology by major stages suggests that these stand in a fixed relationship to one another, though this may not fit all cases. It also suggests that diffusion of technology has only gone on from Europe to the rest of the world, whereas technology is constantly diffused between different countries and between different sectors in the same economy. Quite apart from the growing contribution of the United States, which has a century-old tradition of diffusing technology, techniques have also been provided by more recently industrialized countries such as Japan and Australia. Again, it is not possible to think of the diffusion of western technology in terms of clear-cut stages, either as regards the pace of change, or the areas to which the improved techniques were diffused. In a rough and ready way we can trace, during the past century and a half, the spread of western technology from western Europe to central, southern, and eastern Europe as well as to overseas areas; we can say that the diffusion of European technology was felt in North America before it was felt in China; but the complex, continuous changes cannot be fully reduced to an orderly sequence. Stages of diffusion are a descriptive device, nothing more.

Provided these qualifications are borne in mind it is possible to make a rough division between the different kinds of techniques and their order of diffusion from Europe. For instance, in such a general way, it is possible to say that the earliest techniques diffused were the simple basic manufactures for domestic use, and those employed in food and raw material processing and refining, and that these were followed by the techniques needed for manufacturing capital equipment, as well as the more complicated consumer goods, such as automobiles and electrical wares.

The techniques of light manufacturing industries, such as textile, paper, and glass manufacture, brewing, leather-tanning and several other trades, were generally diffused from Europe first because they were largely concerned with providing simply manufactured articles to meet basic needs. They did not represent a complete break with tradition: in many ways they merely centralized the domestic industries already in existence. They were labour-intensive industries, the capital requirements and the unit of production were relatively small. Most of the industries in which these techniques were used had easy access to raw materials, developments were made in small and continuous stages, and they employed techniques which European migrants could easily take with them and practise on their arrival abroad.

An example is the cotton textile industry. British migrants helped to establish the early textile centres of New England. In 1789 Samuel Slater arrived in the United States having committed to memory the principles of the spinning frame of the English manufacturers Richard Arkwright and Jedediah Strutt. Yet, granted that the early American cotton textile machinery was either imported or constructed according to European designs, the Americans quickly made their own important contributions (Table V/3). Technological leadership in both cotton and woollen manufacturing probably rested with the United States for most of the first if not the second half of the nineteenth century; the Americans were ahead of the British in power weaving and in the ring-spinning process; in wool manufacturing they made important innovations in gigging, shearing, fulling, carding, and nap-cutting. Several of these innovations made their way to Britain. In Latin America the European contribution is undisputed. Europeans were responsible for the development of cotton textile manufacture in Brazil, Mexico, and Peru in the period 1820–50. In Mexico, French and later Spanish immigrants, and in Brazil, Italian, and later German and Polish settlers, developed the textile industry. In Guatemala, Colombia, and Venezuela European technicians helped to establish the industry in the twenty years before the First World War. Deliberate state aid was most evident in Mexico and Brazil.

In the second half of the nineteenth century European textile technology was diffused to parts of Asia. The rapid growth of cotton textiles in Ahmadabad and Bombay was mostly the work of Indian native enterprise, assisted by British managers and technicians. The first modern power-driven cotton textile mills in Japan started operations in the 1860's and 1870's, with the help of British and American technicians. In the period 1870–85 the Japanese government hired several hundred foreign technicians from the West, some of whom were employed in the development of the modern spinning, and later the weaving textile industry. Four-fifths of these foreign specialists were British. So keen was the Japanese government to modernize its economy that some of these foreigners were paid about four times the salary of a government departmental minister.[1] In China, native attempts to establish a mechanized, power-driven, cotton textile industry were made in the late 1880's; but the real growth of the industry came with the influx of British and Japanese companies in the 1890's. In sharp contrast to Japanese domestic developments, modernization of Chinese industry was largely peripheral to the Chinese mind. The modern textile industry in Ceylon, established in the early 1880's, was native owned, employing British technicians and managers. Native attempts to establish a modern cotton textile industry in Egypt were made in the 1820's, but the industry did not get under way until Europeans participated in the last quarter of the century. In many

[1] Hideomi Tuge, *Historical Development of Science and Technology in Japan* (Tokyo, 1961), p. 97.

countries the cotton industry has been developed only in the last half-century. In Persia and Indo-China it was established prior to the First World War, in Burma, Indonesia and the Philippines between the two world wars, and in Afghanistan, Malaya, and Iran since 1945. The importance of European technology has been lessened in the present century by the growing exports of American and Japanese machinery.

The first woollen manufactory in the United States was begun at the end of the eighteenth century by the British woollen manufacturers John and Arthur Scholfield. In the great wool-producing countries of the Southern Hemisphere (Australia, New Zealand, South Africa, Argentina, Uruguay, and Chile), woollen and worsted production has been the most important branch of textiles. By the 1870's British woollen textile machinery was widely used in Australia. It made its appearance in South America and South Africa during the next generation. In the countries where woollen manufacture has predominated, cotton textile production has generally been introduced only since the First World War. In Australia and the Union of South Africa it was introduced in the 1920's, and in Argentina and Chile in the 1930's. Canada is the only British Dominion that has had large cotton and woollen mills from an early date, both having been established in the 1840's.

The diffusion of European processing and refining techniques in the period 1860–1914 was primarily dependent on the expansion of Europe's colonial empires. In contrast to the techniques employed in light manufacturing industries, the development of the rest of the world in order to supply Europe with food and raw materials meant an *integration* of the world economy, a growth of world trade. For these extractive and processing industries are highly localized according to the natural distribution of their raw materials. With European aid canning and refrigerating plants were established in food-exporting countries including Argentina, Chile, Uruguay, Canada, Australia, and New Zealand. Silk-reeling machinery was exported to China and Japan; sugar refining was established in the West Indies and Australia; rice milling in Burma; coffee processing in Brazil; mineral-smelting and refining in Canada, Mexico, Malaya, and Australia; rubber processing in Malaya and parts of south-east Asia. The spread of these techniques was deliberately carried out by European and (increasingly in the twentieth century) by American private commercial organizations.

The impact of refrigeration technology, to take an example from these refining and processing techniques, materially assisted the growth of large-scale international trade in meat and other perishable commodities. The introduction of mechanical refrigeration was dependent upon the groundwork laid by a group of European scientists. Galileo provided an accurate thermometer in the sixteenth century; Robert Boyle discovered the law of compression of gases; Joseph Priestley improved the apparatus for collecting gases, and discovered and isolated carbon dioxide and ammonia (not knowing this had been done a few years earlier by the Swedish chemist C. W. Scheele); and Michael Faraday studied the behaviour of gases under pressure. Building on these and other past efforts William Thomson was then able to set down the chemistry of refrigeration.

The earliest patents for mechanical refrigeration, by the expansion of compressed air, were taken out in Britain by L. W. Wright and Jacob Perkins in 1834, and by Piazzi Smyth in 1839. Refrigeration techniques using ammonia were developed principally by the Frenchmen Ferdinand Carré and Charles Tellier in the 1850's, and by the German Karl von Linde in the 1870's. Similar experiments were being made at the same time in America and Australia. In the 1840's the American John Gorrie developed a compressed-air icemaking machine which was used for air-conditioning. In the 1850's the Australian James Harrison applied refrigeration to brewing, and later (in 1860) to the manufacture of paraffin. This is thought to be the first refrigeration plant to be applied to a manufacturing process, though the Americans claim to have used an ether refrigerator in Cleveland at the same time. In 1861 the world's first meat-freezing works were established by an Australian, T. S. Mort, and a French engineer, E. D. Nicolle, in Sydney.

The need for refrigeration is reflected in the speed with which meat-freezing plants were constructed in the world, once the technical difficulties of refrigeration and shipping meat had been solved. By 1875 chilled beef was being carried successfully from the United States to Europe, and in the late 1870's, after several attempts, the first successful shipments of frozen meat were made from Argentina and from Australia. Freezing plants became common in the United States from the 1870's. In Australia, the pioneer establishment in New South Wales was followed by other works in Victoria (1881) and Queensland (1884), centres of the cattle-raising and meat industry. By 1900 there were more than twenty freezing plants in Australia. Refrigerated meat, however, remained a small part of the total value of Australian exports, and a very small fraction of the world market compared with United States exports of meat, say, in 1900, or the exports from Argentina from the mid-1900's to the 1940's. In 1881 the first works were established in New Zealand (soon to become the greatest exporter of lamb and mutton), and within ten years another sixteen had been constructed. Three plants came into operation in Argentina during the 1880's, and by the First World War others had been constructed in Uruguay, Chile, Brazil, and Venezuela. By this time South America supplied most of the world's chilled beef. The export of chilled meat — in contrast to frozen meat — has increased since the

1930's, when it was discovered that a 10 to 12 per cent carbon-dioxide atmosphere would prolong good quality. This has greatly improved the position of Australia and New Zealand, whose trade in frozen meat had proved uncompetitive against the chilled-meat exports of Argentina and the United States.

The rapid development of the frozen-meat trade in response to the demands of Europe during the period 1880–1914 owes much to the skill and enterprise of Americans as well as Europeans, especially in the Southern Hemisphere. While the pioneers of refrigeration in Australia were all European immigrants, and the plants they and the graziers had established depended upon Australian and European initiative and capital, by 1914 control of the Australian meat-freezing industry had passed to large, foreign mercantile companies, some of which had American as well as British holdings. In South America the industry was dominated by foreign companies. British enterprise was responsible for the establishment of meat-freezing works in Argentina and Venezuela. In Brazil and Uruguay British and American interests have predominated. The major importer of meat has always been Britain.

Until the First World War the frozen-meat trade was by far the most important application of refrigeration principles, and in helping to lay the foundation of the economies of countries such as Argentina and New Zealand it greatly encouraged the economic integration of the Southern and the Northern Hemispheres. Refrigeration techniques came to be applied also to the world dairying, fruit, and vegetable industries. By 1914 most of the techniques of the freezing of food had been perfected and it remained for the British biologist Clarence Birdseye and others to develop in recent years modern methods of quick freezing, which must be regarded as a major improvement in fruit and vegetable preservation.

Between 1890 and the 1920's modern techniques of production in heavy industry, such as steel and heavy chemicals, for which Europe and the United States were almost entirely responsible, were diffused for the first time on a general and significant scale. Prior to this date heavy industrial techniques had spread from Europe only to the United States and, to a lesser extent to Canada, Japan, and Australia. In the thirty or forty years after 1890 the techniques of steel production, electric power, heavy engineering (heavy armaments, machine tools, ship-building, locomotive construction, etc.), cement and heavy chemical manufacture (sulphuric acid, soda-ash, caustic soda, and chlorine; Table V/6) became widespread in areas influenced by European technological developments. These industries supplied the needs of producers rather than consumers, and the home market rather than the export market. They were complex, requiring great amounts of capital, high levels of skill, and large plants. Before their diffusion from the West they were unknown outside Europe and America. Their influence in stimulating the further industrialization of an economy was much greater than that of the light manufacturing industries.

Because of the size and complexity of the heavy industries, the part played by the individual migrant was less important than that of the European or American technician, engineer, or manager. For the same reasons the reliance of foreign countries on European funds and equipment was considerable in the early stages of development. Sometimes complete production units were transferred from Europe to other continents. Usually it was only after considerable growth of other sectors of the internal economy, particularly other branches of manufacture, that the home demand for iron and steel, chemicals and machinery, to take several examples, was sufficiently great to justify local production. The recent history of Russia and mainland China, however, shows how difficult it is to dogmatize about the time-sequence of industrial diffusion. In these countries, as in the emergent lands of Asia and Africa today, the desire for rapid industrialization has often meant that the heavy (and more strategic) industries are introduced before other sectors of the domestic economy have been developed. The Russians argue that any country wishing to modernize its economy rapidly should concentrate on the development of the producer rather than the consumer-goods industries. They do so partly for ideological as well as economic reasons; to foster the consumer goods industries is to encourage the rise of a class of little manufacturers and capitalists with political as well as economic ambitions. It is true that, as a result of giving priority to heavy industry, the industrialization of the Soviet Union was completed 'within a historically short period'; but Russia had already undergone considerable industrialization before the economic reconstruction under Communism began to take place. Even in the non-Communist world, however, the introduction of heavy industries has relied upon extensive government support.

The establishment of most branches of the iron and steel industry, to take an example from the heavy industries, has depended to a greater or lesser extent on state action. The growth of the iron and steel industry in Canada, for example, owes much to the tariffs introduced in 1879 and 1887, as well as to the bounty of 1884. Throughout Latin America high tariffs on imported iron and steel were established to stimulate the industry. Other devices were employed such as duties on the export of scrap from Mexico, and grants of forest land for charcoal furnaces in Chile. Production in India was helped by government orders, by protective tariffs, and by railway freight concessions, and in Australia by the increased federal duties on imported iron and steel, and the bounties paid by the government of New South Wales on home-produced iron and steel. In more recent years governments have been directly responsible for the development of steel manufacture. The first large-scale works in Japan, the Union of South Africa, Argentina, and Turkey, as well as subsequent major developments in China, Brazil, and other Latin American and African countries, have all sprung from direct government enterprise. The first integrated iron and steel operations in many of these countries — especially in the Union (now the Republic) of South Africa, Brazil, and China — grew out of the First World War.

All this has tended to make for few centres of steel production. Advanced technology has frequently been in the hands of a single plant. The Yawata steel works in Japan (which accounted for most of the country's iron and steel thirty years after its establishment in 1901), and the much more recently established government-sponsored Volta Redonda plant in Brazil (which, until the opening of two new integrated steel plants in the 1960's, dominated Brazil's iron and steel production), are examples. Iron and steel production in Australia has largely been confined to the Broken Hill Proprietary Company Limited, and, in India, to the Tata Iron and Steel Co. Ltd. In Mexico the Monterrey Iron and Steel Company dominated the industry until the Second World War.

In the diffusion of ferrous techniques Europe has played a consistently important role. The only country outside Europe to have employed modern iron and steel techniques on any scale before the 1890's was the United States. Here the adoption of modern techniques followed closely, if tardily, upon European developments. Puddling (for refining pig-iron to wrought iron), and rolling of iron (instead of using trip-hammers) were begun in Pennsylvania in 1816. A Welsh iron-founder, David Thomas, started anthracite smelting in Pennsylvania in 1839; and the William Kelly (American) and Henry Bessemer (British) method of making steel was adopted in the 1860's. Their largely duplicative invention, which we call the Bessemer process, was more quickly taken up by the Americans than by Bessemer's own countrymen. Friedrich Siemens's gas regenerative furnace and the Gilchrist and Thomas basic process were adopted soon after. The open-hearth process of steel-making was further developed in the United States in the nineties by the Yorkshireman Benjamin Talbot. By the end of the nineteenth century, as a result of the innovation of European (and American) techniques, the United States led the world in its output of steel.

The United States also led the world in devising machine tools such as the automatic turret-lathe, for the reproduction of identical machined parts. In these developments American industry had drawn upon the work of earlier British engineers including John Wilkinson, Joseph Bramah, Henry Maudslay, James Nasmyth, and Joseph Whitworth, who between 1775 and 1850 devised important metal-working machinery, including lathes, borers, planers, shapers, hammers, taps, and dies. Equally important contributions to the development of machine tools were made by the Americans James Harkness and C. H. Norton. The British concentrated on providing the tools and equipment required to construct steam engines, mining equipment, textile machinery, railways, and ships, while the Americans, beside their inventions for traditional industries, developed the tools and the metal-working techniques required for the mass production of guns and firearms, sewing machines, agricultural machinery, footwear, printing, clocks, locks, and, later, electrical equipment. Most of these they produced with interchangeable parts — a system of manufacturing which although first noticed in French musket manufacture really began at the Springfield Armory, Massachusetts, and quickly became known in Europe as the 'American system'.[1] The emphasis in Europe was upon existing production; the emphasis in the United States, with varying degrees of success, was upon technical advance. On both sides of the Atlantic the development of the machine tool industry was vital. Without these tools the new metals and the new machinery would not have been possible.

British enterprise was responsible for the iron and steel works established in India during the nineteenth century. This is in contrast to the ancient order of things when India had exported steel to the West. First attempts to establish a modern iron and steel industry in the 1830's, 1870's, and 1905 all failed. Success came only in 1911 when Jamshedji Tata laid the foundations of India's first major iron and steel works at what later came to be known as Jamshedpur. He was heavily indebted to Americans as well as Europeans for expert help. Belgian and Luxembourg enterprise was the first to produce iron and steel in Brazil, and French enterprise pioneered developments in Chile, as did the combined European-American organization in Mexico. The Chinese iron and steel industry was developed by European technicians, mostly Belgians. Direct European technical assistance was also a conspicuous feature of Japanese developments. Three years before Perry's arrival in 1853, Japanese iron works were erected from Dutch drawings with the aid of British engineers. In 1857 Dutch engineers and workmen erected a foundry at Nagasaki, and later supervised its operation. French assistance was given at Yokohama in the 1860's, and at Yokosuka in the 1870's, and the Germans helped to establish a large plant at Yawata in 1901. At this time the shift from light to heavy industry was beginning to take place in Japan. The first major iron and steel works in South Africa relied upon British and German technical assistance. In some areas, as in Canada, or in parts of Latin America since the Second World War, foreign technical assistance in the development of the iron and steel industry has been provided almost

[1] Robert S. Woodbury, *The Legend of Eli Whitney and Interchangeable Parts*, M.I.T. (Cambridge, 1964).

entirely by the United States. Australia's steel industry has American as well as British origins. Yet since the Second World War most of the improved steel-making techniques have come from Europe. The important L-D (Linz Donawitz) convector method of making steel is one of these. The most recent technique to be introduced into the United States is the continuous process of casting steel, which had been conceived by Britain's Henry Bessemer more than a century ago and was improved by the Germans in the 1930's. (Table V/4.)

In the development and diffusion of industrial technology since the First World War certain changes are evident. One is its increasing complexity and dependence upon scientific progress. Many modern industries were created by science. Yet we should not overlook the reverse causation, science depending upon technology, both for noticing things, and especially for scientists being set to work where their likely discoveries might help an industry. In this general, two-way process the scientific and technical contributions of the United States, together with the most advanced countries of Europe, have grown vastly in absolute importance, though probably not relatively to the rest of the world. The recent development of electronics, synthetic rubber, plastics, rayon, nylon, and especially nuclear energy, by the combined scientific and technical efforts of European and American governments and corporations may be borne in mind. While much of the theoretical groundwork underlying modern industry was laid in Europe, the United States contribution has grown enormously and been applied to practical ends to a greater extent than in Europe.

An interesting example of this combination of the skills of the Old and the New World is the manufacture of automobiles, which grew from about four thousand in 1900 to over eleven million in 1961. This industry, which is often looked upon as signalling a country's arrival as an industrial nation, has stimulated other forms of production such as steel, glass, electrical accessories, and rubber manufacture, and leaves an unmistakable impress upon a people's life. The development of transport technology has not only helped the diffusion of other techniques, but it has been of vital importance in instigating and improving the mechanical efficiency of a nation. In encouraging technical and mechanical skills and aptitudes the automobile occupies in our century a similar position to that occupied by the railway in the nineteenth century. It was the German Gottlieb Daimler, following upon the work in the sixties and seventies of the Austrian engineer Siegfried Markus, who in 1885 patented a high-speed internal-combustion engine and a carburettor, and it was Daimler's automobile of the following year which inspired the work of several engineers on both sides of the Atlantic, especially that of René Panhard, E. Levassor, and

Armand Peugeot in France, and Karl Benz in Germany. While Europeans were responsible for most of the pioneering developments of the automobile (Wilhelm Maybach's float-feed carburettor came into general use in the nineties) many important improvements were made by a group of American automobile pioneers, among them the Duryea and the Dodge brothers, H. P. Maxim, J. W. Packard, J. W. Willys, R. E. Olds, and the best-known Henry Ford. The industry has been centred in the United States since the Americans became automobile-conscious at the end of the nineteenth century, and it is the United States, rather than the nations of north-west Europe, which has had the greatest impact upon automobile development in the world. (A situation which cannot be explained without also taking into account American developments in petroleum technology and the machine-tool industry.) Outside Europe and the United States the development of automobile production has been dominated by three American corporations, General Motors, Ford, and Chrysler. The influence of the German, French, Italian, and British corporations overseas has been more recent and less widespread.

Yet until the last decade of the nineteenth century automobile production was chiefly confined to France, Germany, Austria, and Italy. (In spite of the important contributions to vehicle design made by Herbert Austin and F. W. Lanchester, Britain did not manufacture automobiles until the early years of the present century.) Compared with these countries, the United States made a relatively late start in the 1890's; but the industry grew rapidly and by the First World War American companies had extended their activities to Canada. Since the 1920's the Americans have also established assembly plants in many countries, including Mexico, Argentina, Brazil, India, Japan, the Union (since 1961, Republic) of South Africa, and Australia. Some of these plants have now been developed, as in Australia, to the stage of complete manufacture. European companies, however, have excelled in the diffusion of small-car manufacture.

Although this work is concerned primarily with Europe's impact on the development and diffusion of technology, it might be fitting to add a further note on America's contribution to general technological development. Americans have done far more than adopt and adapt European improvements in technology. For more than a century they have given important technological developments to the rest of the world. The manner in which American technology in almost every field of endeavour — in agriculture, mining, industry, transport and communications, electricity, and commerce — has influenced world development during the past generation has led some European scientists to suggest that America's recent emphasis upon basic research has carried it to a position, particularly in metallurgy and communications, where American technical developments overshadow those of Europe. While the most recent European developments in steel- and glass-making, for example, would suggest that this is an exaggerated view, it is fairly certain that America's contribution to the development of technology in the nineteenth century has been underestimated. The old saying that Europe excelled in pure and America in applied science no longer holds true. Even in the basic discoveries and developments in nineteenth-century industry — the hot blast in steel-making, for instance, or the introduction of power weaving in the early part of the nineteenth century — it is often difficult to say which country led in technological innovation. Because of this uncertainty and the fact that so little is known about the nature and magnitude of invention, the definite ascription of an invention or innovation to one person or country has been largely avoided in this chapter and in the Tables which follow it. To ascribe the origin of any technique to any one inventor is often to becloud the picture of industrial change.

* * *

The diffusion of European technology has introduced an era of world history. While many techniques have originated outside Europe, particularly in North America, and have spread without European assistance, Europe's contribution to the raising of general technical levels in the world has been considerable. Yet it is easy to exaggerate it. The diffusion of Europe's techniques has been erratic and random. When compared with the developments in western Europe and North America, the economically underdeveloped areas of Latin America, Eastern Europe, Africa, and Asia have *relatively* less industry today than they had a generation ago. A comparison of the output of consumer goods, such as cotton fabrics and footwear, and of producer goods, such as steel, in the world shows that the rate of increase has been faster in the developed than in the underdeveloped countries. Although, in absolute terms, Asia (led by Japan) has nearly quadrupled its mining and manufacturing production in the twenty-five years since 1938, and Latin America has increased its output two and a quarter times in the same period, neither area has significantly increased its share of the world's expanding industrialization. Excluding Communist countries, Asia's share of world industrial output in 1961 was only slightly above its share in 1938 (7·9 as against 7·4 per cent); the countries of Latin America only increased their share slightly in the same period (from 3·9 to 4·0 per cent). The most notable gains have been in the United States and Canada, which increased their share of total (non-Communist) industrial production from 39 per cent in 1938 to 47 per cent in 1961.[1] Western Europe has also made a remarkable recovery from the

[1] United Nations, *The Growth of World Industry, 1938–1961: National Tables* (New York, 1963).

damages inflicted by the Second World War. In the past decade western Europe's share of total (non-Communist) industrial production has increased from 32 to 36 per cent. Similarly, when dealing with Europe's contribution to the improvement of world agriculture during the past two centuries, the great progress that has been made is largely in European-settled or European-controlled lands. It is in the United States that farmers are subsidized to grow less rather than more food. Almost all the mechanical-powered farm implements (in 1960 approximately ten of the eleven million tractors in the world) were in Europe, U.S.S.R., and North America.[1] Overwhelmingly, whether we are dealing with industry or agriculture or the especially indicative supply of inanimate energy, the basic point that emerges is not the extraordinary progress that has been achieved by the less economically developed parts of the world, but the slowness of change; not the opportunities seized, but, for some parts of the world today, the opportunities forgone. It is a telling fact that Europe and North America, with less than 30 per cent of the world's population, should be able to produce almost 80 per cent of its income;[2] and the gap between the richer and poorer countries of the world is widening. While the U.S.A. and U.S.S.R. strain to reach the moon, most of the world's people remain poor, short-lived, illiterate, dependent for their livelihood upon ancient ways.

For the first time in history science and technology have made it possible to banish the spectre of want which has haunted the human family for so long. Yet so little of modern science and technology is known in the world. And often where men have knowledge they lack the will or the capital to apply it. The more extraordinary the scientific and technical developments have been, the stronger the conservatism of progress. The real difficulty about technical advance is that it requires changes in man as well as in his machines. If one were pessimistically inclined one might defend a generalization that the more numerous the people to be persuaded to accept change in the interests of economic advance, the slower the rate of progress will be. One of the most powerful instincts man possesses is the instinct to resist change. The harnessing of inanimate energy has been one of the few interesting exceptions to this rule. The titanic struggles which Mother Russia has had during the past four decades to persuade, or most draconically command her peasant sons to improve their agricultural ways, is a lesson on the human difficulties in technical progress. The greatest struggle in trying to improve man's lot is not with nature but with man. We have to relearn a simple fact: that men are at the centre of all technical and economic change.

[1] Food and Agricultural Organization figures quoted in the *Report on the U.N., Conference on the Application of Science and Technology for the benefit of the less Developed Areas*, vol. i, *World of Opportunity* (New York, 1963), pp. 25–26.

[2] United Nations Conference on Science and Technology, already cited. Vol. i, p. 37.

The difficulties in raising the levels of world agricultural and industrial production should not, however, be allowed to blind us to what has been achieved.[1] The rich may be as rich or richer than they were a century ago; the income distribution between the various areas of the world may have become more unequal than it was;[2] but, overall, the poor are not as poor as they were. And, more importantly, it is gradually becoming apparent to the poor that they need not stay as poor as they are. Most men in the world are still borne down by want; their efforts to escape from poverty are often undone by man's inertia, ignorance, stupidity, greed, and hate. It is not the fear of losing worldly riches or the chance of plenty that haunts many men today, it is the fear of famine.[3] Yet man's growing scientific and technical knowledge at least provides hope of better things. And hope is expectation and desire combined; without it there can be no progress. Moreover, there is plenty of evidence before our eyes of the effect of intercontinental diffusion of technology and the ability of the human race to change and improve its ways; witness the manner in which great nations today support themselves by crops and industries of which their ancestors knew not. Ultimately, what matters is not so much the speed of change as its direction. It cannot be denied that during the past two hundred years, and particularly during the past century, Europe has raised the absolute technical levels of world agriculture, industry, transport, and commerce to an unparalleled extent. However slow the process, technical progress is transforming many parts of the world where before European intrusion there was no incentive to change. The question which some men ponder is not the slowness of change but whether non-western societies are ready for the frightening speed of change which western expansion has brought in its train. Technology is the social force of our time. We certainly do not know all the factors (perhaps not even the most important ones) that prompt a nation to undergo rapid economic change, but we can be fairly confident from the history of the past half millennium that the intrusion of western scientific and technological ideas has been one of them. Europe's leadership during the past two or three centuries in the development and diffusion of technology is no longer unrivalled; in particular there is the challenge of the United States. Yet, those who seek to excel Europe will do so only by building on the foundations that Europe and all other past civilizations have helped to lay.

[1] 'Economic Growth: The Last Hundred Years', *National Institute Economic Review* (July 1961), pp. 24–49, The National Institute of Economic and Social Research, New York.

[2] L. J. Zimmerman, 'The Distribution of World Income 1860–1960', ch. ii of *Unbalanced Growth*, ed. by Egbert De Vries (Amsterdam, 1964).

[3] 'Up to half the world's population is still hungry, or malnourished or both.' Mr. R. B. Sen, Director General of the Food and Agricultural Organization, in the introduction to the *Third World Food Survey* (F.A.O. 1963).

TABLES

V/1 to V/7

Table V/1

Some Important Developments in Agriculture, 1700–1960

Approximate date	*Development*	*Usually ascribed to*	*Area of development*	*Major effects*
1701	Seed-drill	Jethro Tull	United Kingdom	This improved drilling machine provided a stimulus to farm-machinery invention.
Last half eighteenth century	Selective animal breeding	Robert Bakewell, Charles and Robert Collins and Lord Coke.	United Kingdom	Pioneers of intensive animal breeding. Coke was one of England's 'improving' landlords.
		A. L. Lavoisier	France	A French scientist who started a model farm in the 1770's.
1782	Seed-drill	James Cooke	United Kingdom	Improvements leading to the modern drilling machine.
1786	Threshing machine	Andrew Meikle	United Kingdom	One of the first mechanical threshing machines. Many improvements followed.
1794	Cotton gin	Eli Whitney	United States	Permitted a rapid extension of the cotton-growing industry.
1797	Cast-iron plough	Charles Newbold, Robert and Joseph Smith	United States	Advanced the process of ploughing. Incorporated some of the principles suggested by Thomas Jefferson.
1800	Hay tedder	Robert Salmon	United Kingdom	An important forerunner of today's hay-making.
1800's	Bone-dust fertilizer	Numerous sources	United Kingdom	Thought to be one of the earliest uses of artificial fertilizer in Europe.
1802–87	Introduction of a scientific approach to agriculture, especially as regards chemical elements	Jean-Baptiste Boussingault	France	A turning-point in the development of a scientific approach to agriculture, based from 1834 onward on systematic field experiments.
1813	*Elements of Agricultural Chemistry*	Humphry Davy	United Kingdom	Provided some of the theoretical groundwork for the later development of soil chemistry.
1819–22	Development of a cast-iron, 3-piece plough, with standardized interchangeable parts	Jethrow Wood, following on the earlier work of Newbold and	United States	The forerunner of the system of interchangeable parts in agricultural machinery. The prejudices against the use of a metal plough were still too great for Wood's ideas to be generally accepted.

				the eighteenth century.
1831–3	Reaper with the first successful cutting bar	Cyrus McCormick and Obed Hussey	United States	One of the most important labour-saving devices. Much superior to the Bell reaper.
1831	Mowing machine	William Manning	United States	One of the names associated with American developments.
1830's–1850's	Introduction and improvement of chilled-iron and chilled-steel walking ploughs	Joel Morse, John Lane, John Deere, William Parlin, and James Oliver	United States	Tougher, lighter, and more efficient than the wooden and cast-iron plough.
1840	*Organic Chemistry in its application to agriculture and physiology*	Justus von Liebig; drew upon the work of Boussingault and others	Germany	Along with Davy's work a landmark in the development of soil chemistry.
1840's	Guano and nitrate fertilizers	Numerous sources	United Kingdom	Rapid spread in use of artificial fertilizers after 1840's. The experiments at Rothamsted in England, which still continue, have provided new knowledge of soils, crops, and livestock. Effects were felt in the work of the Frenchman Georges Ville (1824–97) and in Russian studies of soil morphology.
1840's	Superphosphate experiments and manufacture. Plant nutrition and plant pathology	James Murray, J. B. Lawes, J. H. Gilbert, and others	United Kingdom	
1843	Cylindrical clay pipe	John Read and Thomas Scragg	United Kingdom	Earliest tubular clay pipe *c.*1800, but mass manufacture for soil drainage only from 1840's.
1843	Stripper	John Ridley and John Wrathall Bull	Australia	Rapid stripping of the grain from the straw. Economical in the use of labour.
1840's–1860's	Thresher, portable thresher-winnower	Numerous sources	United States United Kingdom	Reduced time and labour of earlier flailing.
1840's–1860's	Further improvements in the plough	J. C. Pfeil (wheel plough), J. S. Godfrey, and J. M. Cravath (disc plough)	United States	Especially acceptable for the tough sod of the prairie country of the United States.

TABLE V/1

Some Important Developments in Agriculture, 1700–1960 (contd.)

Approximate date	*Development*	*Usually ascribed to*	*Area of development*	*Major effects*
1865	Principle of heredity	Johann Gregor Mendel	Austria	Introduced a 'quantum conception into biology', but only heeded after 1900.
1874–5	Barbed wire	Joseph Glidden and others	United States	Earliest manufacture on a large scale. Important in the settling of the American West and South-West.
1876	Stump-jump plough	R. B. Smith, J. W. Stott, and Chas. Branson	Australia	Made it possible to clear and cultivate scrub-land.
1877	Automatic twine-binder	J. F. Appleby, Jacob Behel, and others	United States	First efficient self-binder. Its importance was in saving labour. Replaced the earlier wire binders.
1870's	Combination-harvester	Numerous sources	United States	Culmination of many attempts to perfect a harvesting machine since 1820's. The combination-harvester cut a wide swath of grain, threshed, cleaned, and sacked in one operation.
1890	'Babcock centrifuge'	S. M. Babcock	United States	A simple machine which rated milk for its butterfat. With the earlier Swedish De Lavel steam cream-separator (1879), one of the landmarks in the history of dairying.
c. 1900	Scientific plant-selection	K. E. Correns, E. Tschermak von Seysenegg, H. de Vries and others	Germany Austria Netherlands	Important only after rediscovery in 1900 of Mendel's (1865) work on genetics. Dramatic accomplishments of plant geneticists in the present century can be seen in the development of hybrid corn and disease-resistant wheat and other food grains.
1901	Tractor, internal combustion	Numerous sources	United States	Lessened labour and greatly assisted the

		others		[illegible] the process of obtaining atmospheric nitrogen to become commercially profitable for artificial fertilizers.
1905–19	Milking machine	Numerous	Australia	Labour-saving.
1929	Mechanical cotton-picker	John Rust of Texas and others	United States	Economical in use of labour.
1936	Completely automatic combination-harvester	Numerous sources	United States	For some years now the culmination of major technological developments in the history of grain harvesting.
1939	Development of insecticide DDT	Paul Müller. Compound prepared by Othmar Zeidler in 1874. Insecticide properties rediscovered by Müller in 1939	Switzerland	A most powerful insecticide used against a broad group of insects.
1960's	Livestock improvement by artificial insemination	Dating back to the artificial insemination of Arab horses in the thirteenth century, its widespread use in animals awaited the development of the microscope by A. van Leeuwenhoek in 1677. Lazaro Spallanzani used this technique in the dog in 1780. It was first employed in woman in 1799. In 1827 Karl Ernst von Baer first described the role of the ovum in reproduction. Studies and experiments continued to be made in Europe and North America. In the 1930's interest was revived in the improvement of dairy cattle. In 1963 about 48 million cattle were bred by this method.		
1960's	Plant and animal hormones and growth regulators	Widespread. A landmark in the development of a science of internal secretions was the work of the nineteenth century German physiologist, A. A. Berthold. The term 'hormone' was first introduced by the English physiologists W. Bayliss and E. H. Starling in 1904. The first demonstration of the presence of growth substances in plants was made by the Englishman F. W. Went in 1928.		Has opened up a new branch of animal and plant science.

Table V/2

Some Important Developments in Mining and Mineralogy, 1800–1960

Approximate date	*Development*	*Usually ascribed to*	*Area of origin*	*Major effects*
Early eighteenth century	Drainage	Thomas Savery and Thomas Newcomen	United Kingdom	First practical steam engines, used for draining tin mines in Cornwall, also achieved success as a pump used in private houses and gardens. Later (1770's) superseded by the Watt engine and, at the end of the nineteenth century, by reciprocating or centrifugal pumps electrically driven.
1800	High pressure non-condensing steam engine	Richard Trevithick	United Kingdom	Suitable for winding duties in deep shaft mines.
Early decades nineteenth century	Crystallography	J. B. L. Romé de l'Isle and R. J. Haüy	France	Laid foundations of crystallography. Effects on the mining industry came much later.
	Chemistry in relation to mineralogy	C. W. Scheele and J. J. Berzelius	Sweden	Analysed new mineral species to discover chemical elements.
1807	First air-pump ventilator	John Buddle and John Nixon	United Kingdom	Extended mining.
1809	Reflecting goniometer	W. H. Wollaston	United Kingdom	Permitted exact measurement of crystalline forms of many minerals.
1813	Rock-boring machine	Richard Trevithick	United Kingdom	Important only in setting a precedent for later developments.
1815	Safety lamp	Humphry Davy, G. Stephenson, and W. R. Clanny	United Kingdom	Provided better illumination and reduced fatalities.
1819–21	Clarification of mineral species	E. Mitscherlich	Germany	Among other things, enunciated the principles of isomorphism and dimorphism.
1820's	Polarization of light	E. L. Malus	France	Stimulated the Englishman David Brewster and others to make optical examination of natural crystals.
1830's	Ventilation	J. Guibal	France	Steam-driven fans to improve ventilation. Permitted deeper mining.
[illegible]	[illegible]	John Buddle	United Kingdom	Economy and efficiency in mineral con-

	hydraulic, or water-flush system of drilling	of Beart and Fauville. Perfected by many others, including the Baker brothers of S. Dakota, United States, in the present century	and France	(especially in oil wells) would largely replace the ancient percussion system.
1850's	Drilling	Numerous	Western Europe and United States	Improvements in rotary drilling by application of industrial diamonds.
1850's	Steam drilling	W. Bartlett	United Kingdom	Following the precedent set by Trevithick and others.
1850's	Safety fuse	W. Bickford	United Kingdom	Made blasting less hazardous.
1863	Coal-cutter	T. Harrison	United Kingdom	A practical rotary motion (in contrast to earlier reciprocating motion) cutter to which steam power could be applied.
1860's	Microscopic examination of minerals	A. des Cloiseaux and others	France	Investigated rocks in their sections under the microscope. Led to an exact determination of the optical constants of rock-forming minerals.
1860's	Power transmission by compressed air	Numerous	Widespread	More convenient than steam and in mines has additional cooling and ventilating effects.
1860's	Geological foundations of modern oil-prospecting laid	T. Sterry Hunt, E. B. Andrews, Alexander Winchell, and Hans Höfer von Heimholt	Canada, United States, and Austria	Provided a theory of petroleum origin, accumulation, and occurrence.
1861	Microscopic examination of metals	H. C. Sorby	United Kingdom	Founded the science of metallography.
1880's	Field investigations for petroleum deposits	I. C. White	United States	Tested the earlier theoretical generalization of Hunt, Andrews, Höfer and others.
1880's	Power transmission by electricity	Numerous	Widespread	Greater productive power and safety.

TABLE V/2

Some Important Developments in Mining and Mineralogy, 1800–1960 (contd.)

Approximate date	*Development*	*Usually ascribed to*	*Area of origin*	*Major effects*
1890's	Torsion balance	Roland von Eötvös	Hungary	Led to more perfect geophysical methods for deducing geological structures.
1902	Coal-face conveyor	W. C. Blackett	United Kingdom	Increased output.
1905–15	Diamond drill as exploratory tool	W. A. J. M. van Watersschoot van der Gracht. Introduced to the United States in 1919. American M. M. Travis introduced the use of the diamond drill independently in searching for oil in Oklahoma in the same year	Holland, United States	Advanced geological knowledge in search for oil-bearing structures.
1919	Seismography	L. Mintrop	Germany	An adaptation of old principles to geophysical prospecting.
1928	Electrical coring of drills	Charles Schlumberger	France	Electrical device which enabled the engineer to 'sound' the various strata through which his drill passed: a major landmark in oil-prospecting.

Some Important Developments in Textiles, 1733–1960

Approximate date	*Technique*	*Usually ascribed to*	*Area of origin*	*Major effects*
1733	Flying shuttle	John Kay	United Kingdom	Made it possible to weave wider cloth, and speeded weaving.
1733	Roller spinning	John Wyatt and Lewis Paul	United Kingdom	Made cotton yarn strong enough to be used as warp in weaving in place of linen.
1764–67	Spinning jenny	James Hargreaves	United Kingdom	Multiplied the spindles operable by one spinner.
1769	Water frame (power-driven spinning)	Richard Arkwright	United Kingdom	Like Wyatt and Paul's invention it provided a cheap strong yarn which could be substituted for the expensive linen warp threads. Gradually superseded in the United States by American developments in spinning machinery.
1779	Spinning mule	Samuel Crompton	United Kingdom	Combined the best principles embodied in the jenny and the water-frame. By 1900 the American ring spindle had triumphed over Crompton's mule.
1785	Power-loom (hardly successful until 1803; important 1830)	Edmund Cartwright, but like so many other developments needed a long chain of improvements	United Kingdom	With further improvements it considerably reduced the cost of weaving. Developments in the United States led by F. C. Lowell (1813) and others.
1802	Jacquard loom	Joseph Jacquard	France	Enabled mass production of figured fabrics. Successfully applied to lace-making in the 1840's.
1809	Bobbin-net machine	John Heathcote	United Kingdom	Mechanized the lace-making process.
1813	Machine-made patterned lace	John Leavers	United Kingdom	A machine capable of producing the most intricate pattern of lace.
1825	Self-acting mule	Richard Roberts	United Kingdom	Following the efforts of John Kennedy, made the operation of the mule automatic.

TABLE V/3

Some Important Developments in Textiles, 1733–1960 (cont.)

Approximate date	*Technique*	*Usually ascribed to*	*Area of origin*	*Major effects*
1826	The Goulding condenser	John Goulding	United States	A series of woollen carding machines which made it possible to increase the number of spindles on the mule or jack.
1828–9	Ring spindle	Charles Danforth and John Thorpe	United Kingdom	Gave coarser but much cheaper yarn, with less skilled labour. A basic device in textile machinery of the greatest significance. Later improvements made possible the spinning of finer thread. There was a delay in the adoption of the ring spindle both in the United States and Europe. Not of much effect in the industry until the last quarter of the nineteenth century.
1836	Crompton's 'fancy loom'	William Crompton, Francis Knowles (1856), and George Crompton (1857)	United States	Made possible the weaving of woollen patterns or designs on power machinery. Further developments towards complete automation.
1840's	'Mercerizing.' The use of strong caustic soda on cotton fabrics and thread under tension	John Mercer	United Kingdom	Beginning of many experiments to give strength and lustre to fabrics. R. Thomas and E. Poérost added to this work in the 1890's. Experiments not only produced a new textile material but also a new era in chemical technology in relation to textile production. It took fifty years to develop Mercer's work.
1850's	Chemical Dyes (see Table V/7)			
1840's	Brussels power loom	E. B. Bigelow	United States	Enabled mechanical weaving of Brussels carpets.
1850's	Circular rib frame machine and rotary movement in	M. Townsend and L. Batton	United Kingdom	Gave impetus to trade in seamless hose and to efforts of B. Shaw a decade later.

		indebted to much earlier European developments such as those of the English sixteenth-century parson, William Lee, and the eighteenth-century Jedediah Strutt	United States	... European developments in mechanization. Knitting was one of the first of the textile industries to be mechanized and is regarded by some authorities as peculiarly European in its contribution to the development of the textile industries.
1867	Knitting-machine	William Cotton (1869), Benjamin Shaw, Charles Fletcher (1883), and others	United Kingdom, United States	Made possible the manufacture of seamless hosiery and women's fully-fashioned stockings. The Englishman William Cotton's machine was adapted by the Americans and the Germans in the construction of the intricate fully-fashioned stocking machine to the entire exclusion of the British hosiery-machine builder.
1890's	Completely automatic loom	J. H. Northrop	United States	Supply of weft replenished automatically. With other improvements, such as an automatic threading device, it enormously increased low-cost production. Northrop was one of many English migrants who felt that his inventiveness would be given greater scope in America.
1930's	Sulzer loom	Rudolf Rossman and engineers of Sulzer Bros. of Switzerland	Switzerland	Use of several shuttles increasing the speed of weaving.
1960's	Following upon Mercer's work in the 1840's, the influence of the chemists (the other great influence was that of the engineers) grew in the textile industry. No single chemical contribution to the textile industry has surpassed the introduction during the past generation of synthetic fibres such as nylon and 'Terylene'. In response to the challenge provided by the synthetic fibres the traditional fibres have introduced many improvements since the Second World War. Most evident is the mixing of synthetic and natural fibres.			

Table V/4

Some Important Developments in Metallurgy, 1709–1960

Approximate date	*Technique*	*Usually ascribed to*	*Area of origin*	*Major effects*
1709	Coke smelting	Abraham Darby	United Kingdom	Alternative fuel to charcoal in smelting iron ore.
1720	Cementation process of making steel	René Antoine de Réamur	France	Réamur's discovery of the metallurgical chemistry of steel is thought to have influenced American as well as European developments.
1740	Crucible or cast steel	Benjamin Huntsman	United Kingdom	Better and cheaper steel.
1750	Carbon content of iron ore discovered	T. O. Bergman	Sweden	Concluded that conversion of iron into steel was due to its combination with carbon.
1761	Air cylinders	John Smeaton	United Kingdom	Water-driven piston improved the air-blast for smelting iron and increased output threefold.
1774	Satisfactory cast-iron cylinders for steam-engine	John Wilkinson	United Kingdom	Stimulated substitution of steam for water power in blowing blast furnaces.
1783–4	Improvements in puddling and rolling	Christopher Polhem (1740's), Peter Onions and Henry Cort	Sweden and United Kingdom	Enabled the production of cheap wrought iron in large quantities.
1780's	Application of steam power to forging. First forge hammer	John Wilkinson	United Kingdom	Reduced cost of production over the water-powered trip-hammer.
1829	Hot blast	James Beaumont Neilson	United Kingdom	Raising air blast temperatures meant greater fuel economies.
1831	Hot blast	Friedrich von Faber du Faur	Germany	Further work on utilization of waste gases.
1838, 1841	Steam drop-hammer	James Nasmyth	United Kingdom	Provided greater power and control in forging metal.
1850's–1860's	Steel converter	William Kelly, Henry Bessemer, Robert Mushet, and C. F.	United States, United Kingdom and Sweden	Facilitated the mass production of steel from phosphorus-free pig-iron. Excess of oxygen in the metal in Bessemer's process removed by Mushet adding spiegel (alloy of

				converter, enlarging the variety of steel. Also valuable for utilizing scrap and waste steel.
1877–8–9	'Basic' process, neutralizing the phosphoric content of certain ores by using lime	Sidney Thomas and Percy Gilchrist. The American Jacob Reese partly anticipated this development ten years earlier	United Kingdom and United States	Enabled the production of steel from ores with a high phosphorus content such as those of French Lorraine and America. The basic process of making steel still accounts for about three-quarters of total world output.
1887	Cyanide process for extraction of gold	J. S. MacArthur, R. W. and W. Forrest, and others	United Kingdom	Made economically possible to exploit ores with only a fraction of the gold content of those worked previously.
1890's	Flotation techniques	Numerous. The first commercially successful plant resulted from the work of the Australians, C. V. Potter, G. D. Delpratt, and A. D. Carmichael, in early years of the twentieth century	Widespread	Much progress in the present century, particularly in the development of the techniques of selective flotation, has come from North America. Applied to a wide variety of ores, flotation techniques facilitated the utilization of vast deposits of low-content ores, as well as complex ores containing several minerals. Especially important for the recovery of sulphide ores of copper, lead, and zinc. Selective flotation is especially valuable to separate copper, lead, and zinc.
1880's–1910	Regenerative electric steel furnace	Wilhelm Siemens and others	United Kingdom	Made possible to produce and maintain steel-smelting temperatures easily and economically, encouraging growth of the industry in areas with cheap electricity. A post-First World War development. The Norwegians were the first to pioneer the electric smelting process on any scale.
1900	Regenerative electric steel furnace	Paul Louis Toussaint Héroult	France	(see above)
1870–1916	Alloy steel	Robert Hadfield, F. W. Taylor, and others. Michael Faraday first produced alloy steel experimentally in 1819	United Kingdom and United States	Development of a high manganese steel superior to mild steel in tensile strength, elongation, and hardness. The beginning of high-speed steel for machine tools. Hadfield is also credited with the development of silicon steel for use with alternating current electrical machinery and apparatus.

Table V/4

Some Important Developments in Metallurgy, 1709–1960 (contd.)

Approximate date	*Technique*	*Usually ascribed to*	*Area of origin*	*Major effects*
1886	Electrolytic method of aluminium production	P. L. T. Héroult and Charles Martin Hall	France and United States	Became the basis of the modern aluminium industry.
1903–1912	Stainless steel	Harry Brearley, F. M. Becket, B. Strauss, and E. Maurer. A long and complex history	United Kingdom, United States and Germany	By adding chromium besides nickel reduced losses caused by corrosion of steel.
Twentieth century	Oxyacetylene and electric welding	Numerous sources	Europe and United States	Enabled a great expansion in the welding operations of steel and alloys.
Twentieth century	Continuous casting and rolling mills	Numerous sources, especially Henry Bessemer, Siegfried Junghaus, J. B. Tytus, H. M. Naugle and A. J. Townsend	United Kingdom, Germany, United States	Much greater efficiency in the casting and rolling process. Eliminated intermediate stages of casting ingots, stripping and soaking pits and primary rolling. Can be completely automated, produces a uniform grade of steel at lower cost. Coupled with a recently developed Austrian process employing liquid oxygen in the steel furnaces these techniques have led to major economies in steel production.
Twentieth century	Direct reduction of iron	Various	One of the first successful applications at the Hojalata y Lamina plant in Mexico	Eliminates the use of the blast furnace. A number of direct reduction methods have been evolved employing a gaseous reducing agent — natural gas or a gas derived from petroleum — and those that employ solid fuels. Chief advantage is economy. The installation of a direct reduction method requires about half the capital investment of a conventional blast furnace, including coke ovens of the same capacity.

to the surface of molten iron.
Usually referred to as the L–D (Linz–Donawitz) process.

open-hearth method of making steel. Of wide application since the Second World War.

Special alloy high-speed steels have been introduced in the twentieth century for machine-cutting tools which retain their hardness at high temperatures. This result is obtained by mixing a considerable amount of tungsten or of molybdenum, along with vanadium, chromium, and carbon. There have also been developed ferrous and non-ferrous materials with high-temperature strength for the gas turbine and the jet engine. The alloy steels contain relatively large proportions of nickel, chromium, and cobalt, with additions of molybdenum, tungsten, niobium, and titanium. The non-ferrous alloys suitable for high-temperature use consist chiefly of nickel and chromium, nickel and molybdenum, cobalt and chromium, and cobalt, chromium, and molybdenum or tungsten. Aluminium alloys, first developed in the 1880's, have provided a challenge to the older metals in some uses. They are now challenged by the alloy beryllium. Experiments in controlled nuclear fusion have been assisted by American developments of an alloy of tin and niobium as a superconductor in strong magnetic fields.

TABLE V/5

Some Important Developments in Power, 1700–1960

Approximate date	*Technique*	*Usually ascribed to*	*Area of origin*	*Major effects*
Early eighteenth century	Atmospheric steam engine	Thomas Newcomen	United Kingdom	See Note, p. 204. More powerful and safer than earlier steam pumps.
1765–9	Improved steam pumping-engine with separate condenser and later use of 'cut-off'	James Watt	United Kingdom	Further fuel economy. Used one-third of the coal of the Newcomen engine of comparable size.
1774	Accurately bored cast-iron cylinders for steam engines	John Wilkinson	United Kingdom	Tremendous improvement in the steam engine.
1781–6	Rotative motion	James Watt	United Kingdom	Made low-pressure steam engines suitable for driving machinery directly.
1781–1804	Compound steam engine	Jonathan Carter Hornblower, Richard Trevithick, Oliver Evans	United Kingdom, United States	Increased the overall efficiency of the steam engine and made it more compact and mobile. Extended the range of industry which could be served by steam power.
1820's–1880's	Electric generator and motor	M. Faraday, Werner von Siemens, Z. T. Gramme, T. Edison, and others	United Kingdom, Germany, France, and United States	Provided a new distributable source of power. The first European hydro-electric power station was inaugurated in Milan in 1883.

1827	Hydraulic (reaction) turbine water-wheel	Benoît Fourneyron	France	Provided a better water-wheel, especially for low heads of water. The first scientifically designed water turbine.
1840's–1850's	Hydraulic turbines	J. B. Francis, James Thomson, C. and P. J. Callon, P. S. Girard, L. A. Pelton	Western Europe and United States	Important advances in design (including introduction of impulse turbine) for special purposes.
1850's	Compound steam engine	John Elder	United Kingdom	Cut the rate of fuel consumption by half. Highly significant for use at sea. Followed by triple and quadruple expansion engines.
1859	*Manual of the Steam-Engine and other Prime Movers*	William John Macquorn Rankine	United Kingdom	Represents the first scientific approach to steam power.
1859	One-cylinder coal-gas engine	Étienne Lenoir	France	First successful internal-combustion engine.
1862	Internal-Combustion engine	Alphonse Beau de Rochas	France	Provided the first scientific analysis resulting in the four-stroke cycle.
1876	Four-stroke coal-gas engine	N. A. Otto	Germany	A better engine, providing a valuable substitute for the steam engine.
1880's	Steam turbine	Charles Parsons and Gustaf de Laval	United Kingdom and Sweden	Better than the reciprocating engine for driving steamships and dynamos.
1886	High-speed gasoline or petrol engine	Gottlieb Daimler	Germany	Lighter, more efficient engine than Otto's. Joined with the work of W. Maybach and K. Benz the automobile became a practical possibility.
1890	Oil engine	H. Ackroyd Stuart	United Kingdom	Much more economical internal-combustion engine, especially in fuel consumption. Diesel's work only used widely in automotive field half a century later.
1892	Diesel engine	Rudolf Diesel	Germany	
1912	Kaplan-Turbine	V. Kaplan	Austria	The provision of adjustable wheel vanes enabled high efficiency to be obtained at all loads.
1937	Jet engine.	Frank Whittle and Hans von Ohain	United Kingdom Germany	A motor for faster aircraft, saving weight and complexity. First jet aircraft flown successfully by the Germans in 1939, and by the British in 1941.
1890's–1960's	Atomic energy	Most recent developments began with the discovery of radio-activity by the		Experiments in releasing energy from the hydrogen atom promise an almost in-

Table V/5

Some Important Developments in Power, 1700–1960 (cont.)

Approximate date	*Technique*	*Usually ascribed to*	*Area of origin*	*Major effects*
		Frenchman A. H. Becquerel in 1896 and the pioneer investigations of the Englishman Ernest Rutherford in the 1900's. Einstein's famous equation of 1905 is significant because it started people thinking of turning matter into energy, which physicists had always regarded as inconvertible. In the 1930's major steps were taken by the British workers J. D. Cockcroft, E. T. S. Walton, and J. C. Chadwick; by the French Irene Curie and F. Joliot; by the Italian-American Enrico Fermi; by the Dane Niels Bohr; and on the eve of the Second World War by the Germans O. Hahn and F. Strassmann, who discovered uranium fission.		exhaustible source of power. But atomic energy has been introduced in such a dramatic manner in the twentieth century that we are in danger of exaggerating its role. There are no grounds for supposing that atomic energy will prove more economical faster than the constantly improving other sources of power. Not only is atomic energy a more expensive source but there are serious health hazards connected with its use. The development of inanimate energy is one aspect of the European era of history; it is not the explanation for it. The first production of electric power from a nuclear reactor was at Arco, Idaho, U.S.A. in 1951. The first regular power station to be built was at Calder Hall, Cumberland, England, in 1956.
1960's	Solar engines based on photo-cells	Numerous sources	North America and Europe	Boiling water by concentrated sun power is an old idea. The progress of the 1960's is electrochemical.
1960's	Great developments of rocket propulsion	Numerous sources	America, Germany, Russia	The modern rocket opens a new age in scientific research, space exploration and warfare.
1960's	Optical maser	Numerous	United States and Western Europe	A possible new source of power at present in the experimental stage.
1960's	Magnetohydrodynamics, the process of generating	Work has been under way since the		As with atomic energy, it is too soon to say what the outcome of these experiments will

world for energy has caused growing attention to be paid since the 1930's to the practical utilization of these sources of energy on a large scale. Chief developments have been in western Europe and North America. See *New Sources of Energy and Economic Development, United Nations* (1957).

The result of these developments since the eighteenth century is that most of the energy consumed for productive purposes in Europe and America today is provided by inanimate sources. In the United States, which uses more mechanical-energy resources than any other nation, inanimate sources of energy furnish practically the total energy consumed in industry.

TABLE V/6

Electrical Energy

In order of electric generating capacity the United States is followed in Europe by the U.S.S.R., the United Kingdom, Western Germany and France; in Asia by Japan, China, and India; in Africa by the Republic of South Africa, the Rhodesias, United Arab Republic, and Katanga; in Latin America by Brazil, Mexico, and Argentina; and in Oceania by Australia.

World electric power in 1960 is set out in Table V/6. In 1960 almost three-quarters of the world's power was generated by steam. Most power is still obtained from coal or, increasingly, by oil and gas. World power supplies in 1963 were divided (approximately) as follows: coal 45%, oil 34%, natural gas 15%, water power 6%. Consumption trebled between 1924 and 1962. Estimates given at the World Power Conference in Melbourne show that nuclear energy will contribute 1% of total fuel requirements by 1970 and not more than 10% by the 1980's. Although Europe has become the largest fuel importer in the world, coal, economically and politically, is the most significant source of power that Europe possesses.

TABLE V/6

Electrical Energy, 1960

Continents and Countries	*Installed Capacity*[1] *Total*	*Hydro*	*Thermal*	*Production*[2] *Total*	*Hydro*	*Thermal*
World	..	..	..	2,299,900	..	..
Europe						
Austria	4,088	2,946	1,142	15,965	11,882	4,083
Belgium	4,752	n.	4,752	15,153	171	14,982
Luxemburg	256	2	254	1,464	20	1,444
Czechoslovakia	5,663	929	4,734	24,450	2,495	19,550
France	21,851	10,231	11,620	72,118	40,344	31,774
Germany — East	7,842	..	..	40,305	617	39,688
Germany — West	27,665	3,349	24,316	116,418	12,992	103,426
Italy	17,686	12,612	5,074	56,240	46,106	10,134
Netherlands	5,262	..	5,262	16,512	..	16,512
Norway	6,245	6,079	166	31,121	30,914	207
Poland	6,316	261	6,055	29,307	659	28,648
Spain	6,567	4,600	1,967	18,614	15,624	2,990
Sweden	8,955	7,005	1,950	34,795	31,090	3,705
Switzerland	5,900	5,700	200	19,072	18,826	246
United Kingdom	37,240	1,170	36,070	136,941	3,133	133,808
U.S.S.R.	66,721	14,781	51,940	292,274	50,913	241,361
North America						
Canada	23,035	18,643	4,392	114,378	105,883	8,495
U.S.A.	185,815	33,092	152,723	841,616	149,123	692,493
Latin America						
Argentina[3]	2,287	317	1,970	7,847	867	6,980
Brazil	4,800	3,642	1,158	22,865	18,384	4,481
Chile	991	571	420	4,423	2,965	1,458
Colombia	911	505	406	3,750	2,587	1,163
Mexico	3,021	1,329	1,692	10,728	5,149	5,579
Venezuela	1,277[4]	130[4]	1,147[4]	2,972[3]	95[3]	2,877[3]
Oceania						
Australia	5,953	1,423	4,530	23,199	4,087	19,112
New Zealand[3]	1,586	1,267	319	6,835	5,512	1,323
Asia						
China Mainland	..	..	..	58,500	..	..
Taiwan[3]	709	448	261	3,628	2,065	1,563
India	5,576	1,846	3,730	20,041	7,779	12,262
Indonesia[3]	308	169	139	1,161	..	..
Japan	23,657	12,678	10,979	115,472	58,471	57,001
Philippines	596[3]	290[3]	306[3]	2,824	1,119	1,705
Malaya	284	38	246	1,190	195	995
Singapore	152	..	152	659	..	659
Turkey	1,272	407	865	2,815	1,002	1,813
Africa						
North — Algeria[3]	439	186	253	1,325	348	977
Morocco[3]	367	290	77	1,012	931	81
U.A.R.[3]	912	350	562	2,639	2,003	636
West — Nigeria	173	20	153	562	104	458
Ghana	103	..	103	374	..	374
Congo (Leopoldville)	845[5]	763[5]	82[5]	2,519[6]	2,419[6]	100[6]
East — Kenya[3]	82	26	56	222	147	75
Tanganyika[3]	41	20	21	155	94	61
South — Federation of Rhod./Nyasaland	1,095	344	751	3,240	1,305	1,935
South Africa	4,193[7]	n.[7]	4,193[7]	23,259	..	23,259

n.=negligible

Notes:

GENERAL: All figures denote totals for enterprises generating for industrial and public use unless stated otherwise.

[1] In thousands kW. [2] In millions kWh. [3] Primarily for public use.
[4] 1959 figures. [5] 1957 figures. [6] 1958 figures. [7] 1956 figures.

Source:

United Nations *Statistical Yearbook, 1962.*

TABLE V/7

Some Important Developments in Industrial Chemicals, 1736–1960

Approximate date	*Technique*	*Usually ascribed to*	*Area of origin*	*Major effects*
1736	New process of sulphuric-acid manufacture with the aid of large glass jars	Joshua Ward	United Kingdom	Reduced cost of making sulphuric acid to about one-twentieth, enabling commercial manufacture.
1746	Lead-chamber process. Preparation by burning sulphur with saltpetre.	John Roebuck and Samuel Garbett	United Kingdom	Beginning of sulphuric-acid industry. Considerable cost reductions. Provided the basic process to satisfy growing needs of industry after 1750, particularly other branches of chemical production. Later became essential to manufacture of dyes, explosives, and refining of oil. First worked on a commercial scale in Bohemia and at Nordhausen, Germany. Sulphuric acid probably the most important single product of the heavy chemicals industry because of its use in many other chemical industries, including the manufacture of fertilizers.
1774 1785	Discovery of chlorine Use of chlorine as bleach	C. W. Scheele C. L. Berthollet	Sweden France	Introduced cheap and powerful bleaching agent for expanding textile industry and the pulp and paper trade.
1787	Leblanc soda-ash process	Nicolas Leblanc	France	Displaced older potash process. Reduced cost considerably. (Soda produced from common salt was dear.) Could satisfy rapidly increasing demands of bleachers, for the scouring of raw wool, and textile fabrics, soap manufacturers, glass-makers and others.
1827	Absorption towers	Joseph-Louis Gay-Lussac	France	Founded modern sulphuric-acid plant. Much improved economy of process.

		Perkin and Natanson discovered the first two dyes, mauve (or purple) and red.		Perkin when researching on alkaloid quinine. Almost simultaneously Natanson discovered aniline red. Further growth of the dyestuffs industry was encouraged by the work of A. Graebe, C. Liebermann, P. Griess, A. Baeyer, and others. An important effect, not lost on the more traditional heavy chemical industries, was to emphasize the value of research.
1866	Ammonia-soda process	Ernest and Alfred Solvay	Belgium	More economical than Leblanc process which it rapidly displaced.
1866	First efficient, safe, high-explosive 'dynamite'	Alfred Nobel and others	Sweden	Provided a strong demand for the products of the heavy chemical industry — Nobel's process was the controlled use of nitro-glycerine — and a more reliable and economical explosive for use in civil engineering and warfare.
1869–70	Chlorine production from hydrochloric acid (by-product of soda production)	Walter Weldon	United Kingdom	Considerably reduced cost and increased production.
1892	Electrolytic production of caustic soda and chlorine	Hamilton Young Castner and Carl Kellner	United Kingdom and Germany	More economical production, and purer product. Greatly extended the use of caustic soda. The process is limited by extent to which accompanying chlorine can be utilized, but has rendered all former methods of chlorine production obsolete. Chlorine today (1960's) is vital in a variety of industries and public health.
1900	In sulphuric-acid production, remedied catalyst poisoning and other problems of the contact process.	Rudolf Messel and Clemens Winkler	Germany	Made the contact process a formidable competitor of the older lead-chamber process.
		The First World War revealed the dependence of other countries upon German supplies of heavy chemicals, with the result that branches of the chemical industry were quickly		

TABLE V/7

Some Important Developments in Industrial Chemicals, 1736–1960 (contd.)

Approximate date	*Technique*	*Usually ascribed to*	*Area of origin*	*Major effects*
		developed in many countries, particularly in the United States and the United Kingdom. Important developments prior to 1914, which have been passed over here, were the conversion of ammonia to nitric acid by Wilhelm Oswald in 1907, and the fixation of atmospheric nitrogen by Fritz Haber in 1909.		
		In more recent years considerable progress has been made by Europeans and North Americans (often developing and adding to much earlier discoveries) in colour chemistry, and what might be loosely called synthetic fibres (e.g. nylon), plastics (e.g. Bakelite), polymers or chemical compounds (e.g. synthetic rubber), water repellents (e.g. silicone), and solvents and detergents (e.g. trichloroethylene used by the dry-cleaning industry). Other major discoveries include selective weedkillers, non-arsenical weed-killers, plant hormone or growth regulators, and benzene hexachloride as an effective insecticide. It hardly needs to be stressed that industrial chemistry in the twentieth century is changing the process of manufacture. Whereas earlier forms of manufacture were primarily of a mechanical nature, the product is now transformed chemically.		

Chapter VI

THE CONQUEST OF DISTANCE

FROM the time of the first recorded civilization the movement of people and merchandise has been a perpetual struggle with nature. On all but the shortest routes travel was slow, perilous, and costly. Because transport facilities were inadequate, vast areas of the earth's surface remained inaccessible and unsettled; economic progress was restricted. During the past hundred years all this has changed. New and increasingly astonishing methods of transport and communications have followed each other with such rapidity as to make the greater unity of mankind a feasible and an imperative aim.

It is perhaps difficult for a generation accustomed to jet propulsion and outer space travel to realize that Europe's greatest achievement in the conquest of distance was the application of steam power to land and sea transport. Less than a century and a half ago the world had neither a single mile of railway nor a single steamship. On land the sledge, the ox-wagon, the pack-horse, the stage-coach, and the human porter and at sea the raft and the sailing-ship, were the only means of transport. Most common was the human beast of burden. European initiative and skill transformed this situation. By the First World War nearly three-quarters of a million miles of railway and more than forty-three million gross tons of steam shipping had joined the world together. On land the steam locomotive replaced many of the traditional forms of transport. At sea the steamship virtually monopolized the ocean routes as well as the coastal and inland waterways. It has been estimated that in 1913 the carrying power of steam vessels was more than forty times the carrying power of the world's sailing vessels.

European improvements in transport and communications affected the whole world. Accompanying the introduction of the steam locomotive and the steamship was a network of land and sea cables encircling the globe. The Suez Canal was cut connecting the Mediterranean and the Indian Ocean. Breakwaters, ports, harbours, lighthouses and other shipping aids were created or improved in every part of the world; roads, tunnels, and bridges that remain to this day masterpieces in engineering were built in every continent. International agreements regarding national identity, classification of vessels, documentation, safety and salvage and territorial rights were gradually evolved to regulate traffic on the high seas. The International Telegraph Union was formed in 1865. In 1875, following upon the International Postal Congress held at Berne in Switzerland, the Universal Postal Union was established; increasingly, the countries of the world came to form a single postal territory. The French gold franc was adopted as the common unit for the establishment of world telegraph tariffs; French, the language of diplomacy, became the international postal language; English became the language of world commerce.

One of the most illuminating ways to trace the growing influence of European man is through the changing number of people speaking the principal European languages in the world. Whereas in the early eighteenth century English was little known (compared with Italian, French, German, and Latin), by 1900 more than two-thirds of the total English-speaking people lived outside Europe. In the 1960's English has not only become the chief language used in the western world, it has also become an important means of communication in many Asian, African, and (to a lesser extent) Latin American countries.[1]

The extension of the European system of transport and communication to other continents was of enormous importance to the development of a world economy. Steam transport on land and sea reduced transport costs to a fraction of their earlier level; routes were shortened and shipments made more regularly and with a greater degree of certainty. Without these changes world commerce could not have grown (even allowing for the great depreciation of world currencies during this period) from less than $2 billion in 1800 to $20 billion in 1900 and to more than $260 billion in 1960; had world economic unity and world commerce not been encouraged and stimulated in this way it would not have been possible for the world's population — which more than doubled in the period 1850–1950 — to have raised its standard of living. More recently, the internal-combustion engine has partly superseded steam power; radio communication has partly superseded land and sea cables, and a new age of jet propulsion and nuclear energy has begun. Extraordinary as these recent changes have been, it still remains true that it was the European steam-engine — employed in land and sea transport — and the European submarine cable which first linked the world together. These two agencies affected the life of mankind to a greater extent than any other improvement in transport and communications evolved before or since.

* * *

[1] See 'Trends in the number of people speaking the principal languages of the world and the role of these languages in international intercourse in the 18th–20th centuries'. Paper given by V. K. Yatsunsky to the Seventh International Congress of Anthropological and Ethnological Sciences, Moscow, August 1964.

In the history of the technology of transport the steam railway occupies a special place. With the transfer of the steam engine from the mines to the early railways (and river boats) the use of inanimate energy in transport had begun: an extraordinary chapter had opened in the life of mankind. The effect of railways varied from country to country, according to the relative efficiency of river and road transport and the expense of constructing and operating railways. In most developing countries in the second half of the nineteenth century, the repercussions of railway building and operation extended far beyond the region in which railways were built or the traffic which the railways were meant to serve. Many industries and many trades were affected by the railway; the iron and steel industries and the engineering trades of the various countries were particularly affected by the growing demand for railway equipment. Much depended on whether railways, as in India, remained a foreign importation, or whether, as in Japan, they quickly stimulated the development of the home industry. Most significantly, wherever railways were introduced, there was an immediate and dramatic fall in carrying charges (Table VI/2). For instance, during the early development of railways in Britain in the 1830's, a ton of goods carried by road cost in the region of 1*s*. ($0·20) a mile. By the 1840's the steam locomotive was carrying a ton of goods for as little as 2*d*. to 3*d*. ($0·3 to $0·5). In the United States 12 to 17 cents per ton mile was considered the most common rate for road transport in the 1830's. Yet one of the earliest railways to be opened from Boston to Worcester, in 1833, carried goods for little more than 6 cents per ton mile. To move a ton of freight from Pittsburgh to Philadelphia in 1817 cost $140; in 1886 the Pennsylvania railroad was charging less than three dollars for the same service. Railways constructed in other countries showed similar immediate cost reductions. It was estimated in 1862 that to transport a ton of cotton for one mile in India cost about 4½*d*. by bullock cart, but less than 1½*d*. by railway. In 1872, the early railways of New South Wales, Australia, charged an average rate of more than 3*d*. per ton mile compared with a rate by road of about 7*d*. per ton mile. In the less developed parts of the world the coming of the railway had a dramatic effect on freight charges. As late as 1926, in Nigeria, the transport of one ton per mile by head porterage cost 2*s*. 6*d*. by motor transport 1*s*., and by railway 2*d*.

Not only were railways immediately cheaper, but over the years successive improvements reduced the carrying rates on rail still more. Between the 1840's and the end of the nineteenth century railway rates in Britain and France fell by almost a half, and in the United States and Germany by more than three-quarters. In the forty years after 1872, carrying rates in New South Wales alone fell by more than two-thirds. The decrease of real transport costs per ton mile on the vitally important Congo Matadi–Léopoldville railway between its opening in 1898 and

1954 has been estimated to be of the order of 50 to 1.[1] Equally spectacular was the economic effect of the 580-mile railway opened in 1901 between Mombasa and Lake Victoria. Only ivory could bear the cost of transport to the coast before the railway was built (approximately 6*s*. per ton mile). In 1960, allowing for the increased operating costs of the railway, the average cost of transport per ton mile was less than one-third of this figure. And this in a country where geographical factors and the dispersion of the population make railways costly to build and operate. These figures are only estimates, but in the eighty years before the First World War the steam locomotive (where its influence was felt) at least halved the cost of transport on land. From a world point of view the economies are likely to grow as railways are introduced in the twentieth century to many of the underdeveloped regions of the world. For the carriage overland of bulk freight railways remain largely unsurpassed.

Some of the earlier canal and river systems were as economical as the steam locomotive; and for much of the bulk traffic on the canals slowness was no drawback. Estimates for the average cost of transport by canal in early-nineteenth-century England varied from 2½*d*. to 4*d*. (5 to 7 dollar cents) per ton mile, and for most of the nineteenth century the all-important Erie Canal in the United States remained appreciably cheaper than the competing railway system. But even where canals could compete in building costs and operation they did not have the ubiquity of the railways; no other existing form of inland transport was as little affected by topography, climate or local conditions. Railways crossed the great mountain ranges of the Andes and the Rockies, pierced the Alps, remained unaffected by the extremes of climate, and opened up the remotest part of every continent. It was said in the early days of railway building in North America that railways could 'go where a mule could go'; this they did in all continents, but in Africa and Asia the 'iron horse' triumphed over conditions where no mule would have survived. The reduction of transport costs and the ubiquitous nature of the steam locomotive provided an effective instrument for the penetration of the great continental areas.

The steam locomotive not only introduced to the world a more economical form of transport, as well as an exhilarating and bewilderingly new kind of freedom, but also new conceptions of speed and time; exact time and the duration of time (like the straight line and the plane surface) are concepts without which the present western civilization could never have been developed. Operated to a strictly kept timetable, railways imposed on many countries the necessary psychological adaptation to time

[1] A. Huybrechts, 'La Formation des prix du chemin de fer Matadi à Léopoldville, 1898–1954', *Bull., Inst. Rech. Econ. et Soc.* (1955), p. 550. Quoted by Léon H. Dupriez, *Economic Development for Africa South of the Sahara*, I.E.A. Conference (1963), ed. E. A. G. Robinson, p. 508.

demanded by an industrial civilization. Before the railway age towns kept local time. When the railways came the British system was run on Greenwich time, the French system on Paris time, the German system on Berlin time, and so on. In North America each company set its own time with subsequent confusion. During the 1870's Sandford Fleming in Canada and Charles F. Dowd in the United States proposed the adoption of a system of standard time. In 1880 the Canadian and American railways introduced a system of zone time, based on the Greenwich meridian, which is now employed throughout the world.

Speed was the distinct advantage which railways had over canals and roads. Railways excelled at moving people quickly from one urbanized centre to another. As the emphasis gradually shifted from freight to passengers so the relative advantage of the railways grew. The stage-coach of the early nineteenth century, then the most rapid form of inland transport, rarely travelled at more than eight miles per hour and usually averaged little more than four miles per hour. By the middle of the century speeds of thirty miles per hour by rail were common, and by the end of the century passenger trains travelled up to sixty miles per hour.

In addition to a new awareness of speed and time, the railways introduced a greater degree of comfort, as well as a degree of security for passengers and freight. Grimly uncomfortable as the early railways were, they compared very favourably with the hardships entailed in alternative means of transport. The poorest workman could now travel without enduring much greater discomfort than that experienced by earlier monarchs, a factor of some consequence when it is realized that the reduced cost of travel made it possible for an increasing number of people to take advantage of the new form of transport. Some of the debt in passenger comfort is undoubtedly owing to the North Americans who have led in coach design and passenger facilities from the very beginning.

The leading role in the development of the early steam railway was played by the British pioneers, William Murdock, Richard Trevithick, Timothy Hackworth, George Stephenson, his son Robert Stephenson, and Isambard Kingdom Brunel. The French engineers Marc Sequin and Henri Giffard, and the Belgian Egide Walschaert, were also responsible for improvements in the early locomotive. Concurrently and largely independently, Oliver Evans of the United States developed his own non-condensing high-pressure engine. In 1804 Trevithick operated the first steam locomotive on an iron-works railway in Wales; ten years later in 1814 George Stephenson had adapted the steam locomotive to draw coal from the Tyneside collieries to the river; in 1830 the first steam railway line was opened between Liverpool and Manchester in northern England. British developments in steam locomotion were greatly assisted by parallel developments in the British coal, iron, and engineering industries; until well into the nineteenth century Britain led in all these fields. One of the most important changes in the second half of the nineteenth century (which also affected the construction of ocean-going vessels) was the substitution of the much more durable steel for iron.

The British were not only the first to use a steam carriage on rails; they also pioneered the development of railways throughout the world. British engineers, following the traditions of Trevithick, Stephenson, and Brunel, introduced the basic technical laws of railway construction and operation into every continent. The railway systems of France, Austria, and Belgium were heavily indebted to the British. Outside Europe the British helped to build railways in Asiatic Russia, Egypt, the Turkish Empire, Africa, the West Indies, South America, Oceania, Canada, India, and Japan. Railway construction in Western Russia, Germany, and especially Latin America, however, was indebted to American as well as British skill and experience. Yet there were few names in railway building anywhere in the world more famous than those of the British railway contractors T. Brassey, S. M. Peto, and J. Brunton. Men such as these mobilized an unnamed army of British labourers, skilled masons, joiners, quarrymen, engine drivers, machinists, and fitters, who helped to build the railway systems of the world. Towards the end of the nineteenth century other Europeans undertook railway construction in America, Africa, and Asia, but neither continental Europe nor the United States of America have exerted as great an influence in the world in railway building as Britain.

The extent to which the nations of the world have depended upon British and other European leadership in railway building has varied greatly. It mattered whether a nation was technically and mentally orientated to the development and control of this form of transport. For instance, the development of the American railway system did not rely upon European direction to the same extent as the railway systems of other continents. The Americans not only controlled their own railway building, they also had considerable influence on railway building in Europe and Latin America; in many countries of Latin America, including Cuba, Mexico, Colombia, and Peru, it is difficult to distinguish the American contribution from the British. Railway building in North America (Table VI/1) has exceeded by far the construction of railways in any other continent. In 1920, railway mileage in Africa and Asia, however important it was in the economic development of these continents, only amounted to 89,000 miles, as against a total for North America of 292,000 miles (more than 40 per cent of the world total). Three-quarters of all the world's railway freight was accounted for in 1962 by the U.S.A. and the U.S.S.R. The vast distances, the rapid development of the interior, and the absence of equally satisfactory alternative means of east-west communication, have all encouraged the use of railways in North America.

In no other country have railways had the same pioneering influence as in the United States. Apart from the lines built along the eastern seaboard and in the south in the first half of the nineteenth century, American railways preceded the westward movement of population — especially beyond the Mississippi — and determined in many respects the future development of the country. They ensured the exploitation of the great mineral and agricultural wealth of the interior, joined the eastern seaboard with the western, and settled millions of immigrants from Europe. Before the railway age the natural trend of trade was southwards along the great waterways of the Mississippi basin. Stimulated by an enormous export trade in grain and animal produce, which reached a peak in the early years of the present century, this trend, with the aid of the railways, was changed to an east–west, west–east direction. The mileage of United States railways has increased from 31,000 in 1860 — when there were almost no railroads west of the Mississippi — to a peak of 260,000 in 1916; since then it has declined. (Table VI/1.) In the early development of the American railway network, the influence of European technicians, rolling-stock, and capital was pronounced. Imported equipment, however, did not have the power or manœuvrability demanded by American conditions, and the Americans were induced to manufacture their own. As early as the 1850's the British sent technical experts to study American production methods. Yet the dependence of the United States upon European capital continued long after it had been able to meet its needs with its own equipment and skills.

The development of the Canadian railways was also assisted by British railway technology and finance. As in the United States, European equipment was adapted to the Canadian conditions until, by the end of the nineteenth century, Canada was able to provide its own rolling-stock and equipment. Until a generation ago, however, progress continued to be heavily dependent upon European finance. The building of the Grand Trunk Railway (begun in 1852) from Portland in Maine to Sarnia in Ontario, via Quebec, Montreal, and Toronto, gave a particular stimulus to Canadian economic development. By 1879 the vigorous competition of the United States lines south of the Great Lakes forced the Grand Trunk to extend its system into Chicago. The construction of the Great Western and Canadian Pacific Railway (completed in 1885), and later branch lines, was vital to the rapid expansion of the prairie provinces and encouraged the building of two new transcontinental systems, the Canadian Northern to Prince Rupert Isle and the Grand Trunk Pacific Railway to Vancouver, completed in 1915. In certain respects railways have proved even more important in the development of the Canadian than of the American economy. They not only bound the western and eastern parts of the nation together (it is nearly 3,000 miles from the Federal capital, Ottawa, to Vancouver, capital of British Columbia), and provided the means whereby the agricultural and mineral wealth of the country could be exploited, they also provided transport in all seasons — a factor specially important to a country whose waterways are frozen for five months of the year. Railway construction in the Canadian west 'lifted eastern Canada out of its provincialism'. The reorientation of Canadian trade routes on an east–west basis provided Canada with alternative outlets to the traditional trade routes along the Mississippi River to New Orleans, and the Erie Canal and the Hudson River to New York. In both the United States and Canada transcontinental railways ensured the unification of the isolated mountain and Pacific states of the west with the eastern areas. The Canadian Pacific Railway, it is said, in joining eastern and western Canada, saved British Columbia for the British Empire. In contrast to the decline in railway mileage in the United States since 1916 Canadian mileage has increased.

For Australia (in the absence of suitable inland waterways) railways have a special significance. The discovery of gold in the 1850's stimulated their development; the early mining industry of Victoria and New South Wales benefited from the early railways constructed largely with British rolling-stock and railway equipment. Railways were also developed to serve the needs of local settlements along the coast. Migration along the coastal regions between 1880 and 1900 was facilitated by the rapid expansion of railway mileage from about 3,400 to 12,500 miles. (Table VI/1.) Yet once the railways had penetrated the mountain range west of Sydney they also provided a considerable stimulus to the pastoral industry and to primary production.

In 1917 West Australia was attached by rail to South Australia. By 1920 Australian railway mileage had exceeded that of Britain (Table VI/1); only Canada has more railway mileage relative to population. However, the absence of a uniform railway gauge in Australia denied the Australians some of the benefits of railway transport. Only in 1962 were the capital cities of New South Wales (Sydney) and Victoria (Melbourne) united by a uniform railway gauge.

The main network of railways in New Zealand was established between the 1860's and the early years of the twentieth century and, though heavily dependent upon British capital and equipment, promotion and management have come chiefly from the New Zealand government. Practically the whole of New Zealand's railway system is state-owned and controlled. As in Australia, the centres of population and economic activity are concentrated along the coast. By the early years of the present century New Zealand had developed a complete national network of railways linking the chief cities of the two islands; by then New Zealand was able to manufacture much of its own railway equipment.

The railway systems of Latin America, Africa, and Asia have evolved almost entirely from the enterprise, equipment, skill, and capital of western Europe and (in Latin America) of the United States. The manner in which the necessary capital, labour, and technical skill were brought together in many areas of the world, often under the most hostile topographical and climatic conditions, is one of the most remarkable (if less well known) chapters in the story of European expansion.

In the building of the railways of Latin America the British were most active. Lines were also built by the North Americans, the Germans, the French, and other Europeans. The first contracts for the construction of steam railways were signed during the 1830's by Peru, Cuba, Colombia, Mexico, and Brazil, and during the 1840's–1850's by Chile, Honduras, Argentina, Paraguay, and Venezuela. By 1850, however, railroad construction had begun only in Cuba and Mexico. (Table VI/1.) In 1860 Cuba, with 500 miles of railway in operation, had more railway mileage than the rest of Latin America. A century later there were approximately 85,000 miles of railway in Latin America, more than two-thirds of it in Argentina, Brazil, and Mexico. (Table VI/1.) Most of this was heavily concentrated in the neighbourhood of large cities, such as Buenos Aires, São Paulo, and Rio de Janeiro, and in the rich agricultural and mining areas. The greatest proportion was grouped in localized networks along the coast — Chile has its famous longitudinal line — or diverged inland from the ports. There is no complete transcontinental system; the whole emphasis in the development of the railways has been placed upon serving the external trade interests and the existing centres of population rather than, as in Canada and the United States, the opening up and unification of the continent. Only Argentina, Mexico, Chile, and Cuba have anything approaching a national network of railways. In 1960 three-quarters of Latin American territory had no railway communications at all. Topography and climate are barriers to communication; only the oceans and the airways unite the countries of Latin America with each other and with the rest of the world.

However inadequate the railway facilities of Latin America have proved to be, they have played an important role in the economic history of this continent during the past century. Navigation on the great river systems — the Magdalena, the Orinoco, the Amazon, and the La Platte basin — proving costly and largely impracticable, and the road systems having been little improved since the colonial period, extensive mining and agriculture have been heavily dependent upon railway transport. Railway history is closely linked with mining in Mexico, Peru, Bolivia, Colombia, Chile, Brazil, Venezuela, Ecuador, and Honduras, and with the development of agriculture in Argentina and Brazil. Yet valuable as the European (and American) contributions have been, the existing railway networks can only be regarded as the very first step — even if account is taken of the recent spectacular growth of air transport — in providing the improved transport facilities necessary to penetrate and settle such an enormous area of the world.

In many respects the story of railway development in Africa south of the Sahara is similar to that of Latin America. Railway building was begun in the mid-nineteenth century (Table VI/1); its purpose was to meet the same needs in mining and agriculture; developments were imposed from outside, aimed largely at developing the export rather than the domestic sector of the economy; by far the greatest proportion of Africa's railways are grouped in localized networks along the coast, or diverge inland from the chief ports to mining regions and to assembly points and centres of agricultural production (only the Republic of South Africa can claim a railway network of nation-wide proportion). Politics have often thwarted attempts to extend railway systems beyond the borders of one state. On the other hand, Africa is a third larger than Latin America and possesses only half the railway mileage. African railways were much more a foreign importation — often the result of competitive European colonialism. The Berlin Conference of 1884–5 on Africa, having decided that 'a title to territory could only be sustained by effective occupancy', stimulated the building of railways, especially in Central and West Africa; military strategy explains much French railway building in West Africa in the 1880's. Another factor at work has been the traffic in slaves; to rid the area of slavery was the motive behind the building of the Uganda railway agreed to by the British government at the Brussels Conference of 1890 and eventually constructed from Mombasa in Kenya (1895) through to Kisumu on Lake Victoria (1901) where the journey to Uganda was completed by lake steamer. In addition, while Cecil Rhodes's plan for a trans-African line from Cape to Cairo was never realized, his efforts did eventually result in a much greater degree of co-operation between the different railways of East Africa. (A degree of co-operation which also extends to postal, monetary, research, and other services.) The East African railway system today comprises Uganda, Kenya, and Tanganyika, and the Mozambique territory accommodates lines from the Rhodesias, Nyasaland, and the Transvaal. This is in contrast to the West African railways — those of Senegal, Sierra Leone, the Ivory Coast, Ghana, Togoland, Dahomey, and Nigeria — which serve no territory other than their own. The line built by the Belgians during the period 1890–8 between Matadi and Léopoldville, in overcoming the obstacles of the cataracts, made it possible to penetrate the Congo. Railways north of the Sahara are chiefly of French and British construction. Most important are the lines which cross what was French North Africa (Morocco, Algeria and Tunisia) joining the Mediterranean with the Atlantic. The first railroad on the African continent was a line built in the 1850's between Alexandria and Cairo, and later extended to other parts of Egypt and the Sudan (Table VI/1).

Railway building in Asia began relatively late, and is heavily concentrated in India, Japan, and Soviet Asia. Until the 1880's British India accounted for almost the whole of Asia's railway mileage and as late as 1940 exceeded the rest of Asia put together. India has more railway mileage than any other country in the world outside the United States, the U.S.S.R., and Canada. (Table VI/1.) India possessed some good roads before the European invasion, yet the railway network, introduced by the British, had a greater influence than that of any other mechanical device introduced from the West in the nineteenth century. Had the British aimed at an integrated development of the Indian economy rather than internal military security and the fostering of their own commercial interests, the railways might have transformed the sub-continent of India more than they did. But this was expecting too much of any colonial power. Even so, the railways gave a stimulus to the development of commerce. In reducing the cost of inland transport, and in assisting the spread of engineering techniques through the engineering shops established by the British, railways also contributed to the industrialization of the Indian sub-continent. In the early 1960's, although totally inadequate to meet India's needs, they remained the most important form of traffic, carrying 80 per cent of the freight and 60 per cent of the total passenger traffic. It is one of the curious facts of British imperial strategy that while the British were in this way actively improving India's internal communications (and its sea-ways to Europe) they were blocking up the land-ways that had traditionally joined India to the rest of Asia.

After India Japan has the most extensive railway system in Asia. In the nineteenth century Japan was heavily indebted to European railway equipment and technicians. But, unlike the building of India's railways, the prime objective in Japan was to meet Japan's needs and not those of a foreign power. The first line was built by the state, and opened in 1872, with European equipment and technical assistance, between Tokyo and Yokohama. By 1880 the lines between Osaka and Kobe, Kyoto and Osaka, Kyoto and Otsu were in operation. In 1889 the line between Tokyo and Hokkaido was completed. The construction of private railways (authorized in 1881) amounted to 1,368 miles in 1893, compared with 558 miles of government-owned lines. In 1892 a law was passed which prescribed that main lines were to be nationalized, providing Japan with a national, co-ordinated system of railways. From 1890 to 1940 Japan increased its railway mileage from 1,400 to 11,400 miles. These figures are small when compared with early railway growth in Europe and North America, or in

India. Yet Japan, with a degree of industrialization unequalled by any other non-European region, has depended to a high degree (in spite of the great use made of cheap coastal shipping) upon railways for the movement of low-value raw materials and bulky manufactures. The construction of railways between the centres of industry and commerce was a major feature of Japanese government policy. Linking existing centres, over short distances, their economic effect was soon felt. The creation of a national system of railways, together with the important improvements made in water and road transport in the nineteenth century, has greatly assisted the political unification and modernization of the Japanese islands.

In other Asian countries, such as Burma, Malaya, Indo-China, and Indonesia, railway development has followed the pattern set by Latin America and Africa — an almost complete dependence upon European skill, capital, and enterprise, an absence of national railway networks, and a concentration upon routes from the mines and plantations to the ports. Most of the lines were single-purpose railways, running from the hinterland to the main ports. They were intended primarily to assist in shipping the country's produce to the West. Their contribution to the development of a national network of railways was largely unimportant.

Railways in China were similarly the instrument of European colonialism. So opposed at the outset were the Chinese leaders to this foreign contraption that in one instance a complete railway enterprise was purchased from the European 'devils' only to be deliberately destroyed. The action of the European powers in China in the last quarter of the nineteenth century has been aptly described as 'penetration by railway'. In relation to its area and population China has never had a large railway mileage, in spite of the fact that in the years following the Sino-Japanese war (1894–5) Britain, France, Germany, and Russia all obtained territorial bases and railway building concessions. The British built the Tientsin–Taku line which was soon extended to Peking and Mukden. This line was completed in 1896. The Peking–Hankow line (opened in 1897) was built jointly by the French and the Belgians, while the Germans successfully constructed the Shantung railway. Concessions to build the Chinese Eastern railway were obtained by the Russians in 1896 and 1898. This line was meant to serve Russia's strategic and political ambitions in China's North-East, more commonly known as Manchuria. Manchuria's first railway was actually an extension of the Peking–Shanhaikwan railway north-eastwards from the Great Wall to Mukden; mainly due to British enterprise it was constructed in the late 1890's. The control of Manchuria's railways in the twentieth century has been shared by the Chinese, the Russians, and the Japanese. After the Russo-Japanese war of 1904–5 the line was split into two parts: the Chinese Eastern in the north, in Russian hands, and the South Manchuria railway in the south, under Japanese control. In 1924, with the recognition of the U.S.S.R. by China, joint Russo-Chinese control of the Chinese Eastern railways was established, but in the 1930's Japanese power in Manchuria came to predominate over all others.

In 1913 Chinese railway mileage was approximately six thousand miles and in 1920 approximately seven thousand miles. Since 1920 China has almost tripled its railway mileage (Table VI/1). Today, China controls all the railways on Chinese soil. In the 1950's several new lines have been added to the country's railway network; the more important are the Chung–Meng line, forming the shortest connection between Peking and the railways of the U.S.S.R., and the Paotow–Lanchou line which links Peking with China's industrial north-west. In narrow economic terms the stimulus of railways to Chinese economic development, through reduction in the costs of transport, has been limited. In a wider sense, however, railways have affected the traditional way of life and the political structure. They have contributed greatly to national unity and the growth of an effective central government.

Two of the most spectacular railway enterprises, undertaken by the Europeans at the end of the nineteenth century, were the Berlin–Baghdad and the Trans–Siberian railways. The Berlin–Baghdad railway, designed to provide uninterrupted rail communication between the German capital and the Persian Gulf was at the outset an economic project. However, it quickly became a vital factor in the expansion of German political influence in south-west Asia and consequently of the utmost importance in the political relations of Germany with Russia and England. Concessions were given to German companies to build the line linking Constantinople with Ankara (1888); from Ankara through the southern districts of Turkish Anatolia to Konia (1896); and to Basra (1899). The line was incomplete when the outbreak of the First World War halted its construction and put an end — at least for another generation — to German political ambitions in south-west Asia.

The Trans-Siberian railway was successfully completed before the First World War (in 1905), and has proved of vital importance in opening up Siberia, in the political unification of Russia's vast territories in Europe and Asia, and in the extension of Russia's influence as a Pacific Power. Built at a tremendous cost and drawing heavily upon the accumulated experience and technical and financial resources of western Europe, the Trans-Siberian railway extends from Chelyabinsk, in the Urals, via Khabarovsk to the Pacific port of Vladivostock, a distance of 4,607 miles. Linking the Baltic with the Pacific, it is the longest continuous stretch of railway in the world and is undoubtedly one of Europe's greatest transport achievements; especially great when it is remembered that the building of this line measuring one-fifth the circumference of the earth was carried out in the face of immense difficulties. Quite apart from its tremendous political and military significance the Trans-Siberian railway gave a stimulus to the colonization of Siberia. The railway also provided Siberian agriculture with European markets, and an opportunity to tap part of the mineral wealth of Siberia. Railway construction has continued in the U.S.S.R. during the past generation. During the period 1927–30 the Turkestan–Siberia line was constructed. This is of strategic and economic importance to the U.S.S.R. Shortly before the outbreak of the Second World War a second track was added to the old Trans-Siberian railway. A completely new Trans-Siberian railway is under construction both from its western and eastern extremes. Since 1920 no country in the world has increased its railway mileage as much as the U.S.S.R. (Table VI/1); yet in 1960 it only possessed the railway mileage that the United States had almost a century ago. By greatly intensifying the use of its existing railway network, however, the Soviet railways in 1960 were handling as much freight as those of the United States.

* * *

Europe established its economic and political control in the world first through its sailing vessels. All the great European improvements in nautical instruments, the compass, the sextant, and the chronometer, as well as many European developments in shipbuilding and navigation (Table VI/7), were introduced before steam. The fifteenth century is especially important in improvements in construction and rigging. Yet the development of the ocean steamship by the Europeans, and its successive improvements in European shipyards, had a profound effect upon the world economy.

In contrast to developments in land transport during the past century, progress in the art of navigation and shipbuilding has come from the oldest as well as the youngest civilizations. Naval architecture it is claimed by some, is an Egyptian art. The band of Spanish seamen led by the Portuguese Magellan, who first sailed around the world, were themselves dependent upon a compass which was probably known to the Chinese or the Indians many centuries before Christ. In shipbuilding the Chinese probably gave to Europe the principles of the stern-post rudder, the water-tight compartment and a more efficient rigging of a vessel, including fore-and-aft rig and the use of sails arranged on the Chinese mat-and-batten principle. The astrolabe, a graduated brass circle for estimating altitude, was an Arab invention and it was a famous Arab pilot, Ahmad-ibn-Madjid, who showed Vasco da Gama the route to Calicut, the major emporium of the pepper trade on the Malabar coast of India, in 1496. All sea-going nations have made their contribution. In the war of 1812 between the United

States and Britain the speed of an American privateer made her capture by British vessels almost impossible. By the middle of the nineteenth century (Table VI/3) the United States owned an almost equivalent tonnage to Britain. The Americans excelled the Europeans in the design and construction of new types of sailing vessels adapted for rapid ocean transport; so much so that by the 1850's American ships carried a considerable share of all the trade to and from European ports, and were encroaching upon established European routes throughout the world. Only the swiftest vessels could hope to win a share of the lucrative opium trade with China, of the China tea trade with the West, or help to carry an important army of gold 'diggers' to the strikes in California (1849) and Australia (1851). America's answer was the 'clipper ship',[1] which began to appear in growing numbers from the 1840's.

Until the 1860's steamships were neither cheaper nor appreciably faster than sailing vessels, but (especially on the shorter runs) they did ensure that a voyage could be completed in a certain number of days, whereas sailing-ships much more than steamships were at the mercy of the winds. The *Mayflower* in 1620, in spite of the considerable progress that had been made in sailing-ship construction during the fifteenth and sixteenth centuries, had taken sixty-six days to cross the Atlantic; it was forty-four days before news of the American Declaration of Independence in 1776 reached Europe; by the middle of the nineteenth century, sailing-packets on the east-bound trip took about twenty-one days and the fastest clippers about fourteen days. The westbound trip took longer. The earliest European steamships were no faster than this, but better engines and methods of propulsion eventually made for important improvements in speed and regularity. Iron steamships built in the 1850's made the crossing in nine to ten days. This was a great saving on the sailing-ship but until 1860 the majority of cargoes from Europe to North America continued to go by sail. By the 1880's the steam-driven passenger vessels took five to six days, and by the inter-war years as little as three to four days. There were similar reductions on other major routes. The United Kingdom–Australia run was over a hundred days by sailing-ship, though by the mid-century American clippers often completed the passage in little more than sixty days. Today the fastest passenger liner from Europe to Australia takes about twenty-one days.

Experiments in the use of steam for navigation were carried out on American, French, and British rivers during the closing decades of the eighteenth century. In 1807, a steamboat was put to practical use on the River Hudson by the American Robert Fulton. Fulton's 180-ton ship, the *Clermont*, driven by a 20-horsepower engine from Boulton and Watt's factory in England, provided the first regular steamship service in the

[1] See A. H. Clark, *The Clipper Ship Era* (New York, 1911).

world. Beginning in 1810 steamboats penetrated all of the navigable waterways of the Ohio–Mississippi and Missouri River systems. But although Americans were undoubtedly the first to employ steamboats for inland navigation, Europeans were largely responsible for the development of the ocean-going steamship, which over the past hundred years has evolved into the modern cargo-vessel and ocean liner. (Table VI/7.)

Conditions in Europe were peculiarly favourable to the rapid growth of steam shipping in the nineteenth century. There was an abundance of the new building material — iron, a plentiful supply of the new fuel — coal, and an enormous expansion of foreign trade. It was Europe's engineering skill which enabled it to lead the world in shipbuilding. These conditions were most favourable in Britain, whose seafaring traditions, undisputed leadership in technology, especially in the metallurgical industries, engineering skill, mineral resources, ever-expanding commerce and free trade policy enabled it to construct and furnish the new iron and, later, steel vessels at less cost than other nations. In the twenty-five years before the First World War Britain built not less than two-thirds of the ships launched in the world. The British government's policy of subsidizing shipping through lucrative mail contracts was an important factor enabling British lines to out-compete the unsubsidized (after 1868) American lines.

The substitution of iron for wood in shipbuilding from the forties onwards made possible the pioneering work of the British engineer Isambard Kingdom Brunel, who constructed steamers of huge dimensions, such as the *Great Western*, the *Great Britain*, and the *Great Eastern* launched in 1858 and unequalled in size until the present century. With the introduction of the Bessemer and open hearth steel-making processes in Britain, the use of steel in shipbuilding increased gradually. Far from seizing upon Bessemer's improvements, it took British shipowners almost a generation to appreciate what Bessemer and others had done. The conservatism of progress affected Bessemer as it affected a thousand other would-be inventors and improvers.

Steel ships, when they were introduced in the eighties, meant lighter, stronger and ultimately larger ships capable of carrying more cargo. It is not merely the increase in the size of vessels which accounted for the larger carrying capacity of the British and other European mercantile marines after 1870, but the rapid supplanting of sail by steam. In the 1850's the compound engine came into general use. A major defect of the earlier steam-engine was its heavy fuel consumption. The compound engine cut the rate of fuel consumption by half. At the same time an efficient screw propeller superseded the paddle wheel in European shipyards. The greater efficiency and speed of the screw propeller, and the fuel economies of the compound engine, made the ocean steamer from the 1860's profitable as a cargo ship, where previously it had been confined to passengers and mails. In 1881 the *Aberdeen*, the first steamship successfully fitted with a triple expansion engine, which effected still further economies in fuel consumption, was launched from the Glasgow shipyards. In the 1890's twin-screw propellers were generally introduced (they had been used on the Panama–Sydney run in the 1860's), and later multiple-screw propellers, and in 1894 the first quadruple expansion engine was constructed. The same date saw the launching of the *Turbinia* at Newcastle, a vessel fitted with the newly developed turbine engine. The turbine took up less space, and was quieter and more economical at high speeds than the reciprocating engine. It was gradually improved and adopted for new Admiralty and Cunard line vessels. The steel Cunard liners *Campania* and *Lucania* of 1893, and *Lusitania* launched in 1907, probably represent the peak of nineteenth-century developments in ship construction and propulsion. All these improvements permitted astonishing increases in dimensions, strength, power, and speed. So great was the general progress made in maritime communications that in 1912 the British were able to launch the ill-fated *Titanic* which was thought by some authorities to be unsinkable.

The greatest benefit of the steamship, particularly in view of the extraordinary expansion of world commerce in the nineteenth century, was an increase in the carrying capacity of the world's ocean-going fleet. The eventual improvement in speed meant that several times more use could be made of a steam vessel than of a sailing vessel of equal tonnage. Yet the benefits of the steamship were slow to appear. Unlike the steam railway there was no immediate drastic reduction in transport costs. Until the 1850's–1860's, at least for all but the most expensive freight, steamships were an uneconomical means of transport. Certainly, this would be true of conditions on the longer runs. Too much space had to be given up to carrying fuel. The competition of American and European sailing-ship companies had greatly reduced freight rates on the major routes, and it was not until the 1870's and 1880's that steamships began to exert a downward pressure on rates. From then until the First World War a persistent tendency towards over-expansion of the shipping industry, resulting from the greatly increased carrying capacity of steamships and the determination of steamship owners to drive sailing-ships off the world's oceans, added to this downward trend of freight rates.

Much of this reduction in freight rates was accounted for by generally declining price levels. The depression of the 1870's hit shipping rates especially hard. There were many variations between different routes and commodities (Table VI/5b). Rates on low-value goods tended to fall more rapidly than on expensive goods; likewise rates on the more competitive Atlantic, eastern Mediterranean, and Indian routes tended to fall more rapidly than on the distant routes to Australia, the Pacific shores of Asia, and North America. But the general downward trend during the half-century before the First World War is evident. Rates on such staples as wheat from New York and cotton from Bombay to the United Kingdom fell by more than two-thirds between the 1860's and the early years of the present century. A general index of tramp shipping freights (Table VI/5a) shows that while rates fell by about half in the period 1869–1910, general prices fell by about a fifth. Homeward freights to the United Kingdom show a similar fall between 1884 and 1910 (Table VI/5b). The reduction in shipping costs was never as important as that achieved by railways, partly because shipping charges were always a smaller element in the final cost, and partly because their reduction was more gradual and modest. It is unlikely that in real terms they fell by more than a half in the forty years before the First World War. Yet the reductions, together with increased carrying capacity, faster speeds, greater regularity (and consequently lower insurance and interest rates), made it practical to transfer an ever-growing quantity of bulk cargoes from one side of the world to the other. By the First World War trade in bulk cargoes had replaced earlier trade in highly priced luxuries.

Under the stimulus of the steamship international commerce in low-priced commodities expanded at an unprecedented rate in the fifty or sixty years before 1914. During these years exports of grain from the prairies of North America, the pampas of Argentina, the Australian wheat belt, the Sind province of India, and from South and North Africa, increased to enormous proportions. In the 1880's Australian export of wheat doubled, and during the 1890's Argentine wheat exports more than tripled, from just over 300,000 tons to 1,000,000 tons. The value of wheat exports from the United States increased from less than $8 million in 1850 to an annual average of nearly $173 million in the years 1911–15. Trade in meat and other animal produce was made possible by the development of refrigeration. From the 1880's it became increasingly profitable to raise great herds of cattle on the Texas ranges, and in the Rosario Valley of Argentina, and to establish enormous sheep stations in South Africa, New Zealand, and Australia. It was also in these years that the ocean traffic in bulky minerals and other raw materials was developed. Minerals, which could not be mined because of prohibitive transport costs, gradually became available as rail and shipping charges fell. Britain became the world's greatest exporter of coal, Australia the world's foremost supplier of wool, Malaya the source of much of the world's tin, and later, rubber; and from Chile came most of the world's nitrates. In addition to moving animal produce, ships specialized in transporting coal, grains, fibres, ores, and, later, oil. European developments in steamshipping were not the sole cause of this increase in trade but they certainly facilitated and encouraged it. The steamship, particularly when supplemented by the submarine cable, created world markets and world prices. The cheap and easy transport of food and raw materials by sea narrowed the variations in commodity prices between regions and gave rise to new produce markets and exchanges in London, Amsterdam, Paris and other commercial centres. The steamship assisted and accelerated the growing commercial interdependence of the entire world.

The impact of European steamshipping was felt not only in trade but also in the movement of peoples between countries and continents. The speed, safety, relative comfort, and cheapness of the Atlantic crossing by steamship encouraged migration to America from Europe. In fact, European steam shipping companies, under highly competitive conditions, played no small part in attracting immigrants to America. The hazards and cost of the Australian run by sailing-ship were reduced by the steamship. Since the 1880's the majority of British migrants went to Australia as steamship passengers. Most dramatic of all was the effect of improved steam shipping on the South American route. Cut-throat competition among European steamshipping companies reduced the fares to absurdly uneconomic levels, and for a number of years in the early twentieth century there was an important seasonal migration of European agricultural labourers to the estates of Argentina and to the coffee plantations of Brazil.

European steamships supplemented the work of the earlier European steam railways. Goods could leave inland centres of other continents and arrive at European ports according to schedule. The combination of falling railway and shipping rates proved an invaluable stimulus to commerce, and the fluctuations in one were often counterbalanced by the other to give a continuous overall decline in freight rates. In terms of international commerce, development, and integration, there can be little doubt that the introduction of steam railways and steam shipping was most significant in the evolution of the modern world. No one can possibly assess what improved sea transport has meant in terms of the saving of human lives and suffering. One is horrified at the enormous losses in passengers and crew accepted as normal in earlier centuries.

Two further European developments in sea transport before the First World War were the substitution of oil for coal as fuel, and the introduction of the internal-combustion engine. Oil burning was pioneered by the Europeans, but in the absence of European oil supplies it was more readily adopted by American shipping. The diesel engine supplanted the earlier heavy-oil engines and was used for shipping with great fuel-saving as early as 1903; it was also economical in the use of space and labour.

In quantitative terms the most striking results of European developments in shipbuilding over the past one hundred and fifty years has been the enormous increase in world shipping tonnage (Tables VI/3 and VI/4). It has been estimated that the mercantile marines of the world in 1800 totalled about 4 million net tons. By 1850 world net shipping tonnage was approximately 9 million tons; by 1880 it had increased to nearly 20 million tons. Two-thirds of this increase, however, was accounted for by new sailing vessels. It was not until the 1860's that steam was faster than sail and only in the period 1880 to 1910 that European developments in steam shipping made themselves felt on a world-wide scale. In the period 1860–1910 net tonnage of sailing ships fell from 14·5 to 8 million tons, while that of steamships increased from about 5·5 to 26 million tons. World steam tonnage exceeded sailing tonnage for the first time in 1893. Total net tonnage of both sail and steam increased in this period from less than 20 million to almost 35 million tons.

Measured in net tonnage, Europe's share of total world shipping increased from 54 per cent in 1850 to 71 per cent in 1900. Figures for gross tonnage, excluding some of North America's lake and river shipping, show Europe's share of world shipping in 1913 as high as 79 per cent. Measured as a proportion of the world's ocean-going steam shipping, Europe's share was higher still. In contrast, during the sixty years after 1850, the share of total world shipping accounted for by the United States fell from 39 per cent to 12 per cent. The outbreak of the Civil War in 1861 was the turning point. America's ocean-going fleet, one of the world's leading carriers in the middle of the nineteenth century, declined in absolute terms from about 1,600,000 net tons to 800,000 net tons and as a proportion of world ocean-going shipping from more than 22 per cent to less than 3 per cent. As late as 1913, when sailing-ships accounted for barely more than 2 per cent of Britain's fleet, and 8 per cent of the total world's fleet, they still accounted for more than 20 per cent of American shipping. Absorbed with the enormous task of conquering a continent, the Americans, since the 1860's, had fallen behind in shipping developments. In more recent years the situation has changed. While Europe's merchant fleet has grown from 37 million gross tons in 1913 to 71 million gross tons in 1960, Europe's share of world shipping has fallen from 79 per cent to 55 per cent; there has been, as the figures show, an unprecedented expansion in the merchant fleet of the United States. Japan has become the world's greatest ship-building nation.

*   *   *

In addition to these developments in land and sea transport, the Europeans also set themselves the task of piercing the isthmuses of Suez and Panama and so joining together, in the case of one, the Mediterranean and the Red Seas, and, in the case of the other, the Atlantic and the Pacific Oceans. French efforts at Suez met with success in 1869 when a sea-level canal was opened giving access to the Red Sea and the Indian

Ocean. A few years later, at two geographical congresses held at Antwerp in 1871 and Paris in 1875, European scientists considered the building of a canal across Central America. In the spring of 1879 at a further congress in Paris it was resolved that an attempt should be made to pierce the isthmus of Panama. It was estimated that such a canal would take twelve years to construct, and would cost a thousand million francs. Ferdinand de Lesseps, the man responsible for the building of the Suez Canal, closed the congress by reminding the delegates that those 'others who will profit from this inter-oceanic canal will one day say that we have merited well of humanity'. But de Lesseps's singular success at Suez was matched by singular failure at Panama. Humanity has largely forgotten him and those who laboured with him. De Lesseps's statue, which once stood proudly at the Mediterranean entrance to the Canal, now lies in the mud of Port Said harbour.

At one stroke the cutting of the Suez Canal reduced the sea journey between London and Singapore by almost one-third and that between London and Bombay by more than 40 per cent (Table VI/6a). The saving of distance meant a marked increase in the world's effective shipping fleet. The steady growth of shipping movements through the Canal since 1870 (Table VI/6b) reflects the extent to which the Canal provided a new and more acceptable artery of world commerce. The southbound cargoes remain predominantly machinery and metal goods of industrial Europe, the northbound cargoes consist of primary produce and foodstuffs from the areas south and east of Suez, and in recent years of an enormous increase in oil shipments from south-west Asia. Only the two World Wars and the general depression of the 1930's caused any serious set-back in the increased volume of shipping.

The Canal, with its saving of distance, time, and cost of transport, facilitated the development of Asia's trade with Europe. India used the shorter route for its export of grain, jute, tea, and other commodities; China used the Canal for its tea and silk trade. The China clipper was especially hard hit by the opening of the Canal. While the impact of the Canal was not as great for Australasian traffic, the new route meant economies in time, insurance, and transshipment charges. By providing a powerful incentive to the development of the marine engine (sailing vessels had to be towed through the Canal and could not always be safely navigated through the Red Sea) the Suez Canal brought about a premature obsolescence of sailing tonnage. In doing so the Canal indirectly increased and cheapened the amount of sailing tonnage on other routes. Where speed was not important, as in bringing Chilean nitrates to Europe, or jute and grain from India, or wool and grain from Australia, sail could hold its own with steam. Ousted from most other routes, the big sailing-ship, helped by favourable winds, was still carrying timber and grain on the Australian run until the 1940's. The supremacy of the steamship on the Suez route to Australia was established only in the present century and then only because improvements in the marine engine gradually closed the gap between the respective freight rates.

The cutting of the Panama Canal in 1914 was an American not a European achievement. Yet some credit should go to the French whose failure to dig a sea-level canal at Panama in the 1880's had provided an object lesson for the Americans. Credit is also due to a group of Europeans including Patrick Manson, Charles Laveran, Ronald Ross, and Giovanni Grassi, as well as to the Americans Walter Reed and William C. Gorgas. The pioneering achievements of these men in tropical medicine, at the turn of the century, helped to overcome Panama's greatest hazard: disease. The evolution of the science of tropical medicine not only facilitated the cutting of the Panama Canal, but also the colonization of the tropics.

The opening of the Panama lock canal provided an alternative to the historic trade routes overland across Panama and by sea around Cape Horn. It reduced the distance between Liverpool and San Francisco by two-fifths and between New York and San Francisco by three-fifths. In doing so it provided a tremendous stimulus to the sea-borne commerce between the North Atlantic ports and the western seaboard of the American continent. Yet the Panama Canal has never had the same importance in international commerce as the Suez Canal. Most of the shipping passing through the Panama is American, and its total tonnage has been much less than that passing through Suez (Table VI/6b). In building the Panama Canal, however, the Americans did not aim at a greater degree of economic unity, as the French did at Suez, but at a more effective sea defence. Once the Canal was cut the American fleet could pass between the Atlantic and the Pacific much more speedily than by the old Cape Horn route—a fact which helps to explain why the American government took responsibility for the construction and control of the Canal.

* * *

The Europeans and the Americans were also responsible for laying a network of deep-sea cables linking Europe and America with the rest of the world. Before the art of cable-laying was mastered costly lessons had to be learned. The first successful cable was laid between Dover and Calais in 1850. Further cables connected England with Holland and Ireland. In 1866, after many setbacks, a cable between England and Newfoundland was finally and successfully laid. It was this cable which demonstrated the immense possibilities of this new form of communication. Other cables were soon laid from Europe to India and eastern Asia, to Java, Australia, and New Zealand, to the Cape of South Africa, and across the Atlantic to South America. In 1902 Durban in South Africa was linked with Perth in Western Australia; also in 1902 the 'all-Red-Route' (i.e. the route from London across the Atlantic, Canada, and the Pacific to Australia and New Zealand) was completed. London became the world's largest communications centre. By 1903 a world-wide network of submarine telegraph cables had been laid. Success had depended on the earlier efforts of European scientists and engineers, including Francis Ronalds, W. F. Cooke, C. Wheatstone, the brothers John and Jacob Brett, K. F. Gauss, W. E. Weber, K. A. von Steinheil, and W. von Siemens.

The ocean cable reduced the isolation in time of one part of the world from another. Before the first successful Atlantic cable was laid in 1866 it took at least three weeks for a European to get a reply from New York; before the cable reached India in 1870 a reply required at least two months; before the cable reached Adelaide in 1872 a reply (dependent upon whether the Indian or Ceylon extension was used) took at least four months. Once these cables were laid communication took minutes instead of weeks or months. Relatively slow compared with later developments, the early cables revolutionized the system of commercial intelligence between Europeans and the rest of the world. For the first time the merchant was in direct touch with his source of supply. He could buy cotton or wool, sugar or tea, before shipment and be fairly sure of its date of arrival. Fluctuations in supply and demand could be acted upon rapidly. The ability to order supplies from distant continents by cable became an integral part of the activities of the produce exchanges of London, Liverpool, New York, Hamburg, and Amsterdam. Together with steam locomotion on land and sea, deep-sea cables created world markets and world prices. The use of cables was especially important in the control and direction of the world's shipping fleet. With the opening of the Suez and Panama Canals, it increased the carrying power of the world's fleet without another ton of shipping having been launched.

In addition to the improvements in international commerce the submarine cable had important effects upon business organization and international investment. Rapid world-wide communication encouraged the establishing of branches of European and American businesses overseas. Through improved commercial intelligence, submarine cables provided a further stimulus to the international flow of capital.

In 1956 a joint United Kingdom, Canada, and United States undertaking laid the first transatlantic coaxial cable (providing speech and telegraph), from Oban in Scotland to Clarenville in Newfoundland. In 1963 a similar cable was laid between Australia and Canada. The new coaxial cables provide telephone and telegraph channels of greater capacity and efficiency. They have done much to offset the competitive advantage which long-distance radio telephony and telegraphy has had over cable communication during the past generation.

* * *

The development of high-frequency radio service after the First World War also depended on earlier scientific work. The first radio message was sent by the Italian G. Marconi in 1894. In 1901 Marconi made his historic signal across the Atlantic of the letter 'S'; also in 1901 the first radio messages were sent to ships at sea. This practical application of radio communication depended upon the earlier developments in radio engineering made by many European and American scientists. Important contributions were made by the Dane H. C. Oersted, who discovered electro-magnetism; by the Frenchman A. M. Ampère, who worked on electric induction and provided a means of measuring electric current; by the Englishman J. C. Maxwell, who predicted the existence of radio waves and by the German H. Hertz, who verified Maxwell's prediction. Further research was carried out by the Englishman J. A. Fleming, the Americans Lee de Forest and R. A. Fessendon, the Dane V. Poulson, and the German Rudolph Goldschmidt. The drama attending the loss of the ships *Republic* in 1910 and *Titanic* in 1912 drew attention to the vital nature of radio communication and provided a stimulus to its acceptance and further improvement during the next half-century. With the development of the usefulness of shorter wave-bands in the 1920's, broadcasts and radio-telegraphy across the world became technically and economically practicable. Although the use of new methods in the 1950's in ocean cables has reduced the competitive advantage of radio, the introduction of instantaneous and global communication from orbiting satellites in the 1960's is likely to provide a powerful impetus to the increased use of radio communication.

Early European scientific discoveries were also vital in the development of radar (radio detection and ranging) and television. In principle, radar is simple. It consists of sending an electro-magnetic radio wave of very high frequency against an object. The object's position is determined by the direction in which the radio wave is travelling when it hits and is reflected from the object; the object's distance is calculated by measuring electronically the time taken for the echo of the radio wave to return. In practice, radar technology is extremely complicated and it required much effort before it was applied successfully. Early European work on electro-magnetic waves, such as that of Hertz, laid the foundations of later developments. In the 1920's important steps were taken by two Americans, Albert H. Taylor and Lee C. Young. Their work was dependent upon the ionospheric research being conducted by other Americans. During the 1930's scientific research into radio-location was continued by departments of the American Army and Navy. In 1938 the first vessel (U.S.S. *New York*) was equipped with radar. In 1941 when the Japanese carried out their attack on Pearl Harbor radar signals detected the approach of the Japanese planes. Meanwhile, throughout the 1920's and 1930's, similar developments were taking place in Britain and Germany. The need for an improved system of air warning was particularly acute for the British people. Led by the scientists Henry T. Tizard and Robert Watson-Watt, and drawing upon earlier research into the nature of the ionosphere (the Englishmen O. Heaviside and Edward V. Appleton had made important contributions), five radar stations had been built in Britain in 1935. With the outbreak of war in 1939 the need for radar was urgent and research was intensified. The development of radar was a major factor in the outcome of the Battle of Britain in 1940.

The development of television has a similar background. In fact the development of one affected the other. Having discovered how to transmit sound by means of electrical impulse the problem was how to wed sight to sound and transmit and receive them together. Of fundamental importance in solving this problem was the discovery by the Englishman William Crookes in 1876 of cathode rays which were eventually evolved by the German Karl Ferdinand Braun and the Englishman A. A. Campbell-Swinton into the cathode ray oscilloscope — an 'electric gun' producing a beam of electro-magnetic wireless waves which carries the televised image. Other Europeans prominent in the early development of television were the Frenchman C. Senlecq D'Ardres, the Germans Albert Einstein, Paul Nipkow, and the Russian Boris Rosing. After the First World War Russian-born Vladimir K. Zworykin developed the ionoscope (the electronic 'eye') of the television camera. Using the cathode ray tube, Zworykin was able to produce a device which simultaneously saw the object to be televised and converted the image into an electric beam. At the same time the American Philo T. Farnsworth developed his own electronic 'eye' along different lines. There are in fact many other names associated with the development of television during the past thirty years. The first transmission of television signals was made by American engineers in 1927. The first transatlantic telecast was made in 1928 by the Scotsman John Logie Baird. Commercial television was introduced by the British in 1935 and by the Americans in 1939. The growth of the television industry in Europe and America since the Second World War has been more rapid than that experienced by any other branch of communications.

In the more recent developments in transport and communications the Americans have played an ever-increasing role. In those regions of the world which remain to be developed the automobile, which is identified with the Americans, will probably play the part which at an earlier age and in other regions was played by the railway. In so far as the automobile is more ubiquitous and more personal than the railway, its future economic and social effect in the less industrially advanced parts of the world is likely to be even more pronounced. Continental Europeans did much of the pioneering work in developing the automobile. The American contribution was to convert a luxury industry into one of mass production and consumption. Americans carried the automobile industry to many parts of the world, and, along with it, often adding to the road-building efforts of earlier generations of Europeans, many improved ideas and methods in road construction. Yet the impact of the motor vehicle and improved roads outside Europe and North America is slight. In 1962, with more than half the world's population, Asia had only 3 per cent of the world's motor vehicles. Africa and Latin America, with more than a third of the land area of the world, had only 7 per cent of its surfaced roads.

The development of the aeroplane also owes much to the endeavours of both Europeans and Americans. The first important step towards aerial navigation was taken by the French brothers, Joseph and Jacques Montgolfier, when in 1783 they demonstrated the practicability of an air trip by means of a balloon. Their work had been preceded by the Portuguese priest, Father Bartolomeu de Gusmão, who demonstrated his balloon to King John V of Portugal. It was upon the basis of experiments carried out by the Englishmen G. Cayley, W. S. Henson, J. Stringfellow, and H. Maxim, as well as the work of the German O. Lilienthal, the Australian L. Hargrave, and the Americans O. Chanute and S. P. Langley, that the first really successful flight was performed by Wilbur Wright and his brother Orville, at Kitty Hawk, North Carolina, in 1903. The first public flight of a machine heavier than air was that of the Brazilian, Santos Dumont, who in 1904 flew around the Eiffel Tower. The significance of what the Wrights and Dumont had done went largely unnoticed. Further developments followed tardily. Six years passed before, in 1909, the Frenchman L. Blériot achieved the first flight across the English Channel. In 1919 the Britons J. Alcock and Arthur W. Brown first crossed the Atlantic in an aeroplane flying from Newfoundland to Ireland. In 1919 Ross Smith made the first flight from England to Port Darwin in Australia, taking twenty-seven days. American airmen were the first to fly around the world in 1924. Charles A. Lindbergh made his epic solo non-stop flight from New York to Paris in 1927. In 1928 the Australian Charles Kingsford-Smith made the first trans-Pacific flight from California to Brisbane. In 1933 an American, Wiley Post, flew around the world in seven days and eighteen hours. Stimulated by the demands of two World Wars, the aeroplane has been perfected more quickly than any other means of transport.

In improving the system of commercial intelligence, and particularly in providing a more flexible and faster form of transport for the movement of people and high-value freight, the aeroplane has had an enormous effect in the world. It is quite impossible to assess what its effect has been, for instance, in the development of the Australian outback, and the more remote areas of Siberia and the Canadian North. In many parts of the world aircraft have played a vital role in geological survey. They have also broken the traditional pattern of regional isolation. The Americans have exploited commercial air transport more fully than the Europeans, but much of the early pioneering work on new routes and in new areas was conducted by European airlines. British Imperial Airways, for example, developed the air route to East and South Africa, to eastern Asia and Australasia; Royal Dutch Airlines established a route to the East Indies; Air France pioneered the routes to many parts of Africa and Indo-China; the Spaniards, the Portuguese, and the Germans helped to develop the air companies of Latin America. The first successful airline in South America was established in Colombia in 1920 by Austrians and Germans. German influence was also most pronounced in Argentina and Brazil until the outbreak of the Second World War. The first series of internal air flights in Africa were instituted in 1920 by the Belgians between Léopoldville and Stanleyville. By 1932 the British had succeeded in extending a flying-boat service from London down the east coast of Africa to Cape Town. Also during the 1930's, the French commenced a service to French West and French Equatorial Africa. What the aeroplane has meant in terms of military and naval strategy needs no emphasis here. A similar story of joint European-American effort might be told concerning the development of the helicopter and the high-altitude, long-range rocket.

* * *

One of the most dynamic and potent factors in the rise of the modern world has been the revolutionary change brought about in transport and communications. The whole habitable and traversable surface of the planet has been brought together by a system of communications that staggers the imagination. The tiny caravelles which enabled the pioneer mariners of western Europe to make themselves masters of all the oceans have been replaced by the mechanically propelled giant liners and cargo vessels of today; in place of the stage-coach there is the railway and the automobile; the white man's tracks and roadways have pierced every continent; great waterways have been joined together at Suez and Panama; the skies have been conquered. Within the span of a few years there has been conjured up the magic of simultaneous communication provided by telegraph, telephone, wireless transmission, television, and radar. The 'winds of change' are truly electro-magnetic. The white man now probes outer space.

Yet to place undue emphasis upon the more recent and much more spectacular developments in transport and communications is to lose sight of the unparalleled improvements brought by two great agents of European civilization: the steam railway and the steamship. Nothing has equalled the power of steam in the development of a world economy; nothing has affected the life of mankind to a greater extent. It was the steam railway and the steamship (supplemented by the early deep-sea cables) which first conquered distance in such a way as to make it necessary to think in terms of one world. More recent developments in transport and communications have had a more dramatic effect, but it was steam that first caused the shift in the centre of gravity from the nation to the world.

As distance vanishes before the growing marvels of western science and technology, mankind approaches the dawn of a global civilization. Yet the electrifying events of the present day are largely confined to the white world. The network of global communications was built by white men to serve white men's needs; developments which the West takes for granted are for the majority of the world's population still a curiosity. Much of the world has still to reach the bicycle age. The great metal birds that wing their way across the sky, or the voices that splutter and hiss through the ether, remain part of the white man's magic. More than anything else, the barrier that prevents the non-white from hastening in the footsteps of the white man is a social barrier, and men change their social habits so slowly and so reluctantly as to drive their leaders to despair.

TABLES

VI/1 to VI/7

Development of World's Railway Mileage, 1840–1960
(in thousand miles and in percentage of world total)

Continent and Country	First steam line opened	1840 Mileage	1840 %	1860 Mileage	1860 %	1880 Mileage	1880 %	1900 Mileage	1900 %	1920 Mileage	1920 %	1940 Mileage	1940 %	1960 Mileage	1960 %
World	1825	5·49	100·0	66·06	100·0	222·08	100·0	465·91	100·0	674·89	100·0	729·25	100·0	770·06	100·0
Europe[1]	1825	2·54	46·3	30·83	46·7	83·65	37·7	132·23	28·4	159·97	23·7	171·88	23·6	176·74	23·0
Great Britain[2]	1825	1·48	27·0	9·07	13·7	15·56	7·0	18·67	4·0	20·33	3·0	20·23	2·8	18·77	2·4
France	1832	0·26	4·7	5·85	8·9	14·66	6·6	22·87	4·9	25·85	3·8	24·86	3·4	24·15	3·1
Germany	1835	0·34	6·2	7·18	10·9	20·2	9·1	32·29	6·9	35·85	5·3	36·75	5·0	32·79[3]	4·3
Belgium	1835	0·21	3·8	1·05	1·6	2·51	1·1	2·83	0·6	3·05	0·5	3·05	0·4	2·88	0·4
U.S.S.R.[4]	1837	0·02	0·4	0·67	1·0	11·0	5·0	27·65	5·9	44·49	6·6	65·93	9·0	76·77	10·0
North America	1830	2·83	51·5	32·69	49·5	100·46	45·2	211·60	45·4	292·16	43·3	277·11	38·0	262·81	34·1
U.S.A.[5]	1830	2·82	51·4	30·63	46·4	93·27	42·0	193·37	41·5	252·87	37·4	234·18	32·1	218·94	28·4
Canada[6]	1836	0·02	0·4	2·07	3·1	7·19	3·2	18·23	3·9	39·29	5·8	42·93	5·9	43·87	5·7
Latin America	1837[7]	(0·10)[8]	1·8	0·52	0·8	7·15	3·2	34·48	7·4	62·91	9·3	76·48	10·5	85·49	11·1
Mexico	1850	..	..	0·02	n.	0·68	0·3	8·33	1·8	12·99	1·9	14·29	2·0	14·58	1·9
Chile	1851	..	..	0·27	0·4	1·11	0·5	2·71	0·6	5·10	0·8	5·35	0·7	4·81	0·6
Peru	1851	..	..	0·06	0·1	1·26	0·6	1·12	0·2	2·24	0·3	1·72	0·2	1·62	0·2
Brazil	1854	..	..	0·14	0·2	2·11	1·0	9·52	2·0	17·73	2·6	21·28	2·9	23·25	3·0
Argentina	1857	..	..	..	..	1·57	0·7	10·35	2·2	21·18	3·1	25·80	3·5	27·28	3·5
Asia	1853	..	..	0·84	1·3	11·0	5·0	34·74	7·5	62·06	9·2	71·07	9·7	96·92	12·6
India[9]	1853	..	..	0·84	1·3	9·16	4·1	24·75	5·3	36·74	5·4	41·16	5·6	42·26	5·5
Indonesia	1864	..	..	..	..	0·25	0·1	2·23	0·5	3·59	0·5	4·17	0·6	3·79	0·5
Japan	1872	..	..	..	..	0·10	n.	3·92	0·8	6·49	1·0	11·43	1·6	12·68	1·6
Burma	1877	..	..	..	..	..	..	1·35	0·3	1·63	0·2	2·06	0·3	1·86	0·2
China[10]	1883	..	..	..	..	1·35	0·6	1·46	0·3	6·95	1·0	n.a.	n.a.	19·50	2·5
Africa	1854	..	..	0·29	0·4	2·82	1·3	10·44	2·2	27·16	4·0	36·24	5·0	42·15	5·5
Egypt	1854	..	..	0·29	0·4	0·94	0·4	1·39	0·3	1·68	0·2	2·41	0·3	2·95	0·4
South Africa	1860	..	..	n.	n.	1·02	0·5	4·35	0·9	10·12	1·5	13·59	1·9	13·50	1·8
Algeria	1862	..	..	..	..	0·74	0·3	1·87	0·4	2·52	0·4	2·76	0·4	2·53	0·3
East Africa	1897	..	..	..	..	..	..	0·42	0·1	1·87	0·3	3·00	0·4	3·45	0·4
Rhodesia[11]	1897	..	..	..	..	..	..	0·64	0·1	2·14	0·3	2·39	0·3	2·60	0·3
Australasia	1854	..	..	0·21	0·3	4·68	2·1	14·72	3·2	26·14	3·9	30·54	4·2	29·18	3·8
Australia	1854	..	..	0·21	0·3	3·40	1·5	12·51	2·7	23·12	3·4	27·15	3·7	26·15	3·4
New Zealand	1863	..	..	..	..	1·28	0·6	2·21	0·5	3·02	0·5	3·39	0·5	3·03	0·4

n.a. = not available. n. = negligible.

Notes:

General:
The table shows the development of the world's main railways in twenty-year periods.

Mileage (so far as possible) is based on present national boundaries. Because of the difficulty of adjusting earlier mileages to present political boundaries, and the varying definitions as to what constitutes a 'main' railway, the figures are not strictly comparable.

[1] Excluding U.S.S.R.
[2] Ireland not included.
[3] Includes Western and Eastern Germany.
[4] Revised figures of the Ministry of Transport of the U.S.S.R. do not include Finland, Russian Poland, and Manchuria.
[5] Including Alaska.
[6] Including Newfoundland.
[7] Presumably Cuba.
[8] Woytinsky's figure, presumably covering Cuban railways at the time.
[9] Including Pakistan.
[10] Including Manchuria.
[11] Including Bechuanaland.

Sources:

Universal Directory of Railway Officials and Railway Yearbook, 1961/2 (and various earlier issues), London.
Woytinsky, W. S. and E. S., *World Commerce and Governments* (New York, 1955).

Table VI/2

Cost of Inland Transport in Selected Countries, 1800–1960
(In U.S. cents per short ton-mile)

	United Kingdom	*France*	*United States*	*Australia (New South Wales)*	*India*	*Japan*
Road						
1800–20	18–29	..	30–70			
1830's	14–22	5–11	12–17	..	12	
1860's	..	..	..	13[1]	(8)[2]	
Canal						
Early Nineteenth Century	5–7[3]	2–4	(1·7–3·4)[4]			
Railway						
1850	(3–5)[5]	2·2[6]	(4·1)[7]			
1880	2·4[8]	1·7	1·2	4·1	2·0[9]	
1900	2·0[10]	1·3	0·7	2·3	0·9	0·9
1920	2·2	1·2	1·1	1·4	0·8	1·0
1938	2·3	1·7[11]	1·0	2·0	1·0	0·7[12]
1950	2·2	2·1	1·3	1·6	1·0	0·8
1960	3·3	2·5	1·4	3·6	1·1	1·6[13]

Notes:

General: Road and canal figures are mostly approximate. Brackets denote incomplete figures. Railway figures refer to average receipts for goods carried by rail and are from the following dates onwards: U.K. 1820, France 1850, U.S.A. 1870, Australia (New South Wales) 1870, India 1900, Japan 1890.

[1] 1871 figure.
[2] 1861–2 figure for cotton only.
[3] See Jackman.
[4] Erie Canal route, 1830–50.
[5] Yorkshire and Lancashire railways for 1852–3.
[6] 1851 figure.
[7] New York State railways.
[8] 1885 figure.
[9] 1874 figure.
[10] Raper's very rough estimate.
[11] Increase from 1938 partly accounted for by new method of calculation.
[12] 1936–7 figure.
[13] Approximate.

Sources:

Coghlan, T. A., *Wealth and Progress of New South Wales 1900–01* (Oxford, 1902).
Labour and Industry in Australia (Oxford, 1918).
Jackman, W. T., *The Development of Transportation in Modern England* (Cambridge, 1916).
Mulhall, M. G., *Dictionary of Statistics* (London, 1880).
Raper, C. L., *Railway Transportation* (New York, 1912).
Taylor, G. R., *The Transportation Revolution, 1850–1860* (New York, 1951).
Statistical Abstracts of various countries.

Distribution of World Shipping
(*since 1850*)

Area	Net registered tons and percentages						Gross registered tons and percentages[1]					
	1850		*1880*		*1900*		*1913*		*1938*		*1960*	
	'*000 tons*	%	'*000 tons*	%	'*000 tons*	%	'*000 tons*	%	'*000 tons*	%	'*000 tons*	%
U.K.	3,565	39·4	6,575	32·9	9,304	35·5	18,696	39·8	17,781[2]	26·2	21,131	16·3
France	688	7·6	919	4·6	1,029	3·9	2,201	4·7	2,903	4·3	4,809	3·7
Germany			1,182	5·9	1,942	7·4	5,082	10·8	4,244	6·3	4,687[3]	3·6
Netherlands	293	3·2	328	1·6	347	1·3	1,310	2·8	2,855	4·2	4,884	3·8
Norway	298	3·3	1,519	7·6	1,508	5·8	2,458	5·2	4,614	6·8	11,203	8·6
Sweden			503	2·5	614	2·3	1,047	2·2	1,576	2·3	3,747	2·9
Italy			999	5·0	948	3·6	1,522	3·2	3,290	4·8	5,122	3·9
U.S.S.R.			765	3·8	975	3·7	974	2·1	1,281	1·9	3,429	2·6
Rest of Europe[4]	35	0·4	1,208	6·0	2,023	7·7	3,807	8·1	6,306	9·3	12,967	10·0
Europe	4,879	54·0	13,988	69·9	18,691	71·3	37,097	78·9	44,850	66·1	71,979	55·5
U.S.A.[5]	3,485	38·5	4,068	20·3	5,163	19·7	5,429	11·6	11,939	17·5	24,837	19·1
Japan			41	0·2	864	3·3	1,500	3·2	5,007	7·4	6,931	5·3
Rest of World[4]	668	7·4	1,894	9·5	1,486	5·7	2,944	6·3	6,051	8·9	26,023	20·0
World	9,032	100·0	19,992	100·0	26,205	100·0	46,970	100·0	67,847	100·0	129,770	100·0

Notes:

[1] Vessels of more than 100 gross registered tons only. Gross registered tons for steamships, net registered tons for sailing-ships. Sailing-ships of Russia, Japan, Turkey, and Greece, and vessels on the Caspian Sea are excluded.

[2] Including Ireland.

[3] Western and Eastern Germany.

[4] Figures for Rest of Europe and Rest of the World to 1913 are incomplete.

[5] Including the iron vessels on the Great Lakes and the rivers of the U.S.A.

Sources:

Kirkaldy, A. W., *British Shipping* (London, 1914).

League of Nations, Economic Intelligence Service, *Statistical Yearbook 1939/40* (Geneva, 1940).

League of Nations, Economic and Financial Section, *International Statistical Yearbook 1927* (Geneva, 1928).

Lloyd's Register of Shipping, *Statistical Tables 1960*, London.

Mulhall, M. G., *Dictionary of Statistics* (London, 1880).

United Nations, Statistical Office, *Statistical Yearbook 1962* (New York, 1963).

Woytinsky, W. S. and E. S., *World Commerce and Governments* (New York, 1955).

TABLE VI/4

Percentage of Recorded Shipping Fleets accounted for by Steamships, 1860–1913, and Motorships, 1923–60

Area	*Steamships*[1]				*Motorships*[1]		
	1860	*1880*	*1900*	*1913*	*1923*	*1938*	*1960*
U.K.	9·8	41·4	77·5	97·7	2·0[2]	22·8[2]	49·1[2]
France	6·8	30·2	51·3	81·5	0·8	11·9	58·4
Germany	..	18·3	69·4	93·3	3·4	24·6	76·5[3]
Netherlands	2·3	19·6	77·4	98·2	2·6	43·0	62·7
Norway	..	3·8	33·5	76·1	7·5	59·5	85·3
Sweden	..	16·1	53·0	90·2	15·3	44·8	90·1
Italy	..	7·7	39·8	83·7	2·1	28·7	46·9
U.S.S.R.	..	13·3	42·9	81·1	n.a.	26·0	49·5
Europe[4]	7·7	28·7	66·7	93·4	3·0	27·1	60·6
U.S.A.	16·4	29·8	51·5	79·3	0·9	6·3	0·4[5]
Japan	..	66·1[6]	62·9	n.a.	0·1	25·7	69·3
World[4]	10·8	27·3	61·9	91·7	2·1	22·5	43·2

n.a. = not available.

Notes:

[1] Percentages calculated from figures for net registered tons for steamships to 1900, and gross registered tons for steamships 1913 and motorships 1923–60.

[2] Great Britain and Northern Ireland.

[3] Western and Eastern Germany.

[4] Early figures for Europe and World very incomplete.

[5] Including ships of the United States Reserve Fleet.

[6] Figure for 1890.

Sources:

Table VI/3, above.
Whitaker's Almanack 1891, 1901, 1914, 1962.
Lloyd's Register of Shipping, Statistical Tables 1950.
Lloyd's Register of Shipping 1923–4, 1938–9, 1950–1.
League of Nations, Economic Intelligence Service, *Statistical Yearbook 1938/9* (1940).
League of Nations, Economic and Financial Section, *International Statistical Yearbook 1927* (1928).

TABLE VI/5a

Index Numbers of Wholesale Prices and Tramp-shipping Freights

Year	*Wholesale Prices Index*		*Tramp-shipping Freights Index*	
	Isserlis[1] (*1869 = 100*)	*Statist*[2] (*1867–77 = 100*)	*Isserlis* (*1869 = 100*)	*U.K. Chamber of Shipping* (*1935 = 100**) (*1948 = 100†*)
1869	100	98	100	..
1874	104	102	108	..
1879	85	83	85	..
1884	78	76	64	..
1889	73	72	75	..
1894	64	63	58	..
1899	69	68	65	..
1904	71	70	49	..
1909	76	74	46	..
1913	87	85	68	..
1914	87	85	67	..
1919	210	206	490	..
1924	142	139	121	..
1929	117	115	115	..
1934	84	82	85	..
1935	86	84	88	100*[3]
1939	..	95	..	n.a.*[3]
1944	..	160	..	..
1948	..	260	..	100†[4]
1949	..	274	..	82†[4]
1954	..	361	..	95†[4]
1959	..	356	..	80†[4]

Notes:

[1] Based on *The Statist*, London, with 1869 taken as base-year.

[2] Continuing the original calculations of A. Sauerbeck. See *The Economist*, 1843–1943 (Oxford, 1943), pp. 138–54.

[3] The weighted Index Number of Tramp Freights (1935 = 100), issued by the United Kingdom Chamber of Shipping prior to the last war, was discontinued after August 1939.

[4] Index Numbers for 1948, 1949, 1954, and 1959 are based on the Chamber's Revised Index with 1948 as base-year.

Sources:

Chamber of Shipping of the U.K., *Annual Reports 1952–53, 1960–61.*

The Statist, Wholesale Prices in 1939 (part 3, 1940), and in 1960 (part 3, 1961).

Isserlis, L., Tramp Shipping, Cargoes and Freights, *Journal* of the Royal Statistical Society, vol. ci (1938), pp. 53–154. The Sauerbeck index has been published annually in the *Journal* since 1881; also by *The Statist* since 1914.

Table VI/5*b*

Eighty Years' Freight Rates, 1869–1949
(in Sterling currency)

Year	*Coal (per ton)*												*Timber (per standard)*				*Nitrate (per ton)*	
	U.K.–Colombo (or Galle)		*U.K.–Alexandria*		*U.K.–Port Said*		*U.K.–River Plate*		*U.K.–Rio de Janeiro*		*U.K.–U.S.A. or Canada*		*Kronstadt–U.K.*[1]		*Canada–U.K.*		*West South America–U.K.*	
	High	*Low*	*High*	*Low*	*High*	*Low*	*High*	*Low*	*High*	*Low*	*High*	*Low*	*High*	*Low*	*High*	*Low*	*High*	*Low*
	s. d.	*s. d.*	*s. d.*	*s. d.*	*s. d.*	*s. d.*	*s. d.*	*s. d.*	*s. d.*	*s. d.*	*s. d.*	*s. d.*	*s. d.*	*s. d.*	*s. d.*	*s. d.*	*s. d.*	*s. d.*
1869	25 0	22 0	22 7	17 0	24 0[2]	17 0[2]	36 0[3]	30 0[3]	24 0	21 0	..	..	47 6	25 0	75 0	62 6	..	..
1874	31 2½	28 5	22 2	15 7	22 6	15 6	40 0	27 0	33 0	21 0	..	..	57 6	40 0	115 0	80 0	..	..
1879	30 0	23 6	16 0	11 6	15 6	11 6	..	..	..	..	..	..	40 0	30 0	..	..	..	..
1884	21 0	16 6	13 0	7 6	14 0	7 6	..	..	..	..	..	..	45 0[4]	28 0[4]	50 0	45 0	..	..
1889	23 3	17 6	11 0	9 0	12 9	9 9	55 0	43 9	..	..	..	..	42 6	25 0	67 6	60 0	..	..
1894	11 6	8 6	6 6	4 0	6 9	4 3	20 0	15 0	16 0	12 0	..	..	26 0	17 6	45 0	37 6	30 0	27 6
1899	19 0	12 0	12 6	7 6	13 6	7 9	14 3	9 0	14 3	9 0	..	..	42 6	18 0	50 0	42 6	33 9	30 0
1904	10 6	6 9	6 9	4 1	6 4½	4 3	8 0	6 9	10 0	8 0	..	..	30 0	18 6	38 9	33 9	23 0	21 0
1909	9 0	7 0	8 6	4 6	7 0	4 6	14 0	7 0	12 6	8 4½	..	..	30 0	19 0	..	..	22 0	14 9
1913	14 3	9 3	12 6	7 6	13 0	7 0	20 6	14 3	19 6	14 0	..	..	40 0	26 0	..	..	68 0	21 6
1914	21 0	8 6	20 7½	6 10½	21 6	6 9	20 0	11 1½	18 3	11 9	..	..	24 6	23 9	..	..	61 3	16 3
1919	..	..	80 0	47 6	75 0	46 9	60 0	40 0	60 0	42 6	..	..	..	..	380 0	225 0	250 0	200 0
1924	16 6	11 6	14 6	9 6	13 9	9 3	16 0	10 9	14 6	11 3	10 9	6 6	78 0	60 0	80 0	60 0	33 0	23 6
1929	19 0	15 3	14 0	8 9	12 10½	8 6	18 6	11 6	17 0	10 9	15 0	6 6	90 0	60 0	94 0	57 6	31 0	20 0
1934	9 0	8 9	8 6	5 9	8 0	5 9	9 6	8 6	9 0	7 9	9 0	5 6	70 0[5]	40 0[5]	87 6	47 6	20 3	18 0
1939	..	..	25 0	6 0	23 0	6 0	22 0	8 6	22 6	7 6	10 0	5 3	59 6	42 3	145 0	60 0	..	..
1940	..	..	100 0	25 0	35 0	23 6	38 0	27 6	38 0	29 6	12 6	7 6	..	..	375 0	225 0	..	..
1944	..	..	90 0[6]	90 0[6]	90 0[6]	90 0[6]	57 0[6]	57 0[6]	57 0[6]	57 0[6]	10 0[6]	10 0[6]	163 0[7]	156 0[7]	..	..	..	
1949	..	..	31 0	22 6	32 0	21 0	50 0	25 0	45 0	33 9	15 0	10 0	..	..	..	..	102 7	57 6

Notes:

[1] From 1934 to 1939 includes White Sea ports to U.K.
[2] 1870. [3] U.K.–Buenos Aires.
[4] 1883. [5] 1936.
[6] M.W.T. rates (Ministry of War Transport).
[7] Sweden–U.K., 1945.

Eighty Years' Freight Rates, *1869–1949*

(*in Sterling currency*)

Year	Grain (per ton)								Sugar (per ton)						Rice (per ton)		Wool (greasy)	
	River Paraná–U.K.		U.S.A. Atlantic ports–U.K.		U.S.A. Pacific ports–U.K.		Australia–U.K.		West Indies–U.K.		Mauritius–U.K.		Java–U.K.		Burma–U.K.		Australia–U.K. d. per lb.	
	High	Low	High	Low	High	Low	High	Low	High	Low	High	Low	High	Low	High	Low	High[8]	Low[8]
	s. d.	s. d.	s. d.	s. d.	s. d.	s. d.	s. d.	s. d.	s. d.	s. d.	s. d.	s. d.	s. d.	s. d.	s. d.	s. d.		
1869	..	..	29 2	25 8	..	..	..	..	50 0	40 0	..	..	75 0	57 6	72 6	60 0	0·40[9]	
1874	..	..	43 2	28 0	85 0	60 0	..	..	..	..	..	..	115 0[10]	95 0[10]	100 0	82 6	..	
1879	..	..	31 6	23 4	..	..	..	..	..	..	..	..	80 0	60 0	57 6	40 0	0·70[11]	
1884	..	..	25 1	11 8	30 0	27 6	..	..	..	..	..	..	50 0	35 0	47 6	27 6	..	
1889	25 0	18 0	25 8	15 2	40 0	27 6	..	..	..	..	..	..	52 6	42 6	50 0	30 0	0·69	0·44
1894	27 0	14 0	17 6	11 8	28 9	24 6	28 9	23 0	..	..	..	..	35 0	32 6	33 9	26 3	0·44	0·44
1899	31 0	19 0	18 8	10 11	40 0	22 6	33 9	32 6	..	..	..	..	35 0	27 6	33 9	22 6	0·56	0·34
1904	22 0	15 9	12 3	10 6	23 9	14 0	29 0	20 0	..	..	..	..	27 6	22 6	29 0	20 0	0·44	0·44
1909	16 0	7 10½	12 3	7 0	31 3	28 9	27 6	23 0	..	..	..	..	27 6	24 0	24 0	17 6	0·50	0·50
1913	30 6	10 6	18 8	8 2	45 6	29 6	43 9	28 0	..	..	..	..	No fixture		33 0	22 6	0·75	0·75
1914	60 0	9 7½	35 0	8 2	42 6	22 6	31 9	17 6	..	..	..	..	40 0	19 0	32 6	16 3	0·75[12]	
1919	252 6	65 0	81 8	39 8	172 0[13]	90 0[13]	225 0	105 0	..	..	..	..	350 0[14]	170 0[14]	180 0	75 0	0·75	
1924	35 0	19 0	18 8	13 5	41 3	30 0	49 0	30 0	26 6	20 0	30 0	25 0	40 0	27 6	36 3	28 9	1·31[15]	
1929	26 9	11 0	16 4	8 2	33 0	24 0	42 6	22 6	21 6	15 0	26 0	22 6	27 6	17 6	28 9	16 6	1·18[16]	
1934	18 3	13 3	9 4	5 10	21 0	18 3	29 6	21 0	15 0	12 0	18 10½	18 0	..	..	25 0	22 6	1·00	
1939	109 3	19 3	54 3	12 10	57 0	22 3	80 0	33 0	109 3	15 0	..	..	70 0	25 6	50 0	25 6	1·50	
1940	161 4	43 6	110 10	26 5	130 0	57 3	155 0	150 0	130 0	41 0	..	..	160 0	130 0	..	..	1·69	
1944	86 6[17]	82 6[17]	56 0[18]	47 10[18]	110 6[17]	106 6[17]	120 0[17]	95 0[17]	77 6[17]	71 6[17]	..	..	..	..	..	..	1·94	
1949	62 6	..	67 1	29 0	85 0	50 0	100 0	50 0	95 10	52 6	72 6[19]	62 6[19]	..	..	..	..	2·01	

Notes:

[8] 'High' denotes steamers' rate, 'Low' sailing rate.
[9] 1870 (average rate for the year).
[10] 1873. [11] 1880 (average rate for the year).
[12] 1913 onwards — Conference Freight Rates.
[13] 1920. [14] Per ton deadweight. [15] 1·25 plus 5 per cent.
[16] Same as above less 10 per cent. [17] 1945.
[18] 1946. [19] 1948.

Sources:

Angier, E. A. V./Angier Bros. in: *Fair Play Magazine* 1917–50 (various numbers).

Angier, E. A. V., *Fifty Years' Freights 1869–1919* (1920). The only figures published. Where cross-checking with official sources has been possible they were within 3 per cent of accuracy.

Commonwealth of Australia, *Quarterly Summary of Australian Statistics* (various).

TABLE VI/6a

Distance Saved by the Suez and Panama Canals

Suez Canal					*Panama Canal*				
Route		*In Nautical Miles*		*Distance saved (%)*	*Route*		*In Nautical Miles*		*Distance saved (%)*
From	*To*	*via Cape*	*via Suez*		*From*	*To*	*via Magellan*	*via Panama*	
London	Bombay	10,667	6,274	41	Liverpool	San Francisco	13,502	7,836	42
London	Calcutta	11,900	8,083	32	New York	San Francisco	13,135	5,262	60
London	Singapore	11,740	8,362	29	Liverpool	Valparaiso	8,747	7,207	18
London	Hong Kong	13,180	9,799	26	New York	Valparaiso	8,385	4,633	45
London	Sydney	12,690	12,145	4	New York	Hong Kong	16,579	11,539	30
					New York	Sydney	13,000	9,332	29

TABLE VI/6b

Shipping through the Suez and Panama Canals (in millions of net tonnage)[1]

Year	*Suez Canal (opened 17 November 1869)*	*Panama Canal*[3] *(opened 15 August 1914)*	*Year*	*Suez Canal*	*Panama Canal*
1870 . .	0·4	..	1920	16·8	9·4
1880 . .	3·1	..	1930	31·4	30·0
1890 . .	6·9	..	1938	34·4	27·4
1900 . .	9·7	..	1940	13·5	27·3
1910 . .	16·3	..	1950	81·8	28·9
1914 . .	19·4	4·9[2]	1960	185·3	58·3

Notes:

[1] The different systems of measuring net tonnage passing through the Suez and Panama Canals make these figures not strictly comparable.

[2] 1914/15 figure.

[3] Cargo (in millions of long tons).

Sources:

Rabino, J., 'The Statistical Story of the Suez Canal' in *Journal of the Royal Statistical Society* (September 1887), vol. 50, pp. 495–541.

Siegfried, A., *Suez and Panama* (London, 1940).

United Arab Republic, Suez Canal Authority, *Suez Canal Report* (1961).

U.S. Dept. of Commerce, *Historical Statistics of the U.S., Colonial Times to 1957* (1960).

U.S. Dept. of Commerce, *Statistical Abstract of the U.S. 1962.*

Wilson, A. T., *The Suez Canal* (London, 1933).

Some Important Developments in Sea Transport, 1731–1950's

Approximate date	*Technique*	*Usually ascribed to*	*Area of origin*	*Major effects*
1731	Reflecting octant	John Haddley and Thomas Godfrey	United Kingdom United States	Enabled accurate measurement of angles on board ship.
1729–60	Development of marine chronometer	John Harrison	United Kingdom	With its use longitude could now be determined at sea to within half a degree.
1746	*Traité du Navire*	Pierre Bouguer	France	Fundamental work on naval architecture.
1767	Tables of the motion of the moon published in the first *Nautical Almanac*	Johann Tobias Mayer	Germany	First published in Göttingen in 1755, Mayer's tables enabled longitude to be calculated at sea by lunar distance.
1775	British patent for screw propulsion	Samuel Miller and others	United Kingdom	Archimedes' idea put to a new use.
1785	Screw propeller	Joseph Bramah	United Kingdom	Further adaptation of screw principle.
1785	Use of steam jet for shipping	James Rumsey	United States	First known steamboat powered by a jet. Demonstration took place on the Potomac River. John Fitch of the United States ran a steam-driven paddle boat on the Delaware River two years later in 1787.
1787	Use of iron in building the barge *Trial*	John Wilkinson	United Kingdom	One of the earliest known uses of iron in shipbuilding.
1789	Steam propulsion for ships	William Symington and Patrick Miller built Britain's first steamboat.	United Kingdom	Furthered the use of steam propulsion. Success achieved by Symington in 1802.
1795	Establishment of a hydrographical department		United Kingdom	Systematised and made available chart information amassed by outstanding early marine surveyors such as James Cook and Alexander Mackenzie.
1803	Side-paddle steamboat	Robert Fulton	United States	Follows the earlier experiments of J. C. Périer (on the Seine) and the Marquis Jouffroy d'Abbans (on the Saône) in France.
1807	Paddle-steamer *Clermont*	Robert Fulton	United States	First commercially successful steamboat.
1819	Voyage of the *Savannah*		United States	First ship to cross the Atlantic — from Savannah to Liverpool, with auxiliary steam engine.
1821	Iron steamboat (on the Thames) *Aaron Manby*		United Kingdom	One of many experiments taking place at the time.

TABLE VI/7 (*continued*)

Some Important Developments in Sea Transport, 1731–1950's

Approximate date	*Technique*	*Usually ascribed to*	*Area of origin*	*Major effects*
1835	Principles of compass correction	George Biddell Airy	United Kingdom	Necessary for a reliable use of the compass in iron ships.
1836	Practical screw propeller patented	John Ericsson, John Stevens, Francis Pettit Smith and others	Sweden, United States and United Kingdom	First practical application of screw propulsion.
1838	The *Great Western*	Isambard Kingdom Brunel	United Kingdom	Atlantic crossing of the first great ocean steamer.
1848	The *Great Britain*	Isambard Kingdom Brunel	United Kingdom	The first great ocean steamer with screw propellor and iron hull.
1851	A compilation of *Winds and Currents Charts* and Sailing *Directions*; followed in 1855 by *The Physical Geography of the Sea*	Matthew Fontaine Maury	United States	Important scientific study in oceanography. The routes laid down by Maury reduced the sailing time of vessels in many parts of the world.
1850's	Compound engine	John Elder, Alfred Holt and others	United Kingdom	Cut fuel consumption by half.
1862	Paddle steamer *Banshee*		United Kingdom	First steel-hulled vessel to cross the Atlantic. By the end of the century the transition from iron to steel was completed.
1862	Introduction of 'Scotch' marine boiler	Numerous	United Kingdom	Permitted higher pressures than the earlier 'box' boilers.
1871	Triple-expansion engine	Benjamin Normand A. C. Kirk	France United Kingdom	*Aberdeen*, launched in Glasgow in 1881, was the first ship to employ it successfully.
1872	Tide-predicting machine	William Thomson	United Kingdom	Avoided the difficult computation of tide prediction.
1875	Sounding machine	William Thomson	United Kingdom	Enabled soundings to be taken without stopping the ship.
1876	Improvements in the mariner's compass	William Thomson	United Kingdom	Technical improvements which provided more exact and steadier readings.
18[illegible]	Wireless telegraphy	Guglielmo Marconi	Italy	A ship at sea was no longer isolated but had a means of communication.

	Turbinia	Laval		turbine engine soon replaced the reciprocating engine
1903	Caspian steamer *Wandal* launched	Alfred Nobel	Sweden	The first sizeable ship with internal-combustion engine (generating electricity for the main drive).
1908	Practical gyro-compass	Max Schuler, E. A. Sperry, H. C. Ford, and S. G. Brown	Germany, United Kingdom, and the United States	Practical application of the principles enunciated by the French physicist L. Foucault half a century earlier. Replaced existing mariner's compass. Much more stable than ordinary mariner's compass and not affected by magnetic storms.
1924	Radar	Numerous	United States, United Kingdom, and Germany	Radio detection and ranging of reefs, ships, icebergs, aircraft etc. Made navigation safer.
1950's	Use of atomic energy for propulsion. U.S.S. *Nautilus* launched 1954	Numerous	United States and western Europe	Enormously increased the possible range of a vessel and its duration at sea without refuelling.

Chapter VII

THE CHANGING PATTERN OF TRADE

INSEPARABLE from the impact of western civilization was the impact of the western trader. During the past two hundred years the great traders of the world were Europeans. It is they who developed international trade until it embraced not only the luxury items of commerce, but also the indispensable things of daily life.

To some of the less-developed nations of Africa, Asia, and America, trade with Europe, especially during the past century, provided the initial stimulus to their economic development. To the advanced industrial countries in western Europe, as well as to certain regions of other continents, whence Europe obtained growing quantities of food and raw materials, foreign trade became vital to their existence.

Until the expansion of the Portuguese and Spanish empires in the sixteenth century there was very little trade between Europe and the rest of the world. Until the discovery and colonization of the Americas, Europe was largely self-sufficient. There were few things that Europe lacked, even fewer things that it could offer Asia or Africa either as a necessity or a luxury. In the sixteenth century the Spaniards exploited the mineral wealth of the New World, while the Portuguese continued to dominate the spice trade of the East. Only gradually in the seventeenth and eighteenth centuries did new overseas products — chiefly from the new European colonial empires — become principal articles of European trade.

In Asia's trade with Europe, textile products had replaced spices before the end of the seventeenth century. In the middle of the eighteenth century the list of European imports consisted of the more delicate and expensive cottons, as well as a lot of cheap Indian calico prints, chintz, muslins, figured silks, rich brocades, silk carpets, raw cotton and raw silk. Accompanying these products were perfumes, drugs, wines, dried fruits, ginger, sugar and tobacco, tea, coffee, cocoa, slaves, gold and silver, precious stones, ivory, furs, dyes and saltpetre, porcelain and metal work. Most of these items were destined for a relatively small number of wealthy Europeans.

At the beginning of the nineteenth century Europe's chief imports from other continents came primarily from the Americas and the West Indies.

Among the leading items were sugar and tobacco. As Europeans grew in numbers in the nineteenth century and real incomes rose, particularly among the new middle classes, the demand for colonial produce increased. Items of trade such as sugar, tobacco, coffee, tea, and cocoa, unknown to previous generations, came to be regarded as necessities of life.

Cane sugar was brought to Europe from the Atlantic islands by the Portuguese in the sixteenth century and at once began to replace other forms of sweetening (for example, honey). In the sixteenth century the sugar-cane was taken by the Portuguese to Brazil and by the French to the West Indies, becoming the basis of a large plantation industry founded on slave labour. So rapid was the development of the cane-sugar industry in the West Indies in the eighteenth century and so important did the sugar trade become, that at the time of the Treaty of Paris in 1763 some Englishmen considered it more important to retain the sugar-bearing island of Guadeloupe than the whole of Canada.

Growing supplies of raw sugar and improved methods of refining, developed in the eighteenth and nineteenth centuries, placed sugar within the reach of an increasing number of Europeans. Between 1700 and 1760 United Kingdom consumption alone increased sixfold. French refineries were handling twenty million pounds of sugar at the beginning of the eighteenth century. Since then the ability of Europeans to consume growing quantities of cane sugar (supplemented in the nineteenth century by home-grown beet sugar) have exceeded the most liberal earlier estimates. Cane sugar provided two other important articles of trade: molasses and rum. Some idea of the extent of the rum trade in the eighteenth century can be gleaned from the imports of rum into the United Kingdom from Jamaica and other British West Indian islands. These grew from over 600,000 gallons in 1750 to almost 2,000,000 gallons in 1794. The French forbade the distillation of rum in their West Indian colonies because it interfered with their trade in brandy; the Dutch forbade it in their colonies because it interfered with their trade in gin. However, it was one thing to forbid the trade and another thing to stop it. Yankee traders soon took advantage of the lower prices asked for the largely unwanted French and Dutch West Indian molasses, and illicitly distilled rum, and a vigorous and profitable trade sprang up between the West Indies and the North American colonies. In 1769 almost four million gallons of molasses and three million gallons of rum were imported into North America, much of it from non-British colonies. This provided the basis of a triangular trade between the West Indies, North America, and Africa: molasses imported into North America from the West Indies were distilled into rum; this was shipped to Africa where it was exchanged for slaves who were, in turn, sold to the West Indian planters.

British eighteenth- and nineteenth-century legislation, aimed at restricting the molasses and rum trade in the Atlantic to British colonies, also had little effect. Illicit rum-making and illicit rum-trading were too profitable to be stamped out by the edict of any European power. Similarly, the attempts made by European governments to protect the aboriginal people of their colonies from European 'fire-water' (rum, brandy, and gin) were largely disregarded. Highly profitable to the white man, the trade continued; often with disastrous effects upon the native people.

In the nineteenth century the Brazilian, the Cuban, and the Indian — and in the twentieth century the Australian — trade in cane sugar had grown. Until the outbreak of civil war in the late 1950's Cuba led the world in sugar production. This position in 1960 was held by the U.S.S.R. Most Russian supplies, however, are obtained from the beet plant. The supply of beet sugar has grown at such a rate during the past hundred years as to make Europe much less dependent on cane-sugar supplies. In 1960 approximately half the world supply of sugar was obtained from the sugar beet.

Encouraging this seemingly insatiable demand of Europeans for sugar in the nineteenth and twentieth centuries were the new beverages introduced from overseas. Coffee, tea, and cocoa were all known in Europe before the eighteenth century, but it was only then that their use by Europeans became widespread. Coffee was brought to Europe from the Province of Yemen in southern Arabia in the seventeenth century. Famous coffee-houses appeared in the capitals of western Europe. Great businesses, such as Lloyd's Insurance of London, sprang from such origins. In 1607 the coffee plant was introduced into Virginia; in the eighteenth century it was taken by white settlers to Dutch Guiana (1714), to Jamaica (1718), and thence rapidly to many tropical countries. Production eventually became centred in the countries of South and Central America. In the nineteenth century coffee became the most common non-alcoholic drink among the white race everywhere. Only the English prefer tea, in spite of their early historical preference for coffee. The North Americans have increased their consumption of coffee greatly since the Second World War. But the rest of the world did not consume much more coffee in 1960 than in 1913. The trade has been expanded in recent years in Colombia, Mexico, and Central American republics, and in French, Belgian, and Portuguese territories in Africa.

The habit of tea-drinking, first introduced from China to Europe by the Dutch in the early seventeenth century, also grew rapidly in the eighteenth and nineteenth centuries. In 1650 it was taken by the English to America (British attempts to tax American imports of tea helped to rouse the colonists to rebellion). In 1664 the directors of the English East India Company presented Charles II with 2 lb. of tea; tea was evidently at that time a present fit for a king. In the eighteenth century America, which had started as a nation of tea-drinkers, became a nation of coffee-drinkers;

England, a nation of coffee-drinkers, became a nation of tea-drinkers. By 1790 the British were consuming between seven and eight thousand tons of tea annually. The establishment of the great British tea plantations in India and Ceylon in the nineteenth century encouraged British tea consumption. The British introduced the cultivation of the tea plant into Upper Assam in the 1830's. In the 1870's tea replaced coffee (which had been destroyed by rust) in Ceylon. Between the 1840's and 1900 tea cultivation had also been extended by the white man to parts of Africa, Europe, and the Americas. China has remained the greatest producer of tea; India and Ceylon, however, continue to be the greatest exporters. The United Kingdom remains the greatest consumer.

Cocoa was brought to Europe from the West as early as coffee and tea reached Europe from the East, but as a drink it never became as popular. However, consumption of cocoa among the nations with the highest incomes has increased considerably in the present century. The United States and the United Kingdom take about half the world supplies. For parts of West Africa cocoa production is a vital industry. Cocoa accounted for 86 per cent, by value, of Ghana's exports in 1960.

The physical harm done to the American aborigines by the sale of English rum, French brandy, and Dutch gin has been more than offset by the physical harm done by American tobacco to Europeans. This is all the more remarkable when it is remembered that it was thought by the Indians — and many Europeans — to possess medicinal properties. First cultivated by white settlers in Santo Domingo in 1531, tobacco was introduced to Europe (France) in 1556. The use of tobacco throughout Europe grew rapidly. White settlers introduced the plant to Cuba in 1580; Jamestown, Virginia 1612; Maryland 1631. Tobacco facilitated the trade relations between the early English colonists of New England and the mother country. In 1724, 4,000,000 pounds of tobacco entered one British port alone (the Clyde). Since then the rate of consumption has increased steadily and the plant has been introduced by Europeans to many parts of the world. Yet most European governments resisted the introduction of the 'cursed weed', and every kind of punishment, including the death penalty, was decreed for those who persisted in the 'filthy, stinking habit of smoking'. No weed ever flourished under repression as tobacco has done. Unable to suppress the trade, European governments eventually compromised with their consciences either by taking over the entire tobacco manufacturing industry or making tobacco a principal source of state revenue, or by doing both.

Of greater consequence in the world, and especially of greater consequence to the development of European industry during the past hundred years, was the growth during the nineteenth century of international trade in agricultural produce and raw materials. Whereas in the fifteenth and sixteenth centuries the spice trade had been the source of wealth in international commerce, and had later been displaced by the growing demand for colonial products, the period after 1850 is marked by the growing trade in the bulky articles of commerce: grain, minerals, raw textile materials, timber, and perishable commodities like fruit and meat. Most dramatic has been the increase in the production of non-ferrous minerals, from an estimated 48,000 tons in 1800 to more than 100 million tons in 1960 (excluding some non-ferrous minerals such as gold, silver, platinum, mercury, uranium, and beryl). As the tide of white settlement flowed across many parts of the world, growing quantities of these items of trade were sent to Europe from the United States, as well as from Australia, India, Canada, and Argentina. Relatively speaking it did not require much capital to finance the movement of earlier luxuries in trade, but once the western European nations — especially Britain — came to rely upon the natural resources of other continents they were compelled to make large capital investments.

Not only did the staples of commerce change in the nineteenth century, but from the 1850's onwards, as the world shrank and communications improved, world rather than national or local prices came to predominate. Articles produced under such diverse conditions as those prevailing in Europe, America, Asia, and Africa brought approximately the same prices in Europe. This was true of wheat, cotton, wool, rubber, copper, oils, tea, coffee, and sugar: for all these articles the world became one market. It was this kind of trade, and the investments and transport facilities that accompanied it, that provided the most effective stimulus to the economic development of the rising parts of the world.

One of the items that came to dominate inter-continental trade in the half-century after 1850 (and which, like the earlier trade in spices and colonial products, came to be taken for granted) was the trade in wheat and other grains. Only then did the supply of wheat to Europe become practically continuous — arriving in increasing quantities from Australia, Argentina, India, the Middle West of America, and Canada.[1] Whether it was produced under the most primitive conditions, as in Russia and India (with high-cost, intensive methods), or with the aid of the most elaborate labour-saving machinery, as on the great plains of North America (low-cost, extensive methods), it largely brought the same price on the European markets. The United Kingdom, which had undergone rapid industrialization and urbanization, became particularly dependent upon foreign supplies of grain. In 1850, the United Kingdom took 5 million bushels of grain from North America; in 1880, stimulated by growing British numbers, by the advancing American frontier, by transport improvements,

[1] These changes are discussed by W. Malenbaum, *The World Wheat Economy, 1885–1939* (Cambridge, Mass., 1954).

and by the more economical mechanical methods employed in grain production, this figure had increased to 92 million bushels, and the demand was still growing. The wars in the Crimea (1856), in North America (1861–4), and in France (1870) only delayed the impact which these new supplies of grain would eventually have upon the European economy. As world production increased, the price of wheat dropped from about $1·50 a bushel in 1871 to 86 cents in 1885; general business instability and the dramatic fall in freight charges from the Americas, Australia, and Asia encouraged the downward movement. The most rapid expansion of United States wheat production occupied the period 1866–90. Russian exports of grains grew from an annual average of about 41 million bushels between 1851 and 1860 to more than 107 million bushels in 1889. By 1913 they averaged 164 million bushels annually. On the eve of the First World War, as the internal demands of the United States grew, and the relative fertility of its soil declined, Russian supplies came to exceed those of North America. In contrast to the American people who could afford to eat the wheat they were growing, industrializing Russia, hard pressed to find enough foreign currency to finance its development, was forced to sell an increasing quantity of wheat and subsist on cheaper rye.

In the twenty-five years between 1913 and 1938 European wheat imports fell from an average of 555 million bushels to 350 million bushels (Europe's share of world imports of wheat fell from 77 per cent to 57 per cent). As regards imports, the First World War had encouraged home production in western Europe, and the number of Europeans grew less quickly in this period; also consumption was probably curtailed by the great depression in trade and industry in the late twenties and the early thirties. As regards exports, those of the United States declined, while those of Canada, Argentina, and the U.S.S.R. increased. At the time of the outbreak of the Second World War Canadian exports of wheat (and flour) led the world with about 200 million bushels of wheat annually. Argentina's foreign trade in wheat at the time (1940) was about 150 million bushels; the figure for the United States and Australia was about 100 million bushels. Since the Second World War the quantity of wheat imported into Europe has remained well above the pre-war level. Europe's share of world imports of wheat, however, has continued to decline from 49 per cent (466 million bushels) in 1951–2 to 37 per cent (517 million bushels) in 1960–1. Europe's population continued to grow at a slower rate than that of areas in South America (i.e. Brazil) and Asia (i.e. India and Japan), where wheat imports have doubled in the post-war period. There has also been a change in consumer tastes. It is a common experience that as incomes rise people eat less bread and relatively more meat; the higher standards of living resulting from post-war prosperity in Europe have encouraged this trend.

With the revolution in 1917 Russian exports of wheat almost ceased. They were replaced in part, in the inter-war years, by the supply of grain from North America, Argentina, and Australia. Canada became the world's major exporter, to be replaced after the Second World War by the United States. Canada remains, however, the largest exporter of grain to Europe. While the world demand for wheat continues at a high level the grain trade does not contribute as much to the economic development of overseas areas as it did in the closing decades of the nineteenth and the early decades of the present century when the great wheat belts of the world were being developed.

The United Kingdom has always been the chief market in the world for imported meat, and Europe's growing demand for the meat and dairy produce of other continents is largely a British story. In 1913 the United Kingdom took over 80 per cent of world exports, and, while the figure is not so high today, United Kingdom purchases still predominate. Live cattle were brought from the Americas to Europe in the 1860's and 1870's. Only with the development of refrigeration at the beginning of the 1880's, did important quantities of meat and dairy produce enter international commerce. The creation of artificial winter conditions in the meat-packing houses of the Americas and the Antipodes meant that the industry could operate all the year round. Between 1873 and 1896, encouraged by the downward trend of world prices, by the growth of the trade in by-products, as well as by the growth of world supplies and the improvements in land and sea transport, the world prices of meat declined by about a quarter. The United States was the leading meat supplier until the end of the nineteenth century. Exports of frozen meat from the United States grew from just over a thousand hundredweights in 1874, to one and one-third million hundredweights of 'chilled' meat in 1899. By 1900, however, Argentina, Australia, and New Zealand had gained importance as world suppliers of meats. Because of the long journey, meat from the Antipodes had to be frozen. While Europe's demands for meat in the closing decades of the nineteenth century had a considerable effect upon the development of the American mid-west, the overall impact was probably greater on the smaller and much less diversified economies of Argentina and New Zealand.

World trade in agricultural raw materials, such as cotton and wool, also grew in importance in the nineteenth century. Since early times, small quantities of raw cotton were obtained by Europe from the Levant and Asia. With the discovery of the Americas, West Indian cotton was added. Europe had no suitable area large enough for cotton growing, and the Turks were reluctant to develop the industry in Asia Minor. Russian cotton, largely obtained from Asiatic Russia, has only become of world significance during the past thirty years. In these circumstances, Europe came to rely upon the cotton-growing regions of the United States. But the clash between the Northern and Southern States in the 1860's caused a world-wide cotton famine and forced European nations to seek alternative supplies. Additional quantities were obtained from India, the West Indies, Guiana, Natal, Australia, the Ottoman Empire (especially Egypt), Brazil and other regions. The cotton famine of the 1860's also gave an impulse to scientific agriculture in the tropical and semi-tropical areas of British India and parts of Africa, especially in the Sudan and Egypt. Indian cotton has become available in increasing quantities in the present century, but the United States remains the largest single supplier to Europe and the world. Unlike wool, almost two-thirds of the world's cotton is produced in the Northern Hemisphere. This means that the bulk of the supply comes on the world market in the second half of the calendar year, which has important bearing on market conditions.

The extraordinary growth of the European textile industry in the nineteenth century, with the consequent demand for raw cotton, resulted in important economic and social changes in the United States; changes that were partly responsible for the American Civil War. With the rise of other great cotton-growing areas in the present century, however, as well as the relative decline of textile manufactures in the United Kingdom, the United States no longer provides the majority of raw cotton on world markets, any more than Lancashire provides the majority of cotton cloth sold in world trade. The cotton industry of the world continues to grow, but it grows at a faster rate in the more recently industrialized countries (particularly in Japan) than in the older ones, and it draws its supplies from other areas of production. In 1935 the United States produced 10·6 million out of a world production of 27·5 million bales. In 1960 the figures were 14·3 out of a world production of 47·5 million bales.

Cotton became king in the nineteenth century because of the growth of industrialization and the factory production of textiles. Producing practically no cotton of its own, Europe was entirely dependent upon foreign cotton. The tremendous development of man-made polymers during the past two decades, however, coupled with the rise of the cotton and other consumer-goods industries in non-western nations, have caused raw cotton to have a declining importance in European imports. Yet raw cotton remains one of the most important commodities in world trade: it is still the leading textile raw material and in this respect it is still king.

The mechanization of the European woollen industry proceeded more slowly than that of cotton. Only in the second half of the nineteenth century did the woollen industry completely outstrip the domestic supply of wool. Yet Australia was competing seriously with Spanish and German wool in the 1830's; by 1850 Australia supplied half of Britain's total imports. Between 1870 and 1895 wool from the Antipodes had become the mainstay of the British woollen industry. In 1850 Britain imported a total of 74 million lb. of raw wool (39 million from Australia, 9 million from Germany). By 1900 British imports of wool had increased tenfold. To a lesser degree the same is true of the continental countries. Germany, having by the 1830's exceeded Spain in wool production, had, by the 1850's, been displaced by Australia. In 1913 half the world's wool supply was drawn from Australia and New Zealand; over the years, the breeding of stock and the quality and weight of the fleeces had been greatly improved. In 1960 Australia dominated the world supply, with 47 per cent of the total; New Zealand followed with 18 per cent, Argentina 11 per cent, and the Republic of South Africa 8·5 per cent. Sheep flocks in Europe today are kept largely for their meat rather than their wool.

Europe's demand for wool had a different impact upon world development than the impact resulting from Europe's demand for cotton. Sheep could be grazed on the largely unoccupied grasslands of the Southern Hemisphere with relatively little labour and moderate capital outlay. The history of Australia, New Zealand, Argentina, and South Africa, where land was plentiful and labour and capital scarce, shows that wool was the ideal pioneering industry of the first white settlements in these regions.

* * *

A study of European foreign trade during the past two centuries reveals the importance of agricultural produce and raw materials. In the 1870's the value of international trade in primary produce was over 70 per cent higher than in manufactured goods. By 1960, however, with the development of industrialization, only about 40 per cent of the volume of world trade consisted of primary produce. Compared with manufactured goods, the volume of world trade in primary produce has, in fact, shown a slower rate of growth for the past thirty years. Movements in this trade are traced in the following table:

World Trends in Production and Trade, 1876–1959
Index Numbers 1913 = 100

Period	*Production*		*Trade Volume*		*Trade Unit Value (in terms of current U.S. dollar)*	
	Manufactures	*Primary produce*	*Manufactures*	*Primary produce*	*Manufactures*	*Primary produce*
1876–80	25		31	31	102	104
1896–1900	54	76 (1900)	54	62	82	77
1911–13	95	93	94	97	98	98
1926–30	141	123	113	123	145	128
1936–8	158	135	100	125	120	93
1948–50	238	156	132	116	233	259
1957–9	381	203	251	182	259	257

Adapted from A. Maizels, *Industrial Growth and World Trade* (Cambridge, Eng., 1963), p. 80.

The exports of primary produce from industrialized countries during most of the past decade have risen at a faster rate than the exports of primary produce from non-industrialized countries.

The declining importance of primary produce in international trade was to be expected as European industrial ideas were taken up by non-Europeans. The First World War, by interrupting the supply of European goods to eastern markets, and by providing the stimulus of war demands, hastened the growth of the factory system elsewhere. Eventually, other continents were able to challenge the industrial predominance which Europe had held since the seventeenth century. The greatest development of manufactures after 1919 took place in the United States, but industrialization grew elsewhere, especially in the U.S.S.R., Japan, India, China, and Australia. No other eastern country equalled the speed of Japan in adopting European techniques of machine production, commerce, and finance. Japan's exports of manufactures increased sharply during and after the First World War, particularly in the easily imitable textile industry — the mainstay of Britain's exports since the eighteenth century. In 1924 Britain exported almost 4·5 billion yards of cotton goods; Japan exported less than 1 billion yards. By 1936 Britain's exports had declined to less than 2 billion yards, while Japanese exports had expanded to approximately 2·75 billion yards. Among all the European nations, Britain was hardest hit by the subsidized competition of the newly established eastern industries. By the Second World War Asian industrial development had spread from certain staples such as textiles into almost every field of manufacture.

While the composition of world trade has undergone important changes since the eighteenth century, the geographical distribution remains largely what it was: with Europe, the Americas, and, to a lesser extent, Asia, as the main participants. In 1960, western Europe and North America accounted for almost two-thirds of world trade. Western European nations accounted for 40 per cent, in value, of the world total. The rise of the United States and Japan since the First World War has done something to reduce European predominance, but trade with Europe, including that with the Soviet Union whose industrial capacity and exports of machinery and equipment have grown steadily since 1945, remains of overwhelming importance to many countries. For two hundred years Europe has been the chief consumer of the world's surplus foods and raw materials. It has also remained the principal market for its own manufactures, as well as those of other industrialized countries. If the ten leading exporters of manufactured goods in 1960 are compared with those of 1900, the United Kingdom, Germany, and France appear within the first four nations on both occasions. Of the remainder, the most important are Japan and Canada, both of which have made considerable progress since 1900 as the following table shows:

The Ten Leading Exporters in Manufactures, 1899–1960
(per cent of total of these countries)

	1899	1913	1929	1937	1950	1960
United Kingdom	33·8	30·6	23·8	22·4	25·7	16·7
U.S.A.	11·5	13·0	21·4	20·3	29·9	22·5
France	15·1	12·7	11·1	6·1	10·3	10·1
Germany	23·2	27·5	21·9	23·4	7·5	20·2
Belgium	5·8	5·1	5·8	6·1	6·1	6·2
Italy	3·5	3·5	3·8	3·6	3·9	5·4
Sweden	0·9	1·5	1·8	2·6	2·8	3·2
Switzerland	4·2	3·2	2·9	3·0	4·2	3·5
Canada	0·3	0·7	3·4	5·0	6·2	5·0
Japan	1·6	2·5	4·1	7·5	3·5	7·2

Adapted from A. K. Cairncross, *Factors in Economic Development* (London, 1962), p. 235.

The figures given above do not account for the total of world trade in manufactures during this period.

In 1960 manufactures and machinery accounted for 73 per cent of the total exports of the United States. The figures, by value, for West Germany and the United Kingdom were 86 and 88 per cent respectively. Belgian exports, principally of manufactures, in 1960 were 72 per cent; Austria 57 per cent; France 56 per cent; Switzerland 52 per cent; Italy 51 per cent; Norway 41 per cent, and the Netherlands 40 per cent. In the case of Belgium, the Netherlands, Norway, and Switzerland (the United States and India are other examples) manufactures were the leading import as well as the leading export in 1960.

* * *

Until the First World War the growth and expansion of world trade was largely a European story. Between 1750 and 1913 European trade is estimated to have increased from about $500 million to approximately $23,700 million. The expansion was at its greatest during the period 1820–80 when it increased in value nearly nine times. The volume of world trade continued to increase almost continuously from 1876 until 1913. Between 1904 and 1913 its value doubled. In 1913, Europe, including Russia, took 61·5 per cent (by value) of the world's imports and accounted for 55·2 per cent of the world's exports. By the First World War the system of international specialization had been carried by Europe to a higher level of perfection than the world had ever known. Under European leadership the foundations of a world-wide trading and financial system, in which national boundaries played little part, were laid. (Table VII/12.)

It has been the purpose of the other chapters in this book to show that the astonishing impact which Europe had on the development of world commerce in the period 1750–1914 was due to many causes. The Spanish and Portuguese explorations of the fifteenth and sixteenth centuries widened the European horizon immensely. Yet it was only during the nineteenth century, with the growth in the number of Europeans and their needs, as well as the extraordinary developments that took place in European agricultural, industrial, and transport technology, that world commerce grew rapidly, far outstripping the increase in the world's population. Underlying the whole movement was the willingness of Europeans to invest their savings in foreign lands, as well as their ability to devise an adequate international monetary policy. By the 1870's the gold standard had become a yardstick of value of many currencies; a newly evolved system of international law further assisted world commerce. Areas that had previously been closed to trade became accessible; with the collapse of the Spanish and the Portuguese empires in the Americas, in the early decades of the nineteenth century, the door to Latin American trade was thrown open. In the 1840's and 1850's European trade was forced upon the Chinese and the Japanese people. As the political and social thinking of many European leaders underwent a change in the nineteenth century the bonds that had restricted the flow of world trade were loosened, and a new emphasis was placed upon the interdependence of the wealth of nations. Although much more limited in its effect than English authors have led us to believe, the liberalizing of trade in the nineteenth century tended to concentrate world production in those areas with the greatest natural advantages, and thus secured a better allocation of world resources.

As Table VII/12 shows, leadership in world trade has remained in the hands of the British for two centuries or more. By the eighteenth century the influence of the nations of the Iberian peninsula had begun to wane. Holland then played a leading part in trade with its flourishing mercantile marine and abundance of accumulated capital. But the Dutch lacked the necessary military power and sufficient manufacturing industries to take the lead. France, although second to Britain as a trading nation for most of the nineteenth century, spent its strength in the quest for European military supremacy rather than for world markets. In the absence of rapid industrial change France never became as dependent on world trade as Britain did. Germany's star only rose in the closing decades of the nineteenth century. It was only then that Germany, stimulated by political unity and by the growth in population and manufacturing industry, which necessitated a great increase in the imports of industrial raw materials and foods as well as in the exports of manufactured products, replaced France as the second greatest European trading nation. So rapid was Germany's development that by 1913 its share in world trade amounted to about 13 per cent, against Britain's 17 per cent. Yet neither the challenge from Germany nor (until very recent times) from the United States was strong enough to displace Britain from its position as the leader of world trade, finance, and investment. Contrary to the experience of other European powers, the bulk of whose trade was centred within Europe itself, Britain's trade was dispersed over the whole world. Unlike an almost self-sufficient Russia, whose influence until recently on the evolution of a system of world trade was negligible, Britain stood to lose most from the catastrophe that overtook Europe with the outbreak of the First World War.

The First World War halted a limited and short-lived attempt on Europe's part to improve international economic integration. The stimulus given by the Old World to the New, through its trading relations, was greater in the nineteenth century than it was before or has been since. Most important was the stimulus given to the economic development of white settlements overseas.

The following table traces the volume of world and European trade in the period 1913–38:

		1913		1929		1932		1938	
		World	*Europe*	*World*	*Europe*	*World*	*Europe*	*World*	*Europe*
IMPORTS:	Value in $billion	20·8	12·8	35·6	19·8	14·0	7·9	24·2	13·6
	%	100·0	61·5	100·0	55·5	100·0	56·2	100·0	56·3
EXPORTS:	Value in $billion	19·8	10·9	33·0	16·1	12·9	6·6	21·9	10·6
	%	100·0	55·2	100·0	48·8	100·0	51·1	100·0	48·2
TOTAL:	Value in $billion	40·6	23·7	68·6	35·9	26·9	14·5	46·1	24·2
	%	100·0	58·4	100·0	52·4	100·0	53·9	100·0	52·2

Sources: W. S. and E. S. Woytinsky, *World Commerce and Governments* (1955).
League of Nations, *The Network of World Trade* (1943).
League of Nations, *Europe's Trade* (1941).

From a peak in 1929, just before the great depression in world trade and industry, the total value of world trade fell from $68·6 to $26·9 billion in 1932; there was a recovery before the outbreak of the Second World War, but the total in 1938, $46·1 billion, was not very much higher than it had been in 1913. If we allow for the inflation of prices that had taken place between 1913 and 1938 there was little real growth in world commerce between the wars. As the above table shows, percentage-wise, Europe's share of world trade declined throughout the period 1913–38. The share of other continents in European trade in 1938 was as follows: Asia 10 per cent of Europe's imports, and roughly an equal percentage of its exports; North America 7 and 14 per cent respectively; Latin America 6 and 7 per cent; Africa 9 and 7 per cent; the figures for Oceania are in the region of 4 and 5 per cent.

Europe's declining influence in the expansion of world trade between the two World Wars can be put down to the less stimulating general conditions prevailing in the 1920's and the 1930's. In the post-war period the economic progress which took place in Europe did not provide the same stimulus to world trade as earlier developments had done. And when Europe stagnated in the late twenties and early thirties many regions of the world also stagnated. As for the industrial and commercial developments in Japan, Russia, and China in the inter-war years, these sprang more from the expansion of the home economy than from international trade. In addition, the impact of international migration upon the development of world trade was smaller in the inter-war years; European numbers were growing at a relatively slower rate; Europe's agricultural, industrial, and scientific superiority was lessening; and while the globe had continued to shrink, as improved transport and communications were introduced, the new forms of transport — spectacular as some of them were — did not stimulate world trade as the initial application of steam to land and sea transport had done during the nineteenth century. Of equal significance were the changes taking place in the interwar years in international investment and monetary policy. Britain, the nineteenth-century leader in world trade and investment, no longer found itself with vast quantities of wealth available for investment elsewhere. The First World War had markedly reduced Britain's holdings of foreign securities, and left it heavily in debt to the United States. The almost universal pre-war gold standard had collapsed, and the free conversion of currencies had become impossible for most nations.

While there was little recognition in the immediate post-First World War years of the essential change that had taken place, the War had undermined Europe's position as the financial centre of the world; and without adequate finance trade could not prosper. The Bank of England even tried to resume its nineteenth-century role as the controlling agency in the international capital market, and took the initiative in arranging reconstruction loans when the war ended. Long-term lending by Britain, France, and, to a smaller extent, by Belgium, the Netherlands, and Switzerland was renewed. Sweden also emerged as a creditor country. The chief borrowers were Germany inside Europe, and Argentina, Australia, and Canada outside Europe. But only the United States possessed the financial resources needed in the post-war period. As that country assumed some of the responsibilities of the world's greatest creditor nation there began to flow from America to Europe a succession of loans and gifts (charity and business have been inextricably linked) which is without parallel, and which has continued until the present day. Important loans were made immediately after the war and during the reconstruction period of the 1920's. Until the onset of the commercial crisis of 1929 considerable investments were made in Europe, Latin America, and the Caribbean.

Possibly, the efforts made by the United States in the inter-war years to improve international economic integration, and thus restore the flow of world trade, did not equal the spontaneous forces that had worked to this end during the nineteenth century. American loans in the inter-war years were never as large or as significant in influencing international development as was the free flow of capital from Britain and other western European nations during the nineteenth and the early part of the twentieth century. They were neither as complementary to the home economy, nor as integrated with world movements in trade and migration as European investments had been. In some respects, the vast flow of credit from the United States in the years 1925–9 concealed the essential instability of post-war Europe. The reduction of these funds in the late twenties precipitated the crisis and financial panic which spread over Europe in 1930–1, and caused the further collapse of the international marketing system. Moreover, the fact that most of the European and Latin American investments were eventually lost made American private investors reluctant to repeat the experiment immediately after the Second World War. Doubtless Europe would have had its share of economic problems if the First World War had never been fought, or the American continent had never been discovered. But the emergence since 1918 of an almost self-sufficient United States economy (with a far greater capacity to sell than to buy) introduced a structural change in the trade relations between Europe and the rest of the world more difficult of solution than the temporary dislocation of the First World War.

The First World War is the point in history where the hope of establishing a world economic community with Europe at its head began to fade. Henceforth, as severe restrictions were placed upon the movement of labour, capital, and merchandise, the pleas for renewed and closer international economic co-operation went unheard in the growing clamour of national interests. Commerce became increasingly an implement of international power politics and a tool of national vested interests. The national barriers impeding the flow of world trade, that had been removed in the second half of the nineteenth century, were quickly re-erected. Autarchy became rampant.

The abandonment of economic liberalism by European countries in the 1920's and 1930's, was forshadowed by events in the nineteenth century. The rise of exaggerated German nationalism, and the political and military rivalry which grew up between France and Germany after the war of 1870, had strengthened the anti-liberal forces at work in Europe. The trend was further encouraged by the severe trade depression of the 1870's, and the rise of American economic power. Even before the catastrophe of the First World War the tide of economic liberalism had spent itself. By then only Britain, Belgium, Finland, Denmark, and Turkey, and for certain products, Switzerland and Norway, adhered to 'free trade' principles. The conflicts and revolutionary upheavals which followed the First World War — not least the political tensions resulting from the dismemberment of the Russian and Austro-Hungarian empires — further undermined the pre-war European trading system. The introduction of quotas, embargoes, and bilateral trade agreements, made ordinary tariff barriers of secondary importance. Britain's return to the gold standard in 1925 made some people think that the pre-1914 process of international trade was returning. But each country continued to safeguard its own interests at the expense of the rest. Many countries could do little else. At the Geneva Conference on Trade in 1927, at the Conference of Danubian States in 1931, and at the World Economic and Monetary Conference in 1933, hopes were expressed that the trend toward economic self-sufficiency and autarchy would be halted. As if to offset the unfavourable impression created by the Hawley Smoot Tariff of 1930 — the highest in United States history — and the refusal to take a leading part in the World Economic Conference in 1933, the United States introduced the Trade Agreement Act of 1934 which began a reduction of its tariff levels. But so great was the balance of payments problem among the western nations at this time that this gesture passed almost unnoticed. Even the British, who had struggled to keep an element of freedom in their trade policies longer than any other country, were forced to protect themselves from the trade of other nations in 1933. This year saw the coming to power in Germany of the Nazi Party. In Russia the Bolsheviks (who had come to power in 1917) were totally opposed to western European capitalist principles of international trade and competition. These events, resulting in the Second World War, were to jeopardize the foundations of European civilization.

In 1939 Europe was plunged into a second and more disastrous World War. In 1945 there emerged from the struggle an impoverished and divided Europe. And not only was the European house divided among itself; the whole world was ranged into hostile political camps. Peace and prosperity seemed as illusive as they had ever been. Yet world commerce was not to be stifled. In the years 1945–60 there was an extraordinary growth (in real and monetary terms) in world trade. Equally as remarkable as the spectacular revival in the exchange of goods between all parts of the world, has been the general liberalizing of trade that has taken place with the help of many international agencies; great regional trading blocs, the best-known being the European Economic Community, have also appeared.

In 1947 the value of world exports was $48·2 billion, which may be compared with the figures for 1913: $40·6 billion, and for 1938: $21·9 billion. In the immediate post-war period the decline in Europe's exports was offset by the increase in the exports of the United States and Canada. Europe's share in the world's total value of exports in 1937 was 45·9 per cent, which fell to 33·2 per cent in 1947. North America's share, on the other hand, rose from 17·1 in 1937 to 36·1 per cent in 1947. Since then, as the accompanying table shows, Europe has improved its position considerably. Europe's share of world trade in 1960 was 52·9 per cent; its share of world exports 51·8 and of world imports 53·9 per cent. The United States, however, is today the world's leading trading nation.

Growth of World Trade
and the respective shares of Europe, the U.S.A., and Canada
(in billions U.S. $)

Year	*World*		*Europe*[1]		*U.S.A.*		*Canada*	
		%		%		%		%
1948	120·7	100·0	51·0	42·3	19·7	16·3	5·7	4·7
1952	166·5	100·0	75·1	45·1	25·9	15·6	8·4	5·1
1956	211·2	100·0	102·3	48·4	31·8	15·0	10·6	5·0
1960	262·5	100·0	138·9	52·9	35·5	13·5	11·2	4·3

[1] Western and Eastern.

Source: United Nations, *Statistical Yearbook*, 1962.

Europe's resurgence since the end of the war springs not from an economic miracle, but from the willingness of Europeans to meet a desperate economic situation by uniting to stimulate production and the consequent flow of trade. If that spirit prevails — especially if the 'iron curtain' which divides one half of the European family from the other can be drawn aside — European and world trade must prosper.

While Europe's recovery since 1945 is largely due to its own exertions, it would be ungenerous not to record the contribution made by the United States as the world's leading creditor nation. Since the early days of the Second World War, European (and to a lesser extent, Asian, African, and Latin American) living standards have been subsidized by the foods, raw materials, and capital equipment supplied on credit or given by the United States. Some of this aid has inevitably got into the wrong hands; some of it has not had the result it set out to achieve; yet, without it, the post-war world would certainly have been a poorer place for many people. There has been Lend-Lease, military occupation costs, relief and rehabilitation grants, loans from the Export–Import Bank and the American Treasury, and loans and grants from the Economic Co-operation Administration. International institutions, such as the International

Bank and the International Monetary Fund, have also acted as channels through which dollars have flowed to Europe. One of the most important experiments in world history was the Marshall Plan, introduced by the United States in 1947, and devised to enable western Europe, as well as the world, to recover from the worst effects of the Second World War. A conservative estimate of the total net outflow of credit from the United States to Europe since the First World War would be close to $1,000,000,000. A breakdown of financial aid provided by the United States in the decade 1948–58 is as follows: military $36 billion, government spending $28 billion, government loans $5 billion, private investments $15 billion.

Extraordinary as Europe's recovery in trade has been during the past decade and a half, it should not be allowed to conceal the significant change that has taken place in these years in the direction of European trade. In the half-century after 1850 there was a growing volume of trade between the developing and the developed countries, whereas the chief stimulus to world trade today is among the so-called developed industrial nations. As far as Europe is concerned, the volume of intra-European trade has always been more important than intercontinental trade. It still is. The significant feature about developments since the end of the Second World War is that it is intra-European trade that is growing most rapidly. In other words, the trend of world trade since 1945 has been away from the exchange of European (and North American) manufactured goods for the primary products of the less-developed parts of the world, towards the exchange of specialized manufactured goods and primary produce between the industrial nations themselves (particularly the industrial nations of continental Europe and North America).

This change is not necessarily a good thing or a bad thing; it is a different thing. We cannot expect the nineteenth-century pattern to be repeated in the twentieth century. There was a time in the nineteenth century when Europe's demand for primary produce (especially for the produce of the white settled parts of the temperate zones) seemed unlimited. The long and steady nineteenth-century rise in the share of the non-industrial countries in world trade in primary produce continued in volume until 1937 and in value, because of the sharp rise in prices in the post-war period, until 1950. But that particular episode in history has ended. Since the First World War the demand of the western nations has either declined (Europe took about three-quarters of world exports of primary produce in 1913, and about half in 1953), or has remained fairly stationary (as North American demands have done). In addition, western demands on the primary-producing areas of the world are today heavily concentrated in certain areas and in certain products. Take, for instance, the ever-growing importance of the trade in petroleum products, which accounted for about half the increase in the volume of world exports in primary produce in the period 1928–55.

The refining of petroleum, along with other developments in chemical technology, has made the industrial countries even less dependent on other kinds of raw materials. The production of synthetic materials from petrochemicals, for instance, has reduced the dependence of the countries of Europe and North America upon overseas supplies of natural rubber, nitrates, vegetable oils, hides and several other kinds of primary produce. New, man-made, textile materials have also reduced the dependence upon natural fibres; silk, cotton, and wool have all been affected. Plastics are now used to make many products which once were made of imported rubber, metal, or wood. Cheap processes for producing aluminium have encouraged its substitution for imported copper and other more expensive materials. The revival of European agriculture since the Second World War, and the substitution of many home-produced foods (for example meat for grain) for foreign supplies, has also reduced Europe's impact upon the rest of the world. Most significant has been the relative fall in the demand for the agricultural raw materials of the tropics and the foods of the temperate regions.

The changing position of the primary-producing areas is not just a matter of fewer and different western demands; it is also a matter of a different supply situation. Talk of demand and supply makes no sense except in terms of price. In the changed situation of the twentieth century some items of trade are no longer as competitive in world markets as they were. Time and again over the past hundred years primary producers (and in 1960 about half the world's exports in primary produce came from the western industrial countries themselves) have priced themselves out of world markets. Either that or they have found it more profitable to consume their own produce or exchange it with that of other primary producers. At one point in the nineteenth century India (and examples are many) supplied the West with considerable quantities of food (wheat) and raw materials (cotton) which it now consumes itself. It is not simply a matter of western demands having changed. India's total situation has changed. There is no static position in international trade.

Not only have the primary-producing countries been doing relatively less trade than the more industrialized countries since the end of the Second World War; the terms on which the primary-producing countries have traded have probably worsened. A League of Nations' study[1] suggests that from the latter part of the nineteenth century to 1939 there was a

[1] League of Nations Intelligence Service, *The Network of World Trade* (Geneva, 1942). Also *Report on the Conference on Trade and Development*: 'Towards a New Trade Policy for Development', United Nations (New York, 1964) chap. ii.

general fall in the export prices of the primary-producing countries of the world relative to the prices of the manufactured goods these countries imported. With qualification, this trend has been renewed since the mid-1950's. To take only one example, Ghana's cocoa crop in 1964 was earning approximately 60 per cent less money than it did in 1954, although the saleable crop is now larger than it was then. It is one of the paradoxes of the present world commercial situation, that at a time when the developing nations of the world need most assistance, the chief stimulus to trade is felt by the relatively developed manufacturing nations.

Important changes also have occurred in the structure of world manufacture. Europe's overwhelming predominance in world exports of manufactured goods is gradually being reduced as markets are lost to North America and Japanese manufacturers. In 1913 Europe provided 84 and in 1960 65 per cent of world exports of manufactures. The industrialization of North America has diverted from Europe a considerable proportion of world trade, especially with Latin America. Whereas in the first decade of the twentieth century, Latin American imports from Europe were about three times as great as those from the United States, by 1925 imports from the United States were only slightly less than those from Europe. Since the Second World War imports into Latin American countries from the United States have usually been twice as great as those from Europe. Similarly, at the turn of the present century, Europe was by far the largest market for Latin American produce. In the inter-war period Europe still took more Latin American exports than did any other area. Since then, Europe's importance as a market for Latin American produce, relative to the United States, has declined. Yet in 1937 Latin American exports to Europe were still twice as great as those to the United States. Since the Second World War, however, Europe's share of the Latin American export trade has fallen below that of the United States. Finally, the fact that the new industrial centres of Asia, Africa, Latin America, and Australasia are more concerned with internal rather than external needs, means that the impact of the newer areas of industrialization upon intercontinental trade is less stimulating than the impact provided by Europe in its early stages of industrial development.

* * *

The changes taking place in Europe's trading position since the eighteenth century are illustrated in the experience of some of Europe's major trading nations. To no other European nation has international trade played a greater role than it has to the British people. The United States has a greater volume of trade than the United Kingdom, but Britain still excels in the far-flung nature of its trade. Between 1800 and 1850 British imports increased more than fourfold from $118 million to $485 million; between 1850 and 1913 the increase was eightfold to $3,767 million. Between 1913 and 1938 imports rose to $4,161 million and from $8,070 million in 1948 to $11,322 million in 1960 (Table VII/13). Measured in volume, Britain's share of world imports fell from 16·0 per cent in 1913 to 11·1 per cent in 1960. Britain's principal imports in order of importance in selected years during the last century came from the following countries:

1864: India, France, Egypt, U.S.A., China, Russia, Germany, Netherlands.

1880: U.S.A., France, India, Netherlands, Germany, Australia, Russia, Canada.

1900: U.S.A., France, Netherlands, Germany, India, Australia, Belgium, Canada.

1913: U.S.A., Germany, India, France, Argentina, Russia, Australia, Canada.

1938: U.S.A., Canada, Australia, India, New Zealand, Argentina, Denmark, Germany.

1960: U.S.A., Canada, Australia, New Zealand, (W.) Germany, Netherlands, Sweden, Kuwait.

The United Kingdom's leading import in 1800: sugar (followed by tobacco) had given way by 1831 to cotton (followed by sugar and grain). The amount of raw cotton consumed by Britain increased nearly fivefold between 1800 and 1830. From the 1850's until the First World War these two items, grain (including flour) and raw cotton, continued to occupy leading positions in British imports (Table VII/1).

Britain's dependence upon other continents for food continued to grow throughout the nineteenth century as its standard of living was raised and its industry increased. However, as late as the 1860's, most of the meat and wheat consumed by the British came from their own countryside. British imports of grain rose sharply in the last quarter of the century encouraged, among other factors, by the fall in world prices. After the introduction of refrigerated transport in the 1880's, there was a similar fall in the prices of animal products. British agriculture, and, to a lesser degree, western European agriculture, was the first great staple industry to feel the effects of the development by the white race of the great grasslands of the Northern and Southern Hemispheres. Yet only Britain was prepared to sacrifice its agriculture to world economic integration. It took the German submarine campaign of the First World War to bring home to the British people the full import of what they had done. Had the British people lost control of the high seas there would have been widespread famine in the land.

Britain's growing reliance for food supplies upon foreign countries was matched by its growing dependence for raw materials. Whereas in the eighteenth century Britain provided all the essential raw materials for its industries, especially for its staple manufacture, wool, in 1913 Britain was self-sufficient only in the supply of coal. At that time Britain obtained most of the timber, most of the wool, a growing part of the iron ore, all the cotton, petroleum, and rubber needed by its economy from overseas.

Changes in the British economy since 1914 are reflected in the declining importance of textile raw materials relative to the growing importance of machinery, chemicals, rubber, petroleum and petroleum products. In the 1950's the United Kingdom was importing about half the quantity of cotton that it did in the period 1934–8. These changes resulted from the industrialization of other parts of Europe, Asia, and North America. For many of the inter-war years, for example, the increase in the Japanese demand for raw cotton largely offset the decline of the British demand. The appearance of new industries, such as the automobile industry, also contributed to the changing character of British imports. In 1960 the imports of petroleum and petroleum products were at a higher level than either the imports of meat or grain. (Table VII/2.)

The second greatest trading nation in the world at the beginning of the nineteenth century was France. Like the other nations of continental western Europe, France's best customers were its neighbours: Britain, Germany, and Belgium. Outside Europe, the most important area for French trade was North America. (Since 1913, however, Africa has replaced North America as France's best non-European customer.) In the last century, France's principal imports in order of importance in selected years came from the following countries:

1863: Britain, Belgium, Italy, Turkey, Germany, U.S.A., India, Russia.
1880: U.S.A., Britain, Belgium, Germany, Italy, Algeria, India, Argentina.
1900: Britain, U.S.A., Germany, Belgium, Argentina, Russia, Spain, Algeria.
1913: Britain, Germany, U.S.A., Belgium, Russia, Argentina, Algeria, Spain.
1938: U.S.A., Algeria, Britain, Belgium, Germany, Indo-China, Australia, French West Africa.
1960: (W.) Germany, U.S.A., Algeria, Belgium, Italy, Netherlands, Britain, Morocco.

French imports grew in value from $147 million in 1840 to $1,636 million in 1913; this fell to $1,322 million in 1938, and rose again to $6,327 million in 1960. Textile raw materials remained the major items throughout the nineteenth century. Coal and coke, woollen and cotton manufactures, and crude sugar were also important. The opening of the

Suez Canal stimulated the growth in the supplies of raw silk from China, Japan, and India. Imports of grain, meat, dairy produce, and fruit into France grew in volume from the beginning of the twentieth century, but they never reached the same proportions as the food imports of the United Kingdom. The benefits of international specialization were never as apparent to the French as they were to the British. The French were especially sensitive to the interests of their agriculture. In their own words 'l'agriculture fait l'homme': agricultural interests were much too valuable to be thrown overboard in the race to a visionary economic cosmos of the world. In order of priority in 1929 imports of cereals into France ranked below raw wool and cotton, coal and coke. In 1960 cereals do not appear among the first eight items. To make concessions to the wine growers of Algeria and Tunisia was another matter. North Africa was regarded as part of metropolitan France. But even in this instance there was conflict between the French wine growers in Europe and those in North Africa. In 1960 France was Algeria's greatest customer, taking 73 per cent of its exports. (Table VII/4, VII/5 and VII/15.)

During the nineteenth century, while France preserved its agriculture, it relied on other European countries, especially Britain, for imports of machinery. In 1913 about one-fifth of French imports of machinery was supplied by the United States. The development of industrialization in France in the present century is reflected in the growing French imports of machinery and mechanical equipment, as it is in the growing imports of petroleum and industrial chemicals. Altogether, the rate of change of the French economy in the nineteenth and twentieth centuries was much slower than that of Britain or Germany. Economic progress in France proceeded at a much more moderate pace than in other western nations, but, of course, in narrow economic terms for the French nation it also proceeded much less profitably.

The German States prior to their unification in 1871 were predominantly rural areas. A very rough guess of the foreign trade of these States in the mid-nineteenth century would be in the region of $350 million. Although the expansion of German railways in the fifties and sixties had led to the development of the coal mining industry, German manufacturing was still organized along traditional lines and the great majority of the population was engaged in rural occupations. During the early decades of the nineteenth century the German States had been net suppliers of food and fine wool to other European countries, especially the United Kingdom, but as the century progressed Germany lost its position as a leading exporter of home-produced wool and grain to the temperate zones of North and South America, Australasia, and South Africa. However, throughout the past two hundred years Germany has been self-sufficient in most temperate foods; the bulk of its food imports during the past century has consisted of tropical and semi-tropical foods and beverages.

While Germany never lost the ability to feed itself as Britain did in the nineteenth century, the German Industrial Revolution proceeded with exceptional momentum once it got under way in the 1870's. Had not the efficiency of German agriculture increased and production expanded during the nineteenth century, Germany's reliance upon eastern European and overseas areas for food would have been much greater than it was. Even so, the rapid transformation of Germany during the last quarter of the nineteenth century, from a predominantly rural and agricultural to a predominantly urban and industrial society, meant that Germany had to find extra food overseas. Whereas in 1870 only about one third of German population was urban, by the end of the century the proportion of urban dwellers was over one half, and on the eve of the First World War nearly two-thirds. Both the rapid industrialization and urbanization in this period helped to change the nature of German trade not only in food but also in raw materials.

In the period 1870–1913, as the German cotton and woollen textile industries expanded, increasing quantities of raw wool and cotton were imported. After the First World War while Germany's reliance upon Egyptian, South American, and Turkish cotton producers grew, the relative importance of United States cotton supplies to Germany declined. In the first decade of the twentieth century Germany had the most rapidly growing cotton textile industry in Europe, relying on the United Kingdom for supplies of the finer type of yarn.

The extremely quick rise to pre-eminence of the German iron and steel industry is probably the most important aspect of Germany's industrialization. With the rapid expansion of German industry since the 1880's Germany came to rely upon outside supplies of iron ore. Until the Second World War Europe provided the overwhelming bulk of this material, but since then Germany has obtained more iron ore from countries outside Europe, particularly India, as well as from parts of South America and North and West Africa. (Table VII/7, VII/8 and VII/17.)

The appearance of new German industries in the twentieth century has created a demand for new kinds of imports. Although Germany still depends on outside supplies of textile raw materials, the rise of the automobile and engineering industries has created new demands for petroleum and metals. In the inter-war years Germany was a large importer of vegetable oils, most of which came from Argentina and the tropical and sub-tropical countries of Asia and Africa. The rise of the petroleum-refining industry, however, has provided the raw materials for synthetic oil substitutes. Since the division of Germany after the Second World War, the European trade of the Federal Republic has been almost entirely with the countries of western Europe; at the present time over 60 per cent of total West German trade is with these countries. The division of Germany has caused the Federal Republic to replace much of its former eastern European supplies of petroleum by supplies from Asia and South America. The eastern German Democratic Republic trades almost exclusively with the communist countries of the U.S.S.R. and eastern Europe.

In the present century, Germany's principal imports came from the following countries, listed in order of importance:

1900: U.S.A., Britain, Austro-Hungary, Russia, France, Argentina, Belgium, Netherlands.
1913: U.S.A., Russia, Britain, Austro-Hungary, France, India, Argentina, Belgium.
1938: U.S.A., Britain, Sweden, Italy, Argentina, Brazil, Netherlands, Belgium.
1960: U.S.A., France, Netherlands, Italy, Belgium, Britain, Sweden, Switzerland.

Europe's leading export in the period 1750–1914 was textile products; sales of manufactured woollens, silks, linens, and, especially during the nineteenth century, cotton goods, provided the largest volume of trade. With the development of the European cotton textile industry the earlier restricted trade of eastern luxuries for western bullion declined. Europe also provided the machinery and railroad equipment needed to develop other lands. In contrast to the exports of textile products, which tended to decline from the end of the nineteenth century, demand for other kinds of manufactured goods and capital equipment continued to grow. Thus the rise and expansion of local manufacturing industry in other continents before the First World War resulted, on the one hand, in a decline in the demand for certain European consumer goods, particularly for cotton textiles, and, on the other hand, in an increased demand for European equipment, especially for textile machinery.

The importance of exports to the different European nations has depended upon the nature of their economy and the stage of their development. Some of the smaller nations of Europe, such as Denmark, the Netherlands, Belgium, and Switzerland, became so involved in foreign trade that their economic existence came to depend upon it. For most European nations, however, it was the intra-European rather than the intercontinental trade that was vital.

The changing nature of British exports is traced in Tables VII/1, VII/3, and VII/14. By the 1830's the sales of woollen cloth, Britain's most important single export, were far exceeded in value by the exports of cotton fabrics. Until the rise of other great industrialized nations — especially the rise of the United States and Germany in the closing decades of the nineteenth century — Britain continued to supply the bulk of world cotton and woollen textiles, as it continued to supply the bulk of manufactures. The decline in the export of British textiles after the First World War was offset partly by the exports of textile machinery.

Total British exports rose from $185 million in 1800 to $350 million in 1850, an increase of approximately 60 per cent. By 1913 the figure was $2,573 million, a seven and a half-fold increase. In 1938 the figure was $2,307 million, a slight decline. It rose again after the war until in 1960 the value of foreign trade was $9,953 million, a fourfold increase. The list of principal markets in order of importance in selected years during the past hundred years are given below:

1864: India, U.S.A., Germany, Australia, France, Turkey, Netherlands, Brazil.

1880: U.S.A., India, Germany, France, Australia, Netherlands, Russia, Canada.

1900: India, Germany, Australia, France, U.S.A., Russia, Netherlands, Belgium.

1913: India, Germany, Australia, U.S.A., France, Canada, Argentina, Russia.

1938: Union of South Africa, Australia, India, Canada, Germany, U.S.A., Ireland, Argentina.

1960: U.S.A., Australia, Canada, (W.) Germany, South Africa, India, Sweden, New Zealand.

The greatest increase in the growth of British exports was during the period 1824–72. Between 1876 and 1880 Britain had 38 per cent of world trade in manufactured goods, a position it could not hope to maintain as other nations industrialized. In the last quarter of the nineteenth century the gradual expansion in the volume of British exports was concealed by a fall in prices.

Britain's Changing Export Position in the period 1800–1960

Year	*Total export trade (in millions U.S. $)*	*Exports and re-exports*	*Share of world exports* (%)	*Year*	*Total exports of manufactures (in millions U.S. $)*	*Share of world manufactures—exports* (%)
1800	185	257				
1850	350	409				
1880	1,093	1,405	16			
1900	1,427	1,737	15	1899	1,031	33
1913	2,573	3,111	14	1913	1,960	30
1929	3,574	4,111	11	1929	2,735	23
1938	2,307	2,608	10	1937	1,935	21
1948	6,375	6,565	11	1950	5,100	25
1960	9,953	10,349	7	1959	7,713	18

Sources: Table VII/14 and calculations based on A. Maizels, op. cit.

During the past century and a half Britain has usually imported more merchandise than it exported, the balance being paid for by providing world shipping, banking, brokerage, and insurance services. Imports also expanded relative to exports because of the steady improvement of the terms on which Britain did business with other nations. Britain, like other industrialized countries in their trading relations with primary producers, obtained a greater quantity of imports for a smaller quantity of exports. Britain also had a large unearned income from vast investments overseas. To a greater extent than other European nations, the British people in the twentieth century have been able to draw upon the overseas wealth created (but not consumed) by their nineteenth-century forbears. Britain's growing difficulty to pay its way during the past generation springs partly from the fact that much of its accumulated wealth has been consumed by warfare and in subsidizing current income. For some time now, the British have been enjoying a higher standard of living than current production warranted, or, to put it more simply, the British have been living beyond their means. Intense specialization brought great wealth and power to Britain during the past century and a half. But it is one thing to reap the benefits of an early start as a great manufacturing and trading nation, and another thing to struggle to retain one's position in a world in which Britain no longer has political, financial, industrial, and commercial supremacy.

Britain's present efforts to enter the European Economic Community (and at the same time honour its longstanding and historic ties with the other nations of the British Commonwealth) illustrate the changed trading conditions of the twentieth century. In the nineteenth century in its search for markets for its manufactures, and for supplies of raw materials, Britain dovetailed its economy with the primary-producing regions of the world. In the 1960's, the most rapidly expanding markets in the world for the manufactured goods Britain wishes to sell are no longer in the rising parts of the world, they are in western and, increasingly in the mid-1960's, in eastern Europe.

French exports grew from $119 million in 1840 to $1,324 million in 1913; they fell to $876 million in 1938, and rose again to $6,914 million in 1960 (Table VII/16). Cumulatively, the export trade never was as important to the French economy as exports were to the United Kingdom or (since 1871) to Germany. Nevertheless, the ratio of foreign trade to National Income rose from about 8 per cent in the 1840's to 16·5 per cent in 1900. In the 1920's it was as high as 24·5 per cent, but during the depression of the late twenties and early thirties the ratio of foreign trade to national income dropped considerably. Until the early 1950's, the ratio averaged only about 12 per cent.

Throughout the nineteenth century the main items in French exports were high-quality textile goods, wines and spirits, leather manufactures, articles of food such as refined sugar and dairy produce, and luxury goods (Table VII/4). Most of France's high quality silk, cotton, and woollen textiles were sold in Europe, particularly to Britain. The chief market for French textile products outside Europe was the United States. Yet the United States market for France's most important textile export, silk products, declined from 28 per cent of total foreign sales in 1913 to 12 per cent in 1930. In the same period the share taken by the rest of Europe rose from 54 per cent to 73 per cent.

Although overtaken by Germany as an exporter of manufactured products in the last fifteen years of the nineteenth century, France at the beginning of the twentieth century was the third most important exporter of manufactures with 15 per cent of the total (United Kingdom 33·8 per cent and Germany 23·2 per cent). However, France's share of the world market for manufactures declined rapidly in the inter-war years. In addition to the general absolute decline in the volume of trade in manufactures during the 1930's (in 1937 world exports were 87 per cent of the 1929 level) France suffered a sharp fall in its position relative to the other exporters of manufactured goods; in 1929 the French share of world exports was 11 per cent, by 1937 it had fallen to 6 per cent; since 1950 France's share has been stable at around 9 or 10 per cent.

The changes in the nature of French exports of manufactures since 1900 have followed the general twentieth-century trend of western European nations. Textiles, which in 1899 comprised 35·8 per cent of French exports of manufactures, accounted for only 18·6 per cent in 1953. In the same period the share of engineering products rose from 5·7 per cent to 25·7 per cent, and metals and chemicals increased from 13·6 per cent to 32·5 per cent. Until the First World War silks and woollens occupied the most important positions. The two leading exports in 1935 were iron and steel products and chemicals. By 1960 iron and steel products, automobiles, non-electrical machinery, textiles and mineral fuels predominated. (Table VII/6.)

France's chief customers in selected years in order of importance were as follows:

1863: Britain, Germany, Belgium, Italy, Switzerland, Spain, U.S.A., Brazil.

1880: Britain, Belgium, Germany, U.S.A., Italy, Algeria, Argentina, Brazil.

1900: Britain, Belgium, Germany, Algeria, U.S.A., Switzerland, Italy, Spain.

1913: Britain, Belgium, Germany, Algeria, U.S.A., Switzerland, Italy, Argentina.

1938: Belgium, Algeria, Britain, Switzerland, Germany, U.S.A., Netherlands, Indo-China.

1960: Algeria, (W.) Germany, Belgium, U.S.A., Italy, Britain, Switzerland, Morocco.

While Europe still remains France's best customer there has been a marked development in the period 1900–60 of intercontinental trade, particularly with Africa (Table VII/16). For much of the nineteenth century Britain was the most important country both in respect to imports and exports. Since the First World War this was no longer true. In 1960 Algeria was France's best customer, taking 12 per cent of its total exports.

Trade and industry in Germany were encouraged by the establishment of the Zollverein or 'Customs Union' which began with the union of Prussia with Hesse-Darmstadt in 1828. By the time of the formation of the Empire in 1871 the Zollverein embraced the whole of Germany, save for Hamburg and Bremen. Germany was about to challenge Britain's position as the greatest trading nation in the world.

Like Britain, Germany's export trade since 1871 has consisted largely of factory products, sold to its industrial neighbours in Europe. The sales of beet sugar was the chief exception. Unlike Britain, in its dealings with primary-producing countries, Germany has always bought much more than it has sold to them. Thus, in 1913, India, China, and Japan took only 4 per cent of Germany's exports, and about 20 per cent of the United Kingdom's exports. By 1900 Germany had the largest iron and steel industry in Europe, and iron and steel products, together with machinery, became important items of German exports. Germany's favourable endowment of natural resources, added to the availability of technological skill,[1] enabled it to develop leadership in the chemical industry. To a greater extent than was true of any other major German industry, the export markets for German chemical products were outside Europe.

The value of German exports has increased from $1,132 million in 1900 to $2,403 million in 1913, fell to $2,103 million in 1938, and rose again to $11,416 million in 1960 (Table VII/18). Germany's chief customers in order of importance were:

1900: Britain, Austro-Hungary, U.S.A., Netherlands, Russia, Switzerland, France, Belgium.

1913: Britain, Austro-Hungary, Russia, France, U.S.A., Netherlands, Belgium, Switzerland.

1938: Netherlands, Britain, Italy, Sweden, Belgium, France, Switzerland, Denmark.

1960: Netherlands, France, U.S.A., Switzerland, Belgium, Italy, Sweden, Austria.

[1] Germany, like the United States, encouraged the development of their technical skills by a nation-wide system of technical education. In Britain this was badly neglected. See 'Education for an Age of Technology', Eric Ashby, V. 5, *A History of Technology* (Oxford, 1958).

Since its rise as an industrial nation Germany has occupied an important place amongst the leading exporters of manufactured goods. Its exports of manufactures increased rapidly between 1900 and 1929. Although German exports fell during the 1930's, Germany, unlike the United Kingdom and France, maintained its relative position in world trade in manufactures. In 1899 Germany's share of world exports of manufactures was 23·2 per cent; in 1937, 20 per cent. Since the Second World War Western Germany has made a remarkable trade recovery. In 1950 Germany's share of the world export market in manufactures had fallen to 7 per cent; by 1960 it had increased to 19 per cent.

Germany's experience during the last generation is characteristic of the growing capacity of industrial nations to do an increasing proportion of trade with each other. German exports of manufactures increased many times between 1937 and 1960, yet German imports of manufactured goods in 1960 remained about one-third of its total foreign purchases. Similarly, German exports of manufactures since the 1930's have followed the trend of that of the other industrialized nations of western Europe: while there has been a decline in sales of the traditional textile products, there has been an increase in the sales of the products of the newer industries requiring highly complicated and costly skills and equipment.

Because of the lack of adequate, comparable data, figures illustrating the changing composition as well as the changing direction of the foreign commerce of the Netherlands, Belgium, Switzerland, and Sweden have been given only since 1900 in Tables VII/10, VII/11, VII/19, VII/20, VII/21 and VII/22.

* * *

International trade during the past two hundred years has been dominated by the white man. Trade became world trade because the European caused the human drama to be played out on a world stage. Yet no people have traded with each other during this period as much as the Europeans have done within Europe; no intercontinental trade can compare with that between Europe and white communities overseas — particularly with Anglo-America.

Trade between the white and the non-white has always been relatively unimportant. The trade of earlier centuries with Asia and Africa hardly affected the life of the common man. Similarly, the trade between European countries and European colonies in Africa and Asia in more recent times has never been significant. Only India's trade with Britain reached important proportions. Colonies were important neither as a source of raw materials or food (perhaps cane sugar is the outstanding exception), nor as markets for European wares. A survey[1] of the value of colonial trade made in 1938 by the League of Nations, showed that colonial trade was an unimportant percentage of total trade. For instance, in 1938, the percentage of total British imports, excluding those from India and the self-governing Dominions, was 7·5 per cent; the percentage of total exports was 10·4 per cent. In 1935 Britain obtained only 8 per cent of its food and 11 per cent of its raw materials from the dependent empire. Except for sugar, the overseas colonies of France did not play a large part in French trade during most of the nineteenth century. As for the German colonial empire, it was well-suited neither as a supplier of raw materials or food, nor as a market for German wares.

Unimportant — at least quantitatively — as the trade between white and non-white may have been, the colonial past helps to explain the present foreign-trade pattern of many nations. By the time a colony obtained its political liberty, and was able to make economic decisions for itself, the whole pattern of past events made a continuance and even a closer economic unity with European countries likely. Certainly this was Britain's experience with its overseas territories: the greater the political freedom obtained, the more trade has flourished. Between 1870–74 and 1910–13, for instance, Britain's trade with its empire (dependent colonies and independent dominions) increased from a quarter to more than a third of Britain's exports. The figures for 1938 and 1960 were 44 and 45 per cent respectively (Table VII/14). In 1960 Australia was the United Kingdom's second best customer, taking almost 8 per cent of Britain's exports. Similarly, the proportion of United Kingdom imports from the British Empire increased in the period 1860–1960, from approximately 20 to 36 per cent (Table VII/13). In 1960 United Kingdom purchases were vital to the Republic of South Africa (Britain took 28 per cent of South Africa's total exports), India (27 per cent), and Australia (26 per cent). During the twentieth century the French overseas possessions have also increased their trade with France. As a result of the Customs Union between France and its empire in 1928 a closed system of imperial preference was established; France committed itself to a policy of reliance upon colonial supplies and markets, and between 1929 and 1935 France's imports of food from the colonies doubled. As the supplies of food from the rest of Europe declined from 63 per cent of French food imports in 1880 to 15 per cent in 1935, the share of the French colonies rose from 7·5 per cent to 64 per cent. And while the French colonies were never important as a source of raw materials, nearly half the oil seeds imported into France in 1935 came from French West Africa. In 1938 France did more trade with its colonial empire than any other imperial power, except Britain (Tables VII/15 and VII/16). Imports from the French colonies, which in 1860 had been

[1] League of Nations, Economic and Financial Section, *Review of World Trade 1932–1938*.

9 per cent of total French imports, and about the same in 1913, had by 1938 become slightly more than a quarter of the whole; they were of a similar proportion in 1960. Exports to the French empire, which in 1860 were about 10 per cent, and approximately 13 per cent in 1913, had risen to about 30 per cent in 1938; the figure for 1960 was about the same.

The colonial past also helps to explain why so many countries in Africa, Latin America, Asia, and Australasia trade with European countries thousands of miles away and do almost no business at all with their immediate neighbours. Foreign countries, once having become orientated to meeting the demands of a particular European country, have usually found it easy on the one hand to extend their trade in Europe, and hard on the other hand to think in terms of trade with other continents. There develops a mental rigidity to change. Until the last twenty years Australia, for instance, did very little trade with its Asian neighbours.

If we include in inter-imperial trade the growing power of the international capitalist corporation (what is crudely known as 'dollar imperialism' although it includes both European and American interests) with its large investments in the primary and extractive industries of many lands, then imperial trade is still very much with us. To take one example, the principal reason why Liberia trades primarily with the United States rather than with its neighbours or with Europe is because the Liberian economy depends upon the sale of plantation rubber owned and operated by American rubber corporations.

* * *

The essential benefit of international trade is to have enlarged and concentrated production in the areas of the world most suitable, as well as to create a closer economic and commercial integration of mankind. The extent to which these benefits have been enjoyed by non-white people has depended upon the degree of specialization which European intrusion has brought about, and the extent to which the export earnings of the developing countries have been siphoned off to the West in the form of profits, interest on loan capital, and charges for foreign shipping, banking and insurance services.

Where European foreign trade has been confined to a relatively small sector of a country's economy, overshadowed by a much larger subsistence, and non-commercial sector, Europe's effect overseas has been limited. European mining in Africa and Asia, for instance, often resulted in the development of 'dual economies', with the European-controlled sector almost self-contained and independent of the much larger and economically more important native subsistence economy; although it is hard to believe that some aspects of European life did not 'rub off' on to the native economy. Where European trade has penetrated an entire country, and especially where trade was intensely specialized as in many European colonies, the white man's interests often took precedence over those of the native people. The more highly specialized a primary-producing country became in response to world (chiefly European) demands, the more unstable its economy was likely to be. A marked change in world prices could mean economic life or death to the native people. In 1953 thirty countries depended upon a single product for at least half of their export earnings. How intense this specialization could be is shown in the following examples for 1960 (the figure is for the proportion of the value of total exports): Mauritius, sugar, 99 per cent; Colombia, coffee, 86 per cent; Ghana, cocoa, 85 per cent; Ceylon, tea, 85 per cent; Liberia, rubber, 95 per cent; Egypt, cotton, 87 per cent; Bolivia, tin, 97 per cent; Surinam, bauxite, 93 per cent; Brunei, petroleum, 99 per cent.[1] Intense specialization which has resulted from meeting western wants often proved to be a dangerous way of life for a developing country. Yet, there is hardly an important country in the West (and some in the East, if we think of Japanese silk or Malayan rubber) that cannot trace its economic quickening to intense specialization. Is this not the story of Australian wool, or Canadian grain, or British woollens and, later, cottons? Conversely, the history of the United States and the more recent history of the U.S.S.R. show that the economic development of a country is not inseparably linked with its ability to earn foreign currency. Economic development of any area, country, region, or continent is a complex process which cannot be ascribed to the effect of any one factor such as domestic or international trade. Ultimately, what a country has gained or lost from the impact of European foreign trade has depended largely on complex social factors. The impact of the western trader cannot be separated from all the other influences accompanying the intrusion of western man. The native people of the world did not simply exchange their natural resources for western merchandise; they received not only cheap, coloured beads, a reel of bright ribbon, or a gaudy cotton dress, gunpowder, and alcohol — for better or worse, they received with these things the aims and objectives of western civilization. Western man took with him western enterprise, industry, thrift, literacy, leadership, commercial, industrial, administrative, and managerial skills. As the western trader went his way, new wants were aroused, new needs created, new efforts begun, new horizons observed, new ambitions felt.

The present position is one where Europe's old economic predominance on the developing areas — particularly on the non-white areas of the world — has gone for good. Yet world economic unity has never been as imperative and urgent as it is today. It is urgent now not only because we

[1] Figures are drawn from United Nations *Yearbook of International Trade Statistics* (various). Also J. W. Alexander, *Economic Geography* (New Jersey, 1963), p. 500.

live in a divided world where tolerance for conflicting economic and social philosophies is fast disappearing, but also because of the unprecedented increase taking place in world population. For unless something can be done to improve the economic position of the under-developed countries — and international trade is surely one if only one of the channels through which this can be done — the relatively poor of the world are certain to become relatively poorer.

TABLES

VII/1 to VII/22

THE CHANGING PATTERN OF TRADE

General Notes on Trade Tables

Although an attempt has been made in the chapter to give a picture of Europe's changing position in international trade since the eighteenth century, reliable figures are not generally available much before the mid-nineteenth century. The nations selected are thought to have been the major world traders during the past century.

Because of changes in place-names and national boundaries over the period, it has been necessary to use rather arbitrary boundaries for the regional divisions. Except where footnotes indicate to the contrary:

West Africa includes the former British, French, Spanish, and Portuguese West African possessions, and the Congo.

East Africa includes the former British, German, and Portuguese East African possessions, and Abyssinia, Somaliland, Madagascar, and Mauritius.

In the French tables East Africa is included in Other Africa, and this also includes Réunion.

South Africa includes the Republic of South Africa, Malawi, Zambia and Southern Rhodesia.

British India includes the present India, Pakistan, Ceylon, and Malaysia.

South-west Asia includes Iran, Iraq, Asiatic Turkey, the countries of the Arabian Peninsula, and the Levant.

Unspecified includes all areas, whether listed in the tables or not, which have exports or imports of less than 1 per cent of the total in a particular commodity, and also areas which have not been sufficiently differentiated in the sources. n. = negligible; n.a. = not available.

Tables 1 to 11 deal with the changes in the composition of imports and exports, as well as the area of provenance and destination in the period 1830–1960.

It has not always been possible to adopt a consistent definition for commodity classification to cover all the countries for the whole period. For this reason, and also because of rounding to the nearest percentage whole number, these figures can only be regarded as very approximate. However, it is hoped that they convey some impression of changes in relative importance of the major commodities in trade as well as changes in the regions of provenance and destination.

The fact that no attempt has been made to differentiate between direct imports and exports of the regions of provenance and destination, and re-exports and re-imports, means that these figures are not an absolutely accurate guide to the qualitative changes taking place in the trade of the countries concerned.

Tables 12 to 22 are an attempt to show the quantitative changes in European trade between 1840 and 1960. As wide variations exist between the estimates prepared by different authorities, overall figures are, at the best, no more than rough approximations. On a world scale, we simply do not know how much trade was done by the different nations during the past two hundred years. Even the more recent United Nations figures are incomplete (Communist China, for instance, does not report its foreign trade to the United Nations). However, the few countries that do not submit trade data to the United Nations cannot account for an important volume of exports and imports — as at 1960 perhaps 3 to 5 per cent of international trade. The wide variety of sources used for earlier periods has made certain inconsistencies in the tables as well as the text inevitable.

The conversion rates used in the tables are as follows:

Year	*Currencies*	
1840 1860 1880 1900 1913	U.K. (sterling) £1	=U.S. $4·90
	France, Belgium (franc) 5·1	=U.S. $1·00
	Germany (mark) 4·2	
	Netherlands (guilder) 2·4	
1938	U.K. (sterling) £1	=U.S. $4·90
	France (franc) 35	=U.S. $1·00
	Belgium, Luxemburg (franc) 29	
	Germany (mark) 2·5	
	Netherlands (guilder) 1·8	
1960	U.K. sterling £1	=U.S. $2·80
	France (new franc) 4·9	=U.S. $1·00
	W. Germany (mark) 4·2	
	Belgium, Luxemburg (franc) 50	
	Netherlands (guilder) 3·8	

Because of the marked depreciation of European currencies during the past century, the growth of trade in monetary terms can be deceiving: trade appears to grow at a much faster rate than was actually the case.

TABLE VII/1

UNITED KINGDOM

Principal Imports and Exports by Approximate Percentage of Total Value

Selected Years, 1831–1960

1831		*1850*		*1875*		*1900*		*1913*		*1935*		*1960*	
Imports													
Cotton	19	Cotton	24	Grain	15	Grain	12	Grain	11	Meat	10	Petroleum	10
Sugar	15	Grain	12	Cotton	12	Meat	9	Cotton	9	Dairy produce	8	Meat	7
Grain	9	Sugar	10	Wool	6	Cotton	8	Meat	7	Grain	7	Non-ferrous base metals	6
Tea	6	Tea	5	Sugar	6	Timber	5	Wool	4	Beverages	6	Fruit and vegs.	5
Coffee	5	Timber	4	Meat	4	Wool	4	Timber	4	Fresh fruit	5	Grain	5
Flax and hemp	5	Flax and hemp	4	Timber	4	Sugar	4	Butter	4	Cotton	5	Machinery (non-elec.)	4
Wines	3	Hides	2	Tea	4	Butter	4	Sugar	3	Wool	5	Timber	4
		Wool	2	Wines	3	Hides	2	Hides	2	Timber	5	Chemicals	4
				Hides	2			Tea	2	Oilseeds and nuts	3	Beverages	4
				Butter	2							Dairy produce	4
												Metalliferous ores and scrap	4
												Wool	3
Exports													
Cotton yarns and tex.	24	Cotton yarns and tex.	14	Cotton yarns and tex.	26	Cotton yarns and tex.	20	Cotton yarns and tex.	20	Cotton yarns and tex.	12	Machinery (non-elec.)	19
Woollen yarns and tex.	7	Woollen yarns and tex.	5	Woollen yarns and tex.	9	Coal	11	Iron and steel goods	8	Machinery	8	Veh. and aircraft	14
Linens	3	Iron and steel	3	Iron and steel	3	Iron and steel	9	Coal	8	Iron and steel goods	8	Chemicals	8
Cutlery, hardware, etc.	2	Linens	2	Coal	3	Woollen yarns and tex.	7	Woollen yarns and tex.	6	Coal	6	Elec. machinery	6
Iron and steel	1	Cutlery, hardware, etc.	1	Linens	3	Machinery	5	Machinery	6	Woollen yarns and tex.	6	Iron and steel	6
		Coal	1	Machinery	3	Chemicals	4	Chemicals, dyes, etc.	3	Vehicles	6	Metal manufactures	4
				Chemicals	2							Petroleum products	3
												Woollen yarns and tex.	2

Table VII/4

FRANCE

Principal Imports and Exports by Approximate Percentage of Total Value
Selected Years, 1830–1960

1830		1875		1900		1913		1935		1960	
Imports											
Cotton	11	Wool	10	Wool	9	Wool	8	Coal and coke	9	Mineral fuels, lubricants and by-products	14
Sugar	9	Silk	9	Cotton	9	Coal and coke	7	Wines	6	Non-elect. machinery	9
Silk	6	Hides and skins	8	Coal	9	Cotton	7	Wool	5	Textile fibres, waste, etc.	8
Hides and skins	3	Cotton	6	Silk	5	Grain and flour	7	Oilseeds	6	Base metals	7
Wool	3	Oils	5	Oilseeds	4	Oilseeds	5	Petroleum	5	Fruit and vegetables	4
Oils	2	Sugar	2	Timber	4	Machinery	4	Cotton	5	Transport materials	4
		Machinery	1	Hides and skins	3	Silk	4	Cereals	5	Coffee, tea, cocoa, spices, etc.	3
				Machinery	3	Wines	3	Fruits	4	Grains, nuts, etc.	3
Exports											
Silk cloth	25	Silk cloth	10	Silk cloth	6	Silk cloth	6	Iron and steel	6	Base metals	14
Cotton cloth	12	Woollen cloth	7	Wines	6	Cotton cloth	6	Chemical products	5	Transport materials	12
Wines	8	Wines	6	Woollen cloth	5	Clothing	4	Cotton cloth	5	Non-elect. machinery	8
Woollen cloth	6	Silk goods	3	Wool	5	Wool	5	Wool	4	Yarns, cloth, textile goods, etc.	8
Prepared hides	4	Fancy goods	3	Fancy goods	4	Motor vehicles	3	Metal manufactures	4	Mineral fuels, lubricants and by-products	4
Linen cloth	2	Prepared hides	2	Cotton cloth	4	Woollen cloth	3	Motor vehicles	3	Elect. machinery and equipment	4
Fancy goods	1	Cotton cloth	2	Silk	3	Chemical products	3	Silk and artificial silk	3	Drinks and beverages	3
						Wines	3	Minerals (all kinds)	3	Cereals and cereal products	3

Table VII/7

GERMANY

Principal Imports and Exports by Approximate Percentage of Total Value
Selected Years, 1880–1960

1880		*1900*		*1913*		*1935*		*1960*	
Imports									
Wool, cotton etc.	17	Cotton	5	Cotton	6	Cotton	8	Iron, steel and prod.	7
Grain	10	Wool	4	Wheat	4	Wool	6	Petroleum and prod.	7
Textile yarns	9	Wheat	3	Wool	4	Petroleum	4	Non-ferrous metals	6
Cattle	6	Coffee	3	Barley	4	Oilseeds	4	Fruit and vegetables	6
Coffee, cocoa, tea	6	Coal	2	Copper	3	Timber	4	Chemicals	6
Foodstuffs (animal)	5	Maize	2	Hides	3	Fruits	4	Machinery (non-elec.)	5
Hides and skins	5	Copper	2	Iron ore	2	Iron ore	3	Raw textile materials	5
				Coffee	2	Coffee	3	Iron ore	4
				Coal	2				
Exports									
Textile goods	15	Iron, steel and products	8	Iron, steel and products	13	Iron, steel and products	17	Machinery (non-elec.)	19
Salt and chemicals	8	Cotton goods	5	Machinery (non-elec.)	7	Machinery (non-elec.)	9	Iron, steel and products	15
Textile yarns	5	Woollen goods	5	Coal	5	Chemicals	8	Chemical products	12
Grain	5	Machinery	5	Cotton goods	4	Coal	6	Elec. machinery etc.	9
Wool, cotton, silk	4	Coal	5	Woollen goods	3	Paints and varnishes	5	Textiles and clothing	5
Metal goods	4	Sugar	5	Sugar	3	Elec. machinery etc.	5	Coal and coke	5
		Silk products	3	Paper and products	3	Paper and products	3		
		Clothing	2			Glass and glassware	3		

Note: The 1960 figures are for the Federal Republic of Germany (incl. West Berlin) only.

Source: Statistisches Jahrbuch für das Deutsche Reich (various years).

Table VII/8

Principal Imports for Selected Years, 1880–1960

Region of Provenance	*1880*							*1900*										
	Wool, cotton etc.	*Grain*	*Textile yarns*	*Cattle*	*Coffee, cocoa, tea*	*Foodstuffs (animal)*	*Hides and skins*	*Cotton*	*Wool*	*Wheat*	*Coffee*	*Coal*	*Maize*	*Copper*	*Cotton*	*Wheat*	*Wool*	*Barley*
Europe	74	91	100	100	79	80	87	1	24	27	15	100	11	16	..	24	17	93
North America	15	7	..	..	1	20	9	81	..	36	..	..	81	79	76	52	..	6
Canada	..	1	..	..	..	1	..	..	..	..	..	..	..	..	..	12	..	..
U.S.A.	15	6	..	..	..	19	9	81	..	36	..	..	81	79	76	40	..	6
Latin America	4	..	..	..	4	..	2	..	35	37	51	..	8	1	..	18	28	..
Argentina	3	..	..	..	..	..	..	..	35	37	..	..	8	..	..	18	22	..
Brazil	1	..	..	..	3	..	..	..	..	..	47	..	..	..	..	..	..	..
Chile	..	..	..	..	..	..	..	..	..	..	..	..	..	1	..	..	2	..
Peru	..	..	..	..	..	..	..	..	..	..	..	..	..	..	..	..	..	..
Venezuela	..	..	..	..	..	..	..	..	..	..	3	..	..	..	..	..	..	..
Other	..	..	..	..	..	..	..	..	..	..	20	..	..	..	..	..	4	..
Asia	5	1	..	..	16	..	1	7	..	..	12	..	..	3	11	2	..	[illegible]
British India	2	1	..	..	2	..	..	7	..	..	2	..	..	..	10	2	..	..
China	..	..	..	..	..	..	..	..	..	..	..	..	..	..	1	..	..	..
Indonesia	..	..	..	..	..	..	..	..	..	..	10	..	..	..	..	..	..	..
Japan	..	..	..	..	..	..	..	..	..	..	..	..	..	3	..	..	..	..
South-west Asia	..	..	..	..	..	..	..	..	..	..	..	..	..	..	..	..	..	..
Other	..	..	..	..	..	..	..	..	..	..	..	..	..	..	..	..	..	..
Africa	..	..	..	..	..	..	..	10	7	..	1	..	..	..	12	..	13	..
East Africa	..	..	..	..	..	..	..	..	..	..	..	..	..	..	..	..	..	..
North Africa	..	..	..	..	..	..	..	10	1	..	..	..	..	..	12	..	1	..
South Africa	..	..	..	..	..	..	..	..	6	..	..	..	..	..	..	..	12	..
West Africa	..	..	..	..	..	..	..	..	..	..	1	..	..	..	..	..	..	..
Australia	1	..	..	..	..	..	..	..	34	..	..	..	..	1	..	4	42	[illegible]
Unspecified	..	..	..	..	..	..	..	..	..	..	..	..	..	..	..	..	..	[illegible]

Note: The 1960 figures are for the Federal Republic of Germany (incl. West Berlin) only.

ERMANY

pproximate Percentage by Region of Provenance

13				*1935*								*1960*						(Raw textile materials)		
Hides	*Iron ore*	*Coffee*	*Coal*	*Cotton*	*Wool*	*Petroleum*	*Oilseeds*	*Timber*	*Fruits*	*Iron ore*	*Coffee*	*Iron and steel prod.*	*Petroleum and prod.*	*Non-ferrous metals*	*Fruit and vegetables*	*Chemicals*	*Machinery (non-electrical)*	*Cotton*	*Wool*	*Iron ore*
27	93	..	100	11	42	42	4	81	80	95	..	90	26	36	70	53	75	15	32	51
2	1	..	..	22	1	26	..	5	..	..	..	9	4	30	5	33	25	35	1	6
..	1	..	..	..	..	..	..	..	..	..	..	1	..	10	..	1	1	..	..	6
2	..	..	..	22	..	26	..	5	..	..	..	8	4	20	5	32	24	35	1	..
38	..	70	..	40	26	25	19	..	3	..	60	..	10	19	9	5	..	15	13	22
22	..	..	..	4	13	..	18	..	..	..	..	..	..	..	1	3	..	..	8	..
8	..	64	..	28	3	..	..	..	..	..	38	..	..	..	1	1	..	6	..	6
1	..	..	..	..	5	..	..	..	..	..	..	..	..	15	1	..	..	..	..	2
1	..	..	..	8	1	2	..	..	..	..	..	..	..	4	..	..	..	7	1	6
..	..	4	..	..	..	..	..	..	..	..	6	..	9	..	..	..	..	..	..	8
10	..	25	..	1	4	26	..	..	2	2	52	..	3	1	8	2	..	13	4	..
22	..	6	..	10	2	3	55	1	7	..	2	..	56	4	5	3	..	4	3	9
15	..	2	..	6	..	..	15	1	..	..	..	..	..	..	..	1	..	1	1	..
5	..	..	..	2	1	..	31	..	..	..	..	..	..	1	..	..	..	..	2	..
1	..	4	..	..	..	2	6	..	..	..	2	..	..	..	..	..	..	..	..	..
..	..	..	..	1	..	..	..	..	..	..	..	..	..	..	1	1	..	..	..	..
..	..	..	..	1	..	1	..	..	4	..	..	..	55	..	3	..	..	3	..	..
..	..	..	..	..	..	..	2	..	3	..	..	..	1	3	1	..	..	..	..	8
5	6	..	..	16	16	..	21	11	9	3	1	1	1	9	8	4	..	20	12	12
3	..	..	..	1	..	..	2	..	..	..	1	..	..	1	..	1	..	13	..	..
..	6	..	..	12	..	..	..	..	4	2	..	..	1	..	4	3	..	7	..	4
..	..	..	..	..	16	..	..	..	..	..	..	1	..	8	3	..	..	..	12	..
1	..	..	..	3	..	..	19	11	5	1	..	..	..	..	1	..	..	..	..	8
2	..	..	..	..	13	..	1	..	..	..	..	..	..	..	1	1	..	..	38	..
..	..	..	..	..	..	..	..	..	..	..	..	..	1	..	..	..	..	..	..	..

Sources: Statistisches Jahrbuch für das Deutsche Reich (various years).
Statistik des Deutschen Reichs (various years).
Monatliche Nachweise über den Auswärtigen Handel Deutschlands incl. *Ergänzungsheft I* (Dec. 1935).
Aussenhandel der Bundesrepublik Deutschland, Teil 3 (1960).

Table VII/[illegible]

Principal Exports for Selected Years, 1880–196[illegible]

Region of Destination	*1880* Textile goods	Salt and chemicals	Textile yarns	Grain	Wool, cotton, silk	Metal goods	*1900* Cotton goods	Woollen goods	Machinery	Coal	Sugar	Silk products	Iron and steel products	Clothing	Machinery (non-elec.)
Europe	77	87	99	100	100	84	55	73	88	100	58	70	80	84	81
North America	19	13	1	..	..	6	15	6	1	..	37	24	1	4	[illegible]
Canada	1	..	..	..	..	..	..	1	..	..	2	1	..	1	..
U.S.A.	18	13	1	..	..	6	15	5	1	..	35	23	1	3	[illegible]
Latin America	2	..	..	..	..	2	15	6	3	..	1	2	5	3	[illegible]
Argentina	..	..	..	..	..	..	4	2	1	..	..	1	2	1	[illegible]
Brazil	..	..	..	..	..	..	3	1	1	..	..	..	1	1	[illegible]
Chile	..	..	..	..	..	..	4	2	1	..	..	..	1	..	[illegible]
Peru	..	..	..	..	..	..	1	..	..	..	..	..	..	..	..
Venezuela	..	..	..	..	..	..	1	..	..	..	..	..	..	..	..
Other	..	..	..	..	..	..	3	2	1	..	1	..	1	2	[illegible]
Asia	2	..	..	..	..	8	9	12	5	..	2	3	9	3	[illegible]
British India	..	..	..	..	..	..	3	6	..	..	..	1	2	2	[illegible]
China	..	..	..	..	..	..	1	2	..	..	..	..	2	..	[illegible]
Indonesia	..	..	..	..	..	..	..	..	3	..	..	..	3	..	[illegible]
Japan	..	..	..	..	..	..	3	4	1	..	2	1	2	..	[illegible]
South-west Asia	..	..	..	..	..	..	..	..	..	..	..	..	..	..	[illegible]
Other	..	..	..	..	..	..	2	1	..	..	..	1	..	1	[illegible]
Africa	..	..	..	..	..	..	3	1	1	..	1	..	1	3	[illegible]
East Africa	..	..	..	..	..	..	..	..	..	..	1	..	..	2	[illegible]
North Africa	..	..	..	..	..	..	1	1	..	..	..	..	..	..	[illegible]
South Africa	..	..	..	..	..	..	1	..	..	..	..	..	1	1	[illegible]
West Africa	..	..	..	..	..	..	1	..	..	..	..	..	..	..	[illegible]
Australia	..	..	..	..	..	..	2	1	1	..	..	..	3	1	[illegible]
Unspecified	..	..	..	..	..	..	..	..	..	..	..	..	..	..	[illegible]

Note: The 1960 figures are for the Federal Republic of Germany (inc. West Berlin)only.

…ERMANY

…pproximate Percentage by Region of Destination

1913 Coal	1913 Cotton goods	1913 Woollen goods	1913 Sugar	1913 Paper products	1935 Iron and steel products	1935 Machinery (non-electrical)	1935 Chemicals	1935 Coal	1935 Paints and varnishes	1935 Electronic and electrical machinery	1935 Paper and products	1935 Glass and glassware	1960 Machinery (non-electrical)	1960 Iron and steel products	1960 Vehicles	1960 Chemical products	1960 Electronic and electrical machinery	1960 Textiles and clothing	1960 Coal and coke
98	58	75	87	74	63	72	59	94	60	78	69	69	68	72	51	65	69	72	99
..	13	5	2	11	3	1	9	1	5	1	4	6	5	7	22	5	6	7	..
..	1	1	1	..	..	..	1	1	1	..	..	1	1	1	3	1	1	1	..
..	12	4	1	11	3	1	8	..	4	1	4	5	4	6	19	4	5	6	..
..	13	9	7	9	13	9	11	3	8	8	8	8	7	6	5	7	5	2	..
..	6	4	3	5	4	3	3	1	3	4	4	2	2	2	2	1	1	..	..
..	3	1	..	3	5	4	5	2	2	2	2	3	2	1	1	2	1	..	..
..	2	2	1	1	1	1	1	..	1	1	1	1	1	..	1	..	1	1	..
..	..	..	..	..	..	..	..	..	1	..	..	..	..	..	..	1	..	..	..
..	..	..	..	..	1	..	..	..	..	..	..	..	1	1	1	1	1	..	..
..	4	3	2	1	4	2	5	..	3	2	2	3	3	2	2	5	3	1	..
..	8	7	1	3	13	13	14	..	23	8	13	10	12	10	8	14	11	8	..
..	5	3	..	1	4	2	4	..	7	2	3	2	4	2	2	3	2	1	..
..	1	1	..	..	3	2	2	..	8	2	6	3	1	2	..	1	..	1	..
..	1	..	..	..	1	1	1	..	2	1	1	..	..	1	1	1	1	..	..
..	..	1	..	1	2	4	5	..	4	2	1	3	2	..	..	3	..	..	..
..	..	..	..	..	2	2	1	..	1	1	..	1	3	3	3	3	5	4	..
..	1	..	..	..	1	1	1	..	1	..	1	1	2	2	2	3	2	1	..
1	4	2	3	..	5	3	3	1	1	3	3	3	5	3	10	4	6	7	1
..	1	..	..	..	1	..	..	..	..	..	..	..	1	1	2	1	1	1	..
1	1	2	1	..	1	1	1	1	1	1	1	1	2	1	1	1	2	1	..
..	1	..	..	..	2	1	1	..	..	1	1	1	1	..	4	1	2	3	..
..	1	..	1	..	1	..	..	..	..	..	..	..	1	1	3	1	1	2	..
..	2	1	..	1	1	1	1	..	1	1	1	2	2	1	2	2	1	3	..
1	..	..	..	..	..	..	..	1	..	..	..	..	..	..	..	..	..	..	..

Source: as Table VII/8.

Table VII/10

Leading Articles of Trade of the Netherlands, Belgium, Switzerland, and Sweden, Percentage Distribution by Value, 1900, 1913, 1938, and 1960

Imports 1900		Imports 1913		Imports 1938		Imports 1960		Exports 1900		Exports 1913		Exports 1938		Exports 1960	
Netherlands															
Cereals and flour	17	Cereals and flour	17	Textiles, raw and manufactured	10	Machinery and transport equipment	22	Cereals and flour	14	Cereals and flour	14	Textiles, raw and manufactured	8	Food and live animals	25
Iron and steel	10	Iron and steel	14	Cereals and flour	8	Crude materials, inedible, except fuels	14	Iron and steel	11	Iron and steel	11	Coal	6	Machinery and transport equipment	18
Textiles, raw and manufactured	6	Textiles, raw and manufactured	6	Iron and steel	8	Mineral fuels, lubricants and related materials	13	Textiles, raw and manufactured	6	Textiles, raw and manufactured	6	Butter	4	Mineral fuels, lubricants and related materials	12
Copper	5	Copper	4	Wood	5	Food and live animals (including cereals and flour)	12	Copper	5	Copper	5	Tin	4	Chemicals	7
Coal	3	Coal	4	Coal	4	Iron and steel	7	Paper	3	Paper	3	Iron and steel	3	Textile yarns, fabrics, etc.	7
Wood	3	Wood	4	Mineral oil	3	Chemicals	7	Sugar	3	Sugar	3	Cheese	3	Crude materials, inedible, except fuels	7
Belgium[1]															
Cereals	14	Wool	9	Cereals and flour	10	Machinery and transport equipment	21	Raw textiles	6	Wool	8	Iron and steel	16	Iron and steel	25
Raw textiles	10	Wheat	8	Food and live animals	8	Crude materials, inedible, except fuels	20	Coal	6	Flax and flax yarns	7	Textile yarns, fabrics, etc.	9	Miscellaneous manufactured goods (excluding textile yarns, fabrics, etc.)	15
Resins, bitumen	4	Cotton	4	Machinery and transport equipment	8	Miscellaneous manufactures (including textile yarns, fabrics, etc.)	18	Yarns, linen, etc.	4	Iron and steel	7	Raw wool and other textile fibres	8	Machinery and transport equipment	13
Timber	4	Rawhides	4	Raw wool	6	Food and live animals	11	Railway carriages	4	Zinc	3	Machinery and transport equipment	7	Textile yarns, fabrics, etc.	10
Crude minerals	3	Coal	3	Coal and briquettes	5	Mineral fuels	10	Glass	4	Railway carriages	3	Precious and semi-precious stones	7	Non-ferrous metals	9
Chemicals	3	Seeds	3	Precious and semi-precious stones	5	Non-ferrous metals	7	Cereals	4	Rawhides	3	Coal and briquettes	6	Crude materials, inedible, except fuels	7

SWITZERLAND							
Foodstuffs, tobacco, spirits, etc. 23 Silks 12 Metals 9 Mineral substances 8 Cottons 7 Wools 5	Cereals 12 Silk goods 10 Cotton goods 7 Minerals 7 Colonial wares 5 Iron work 5	Cereals 11 Minerals 10 Iron work 9 Chemicals 5 Fruits and vegetables 5 Cotton goods 5	Machinery and transport equipment 21 Food and live animals 14 Crude materials, inedible, except fuels 9 Miscellaneous manufactured goods 9 Chemicals 9 Iron and steel 9	Silk 25 Cottons 19 Clocks and watches 14 Foodstuffs, etc. 12 Machinery, carriages 6 Wools 2	Silk goods 14 Cotton goods 14 Clocks and watches 10 Animal food substances 6 Machinery 5 Colonial wares 3	Clocks and watches 18 Machinery 16 Cotton goods 8 Silk goods 7 Dyes 6 Animal food substances 4	Machinery and transport equipment 30 Chemicals 19 Clocks and watches 15 Textile yarns, fabrics, etc. 10 Miscellaneous manufactured goods 9 Food and live animals 5
SWEDEN							
Minerals, mostly coals 16 Metal goods, machinery, etc. 15 Corn and flour 10 Textile manufactures 9 Colonial wares 8 Hair, hides, and other animal products 5	Minerals, mostly coals 18 Metal goods, machinery, etc. 11 Raw textile material and yarn 10 Corn and flour 8 Textile manufactures 8 Colonial wares 7	Minerals and mineral manufactures 18 Textile manufactures 14 Non-precious metals and manufactures thereof 13 Vegetable products 11 Machines, apparatus and electrical plant 10 Chemical products 8	Machinery and transport equipment 15 Manufactured goods 14 Mineral fuels, lubricants and related materials 8 Petroleum and products thereof 7 Food and live animals 6 Machinery, non-elect. 6	Timber 50 Live animals and animal food 14 Metals 12 Metal goods, machinery, etc. 6 Minerals 6 Paper and paper products 3	Timber 25 Wood pulp, paper and products 17 Minerals 12 Live animals and animal food 12 Metal goods, machinery, etc. 11 Metals 10	Paper, pulp and paper products 26 Non-precious metals, etc. 17 Minerals and mineral manufactures 14 Wood and cork and manufactures thereof 11 Machines, apparatus and electrical plant 10 Live animals and animal food 6	Crude materials, inedible, except fuels 18 Machinery and transport equipment 16 Manufactured goods 14 Pulp and waste paper 7 Machinery, non-electric 7 Transport equipment (motor vehicles, etc.) 7

Note:

[1] Since 1922 the Belgo-Luxemburg Union.

Sources:

The Statesman's Yearbook (various).
United Nations, *Yearbook of Trade Statistics* (various).

TABLE VII/11

Direction of the Foreign Trade of the Netherlands, Belgium, Switzerland, and Sweden, by value, 1900, 1913, 1938, and 1960

Importing countries	*Year*			*Principal sources of imports*			
Netherlands	1900	Prussia[2]	Britain	U.S.A.	Dutch E. Indies	Belgium	Russia
	1913	Prussia[2]	Dutch E. Indies	U.S.A.	Russia	Belgium	Britain
	1938	Germany[4]	Belgium[1]	U.S.A.	Britain	Dutch E. Indies	France
	1960	Germany[5]	Belgium[1]	U.S.A.	Britain	France	Sweden
Belgium[1]	1900	France	Germany	Britain	U.S.A.	Netherlands	Russia
	1913	France	Germany	Britain	U.S.A.	Netherlands	Argentina
	1938	France	Germany	U.S.A.	Netherlands	Belg. Congo	Britain
	1960	Germany	Netherlands	France	U.S.A.	Britain	Congo
Switzerland	1900	Germany	France	Italy	Austro-Hung.	Britain	Russia
	1913	Germany	France	Italy	U.S.A.	Britain	Austro-Hung.
	1938	Germany	France	U.S.A.	Italy	Britain	Argentina
	1960	Germany	France	U.S.A.	Italy	Britain	Sweden
Sweden	1900	Germany	Britain	Denmark	Russia[6]	Norway	Belgium
	1913	Britain	Germany	U.S.A.	Denmark	Russia[6]	France
	1938	Germany	Britain[7]	U.S.A.	Denmark	Netherlands	Belgium[1]
	1960	Germany[5]	Britain	U·S.A.	Netherlands	Denmark	France
Exporting countries	*Year*			*Chief markets*			
Netherlands	1900	Prussia[2]	Britain	Belgium	U.S.A.	Dutch E. Indies	France
	1913	Prussia[3]	Britain	Belgium	Dutch E. Indies	U.S.A.	France
	1938	Britain	Germany[4]	Belgium[1]	Dutch E. Indies	France	U.S.A.
	1960	Germany[5]	Belgium[1]	Britain	France	U.S.A.	Sweden
Belgium	1900	Germany	France	Britain	Netherlands	U.S.A.	Spain
	1913	Germany	France	Britain	Netherlands	U.S.A.	Argentina
	1938	France	Britain	Germany	Netherlands	U.S.A.	Argentina
	1960	Netherlands	Germany[5]	France	U.S.A.	Britain	Switzerland
Switzerland	1900	Germany	Britain	France	Austro-Hung.	Italy	Russia
	1913	Germany	Britain	France	U.S.A.	Italy	Austro-Hung.
	1938	Germany	Britain	France	Italy	U.S.A.	Argentina
	1960	Germany[5]	U.S.A.	Italy	France	Britain	Sweden
Sweden	1900	Britain	Germany	Denmark	France	Netherlands	Russia[6]
	1913	Britain	Germany	Denmark	France	Norway	Russia[6]
	1938	Britain[7]	Germany	U.S.A.	Norway	Denmark	Finland
	1960	Britain	Germany[5]	Norway	Denmark	U.S.A.	Netherlands

Notes:

[1] Since 1922 the Belgo-Luxemburg Union.
[2] Including Hamburg.
[3] Including Hamburg and Bremen.
[4] Including Austria.
[5] Western Germany.
[6] Including Finland.
[7] Including Ireland.

Sources:

The Statesman's Yearbook (various).
Trade Statistics (various countries).

Table VII/12

Growth of World Trade

and Percentage of it held by Europe, Leading European Commercial Countries, and the United States

(in millions of U.S. $ to the nearest $50 million, and in percentage)

Year	Value of world trade ($ millions)	Europe %	United Kingdom %	Germany[1] %	France %	Netherlands[2]	Belgium	U.S.A.
1750	700	74	15	..	9	4		..
1800	1,500	75	22	..	10	5		..
1840	2,800	71	20	..	12	8		7
1860	7,300	69	25	..	11	6		9
1880	14,900	70	23	10	11	8		10
1900	19,550	66	20	13	9	8	4	11
1913	38,150	58	17	13	8	8	4	11
1938	46,100	52	14	9	5	3	3[3]	11
1960	262,500	53	8	8[4]	5	3	3[3]	14

Note: The value of world trade is arrived at by adding total world imports to total world exports, i.e. the items of trade appear twice.

Sources: The pre-1900 figures are rough estimates based on M. G. Mulhall, *The Dictionary of Statistics* (1899).
Figures for twentieth century are based on Tables VII/13 to VII/22.
For Notes to Tables VII/12 to VII/22 see p. 332 below.

Table VII/13

UNITED KINGDOM

Sources of Imports, Selected Years

Origin	1840 Value in $ millns	1840 % of total U.K. imports	1840 % of total from British Empire	1860 Value in $ millns	1860 % of total U.K. imports	1860 % of total from British Empire	1880 Value in $ millns	1880 % of total U.K. imports	1880 % of total from British Empire
Europe	..	..	..	*419*	*41*	*1*	*796*	*40*	*n.*
Belgium	..	..	..	20	2	..	55	3	..
France	..	..	..	87	8	..	205	10	..
Germany	..	..	..	73[8]	7	..	120	6	..
Netherlands	..	..	..	41	4	..	127	6	..
North America	..	..	..	*252*	*24*	*3*	*590*	*29*	*3*
Canada[5]	..	..	..	33	3	..	65	3	..
U.S.A.	..	..	..	219	21	..	525	26	..
Latin America	..	..	..	*96*	*9*	*3*	*126*	*6*	*2*
Argentina	..	..	..	5	n.	..	4	n.	..
Brazil	..	..	..	11	1	..	26	1	..
Chile	..	..	..	13	1	..	17	1	..
Mexico	..	..	..	2	n.	..	3	n.	..
Peru	..	..	..	13	1	..	13	1	..
Oceania	..	..	..	*32*	*3*	*3*	*126*	*6*	*6*
Australia	..	..	..	32	3	..	100	5	..
Asia	..	..	..	*143*	*14*	*9*	*270*	*13*	*9*
China	..	..	..	46[9]	5	..	58[9]	3	..
British India	..	..	..	85[10]	8	..	164[10]	8	..
Netherlands East Indies	..	..	..	2	n.	..	11	1	..
Japan	..	..	..	n.	n.	..	3	n.	..
Malaya[6]	..	..	..	5	n.	..	18	1	..
Africa	..	..	..	*80*	*8*	*2*	*98*	*5*	*2*
Egypt	..	..	..	50	5	..	45	2	..
West Africa	..	..	..	9[11]	1	..	13[12]	1	..
South Africa	..	..	..	8[13]	1	..	27[14]	1	..
Countries not included above	..	..	..	*9*	*1*	..	*9*	*n.*	..
World	*255*[7]	..	..	*1,031*	*100*	*20*	*2,015*	*100*	*22*
Total World Imports	..	..	..	*n.a.*	..	..	*8,162*	*25%*	*5%*

n.a. = not available. n. = negligible.

For notes to Tables VII/12 to VII/22 see p. 332, below.

Origin	1900 Value in $ millns	1900 % of total U.K. imports	1900 % of total from British Empire	1913 Value in $ millns	1913 % of total U.K. imports	1913 % of total from British Empire	1938 Value in $ millns	1938 % of total U.K. imports	1938 % of total from British Empire	1960 Value in $ millns	1960 % of tota U.K. imports	1960 % of total from British Commonwealth
Europe	*1,100*	*43*	*n.*	*1,548*	*41*	*n.*	*1,421*	*34*	*n.*	*4,038*	*36*	..
Belgium	115	4	..	115	3	..	93	2	..	191	2	..
France	263	10	..	227	6	..	109	3	..	367	3	..
Germany	153	6	..	394	10	..	141	3	..	509	4	..
Netherlands	154	6	..	116	3	..	141	3	..	507	4	..
North America	*789*	*31*	*4*	*848*	*23*	*4*	*906*	*22*	*9*	*2,639*	*23*	*9*
Canada	109	4	..	149	4	..	358	9	..	1,051	9	..
U.S.A.	680	26	..	694	18	..	548	13	..	1,588	14	..
Latin America	*146*	*6*	*n.*	*393*	*10*	*n.*	*471*	*11*	*1*	*1,027*	*9*	*1*
Argentina	64	2	..	208	5	..	181	4	..	269	2	..
Brazil	29	1	..	49	1	..	37	1	..	82	1	..
Chile	24	1	..	26	1	..	26	1	..	67	1	..
Mexico	2	n.	..	9	n.	..	10	n.	..	16	n.	..
Venezuela	..	..	..	3	n.	..	6	n.	..	201	2	..
Oceania	*173*	*7*	*7*	*286*	*8*	*8*	*530*	*13*	*13*	*1,075*	*9*	*9*
Australia	116	4	..	187	5	..	326	8	..	555	5	..
New Zealand	57	2	..	99	3	..	204	5	..	520	4	..
Asia	*231*	*9*	*8*	*458*	*12*	*10*	*530*	*13*	*8*	*1,467*	*13*	*8*
China	12	n.	..	23	1	..	30	1	..	70	1	..
India	134	5	..	237	6	..	291	7	..	500[30]	4	..
Indonesia	1	n.	..	19	1	..	25	1	..	17	n.	..
Japan	7	n.	..	22	1	..	42[45]	1	..	118	1	..
Malaya[6]	34	1	..	95	2	..	48	1	..	178	2	..
Africa	*105*	*4*	*1*	*220*	*6*	*5*	*282*	*7*	*4*	*1,064*	*9*	*8*
North Africa	65	3	..	113[42]	3	..	79[47]	2	..	91	1	..
East Africa	6	n.	..	9[43]	n.	..	27[48]	1	..	88	1	..
West Africa	14	1	..	15	n.	..	44[51]	1	..	288	3	..
South Africa	20[41]	1	..	61[41]	2	..	90[50]	2	..	561	5	..
Countries not included above	*19*	*1*	..	*14*	*n.*	..	*21*	*1*	..	*12*	*n.*	.
World	*2,563*	*100*	*21*	*3,767*	*100*	*28*	*4,161*	*100*	*35*	*11,322*	*100*	*36*
TOTAL WORLD IMPORTS	*10,262*	*25%*	*5%*	*19,857*	*19%*	*5%*	*24,178*	*17%*	*6%*	*134,800*	*8%*	*3%*

n. = negligible.

Table VII/14

UNITED KINGDOM

Destination of Exports, Selected Years

Destination	1840			1860			1880		
	Value in $ millns	% of total British exports	% of total to British Empire	Value in $ millns	% of total British exports	% of total to British Empire	Value in $ millns	% of total British exports	% of total to British Empire
Europe	*105*	*42*	*3*	*358*	*44*	*2*	*397*	*36*	*1*
Belgium	4	2	..	20	2	..	28	3	..
France	12	5	..	62	8	..	76	7	..
Germany	28[8]	11	..	91[8]	11	..	83	8	..
Netherlands	17	7	..	48	6	..	45	4	..
North America	*40*	*16*	*6*	*132*	*16*	*2*	*189*	*17*	*3*
Canada[5]	14	6	..	20	2	..	38	3	..
U.S.A.	26	10	..	112	14	..	151	14	..
Latin America	*53*	*21*	*7*	*74*	*9*	*2*	*109*	*10*	*1*
Argentina	3[20]	1	..	9	1	..	12	1	..
Brazil	13	5	..	23	3	..	33	3	..
Chile	7	3	..	8	1	..	10	1	..
Mexico	2	1	..	3	n.	..	6	1	..
Peru	4	2	..	7	1	..	2	n.	..
Oceania	*10*	*4*	*4*	*52*	*6*	*6*	*83*	*8*	*8*
Australia	10	4	..	52	6	..	83	8	..
Asia	*37*	*15*	*12*	*139*	*33*	*12*	*232*	*21*	*17*
China	3	1	..	27[9]	3	..	25[9]	2	..
British India	30	12	..	90[10]	11	..	154[10]	14	..
Netherlands East Indies	2	1	..	7	1	..	9	1	..
Japan	n.	n.	..	n.	n.	..	16	1	..
Malaya[6]	n.	n.	..	8	1	..	11	1	..
Africa	*7*	*3*	*2*	*36*	*4*	*2*	*63*	*6*	*3*
Egypt	n.	n.	..	13	2	..	15	1	..
West Africa	2[11]	1	..	5[11]	1	..	9[12]	1	..
South Africa	4[17]	2	..	11[13]	1	..	32[14]	3	..
Countries not included above	*n.*	*n.*	..	*15*	*2*	..	*20*	*2*	..
World	*252*	*100*	*33*	*806*	*100*	*27*	*1,093*	*100*	*34*
TOTAL WORLD EXPORTS	*n.a.*	..	..	*n.a.*	..	..	*7,042*	*16%*	5%

n.a. = not available. n. = negligible.

Destination	1900 Value in $ millns	1900 % of total British exports	1900 % of total to British Empire	1913 Value in $ millns	1913 % of total British exports	1913 % of total to British Empire	1938 Value in $ millns	1938 % of total British exports	1938 % of total to British Empire	1960 Value in $ millns	1960 % of total British exports	1960 % of total to British Commonwealth
Europe	*585*	*41*	*1*	*917*	*36*	*n.*	*813*	*36*	*n.*	*3,031*	*33*	*n.*
Belgium	53	4	..	65	3	..	40	2	..	181	2	..
France	98	7	..	142	6	..	74	3	..	244	3	..
Germany	137	10	..	199	8	..	101	4	..	446	5	..
Netherlands	53	4	..	75	3	..	64	3	..	323	4	..
North America	*137*[5]	*10*	*3*	*265*	*10*	*5*	*212*	*9*	*5*	*1,781*	*19*	*10*
Canada	40[5]	3	..	117	5	..	111	5	..	878	10	..
U.S.A.	97	7	..	144	6	..	101	4	..	903	10	..
Latin America	*150*	*11*	*1*	*272*	*11*	*n.*	*218*	*10*	*2*	*582*	*6*	*2*
Argentina	35	2	..	111	4	..	94	4	..	117	1	..
Brazil	28	2	..	61	2	..	25	1	..	53	1	..
Chile	41	3	..	29	1	..	8	n.	..	38	n.	..
Mexico	10	1	..	11	n.	..	4	n.	..	57	1	..
Venezuela	3	n.	..	4	n.	..	7	n.	..	78	1	..
Oceania	*133*	*9*	*9*	*223*	*9*	*9*	*281*	*12*	*12*	*1,063*	*12*	*12*
Australia	106	7	..	169	7	..	187	8	..	726	8	..
New Zealand	27	2	..	53	2	..	94	4	..	337	4	..
Asia	*282*	*20*	*13*	*620*	*24*	*16*	*385*	*17*	*11*	*1,583*	*17*	*12*
China	27	2	..	73	3	..	22	1	..	88	1	..
India	147	10	..	344	13	..	196	9	..	672	7	..
Indonesia	12	1	..	35	1	..	18	1	..	54	1	..
Japan	48	3	..	71	3	..	9	n.	..	78	1	..
Malaya[6]	17	1	..	34	1	..	54	2	..	197	2	..
Africa	*137*	*10*	*6*	*248*	*10*	*8*	*361*	*16*	*13*	*1,127*	*12*	*11*
North Africa	36[54]	3	..	61[42]	2	..	52[47]	2	..	77[47]	1	..
West Africa	20	1	..	44	1	..	53[49]	2	..	350[21]	4	..
East Africa / South Africa	64[41]	5	..									
East Africa				18[43]	1	..	35[48]	2	..	128[22]	1	..
South Africa		..	..	113[14]	4	..	219[50]	9	..	559	6	..
Countries not included above	*3*	*n.*	..	*18*	*1*	..	*7*	*n.*	..	*22*	*n.*	..
World	*1,427*	*100*	*32*	*2,573*	*100*	*39*	*2,277*	*100*	*44*	*9,189*	*100*	*45*
TOTAL WORLD EXPORTS	*9,310*	*15%*	5%	*18,285*	*14%*	5%	*21,945*	*10%*	5%	*127,700*	7%	3%

Table VII/15

FRANCE

Sources of Imports, Selected Years

Origin	1840 Value in $ millns	1840 % of total French imports	1840 % of total from French Empire	1860 Value in $ millns	1860 % of total French imports	1860 % of total from French Empire	1880 Value in $ millns	1880 % of total French imports	1880 % of total from French Empire
Europe	*102*	*69*	..	*234*	*63*	..	*629*	*64*	..
Belgium	18	12	..	35	9	..	90	9	..
Germany	10[8]	7	..	26[8]	7	..	86	9	..
Netherlands	2	1	..	6	2	..	8	1	..
United Kingdom	17	12	..	60	16	..	130	13	..
North America	*28*	*19*	..	*47*	*13*	..	*146*	*15*	..
Canada[5]	..	..	..	..	..	..	3	n.	..
U.S.A.	28	19	..	47	13	..	143	14	..
Latin America	*12*	*8*	*6*	*41*	*11*	*3*	*85*	*9*	*1*
Argentina	3	2	..	7	2	..	28	3	..
Brazil	n.	n.	..	5	1	..	10	1	..
Chile	n.	n.	..	2	1	..	6	1	..
Mexico	n.	n.	..	1	n.	..	2	n.	..
Peru	n.	n.	..	4	1	..	4	n.	..
Oceania	*n.*	*n.*	..	*n.*	*n.*	*n.*	*4*	*n.*	*n.*
Australia	n.	n.	..	n.	n.	..	n.	n.	..
Asia	*4*	*3*	*n.*	*16*	*4*	*1*	*65*	*7*	*n.*
China	n.	n.	..	n.	n.	..	20	2	..
British India	4	3	..	14[15]	4	..	32[15]	3	..
Netherlands East Indies	n.	n.	..	2	1	..	7	1	..
Japan	n.	n.	..	n.	n.	..	5	1	..
Malaya[6]	n.	n.	..	n.	n.	..	n.	n.	..
Africa	*2*	*1*	*n.*	*34*	*9*	*6*	*57*	*6*	*3*
Egypt and Algeria	2	1	..	15[16]	4	..	36[16]	4	..
West Africa	n.	n.	..	2[11]	1	..	6[11]	1	..
South Africa	n.	n.	..	3[17]	1	..	1[18]	n.	..
Countries not included above	*n.*	*n.*	*n.*	*1*	*n.*	*n.*	*n.*	*n.*	*n.*
World	*147*	*100*	*6*	*372*	*100*	*9*	*987*	*100*	*5*
Total World Imports	*n.a.*	..	..	*n.a.*	..	..	*8,162*	*12%*	*n.*

n.a. = not available. n. = negligible.

Origin	1900 Value in $ millns	1900 % of total French imports	1900 % of total from French Empire	1913 Value in $ millns	1913 % of total French imports	1913 % of total from French Empire	1938 Value in $ millns	1938 % of total French imports	1938 % of total from French Empire	1960 Value in $ millns	1960 % of total French imports	1960 % of total from French franc zone territories
Europe	*516*	*56*	..	*880*	*54*	..	*471*	*36*	..	*2,742*	*43*	..
Belgium	83	9	..	109	7	..	90	7	..	375	6	..
Germany	84	9	..	210	13	..	90	7	..	997	16	..
Netherlands	9	1	..	22	1	..	34	3	..	235	4	..
United Kingdom	132	14	..	217	13	..	92	7	..	231	4	..
North America	*102*[31]	*11*	..	*187*[31]	*11*	..	*170*	*13*	..	*842*	*13*	..
Canada	2[31]	n.	..	4[31]	n.	..	18	1	..	92	1	..
U.S.A.	100	11	..	175	11	..	152	12	..	750	12	..
Latin America	*125*	*14*	*2*	*183*	*11*	*2*	*120*	*9*	*2*	*351*	*6*	*1*
Argentina	56	6	..	72	4	..	27	2	..	57	1	..
Brazil	15	2	..	34	2	..	22	2	..	62	1	..
Chile	15	2	..	21	1	..	12	1	..	16	n.	..
Mexico	3	n.	..	7	n.	..	4	n.	..	22	n.	..
Venezuela	3	n.	..	6	n.	..	9	1	..	51	1	..
Oceania	*20*	*2*	*n.*	*58*	*4*	*n.*	*56*	*4*	*n.*	*250*	*4*	*1*
Australia	18	2	..	55	3	..	43	3	..	142	2	..
New Zealand	n.	n.	..	n.	n.	..	8	1	..	70	1	..
Asia	*91*	*10*	*1*	*192*	*12*	*2*	*186*	*14*	*4*	*700*	*11*	*1*
China	32	3	..	47	3	..	7[46]	1	..	23	n.	..
India	30	3	..	76	5	..	38[28]	3	..	49	1	..
Indonesia	5	1	..	13	1	..	8	1	..	9	n.	..
Japan	13	1	..	24	1	..	11[45]	1	..	16	n.	..
Malaya[6]	n.	n.	..	n.	n.	..	16	1	..	73	1	..
Africa	*65*	*7*	*5*	*148*	*8*	*6*	*318*	*24*	*18*	*1,429*	*23*	*20*
North Africa	46[47]	5	..	104[42]	5	..	203[47]	16	..	797[47]	10	..
West Africa	5	1	..	22[44]	1	..	64[49]	8	..	445[23]	6	..
East Africa	10[32]	1	..	13[33]	1	..	34[48]			115[24]	6	..
South Africa				9[34]	1	..	15[50]	1	..	72[25]	1	..
Countries not included above	*2*	*n.*	*n.*	*3*	*n.*	*n.*	*1*	*n.*	*n.*	*13*	*1*	*n.*
World	*92*	*100*	*8*	*1,651*	*100*	*9*	*1,322*	*100*	*24*	*6,327*	*100*	*23*
TOTAL WORLD IMPORTS	*10,262*	*9%*	*1%*	*19,857*	*8%*	*1%*	*24,178*	*5%*	*1%*	*134,800*	*5%*	*1%*

n. = negligible.

TABLE VII/16

FRANCE

Destination of Exports, Selected Years

Destination	1840 Value in $ millns	1840 % of total French exports	1840 % of total from French Empire	1860 Value in $ millns	1860 % of total French exports	1860 % of total from French Empire	1880 Value in $ millns	1880 % of total French exports	1880 % of total from French Empire
Europe	*81*	*68*	..	*293*	*66*	..	*492*	*72*	..
Belgium	9	8	..	33	7	..	92	14	..
Germany	15[8]	13	..	36[8]	8	..	71	10	..
Netherlands	2	2	..	4	1	..	7	1	..
United Kingdom	17	14	..	117	26	..	179	26	..
North America	*13*	*11*	..	*49*	*11*	..	*66*	*10*	..
Canada[5]	..	..	..	..	..	..	1	n.	..
U.S.A.	13	11	..	49	11	..	65	10	..
Latin America	*17*	*14*	*7*	*53*	*12*	*2*	*66*	*10*	*1*
Argentina	n.	n.	..	7	2	..	17	3	..
Brazil	4	4	..	12	3	..	15	2	..
Chile	3	3	..	12	3	..	3	n.	..
Mexico	2	2	..	2	n.	..	3	n.	..
Peru	n.	n.	..	6	1	..	1	n.	..
Oceania	*n.*	*n.*	*n.*	*n.*	*n.*	*n.*	*2*	*n.*	*n.*
Australia	n.	n.	..	n.	n.	..	1	n.	..
Asia	*n.*	*n.*	*n.*	*3*	*1*	*n.*	*5*	*1*	*n.*
China	n.	n.	..	n.	n.	..	1	n.	..
British India	n.	n.	..	2[15]	n.	..	1[15]	n.	..
Netherlands East Indies	n.	n.	..	n.	n.	..	1	n.	..
Japan	n.	n.	..	n.	n.	..	1	n.	..
Malaya[6]	n.	n.	..	n.	n.	..	n.	n.	..
Africa	*8*	*7*	*7*	*45*	*10*	*8*	*48*	*7*	*5*
Egypt and Algeria	8[16]	7	..	33[16]	7	..	39[16]	6	..
West Africa	n.	n.	..	n.[11]	n.	..	1[11]	n.	..
South Africa	n.	n.	..	4[17]	1	..	2[18]	n.	..
Countries not included above	*n.*	*n.*	..	*3*	*1*	..	*n.*	*n.*	..
World	*119*	*100*	*13*	*446*	*100*	*10*	*680*	*100*	*7*
TOTAL WORLD EXPORTS	*n.a.*	..	..	*n.a.*	..	..	*7,042*	*10%*	*1%*

n.a. = not available. n. = negligible.

Destination	1900 Value in $ millns	1900 % of total French exports	1900 % of total to French Empire	1913 Value in $ millns	1913 % of total French exports	1913 % of total to French Empire	1938 Value in $ millns	1938 % of total French exports	1938 % of total to French Empire	1960 Value in $ millns	1960 % of total French exports	1960 % of total to French franc zone territories
Europe	*594*	*74*	..	*939*	*71*	..	*487*	*56*	..	*3,557*	*51*	..
Belgium	117	15	..	217	16	..	120	14	..	517	7	..
Germany	91	11	..	170	13	..	53	6	..	950	14	..
Netherlands	11	1	..	16	1	..	38	4	..	187	3	..
United Kingdom	241	30	..	285	22	..	102	12	..	349	5	..
North America	*51*	*6*	..	*89*	*7*	..	*54*	*6*	..	*452*	*7*	..
Canada	1[31]	n.	..	5[31]	n.	..	5	1	..	53	1	..
U.S.A.	50	6	..	83	6	..	48	6	..	399	6	..
Latin America	*41*	*5*	*1*	*94*	*7*	*n.*	*57*	*7*	..	*355*	*n.*	*n.*
Argentina	10	1	..	39	3	..	21	2	..	63	1	..
Brazil	7	1	..	17	1	..	9	1	..	66	n.	..
Chile	3	n.	..	8	1	..	2	n.	..	19	n.	..
Mexico	5	1	..	8	1	..	4	n.	..	29	n.	..
Venezuela	n.	n.	..	1	n.	..	3	n.	..	21	n.	..
Oceania	*4*	*n.*	*n.*	*5*	*n.*	*n.*	*6*	*1*	*n.*	*71*	*n.*	*n.*
Australia	2	n.	..	3	n.	..	3	n.	..	37	1	..
New Zealand	n.	n.	..	n.	n.	..	1	n.	..	6	n.	..
Asia	*21*	*3*	*1*[35]	*36*	*3*	*1*[35]	*56*	*6*	*3*[35]	*403*	*n.*	*n.*
China	3	n.	..	4	n.	..	6[46]	1	..	53	1	..
India	4	n.	..	10	1	..	5[28]	1	..	64[30]	1	..
Indonesia	n.	n.	..	1	n.	..	4	1	..	11	n.	..
Japan	4	n.	..	3	n.	..	3[45]	n.	..	28	n.	..
Malaya[6]	n.	n.	..	n.	n.	..	1	n.	..	7	n.	..
Africa	*83*	*10*	*9*	*181*	*12*	*11*	*215*	*24*	*24*	*2,067*	*30*	*28*
North Africa	64[47]	8	..	155[42]	10	..	166[47]	19	..	1,468[47]	21	..
West Africa	3	n.	..	12[44]	1	..	27[51]	4	..	448[26]	n.	..
East Africa } South Africa }	13[32]	2	..	13[48]	1	..	16[52]	1	..	113[24]	1	..
South Africa				1[50]	n.	..	6	1	..	38[25]	n.	..
Countries not included above	*12*	*1*	..	*5*	*n.*	..	..	..	..	*14*	*n.*	..
World	*806*	*100*	*12*	*1,348*	*100*	*13*	*875*	*100*	*28*	*6,919*	*100*	*30*
TOTAL WORLD EXPORTS	*9,310*	*9%*	*1%*	*18,285*	*7%*	*1%*	*21,945*	*4%*	*1%*	*127,700*	*5%*	*2%*

n. = negligible.

Table VII/17

GERMANY

Sources of Imports, Selected Years

Origin	1900 Value in $ millns	1900 % of total German imports	1900 % of total from German Empire	1913 Value in $ millns	1913 % of total German imports	1913 % of total from German Empire	1938 Value in $ millns	1938 % of total German imports	1938 % of total from German Empire	1960 Value in $ millns	1960 % of total German imports
Europe	*903*	*63*	..	*1,402*	*55*	..	*1,187*	*55*	..	*5,902*	*58*
Belgium	52	4	..	82	3	..	78	4	..	581	6
France	73	5	..	139	5	..	57	3	..	952	9
Netherlands	51	4	..	79	3	..	79	4	..	866	9
United Kingdom	200	14	..	209	8	..	113	5	..	466	5
North America	*243*	*17*	..	*423*	*16*	..	*198*	*9*	..	*1,631*	*16*
Canada	..	..	..	15	1	..	37	2	..	209	2
U.S.A.	243	17	..	407	16	..	162	7	..	1,422	14
Latin America	*134*	*9*	..	*290*	*11*	..	*358*	*16*	..	*887*	*9*
Argentina	56	4	..	118	5	..	87	4	..	130	1
Brazil	27	2	..	59	2	..	86	4	..	120	1
Chile	21	1	..	48	2	..	36	2	..	120	1
Mexico	3	n.	..	6	n.	..	25	1	..	66	1
Venezuela	2	n.	..	5	n.	..	12	1	..	90	1
Oceania	*29*	*2*	*n.a.*	*78*	*3*	*n.*	*25*	*1*	..	*137*	*1*
Australia	29	2	..	70	3	..	21	1	..	96	1
New Zealand	..	..	..	2	n.	..	4	n.	..	36	n.
Asia	*86*	*6*	*n.*	*250*	*10*	*n.*	*248*	*11*	..	*1,006*	*10*
China	8	1	..	31	1	..	72	3	..	69	1
India	49	3	..	129	5	..	57	3	..	66[30]	1
Indonesia	20	1	..	54	2	..	54	2	..	46	n.
Japan	4	n.	..	11	n.	..	10	n.	..	68	1
Malaya[6]	3	n.	..	6	n.	..	20	1	..	110	1
Africa	*25*	*2*	*n.a.*	*118*	*5*	*n.*	*154*	*7*	..	*585*	*6*
North Africa	12[47]	1	..	41[42]	2	..	30[47]	1	..	113[47]	1
West Africa	8[36]	1	..	47	2	..	51[49]	2	..	190[23]	2
East Africa	n.a.[37]	n.a.	..	12[43]	n.	..	19[48]	n.	..	144[24]	2
South Africa	4[14]	n.	..	17[14]	1	..	54[50]	2	..	138[27]	1
Countries not included above	*18*	*1*	..	*3*	*n.*	..	*8*	*n.*	..	*24*	*n.*
World	*1,439*	*100*	*n.a.*	*2,564*	*100*	*n.*	*2,180*	*100*	..	*10,172*	*100*
Total World Imports	*10,262*	*14%*	*n.a.*	*19,857*	*13%*	*n.*	*23,720*	*9%*	..	*119,600*	*9%*

n.a. = not available. n. = negligible.

TABLE VII/18

GERMANY[1]

Destination of Exports, Selected Years

Destination	1900			1913			1938			1960[4]	
	Value in $ millns	% of total German exports	% of total to German Empire	Value in $ millns	% of total German exports	% of total to German Empire	Value in $ millns	% of total German exports	% of total to German Empire	Value in $ millns	% of total German exports
Europe	*879*	*78*	..	*1,828*	*76*	..	*1,466*	*70*	..	*7,692*	*67*
Belgium	60	5	..	131	5	..	91	4	..	688	6
France	66	6	..	188	8	..	87	4	..	1,000	9
Netherlands	94	8	..	165	7	..	179	8	..	1,002	9
United Kingdom	217	19	..	342	14	..	140	7	..	511	4
North America	*109*[5]	*10*	..	*184*	*8*	..	*70*	*3*	..	*1,014*	*9*
Canada	4[5]	n.	..	14	1	..	10	n.	..	128	1
U.S.A.	105	9	..	170	7	..	60	3	..	886	8
Latin America	*54*	*5*	..	*183*	*8*	..	*254*	*12*	..	*798*	*7*
Argentina	15	1	..	63	3	..	59	3	..	150	1
Brazil	11	1	..	48	2	..	65	3	..	129	1
Chile	9	1	..	23	1	..	24	1	..	76	1
Mexico	7	1	..	11	n.	..	18	1	..	75	1
Venezuela	1	n.	..	2	n.	..	15	1	..	91	1
Oceania	*11*	*1*	*n.*	*24*	*1*	*n.*	*19*	*1*	..	*159*	*1*
Australia	11	1	..	21	1	..	16	1	..	133	1
New Zealand	..	..	..	3	n.	..	3	n.	..	23	n.
Asia	*54*	*5*	*n.*	*130*	*5*	*n.*	*209*	*10*	..	*1,114*	*10*
China	12[38]	1	..	30	1	..	51	2	..	95	1
India	13	1	..	36	1	..	43	2	..	258	2
Indonesia	6	1	..	23	1	..	22	1	..	65	1
Japan	17	1	..	29	1	..	37	2	..	120	1
Malaya[2]	3	n.	..	3	n.	..	5	n.	..	38	n.
Africa	*13*	*1*	*n.*	*50*	*2*	*1*	*81*	*4*	..	*603*	*5*
North Africa	4[47]	n.	..	16[42]	1	..	22[47]	1	..	175[47]	2
West Africa	4	n.	..	10	n.	..	15[49]	1	..	172[23]	2
East Africa	1	n.	..	8[43]	n.	..	9[48]	n.	..	85[24]	n.
South Africa	4[14]	n.	..	16[25]	1	..	35[50]	2	..	170	1
Countries not included above	*11*	*1*	..	*3*	*n.*	..	*2*	*n.*	..	*34*	*n.*
World	*1,132*	*100*	*n.*	*2,403*	*100*	*1*	*2,103*	*100*	..	*11,416*	*100*
TOTAL WORLD EXPORTS	*9,310*	*12%*	*n.*	*18,285*	*13%*	*n.*	*21,960*	*10%*	..	*113,700*	*10%*

n.a. = not available. n. = negligible.

TABLE VII/19

NETHERLANDS[2]

Sources of Imports, Selected Years

Origin	1840*			1860			1880		
	Value in $ millns	% of total Dutch imports	% of total from Dutch Empire	Value in $ millns	% of total Dutch imports	% of total from Dutch Empire	Value in $ millns	% of total Dutch imports	% of total from Dutch Empire
Europe	..	..	..	*92*	*70*	..	*274*	*78*	..
Belgium	..	..	..	16	12	..	43	12	..
France	..	..	..	6	5	..	6	2	..
Germany	..	..	..	27[8]	20	..	104	29	..
United Kingdom	..	..	..	28	21	..	88	25	..
North America	..	..	..	*5*	*4*	..	*34*	*10*	..
U.S.A.	..	..	..	5	4	..	34	10	..
Latin America	..	..	..	*3*	*2*	*1*	*5*	*1*	*n.*
Argentina	..	..	..	n.	n.	..	n.	n.	..
Brazil	..	..	..	n.	n.	..	n.	n.	..
Chile	..	..	..	n.	n.	..	1	n.	..
Mexico	..	..	..	n.	n.	..	n.	n.	..
Peru	..	..	..	1	n.	..	2	1	..
Oceania	..	..	..	*n.*	*n.*	..	*n.*	*n.*	..
Australia	..	..	..	n.	n.	..	n.	n.	..
Asia	..	..	..	*32*	*24*	*23*	*34*	*10*	*7*
China	..	..	..	1	n.	..	n.	n.	..
British India	..	..	..	n.	n.	..	n.	n.	..
Netherlands East Indies	..	..	..	30	22	..	23	7	..
Japan	..	..	..	n.	n.	..	n.	n.	..
Malaya[6]	..	..	..	1	n.	..	10	3	..
Africa	..	..	..	*1*	*n.*	..	*3*	*1*	..
Egypt	..	..	..	n.	n.	..	n.	n.	..
West Africa	..	..	..	n.	n.	..	3	1	..
South Africa	..	..	..	n.	n.	..	n.	n.	..
Countries not included above	..	..	..	*n.*	*n.*	..	*n.*	*n.*	..
World	..	..	..	*132*	*100*	*23*	*350*	*100*	*7*
TOTAL WORLD IMPORTS	..	..	..	*n.a.*	..	..	*8,162*	*4%*	*n.*

*No figure available for 1840. n. = negligible.

Origin	1900 Value in $ millns	1900 % of total Dutch imports	1900 % of total from Dutch Empire	1913 Value in $ millns	1913 % of total Dutch imports	1913 % of total from Dutch Empire	1938 Value in $ millns	1938 % of total Dutch imports	1938 % of total from Dutch Empire	1960 Value in $ millns	1960 % of total Dutch imports	1960 % of total from Dutch Empire
Europe	*518*	*63*	..	*624*	*38*	..	*479*	*62*	..	*2,886*	*64*	..
Belgium	87	11	..	147	9	..	88	11	..	830	18	..
France	9	1	..	14	1	..	36	4	..	174	4	..
Germany	161[40]	20	..	474[40]	29	..	165	21	..	977	22	..
United Kingdom	120	15	..	142	9	..	63	8	..	311	7	..
North America	*118*	*14*	..	*190*	*12*	..	*97*	*13*	..	*637*	*14*	..
Canada	n.	n.	..	6	n.	..	13	2	..	37	1	..
U.S.A.	118	14	..	184	11	..	84	11	..	600	14	..
Latin America	*49*	6	*n.*	*87*	*5*	*n.*	*77*	*10*	*n.*	*213*	*5*	*n.*
Argentina	20	2	..	53	3	..	35	4	..	69	2	..
Brazil	14	2	..	18	1	..	9	1	..	36	1	..
Chile	5	1	..	11	1	..	2	n.	..	39	1	..
Mexico	n.	n.	..	n.	n.	..	2	n.	..	17	n.	..
Venezuela	1	n.	..	n.	n.	..	..	..	..	19	n.	..
Oceania	*1*	*n.*	..	*5*	*n.*	..	*2*	*n.*	..	*8*	*n.*	..
Australia	1	n.	..	5	n.	..	1	n.	..	7	n.	..
New Zealand	n.	n.	..	n.	n.	..	1	n.	..	1	n.	..
Asia	*130*	*16*	*14*	*274*	*17*	*13*	*94*	*12*	*7*	*481*	*11*	..
China	n.	n.	..	5	n.	..	9[46]	1	..	21	n.	..
India	n.	n.	..	5	n.	..	17[28]	2	..	19[30]	n.	..
Indonesia	114	14	..	220	13	..	56	7	..	62	1	..
Japan	n.	n.	..	1	n.	..	4[45]	1	..	24	1	..
Malaya[6]	17	2	..	42	3	..	1	n.	..	17	n.	..
Africa	*4*	*n.*	..	*14*	*1*	..	*25*	*3*	..	*138*	*3*	..
North Africa	1	n.	..	6	n.	..	6[47]	n.	..	29[47]	1	..
West Africa	2	n.	..	8	n.	..	12[49]	2	..	77[23]	2	..
East Africa	1	n.	..	n.	n.	..	5[48]	1	..	13[24]	n.	..
South Africa	n.	n.	..	n.	n.	..	2[50]	n.	..	19[27]	n.	..
Countries not included above	*n.*	*n.*	..	*n.*	*n.*	..	..	..	..	..	..	..
World	*820*	*100*	*14*	*1,632*	*100*	*14*	*774*	*100*	*7*	*4,531*	*100*	*n.*
TOTAL WORLD IMPORTS	*10,262*	*8%*	*1%*	*19,857*	*8%*	*1%*	*24,178*	*3%*	*n.*	*134,800*	*3%*	*n.*

n. = negligible.

Table VII/20

NETHERLANDS[2]

Destination of Exports, Selected Years

Destination	1840* Value in $ millns	1840* % of total Dutch exports	1840* % of total to Dutch Empire	1860 Value in $ millns	1860 % of total Dutch exports	1860 % of total to Dutch Empire	1880 Value in $ millns	1880 % of total Dutch exports	1880 % of total to Dutch Empire
Europe	..	..	..	*87*	*59*	..	*234*	*89*	..
Belgium	..	..	..	14	10	..	42	16	..
France	..	..	..	4	3	..	4	2	..
Germany	..	..	..	34[8]	23	..	111	42	..
United Kingdom	..	..	..	26	17	..	61	24	..
North America	..	..	..	*2*	*1*	..	*7*	*3*	..
Canada[5]	..	..	..	..	..	..	..	..	..
U.S.A.	..	..	..	2	1	..	7	3	..
Latin America	..	..	..	*1*	*1*	*1*	*1*	*n.*	*n.*
Argentina	..	..	..	1	1	..	n.	n.	..
Brazil	..	..	..	n.	n.	..	n.	n.	..
Chile	..	..	..	n.	n.	..	n.	n.	..
Mexico	..	..	..	n.	n.	..	n.	n.	..
Peru	..	..	..	n.	n.	..	n.	n.	..
Oceania	..	..	..	*n.*	*n.*	..	*n.*	*n.*	..
Australia	..	..	..	n.	n.	..	n.	n.	..
Asia	..	..	..	*14*	*10*	*9*	*20*	*8*	*8*
China	..	..	..	n.	n.	..	n.	n.	..
British India	..	..	..	n.	n.	..	n.	n.	..
Netherlands East Indies	..	..	..	13	9	..	20	3	..
Japan	..	..	..	n.	n.	..	n.	n.	..
Malaya[6]	..	..	..	n.	n.	..	n.	n.	..
Africa	..	..	..	*n.*	*n.*	..	*1*	*n.*	..
Egypt	..	..	..	n.	n.	..	n.	n.	..
West Africa	..	..	..	n.	n.	..	1	n.	..
South Africa	..	..	..	n.	n.	..	n.	n.	..
Countries not included above	..	..	..	*n.*	*n.*	..	*n.*	*n.*	..
World	..	..	..	*147*	*100*	*10*	*262*	*100*	*8*
TOTAL WORLD EXPORTS	..	..	..	..	..	..	*7,042*	*4%*	*n.*

*No figures available for 1840. n. = negligible.

Destination	1900			1913			1938			1960		
	Value in $ millns	% of total Dutch exports	% of total to Dutch Empire	Value in $ millns	% of total Dutch exports	% of total to Dutch Empire	Value in $ millns	% of total Dutch exports	% of total to Dutch Empire	Value in $ millns	% of total Dutch exports	% of total to Dutch dependencies
Europe	*645*	*91*	..	*1,131*	*88*	..	*411*	*72*	..	*2,940*	*73*	..
Belgium	73	10	..	142	11	..	58	10	..	575	14	..
France	9	1	..	13	1	..	33	6	..	237	6	..
Germany	380[40]	54	..	616	47	..	84	15	..	908	23	..
United Kingdom	159	13	..	273	21	..	129	23	..	441	11	..
North America	*27*	*4*	..	*57*	*4*	..	*24*	*4*	..	*228*	*6*	..
Canada	n.	n.	..	2	n.	..	4	1	..	30	1	..
U.S.A.	27	4	..	55	4	..	20	4	..	198	5	..
Latin America	*3*	*n.*	*n.*	*9*	*1*	*n.*	*30*	*5*	*n.*	*123*	*3*	*n.*
Argentina	n.	n.	..	3	n.	..	7	1	..	22	1	..
Brazil	n.	n.	..	n.	n.	..	4	1	..	25	1	..
Chile	n.	n.	..	n.	n.	..	1	n.	..	8	n.	..
Mexico	n.	n.	..	n.	n.	..	1	n.	..	10	n.	..
Venezuela	n.	n.	..	1	n.	..	3	1	..	23	1	..
Oceania	*n.*	*n.*	..	*1*	*n.*	..	*4*	*1*	..	*36*	*1*	..
Australia	n.	n.	..	1	n.	..	3	1	..	35	1	..
New Zealand	n.	n.	..	n.	n.	..	1	n.	..	1	n.	..
Asia	*29*	*4*	*4*	*73*	*6*	*5*	*75*	*13*	*10*	*241*	*6*	..
China	1	n.	..	1	n.	..	1[46]	n.	..	2	n.	..
India	n.	n.	..	n.	n.	..	7[28]	1	..	33[30]	1	..
Indonesia	27	4	..	68	5	..	55	10	..	26	1	..
Japan	n.	n.	..	1	n.	..	2[45]	n.	..	22	1	..
Malaya[6]	1	n.	..	4	n.	..	3	1	..	28	1	..
Africa	*2*	*n.*	..	*14*	*1*	..	*24*	*4*	..	*141*	*4*	..
North Africa	n.	n.	..	4	n.	..	6[47]	1	..	35[47]	1	..
West Africa	1	n.	..	5	n.	..	3[49]	1	..	57[23]	1	..
East Africa	n.	n.	..	3	n.	..	4[48]	1	..	8[24]	n.	..
South Africa	n.	n.	..	1	n.	..	10[50]	2	..	42	1	..
Countries not included above	..	..	..	*n.*	*n.*	..	..	..	..	..	..	..
World	*706*	*100*	*4*	*1,285*	*100*	*6*	*568*	*100*	*10*	*4,028*	*100*	*n.*
TOTAL WORLD EXPORTS	*9,310*	*8%*	*n.*	*18,285*	*79*	*n.*	*21,945*	*3%*	*n.*	*127,700*	*3%*	*n.*

n. = negligible.

TABLE VII/21

BELGIUM

Sources of Imports, Selected Years

Origin	1840			1860			1880		
	Value in $ millns	% of total Belgian imports	% of total from Belgian Empire	Value in $ millns	% of total Belgian imports	% of total from Belgian Empire	Value in $ millns	% of total Belgian imports	% of total from Belgian Empire
Europe	*31*	*77*	..	*80*	*80*	..	*251*	*76*	..
France	8	20	..	21	21	..	66	20	..
Germany	4[8]	10	..	11[8]	11	..	48	15	..
Netherlands	8	20	..	20	20	..	46	15	..
United Kingdom	9	22	..	16	16	..	50	15	..
North America	*4*	*10*	..	*5*	*5*	..	*53*	*16*	..
U.S.A.	4	10	..	5	5	..	53	16	..
Latin America	*5*[19]	*12*	..	*15*	*15*	..	*18*	*5*	..
Argentina	n.	n.	..	8	8	..	8	3	..
Brazil	2	5	..	2	2	..	4	1	..
Chile	n.	n.	..	n.	n.	..	n.	n.	..
Mexico	n.	n.	..	n.	n.	..	n.	n.	..
Peru	n.	n	..	3	3	..	2	1	..
Oceania	*n.*	*n.*	..	*n.*	*n.*	..	*n.*	*n.*	..
Australia	n.	n.	..	n.	n.	..	n.	n.	..
Asia	*n.*	*n.*	..	*1*	*1*	..	*n.*	*n.*	..
China	n.	n.	..	n.	n.	..	n.	n.	..
British India	n.	n.	..	n.	n.	..	n.	n.	..
Netherlands East Indies	n.	n.	..	n.	n.	..	n.	n.	..
Japan	n.	n.	..	n.	n.	..	n.	n.	..
Malaya[6]	n.	n.	..	n.	n.	..	n.	n.	..
Africa	*n.*	*n.*	..	*1*	*1*	..	*n.*	*n.*	*n.*
Egypt	n.	n.	..	n.	n.	..	n.	n.	..
West Africa	n.	n.	..	n.	n.	..	n.	n.	..
South Africa	n.	n.	..	n.	n.	..	n.	n.	..
Countries not included above	*n.*	*n.*	..	*1*	*1*	..	*n.*	*n.*	..
World	*40*	*100*	..	*102*	*100*	..	*329*	*100*	*n.*
TOTAL WORLD IMPORTS	*n.a.*	..	..	*n.a.*	..	..	*8,162*	*4%*	*n.*

n.a. = not available. n. = negligible.

Origin	1900			1913			1938[3]			1960[3]	
	Value in $ millns	*% of total Belgian imports*	*% of total from Belgian Empire*	*Value in $ millns*	*% of total Belgian imports*	*% of total from Belgian Empire*	*Value in $ millns*	*% of total Belgian imports*	*% of total from Belgian Empire*	*Value in $ millns*	*% of total Belgian imports*
Europe	*309*	*71*	..	*652*	*66*	..	*453*	*59*	..	*2,600*	*66*
France	74	18	..	197	20	..	112	15	..	538	13
Germany	63	15	..	149	15	..	89	12	..	674	17
Netherlands	38	9	..	70	6	..	71	9	..	587	15
United Kingdom	53	13	..	102	11	..	61	8	..	292	7
North America	*55*	*13*	..	*88*	*9*	..	*96*	*13*	..	*440*	*11*
Canada	2	n.	..	6	1	..	11	1	..	48	1
U.S.A.	52	13	..	82	8	..	85	11	..	392	10
Latin America	*40*	*9*	..	*97*	*1*	..	*68*	*9*	..	*149*	*4*
Argentina	23	5	..	62	6	..	32	4	..	46	1
Brazil	8	2	..	11	1	..	11	1	..	26	1
Chile	6	1	..	18	2	..	3	n.	..	4	n.
Mexico	n.	n.	..	3	n.	..	5	1	..	15	n.
Venezuela	n.	n.	..	n.	n.	..	2	n.	..	14	n.
Oceania	*7*	*2*	..	*39*	*4*	..	*24*	*3*	..	*78*	*2*
Australia	7	2	..	39	4	..	22	3	..	55	1
New Zealand	n.	n.	..	n.	n.	..	2	n.	..	23	1
Asia	*10*	*2*	..	*58*	*6*	..	*46*	*6*	..	*221*	*6*
China	1	n.	..	4	n.	..	2	n.	..	10	n.
India	8	2	..	47	5	..	24	3	..	29	1
Indonesia	1	n.	..	1	n.	..	5	1	..	6	n.
Japan	1	n.	..	4	n.	..	3	n.	..	21	1
Malaya[6]	n.	n.	..	n.	n.	..	2	n.	..	8	n.
Africa	*11*	*3*	*2*	*21*	*2*	*1*	*78*	*10*	*7*	*363*	*9*
North Africa	2[47]	n.	..	7	1	..	7[47]	1	..	17[47]	n.
West Africa	n.	n.	..	n.	n.	..	3[49]	n.	..	6[23]	n.
East Africa	9[53]	2	..	10[53]	1	..	55[48]	7	..	264[53]	7
South Africa	n.	n.	..	4[14]	n.	..	15[50]	2	..	54[27]	1
Countries not included above	*3*	*1*	..	*36*	*4*	..	..	..	..	..	..
World	*434*	*100*	*2*	*990*	*100*	*1*	*765*	*100*	*3*	*3,957*	*100*
TOTAL WORLD IMPORTS	*10,262*	*4%*	*n.*	*19,857*	*5%*	*n.*	*24,178*	*3%*	*n.*	*134,800*	*3%*

n. = negligible.

Table VII/22

BELGIUM

Destination of Exports, Selected Years

Destination	1840 Value in $ millns	1840 % of total Belgian exports	1840 % of total to Belgian Empire	1860 Value in $ millns	1860 % of total Belgian exports	1860 % of total to Belgian Empire	1880 Value in $ millns	1880 % of total Belgian exports	1880 % of total to Belgian Empire
Europe	*26*	*96*	..	*86*	*93*	..	*223*	*94*	..
France	11	47	..	32	35	..	61	25	..
Germany	6[8]	22	..	14[8]	15	..	46	20	..
Netherlands	6	22	..	12	13	..	30	13	..
United Kingdom	2	7	..	19	21	..	48	20	..
North America	*n.*	*n.*	..	*2*	*2*	..	*7*	*3*	..
Canada	..	..	..	..	..	..	..	..	..
U.S.A.	n.	n.	..	2	2	..	7	3	..
Latin America	*n.*	*n.*	..	*4*	*4*	..	*7*	*3*	..
Argentina	n.	n.	..	1	1	..	3	1	..
Brazil	n.	n.	..	1	1	..	3	1	..
Chile	n.	n.	..	n.	n.	..	1	n.	..
Mexico	n.	n.	..	n.	n.	..	n.	n.	..
Peru	n.	n.	..	1	1	..	n.	n.	..
Oceania	*n.*	*n.*	..	*n.*	*n.*	..	*n.*	*n.*	..
Australia	n.	n.	..	n.	n.	..	n.	n.	..
Asia	*n.*	*n.*	..	*n.*	*n.*	..	*n.*	*n.*	..
China	n.	n.	..	n.	n.	..	n.	n.	..
British India	n.	n.	..	n.	n.	..	n.	n.	..
Netherlands East Indies	n.	n.	..	n.	n.	..	n.	n.	..
Japan	n.	n.	..	n.	n.	..	n.	n.	..
Malaya[6]	n.	n.	..	n.	n.	..	n.	n.	..
Africa	*n.*	*n.*	..	*n.*	*n.*	..	*n.*	*n.*	..
Egypt	n.	n.	..	n.	n.	..	n.	n.	..
West Africa	n.	n.	..	n.	n.	..	n.	n.	..
South Africa	n.	n.	..	n.	n.	..	n.	n.	..
Countries not included above	*n.*	*n.*	..	*n.*	*n.*	..	*5*	*1*	..
World	*27*	*100*	..	*92*	*100*	..	*238*	*100*	..
Total World Exports	*n.a.*	..	..	*n.a.*	..	..	*7,042*	*3%*	..

n.a. = not available. **n.** = negligible.

Destination	1900			1913			1938[3]			1960[3]	
	Value in $ millns	*% of total Belgian exports*	*% of total to Belgian Empire*	*Value in $ millns*	*% of total Belgian exports*	*% of total to Belgian Empire*	*Value in $ millns*	*% of total Belgian exports*	*% of total to Belgian Empire*	*Value in $ millns*	*% of total Belgian exports*
Europe	*320*	*85*	..	*587*	*84*	..	*523*	*72*	..	*2,713*	*72*
France	84	21	..	149	21	..	110	15	..	392	10
Germany	84	21	..	184	26	..	90	13	..	596	16
Netherlands	43	11	..	63	9	..	88	12	..	803	21
United Kingdom	70	18	..	107	15	..	98	14	..	210	6
North America	*18*	*5*	..	*24*	*3*	..	*59*	*8*	..	*408*	*11*
Canada	3	1	..	4	1	..	7	1	..	42	1
U.S.A.	15	4	..	21	3	..	52	7	..	366	10
Latin America	*7*	*2*	..	*39*	*6*	..	*43*	*6*	..	*116*	*3*
Argentina	4	1	..	18	2	..	24	3	..	27	1
Brazil	2	1	..	14	2	..	9	1	..	16	n.
Chile	1	n.	..	3	n.	..	1	n.	..	5	n.
Mexico	n.	n.	..	1	n.	..	1	n.	..	7	n.
Venezuela	n.	n.	..	n.	n.	..	2	n.	..	29	1
Oceania	*3*	*1*	..	*6*	*1*	..	*5*	*1*	..	*35*	*1*
Australia	3	1	..	5	1	..	4	1	..	27	1
New Zealand	n.	n.	..	1	n.	..	1	n.	..	8	n.
Asia	*8*	*2*	..	*27*	*4*	..	*44*	*6*	..	*217*	*6*
China	3	1	..	10	1	..	9[46]	1	..	45	1
India	3	1	..	9	1	..	13[28]	2	..	42[30]	1
Indonesia	1	n.	..	3	n.	..	6	1	..	12	n.
Japan	2	1	..	5	1	..	4[45]	1	..	24	1
Malaya[6]	n.	n.	..	n.	n.	..	1	n.	..	11	n.
Africa	*8*	*2*	*1*	*17*	*2*	*1*	*50*	*7*	*2*	*127*	*3*
North Africa	4[47]	1	..	8	1	..	16[47]	2	..	22[47]	1
West Africa	n.	n.	..	n.	n.	..	4[49]	1	..	6[23]	n.
East Africa	2[53]	1	..	5[53]	1	..	17[53]	2	..	59[29]	2
South Africa	2[14]	1	..	3[14]	n.	..	19[50]	3	..	24	1
Countries not included above	*12*	*3*	..	*29*	*4*	..	..	..	..	..	..
World	*377*	*100*	*1*	*729*	*100*	*1*	*724*	*100*	*6*	*3,775*	*100*
TOTAL WORLD EXPORTS	*9,310*	*4%*	*n.*	*18,285*	*4%*	*n.*	*21,945*	*3%*	*n.*	*127,700*	*3%*

n. = negligible.

Notes to Tables VII/12–VII/22

[1] Data on German trade before the end of the nineteenth century are very incomplete. The value of German trade in 1880 was $1,364 million, of which $668 million were imports and $696 million exports.

[2] According to Dutch official information, most of the country's nineteenth-century foreign trade was registered under that of its neighbours, particularly Belgium.

[3] Belgian figures for 1938 and 1960 include Luxemburg.

[4] 1960 figures are for the German Federal Republic.

[5] Including all British possessions in North America.

[6] Including Singapore.

[7] Estimates range from $255 million (Bartholomew's) to $330 million (McCulloch's) and $447 million (Mitchell and Deane). The real value of British imports (in contrast to its exports) was first stated in 1854.

[8] Deutsches Wirtschaftgebiet, Hanover, and Hanse towns.

[9] Including Hong Kong.

[10] Including Ceylon.

[11] West Coast of Africa.

[12] British and French West Africa.

[13] Cape of Good Hope and Natal.

[14] British South Africa.

[15] French and British India.

[16] Mainly Algeria.

[17] Cape of Good Hope and Mauritius.

[18] Including all British possessions in Africa.

[19] Nearly half the amount represents Belgian imports from Cuba and Puerto Rico.

[20] Including Uruguay.

[21] Ghana and Nigeria.

[22] Including former French and Belgian colonies, but mainly Kenya–Uganda, and Tanganyika.

[23] Mainly Cameroons, Ivory Coast, Nigeria, Gabon, and other former French West African territories.

[24] Including former French and Belgian Congos, former French Equatorial African territories, Kenya–Uganda, Tanganyika, and Somali.

[25] Union of South Africa.

[26] Mainly former French West African territories, Cameroons, Ghana, and Nigeria.

[27] Union of South Africa and the Rhodesia–Nyasaland Federation.

[28] Including Burma and Ceylon.

[29] Mainly former Belgian and French colonies.

[30] Including Pakistan.

[31] Including all British possessions in North and Latin America.

[32] All French Africa with the exception of French West Africa.

[33] Réunion, Madagascar, and Somali Coast.

[34] All British possessions in Africa.

[35] Mainly Indo-China.

[36] British and Portuguese West Africa.

[37] Figure included in 'Countries not included above'.

[38] Including Kiaochow.

[39] Including the import of diamonds.

[40] Prussia and Hamburg.

[41] British South and East Africa.

[42] Algeria, Morocco, and Egypt.

[43] Including Belgian Congo.
[44] French West and Equatorial Africa and West Coast of Africa.
[45] Including Korea and Formosa.
[46] Including Manchuria.
[47] Algeria, Tunisia, Morocco, and Egypt.
[48] Kenya–Uganda, Tanganyika, other British East Africa, Belgian Congo, Ruanda-Urundi, French Equatorial Africa, and French Cameroons.
[49] Nigeria, British and French West Africa, and French Togoland.
[50] British Nyasaland, South-West Africa, Northern and Southern Rhodesias, and Union of South Africa.
[51] Mainly French West Africa and French Togoland.
[52] Mainly French Equatorial Africa and French Cameroons.
[53] Mainly Belgian Congo.
[54] Mainly Egypt.

Sources for Tables VII/13 to VII/22

1840

BARTHOLOMEW, J. G., *Atlas of the World's Commerce* (London, 1907).
KOLB, G. F., *The Conditions of Nations Social and Political* (London, 1880).
McCULLOCH, J. R., *A Dictionary of Commerce and Commercial Navigation* (London, 1856).
BELGIUM, MINISTÈRE de L'INTÉRIEUR, *Annuaire Statistique de la Belgique 1874*.
FRANCE, 'Annuaire de l'Économie Politique pour 1846', *Journal des Économistes* (1846).
UNITED KINGDOM, HOUSE OF LORDS, *Statistical Abstract for the United Kingdom, 1840–1854*, Sessional Papers (session 1854, vol. 8).

1860

BLOCK, M., and GUILLAUMIN, G. U., *Annuaire de l'Économie Politique et de la Statistique 1844 etc.*, Paris.
BELGIUM, MINISTÈRE DE L'INTÉRIEUR, *Annuaire Statistique de la Belgique et du Congo Belge 1914* (1920).
NETHERLANDS, CENTRAAL BUREAU VOOR DE STATISTIEK; foreign trade figures for the nineteenth century were supplied by this Bureau in April 1964.
The Statesman's Year-book 1864, and *1866*.
UNITED KINGDOM, *Statistical Abstract for the United Kingdom, 1849–1863* (no. 11, 1864).

1880

BLOCK, M., *Annuaire de l'Économie Politique et de la Statistique 1882*.
BELGIUM, *see* source for 1860.
NETHERLANDS, *see* source for 1860.
The Statesman's Year-book 1882.

1900

AUSTRALIA, COMMONWEALTH BUREAU OF CENSUS AND STATISTICS, *Official Yearbook of the Commonwealth of Australia* (no. 8, 1915).
BELGIUM, *see* source for 1860.
FRANCE, MINISTÈRE DES FINANCES, *Statistiques et Études Financières, Supplément Retrospectif 1900 à 1930* (supplement 175, July 1963). *Annuaire Statistique de la France 1901*.
GERMANY, STATISTICAL BUREAU, *Statistisches Jahrbuch für das Deutsche Reich 1901, 1923*, and *1936*.
NEW ZEALAND, REGISTRAR GENERAL, *Official Yearbook 1901*.
The Statesman's Year-book 1902 and *1903*.
UNITED NATIONS, DEPARTMENT OF ECONOMIC AFFAIRS, *Public Debt 1914–1916* (1948).

1913

AUSTRALIA, *see* source for 1900.

BELGIUM, *see* source for 1860.

FRANCE, *see* source for 1900.

GERMANY, *see* source for 1900, 1914 and 1936.

LEAGUE OF NATIONS, ECONOMIC AND FINANCIAL SECTION, *International Statistical Yearbook 1926* (1927).

NEW ZEALAND, *The New Zealand Official Yearbook 1914*.

The Statesman's Year-book 1915, 1916, 1920, and *1921*.

UNITED NATIONS, *see* source for 1900.

1938

LEAGUE OF NATIONS, *The Network of World Trade* (Geneva, 1942).

Europe's Trade (Geneva, 1941).

UNITED NATIONS, DEPARTMENT OF ECONOMIC AND SOCIAL AFFAIRS, Yearbook of International Trade Statistics 1950 (1952).

1960

FRANCE, *Annuaire Statistique de la France 1961*.

The International Yearbook and Statesman's Who's Who 1962.

The Statesman's Year-book 1961.

UNITED NATIONS, DEPARTMENT OF ECONOMIC AND SOCIAL AFFAIRS, *Statistical Yearbook 1962* (1963).

UNITED NATIONS, *Yearbook of International Trade Statistics 1961* (1963).

WEST GERMANY, STATISTICAL BUREAU, *Statistisches Jahrbuch für die Bundesrepublik Deutschland 1962*.

Chapter VIII

EPILOGUE

WHEN future generations look back upon the moment of time when the Europeans held sway in the world they will not see the European Age as we see it now. Except for the prophets among us, we cannot hope to know how the future will see the past; we can only guess what the verdict of the future will be; past and future are essentially unknowable. Europe's real impact in the world does not lie in what it has done, or what its legacy will prove to be; Europe's real importance lies in what it has contributed to what is being done now. Measured in these terms, what is the world that the Europeans have helped to create?

It is a world in which the drama of life has been shifted increasingly by the white race from a tribal to a national and from a national to a world stage. In peace and war, industry and agriculture, labour and capital, trade, fishing, transport and communications, health regulations, sport, in culture and art, in all these fields and many others, world influences have come to play a larger part in the life of man. Compared with the world of two hundred years ago, the world has shrunk to a fraction of its former size, and the conquest of distance continues. Fundamental technological change, initiated by the western nations during the past century, has brought increasing world-wide economic integration and interdependence.

It is a world in which the common material lot has been improved. With the aid of western science and technology the incidence of widespread and customary famine has been reduced. Great areas of the earth have been made to fructify, the desert made to flower, the atom split. There are those who will say that man cannot live by bread alone; but man cannot live without bread either. It is easy to ridicule the worship by the West of an all-eclipsing material standard of living and to forget that it is only by lifting man above an animal existence that he can display those human qualities which distinguish him from the beast. Whether western technology will alienate man from himself does not depend on the machine — ultimately it depends upon man. In the development of productive forces devised by the West lies a new hope for mankind; increasingly, what the world will yield depends not only on nature but also on man's ingenuity. Western forms of industrialization, once looked upon with hostility and enmity by older civilizations, have become the new hope of mankind; unbroken and rapid technical advance has come to be taken for granted; western economists claim to have discovered the secret of continuous economic growth. Except where wars destroy wealth, the national income of most countries under European influence continues to rise. Here is the philosopher's stone of twentieth-century man. Is it surprising that when in recent times a new great western faith arose in communism it should have chosen the hammer and the sickle as its emblem?

It is a world in which the force of death has been weakened and pain dulled. The world is not free of plague or major epidemics (the influenza epidemic of 1918 took between eighteen and nineteen million lives), but western man has reduced their toll. The western nations have not banished suffering — no man can do that — but they have devised means whereby much physical suffering can be relieved. If the West has not cured, it has certainly lessened the scourges of tuberculosis, syphilis, diphtheria, diabetes, pneumonia, malaria, dysentery, sleeping sickness, yaws, and leprosy. In many parts of the world today great killers of the past such as cholera and typhoid are virtually unknown. The development of tropical medicine during the past fifty years has revolutionized the lives of many people in the tropics. White men and women willingly laid down their lives that the burden of sickness might be lifted from the shoulders of their coloured brethren. Fearful tropical diseases were deliberately contracted by western man that a cure might be found. To argue that western man was simply concerned with preserving his own skin is to do less than justice to those who gave their lives. Self-sacrifice, not self-gain, was the dominant motive of this curiously little-known chapter of the white man's story. Through these pages of history walks the Nazarene.

It is a world of growing law and order. Most men can now move beyond the area of their kinsmen and friends without falling prey to others. Without the European urge to extend over the entire world a system of security for persons and property, this growing law and order might never have come about. In many parts of the world where, prior to European invasion, there was constant tribal warfare, there is now the rule of law. The end of inter-tribal warfare and the establishment of a central administration able to uphold the law was one of the most startling innovations made by Europeans in other parts of the world. It did not necessarily require European conquest to establish a general peace. Many tribes lacked the will to resist the West; they acquiesced; they were accustomed to subjugation; they were glad of the protection afforded.

It is a world of growing enlightenment. The European often brought light where prior to his intrusion there was darkness. In place of ignorance the white man offered education; in place of magic, witchcraft, and superstition the white man offered reason. There has been a liberation of man from many kinds of authority; the individual has emerged with growing liberty to seek every kind of knowledge, to apply knowledge, to pursue every occupation; to compete for wealth, to take part in government. It is easy to be dazzled by the marvels of modern communications, but at least the white man's conquest of distance has made the world more fully aware of its collective dilemmas.

But in all these things the white men acted not as gods but as men, and as men they sometimes erred; they were the children of vice as well as virtue, of darkness as well as light, of evil as well as good. They erred in plundering without moral scruples, they violated man and nature; in the enslavement of Negroes they set black upon black; they bent their knee to the god of power and were corrupted, false pride consumed them, frenzy possessed them; they robbed men of their liberty, humiliated them, destroyed them; they committed all the crimes known to God and man. And they did it with such seeming hypocrisy; they were able to employ a vessel called the *Jesus* to carry slaves from Africa. Ours is an age when much is said about man as an end in himself; it is also an age when man is much used as a means. In justice to the Europeans, it is well to remember that the European Age, especially the past two centuries, was an age of tumult, of commotion, of confusion, of great disturbance, of extremes, of wonder and shame; such an age always produces the greatest saints and the greatest sinners.

Many men have looked upon the destructive element of western civilization and have wondered.

In this connection, let me quote the Moslem shopkeeper Alihodja contemplating the acts of the Christian Europeans who had 'annexed' part of the Ottoman Empire:

Yes, thought the *hodja* more animatedly, . . . now one can see what all their tools and their equipment really meant, all their hurry and activity. . . . For so many years he had seen how they had always been concerning themselves with the bridge, they had cleaned it, embellished it, repaired it down to its foundations, taken the water supply across it, lit it with electricity, and then one day blown it all into the skies as if it had been some stone in a mountain quarry and not a thing of beauty and value, a bequest. Now one could see what they were and what they wanted. He had always known that but now, now even the most stupid of fools could see for himself. They had begun to attack even the strongest and the most lasting of things, to take things away from God. And who knew where it would stop! Even the Vezir's bridge had begun to crumble away like a necklace; and once it began no one could hold it back.[1]

Under the impact of western civilization much more was lost than the beautiful bridge on the Drina. In the name of material progress tribes were

[1] Ivo Andrič, *The Bridge on the Drina*, 2nd imp., p. 315. Translation by L. F. Edwards (Allen & Unwin, London, 1962).

enslaved, blotted out; nature was despoiled; species of animals and plants were devoured by Europe's demoniacal energy; ancient agricultural systems were cast aside; an individualist form of consciousness took the place of the wholeness of society; great social and cultural values were ignored; plant and animal diseases, which were highly localized before the period of European expansion, became world-wide. Whatever past ages intended, it is only in the European Age that man has been bold enough, or fool enough, to talk of 'conquering nature'. The fault of western man lies not in striving for better things, but in treating complex and uncertain actions as simple and predictable.

The world has not only suffered from the destructive element in the western kind of capitalist economy; the world has also had to pay for the anarchistic tendencies of western capitalism. There is about western industrial capitalism — in its ever-differing and changing form — a deep psychological fear of instability. That instability is felt in the western world as it is felt in those parts of the world that have developed their economies to serve western demands. Those who spring to the defence of western capitalism will argue that the capitalist economy is better understood now than formerly; that the great commercial catastrophes that have beset the western world in the past can now be prevented by the application of a suitable world-wide economic and fiscal policy; that it does not require war and foreign exploitation to keep the capitalist system on an even keel; that western capitalism can function efficiently without casting a great part of its labour force at home and overseas on a temporary or a permanent scrapheap; that it can function without robbing man of his identity. All these things are partly true, and yet, the fear of instability in the western capitalist economy remains. It remains because the memory of capitalism's excesses and abuses are still fresh in many people's minds. While man thinks that he can ignore the past he remains its prisoner. The price of world specialization is growing uncertainty.

How one measures the contribution of a civilization depends on one's criteria of success. The 'good life' is never the same for all men at all times. If the Europeans are to be judged by their achievements during the past two centuries in science and technology, if the present criterion of material progress is an adequate test of civilization, if a 'progressive' civilization is one that (following our present cult of numbers) can satisfy certain numerical tests, if economic efficiency and material success are to be ends in themselves, if wealth can be confused with output or the sum total of profits, if calculation can be confused with originating, measuring with causation — if these tests are to be the yardstick of progress, then the Europeans may consider themselves to have been fairly successful. And they are not short of imitators in the world. However, such a yardstick was inadequate in the past, and it is likely to be inadequate in the future.

What we have to ask of a society is the kind of human life it produces. The wealth of nations is the weal, the wellbeing, of nations; it is something that can never be expressed satisfactorily in quantitative terms.

Even measured in material, quantitative terms the white people of the world have emerged from the Age of European expansion with the best of the bargain. Partly as a result of western growth and expansion the poor of the world are not as poor as they were; they can see in western achievements the hope of better things; but in food, in shelter, in the ordinary facilities of life, in industrial might, it is the western nations (including European settlements overseas) which benefited more than anyone else. Today the white people of the world continue to grow richer at a faster rate than all others.

The white man thinks he is rich because he works harder and more effectively than the others. The poor non-white thinks he is poor because he was exploited by foreign invaders. Both explanations are partly true. But many non-whites have never worked as hard as they are doing now, they have never been so free of foreign domination, and they grow relatively poorer, not richer. It is a complex situation. Some of us Europeans are rich now because we were rich two hundred years ago; we entered the period of European expansion relatively rich; others entered it relatively poor and they remain relatively poor. Some of us Europeans are rich now because we possess the human, climatic, and geographical factors necessary for success in the age of the machine. Yet we have become so accustomed to rapid economic growth and high standards of living in the West that it is only by an effort that we can question its continuance, or ask ourselves whether it is something peculiar to western nations at a particular point in their development. We do not seem to realize that expansionist economic growth is a phenomenon as unusual in the history of the world as the development of western technology; it is restricted to few countries and for a period as recent as the last century and a half. We have become so accustomed to technical mechanical dominance in the West that we never stop to ask whether mechanical inventions are singularly appropriate to western life, whether the trend of mechanical inventions will continue, and whether they are the means by which the life of society will go quickly upwards or quickly downwards. The lesson of Antaeus, who was safe only as long as he remained in touch with the good earth, has been lost upon us. Those who would follow in the white man's footsteps would do well to think on these things.

The western era of history has also left us with the possibility of an explosion of population. Western hygiene, western medicine, western technology and western peace have removed the natural checks on population growth to the point where numbers are increasing faster than the basis of livelihood. If we are to be guided simply by statistics, then in

AD 2000 — i.e. in the lifetime of our children — world population will have doubled and misery and starvation will stare mankind in the face.

The fear that mankind will outstrip its food resources is not new; man has often been fearful of himself. Yet population numbers are relative to given conditions and we can only guess what those conditions will be a generation hence. Moreover, it is doubtful if the great upsweep in the numbers of certain Asian nations can be put down to western influence; this rise in numbers might well have come about without western intrusion. We are likely to harbour illusions about population control if we make the Europeans responsible for something which in the main they did not cause. The initiative in the control of world population has never been in western hands. The West may refer to the 'irresponsible and uncontrolled population increases of the East', but great non-European groups, such as the Chinese, while they are conscious that an infinite number of people cannot occupy a finite area, show no desire to fix the ratio of world population at a moment favourable to the European proportion, which, as we showed earlier in this book, has risen rapidly in the last century or two. Most calls from the West to the East for the limitation of eastern numbers are likely to go unheeded. It is not the East that have most to lose, but the West; hence the growing anxiety in the West. It is largely irrelevant to mention it, for the two situations are essentially dissimilar, but the growing fear of children now felt by the West was also felt by the childless aristocracy of Rome before the collapse of the Empire.

It is difficult to assess what the contribution of the white man has been in removing or alleviating human diseases; it is also difficult to know how many of the diseases of epidemic proportion have been the white man's doing. One of the most agonizing chapters of European expansion describes the manner in which many of the aboriginal people of the world fell prey to the diseases introduced by the European. European influenza, tuberculosis, diphtheria (we are not sure whether syphilis was inflicted upon the aboriginal Americans by the Europeans or vice versa) outran the white man and often emptied the land for him. European sicknesses were far more devastating upon aboriginal people than European arms and European fire-water. Sicknesses cannot really be divided into eastern and western, tropical and temperate (i.e. malaria, which is today identified with the tropics, was at one time very common in Europe) but the European certainly introduced diseases that were relatively benign in Europe and proved to be a scourge elsewhere.

Whether the West has done anything very substantial in substituting reason for religion (faith, vision, or mysticism) really depends on one's view of life. It really depends on one's view of reality. If reality can be achieved only through factual, objective evidence, then the present stress upon precision and certainty is well placed. Yet we are plagued by so much doubt, and an all-embracing synthesis of life escapes us. It is hardly surprising that certain western nations find themselves unable to equate material progress with happiness. A lesson that many primitive societies could teach the West is that happiness of a people consists in how its imagination is satisfied as well as its material needs. Which is not to condone the practices and beliefs of certain primitive religions based on horror and fear, but merely to emphasize the lasting importance in life and human motivation of religion and of what Westerners scathingly refer to as magic.[1] The West has swung from the worship of God to the worship of reason. But the basic forces of life are imagination, emotion, and passion; only when we are fortunate is reason the regulator of these more powerful forces.

Yet if reason is lost, the nemesis of the human race is certain. For the white man has now perfected forms of power which leave the fate of the world hanging on a nuclear thread. Since Cain murdered his brother Abel man has always had the power to destroy his fellow man. The new factor is that man for the first time now has the power to destroy life upon the entire planet. This is new in world history and this is alarming. It pushes all other considerations into the background; it makes nonsense of international name-calling and stone-throwing. Never has mankind been faced with such a stark, terrifying choice between world progress and world annihilation. It is a choice that the white man has placed before the human family, and the hour-glass of decision is running low.

For a moment of time the white man played the chief role on the world stage he created; his word was law. Most other men acquiesced keeping their place at the back of the stage or well in the wings. The greatest struggles for position have not been between whites and non-whites, but between the whites themselves. The great clash of arms in the world these past two hundred years has been the clash of European arms. European man has bitterly fought European man for pride of place in the world. Yet no European nation dominated the world stage for long.

Now, as a result of European expansion and the unprecedented mixing of blood that has taken place in the world, the numbers and the political power of the non-whites grow rapidly. The signs in North America, Latin America, Africa, and Asia all point in the same direction: the chapter of history in which the white people had predominance over the coloured people is ending. Racial integration, although it has been achieved in most of Latin America and in New Zealand, is one of the most acute problems in the world today. Whatever our dreams may be, the reality is that we now live in a world of growing racial enmity between whites

[1] It is salutary to remember that down to quite modern times 'knowledge' meant also 'magic'. The Sanskrit word 'Vidyā' has this double meaning.

and non-whites. And much of this is Europe's doing.

Under European influence the problem of world political unity has also become more acute. All the classical social and political doctrines which sway most of the modern world spring from Europe; each of them is an expression of something in western civilization; each of them a product of western social conditions; all of them claiming to be of universal application; all of them professing to conceive the nature and the earthly destiny of man. Much of the world is now divided between those who believe in the social and political doctrine of western liberal capitalism and representative democracy, and those who believe its authoritarian opposite, Marxist–Leninism. Man has become the prisoner of European social and political ideas.

In a world of growing racial and political bifurcation, the European has begun to cede the central position in world society to other men. Yet, if a transfer of power and authority is taking place before our eyes, it is not because the European has been elbowed off the centre of the world stage by the black, the brown, and the yellow. On the contrary, and in the main, he is quietly withdrawing; for some time now the European has allowed the initiative to pass to his white cousins overseas, particularly in North America. The European's role, however, is still a major role. The leading speaking parts are still held by white men, but new faces are appearing in the centre of the world stage — faces that have not been seen there for many generations. Some of them, particularly the Africans, have perhaps never occupied the centre of the stage before; that they do so now, paradoxically as it may seem, is largely the work of the white man.

It is not difficult to extol the richness, the grandeur, the variety, the vitality, the catholicity of European life; nor is it difficult to dwell upon the profound religious experience and influence of Christianity. Yet the European is only one of many civilizations, and not necessarily the one with the greatest impact upon others. Islam has had great influence on other people's art, architecture, and religion. It was through an Arab window that the West first saw the East. It was a group of Arab scholars who kept watch in the West when others slept. Buddhism was sweeping Asia when Europe was in the Dark Ages. Christianity is an Asian religion. The Europeans did not become Lords of Empires because they were more noble, more refined, more gifted, more spiritually inclined, more courageous than other folk. The Europeans show no more ingenuity, no more skill, no more foresight than that shown by primitive man in his struggle with the hard conditions of nature. What distinguishes the European Age from past ages is its acceptance of *change*; unprecedented change at unprecedented speed. More than any other civilization it is Europe that has made change itself part of a common process of thought. This is the most disturbing if not the greatest contribution that western man has made. Only in the acceptance of change, only in the development of productive (and destructive) forces have the Europeans excelled. It is this which caused the world to shrink; it is this which enabled little Europe to have dominion over the earth; it is this which enabled it to reach its greatest heights of power; it is this which has placed within the grasp of man undreamt of possibilities of human progress. Yet it is also this which has provided mankind with an enigma larger and more desperate than any it has known before; which has cast a shadow across the face of all that Europe has done. Having brought the world to this pass, we Europeans now carry an almost insupportable responsibility. It is to ensure that mankind does not fall into the abyss which, unwittingly, we have dug before its feet. Here, in a deeper, more tragic sense than was ever imagined, is 'the white man's burden'. Now more than ever must Europe examine the principles from which its greatness sprang. Now more than ever must the white man marshal all the faith, vitality, resourcefulness, wisdom, courage, sympathy, and compassion which enabled him to emerge from his tiny homeland in the western seas. Humanity and history shall be our judge. The voice of Europe's past not only inspires hope — it forbids despair.

BIBLIOGRAPHY

In this bibliography I have merely set down those works which I think will be of most value to those who seek further reading, and which I have found most helpful in writing this book. I have not repeated the references given elsewhere in this volume.

CHAPTER I

In attaching meaning to history I found most valuable N. A. Berdyaev's essay, *The Meaning of History* (London, 1936), also R. G. Collingwood, *The Idea of History* (Oxford, 1946), Pieter Geyl and others, *The Pattern of the Past* (Boston, 1949); also by Geyl, *From Ranke to Toynbee* (Northampton, Mass., 1952), Herbert Butterfield, *Man on His Past* (Camb., Eng., 1955), and A. J. Toynbee, *A Study of History*, vol. I–[X] (Oxford, 1934–1954). Toynbee's work is summarized by D. C. Somervell, *A Study of History* (Oxford, vols. i–vi, 1947; vols. vii–x, 1957).

In dealing more specifically with the history of western philosophy and the development and impact of European ideas and beliefs I made use of F. S. Marvin (ed.), *Recent Developments in European Thought* (London, 1920), C. H. Dawson, *The Making of Europe* (London, 1932), H. E. Barnes, *An Intellectual and Cultural History of the Western World* (New York, rev. ed. 1963), Karoly Polanyi, *Origins of our Time* (London, 1945), F. H. Knight, *Freedom and Reform. Essays in Economics and Social Philosophy* (New York, 1947), Ferdynand Zweig, *Economic Ideas: A Study of Historical Perspective* (New York, 1950), J. A. Schumpeter, *Capitalism, Socialism and Democracy* (London, 1950), Crane Brinton, *Ideas and Men; the Story of Western Thought* (New York, 1963), F. Le Van Baumer (ed.), *Main Currents of Western Thought* (New York, 1952), J. B. Bury, *The Idea of Progress* (New York, 1932), Morris Ginsberg, *The Idea of Progress, A Revaluation* (London, 1953), Bertrand Russell, *History of Western Philosophy* (London, 1961). See also Oswald Spengler, *Decline of the West* (New York, 1926) and H. S. Hughes, *Oswald Spengler, a critical estimate* (New York, 1952). Valuable are Oskar Halecki, *The Limits and Divisions of European History* (London, 1950) and Geoffrey Barraclough, *History in a Changing World* (Norman, Oklahoma, 1955).

In tracing the influence of Christianity upon economic development I have relied upon C. A. H. Guignebert, *Christianity, Past and Present* (New York, 1927), H. M. Robertson, *Aspects of the Rise of Economic Individualism* (Cambridge [Eng.], 1933), Amintore Fanfani, *Catholicism, Protestantism and Capitalism* (London, 1955), C. H. Dawson, *Religion and the Modern State* (London, 1935), R. H. Tawney, *Religion and the Rise of Capitalism*

(London, 1936), Jacques Maritain, *True Humanism* (London, 1938), Herbert Butterfield, *Christianity and History* (London, 1949), K. E. Boulding, 'Religious Foundations of Economic Progress', *Harvard Business Review*, vol. 30, no. 3, May–June 1952, pp. 33–40, A. J. Toynbee, *Christianity Among the Religions of the World* (London, 1958). I have also made use of various papal encyclicals, especially those of Pope Leo XIII, *Rerum Novarum* (given 15 May 1891), and Pope Pius XI, *Quadragesimo Anno* (given 13 May 1931).

The other great belief of the West, Marxism, is best studied in the works of Marx (and Engels and Lenin). In addition, I found most illuminating the writings of Isaiah Berlin, *Karl Marx: his life and environment* (London, 1939), and P. M. Sweezy, *The Theory of Capitalist Development. Principles of Marxian Political Economy* (New York, 1956).

In tracing the development of modern science I gained most help from Herbert Butterfield's *Origins of Modern Science, 1300–1800* (London, 1949). I also profited from reading F. S. Marvin (ed.), *Science and Civilization* (London, 1923), and A. N. Whitehead, *Science and the Modern World* (Cambridge [Eng.], 1930). Other references will be found in the bibliography provided for Chapter V below.

Useful in understanding the sociological aspects of economic development are M. J. Herskovits, *The Economic Life of Primitive Peoples* (New York, 1940), F. R. Cowell, *History, Civilization and Culture; an Introduction to the Historical and Social Philosophy of Pitirim A. Sorokin* (Boston, 1952), M. J. Levy, 'Contrasting Factors in the Modernization of China and Japan', *Economic Development and Cultural Change*, vol. 2, no. 3, October 1953, pp. 161–197, B. F. Hoselitz (ed.), *Sociological Aspects of Economic Growth* (Glencoe, Ill., 1960), Ralph Braibanti and J. J. Spengler (eds.) *Tradition, Values and Socio-economic Development* (Durham, N. C., 1961).

More specifically see R. W. Firth, *Primitive Economics of the New Zealand Maori* (London, 1929), also R. S. Merrill, 'Some Social and Cultural Influences on Economic Growth: The Case of the Maori', *Journal of Economic History*, vol. 14, no. 4, 1954, pp. 401–408.

The general impact of Europeans outside Europe can be traced through such works as F. S. Marvin (ed.), *Western Races and the World* (London, 1922), H. Kohn, 'The Europeanization of the Orient', *Political Science Quarterly*, vol. LII, no. 2, June 1937, pp. 259–270. In tracing western influence in particular areas and countries I have also drawn upon Adolf Reichwein, *China and Europe; Intellectual and Artistic Contacts in the Eighteenth Century* (New York, 1925), and V. W. W. S. Purcell, *China* (London, 1962). In understanding Indian and Pakistan developments, in addition to the various volumes of *The Cambridge History of the British Empire*, I found stimulating L. S. S. O'Malley (ed.), *Modern India and the West; A Study of the Interaction of Their Civilizations* (London, 1941), P. S. Griffiths, *The*

British Impact on India (London, 1952), and Jawaharlal Nehru, *The Discovery of India* (New York, 1959). For Burma I found valuable G. E. Harvey, *British Rule in Burma, 1824–1942* (London, 1946) and F. S. V. Donnison, *Public Administration in Burma. A Study of Development during the British Connexion* (London, 1953). Also valuable on Pakistan, Turkey, and other Islamic countries are W. C. Smith, *Islam in Modern History* (Princeton, 1957), Bernard Lewis, *The Emergence of Modern Turkey* (London, 1961), Ian Stephens, *Pakistan* (New York, 1963). Two studies I used in dealing with particular parts of Africa are L. H. Gann, *The Birth of a Plural Society: the Development of Northern Rhodesia Under the British South African Company, 1894–1914* (Manchester, 1958), and F. A. Wells and W. A. Warmington, *Studies in Industrialization: Nigeria and the Cameroons* (London, 1962).

Much more particular aspects of western-induced change can be studied in W. C. Mitchell 'The Role of Money in Economic History', *Journal of Economic History*, vol. 4, suppl., December 1944, pp. 61–67, C. K. Meek, *Land Law and Custom in the Colonies* (London, 1946), F. W. Riggs, 'Public Administration: A Neglected Factor in Economic Development', *The Annals of the American Academy of Political and Social Science*, vol. 305, May 1956, pp. 70–80, Wyndham Lewis, *Time and Western Man* (Boston, 1957).

Excellent overall studies of European developments are contained in W. A. Lewis, *Economic Survey 1919–1939* (London, 1949), Herbert Heaton, *Economic History of Europe* (New York, 1948), S. B. Clough, *The Economic Development of Western Civilization* (New York, 1959), and *The Cambridge Economic History of Europe*, especially Vol. VI, pts. I and II (Cambridge [Eng.] 1965).

CHAPTER II

Indispensable in tracing the course of European empires is a good historical atlas. I have used W. R. Shephard, *Historical Atlas* (Pikesville, Maryland, 1956), Frank Debenham, *Discovery and Exploration: An Atlas History of Man's Wanderings* (New York, 1960), is an excellent introduction to the discovery and exploration which preceded and accompanied European expansion.

A succinct survey of Portuguese expansion is given by C. R. Boxer, *Four Centuries of Portuguese Expansion, 1415–1825* (Johannesburg, 1961). Aspects of Spanish colonial rule are dealt with by Salvador de Madariaga, *Rise of the Spanish American Empire* (London, 1947). On Dutch expansion see J. J. van Klaveren, *The Dutch Colonial System in the East Indies* (Rotterdam, 1953), and C. H. Wilson, 'The Economic Decline of the Netherlands', *Economic History Review*, vol. 9, May 1939, pp. 111–127. French developments are dealt with by F. Roepke, 'Erscheinungsformen des Französischen Imperialismus vor dem Weltkrieg' *Vierteljahresschrift für Sozial- und, Wirtschaftsgeschichte*, Band 25, 1932, pp. 130–140, and Jean Gaillard

L'Expansion Française dans le Monde (Paris, 1951). A work casting light on both French and British developments in Canada is E. E. Rich, *The History of the Hudson's Bay Company, 1670–1870* (London, 1958–59), 2V. The expansion (if not the decline) of the British Empire receives adequate treatment in the relevant volumes of *The Cambridge History of the British Empire*. See also C. E. Carrington, *The British Overseas; Exploits of a Nation of Shopkeepers* (Cambridge [Eng.] 1950). Two important works on Australia are those of W. K. Hancock, *Australia* (London, 1930) and Brian Fitzpatrick, *The British Empire in Australia, 1836–1939* (Melbourne, 1941). E. Shann's *Economic History of Australia* (1930) is also valuable. See also the scholarly treatment of West Indian developments by Richard Pares, *Merchants and Planters* (Cambridge [Eng.], 1960). Two important books on German developments are: Mary E. Townsend, *Origins of Modern German Colonialism, 1871–1885* (New York, 1921), and by the same author, *The Rise and Fall of Germany's Colonial Empire, 1884–1918* (New York, 1930).

A neglected aspect of European expansion is Russia's colonization of parts of Europe and Asia. See F. H. B. Skrine, *The Expansion of Russia, 1815–1900* (3rd ed., Cambridge, Mass., 1915), R. J. Kerner, *The Urge to the Sea: The Course of Russian History* (Berkeley, 1942), W. Kolarz, *Russia and Her Colonies* (New York, 1952), and by the same author, *The Peoples of the Soviet Far East* (New York, 1954), also C. M. Foust, 'Russian Expansion to the East Through the Eighteenth Century', *Journal of Economic History*, vol. 21, no. 4, December 1961, pp. 469–482, and V. N. Semenov, *Siberia: its conquest and development* (Baltimore, 1963).

Quite indispensable in obtaining an overall view of Western intrusion is A. Grenfell Price, *The Western Invasions of the Pacific and Its Continents; A Study of Moving Frontiers and Changing Landscapes, 1513–1958* (Oxford, 1958).

On the relations between Asian and European nations see K. M. Panikkar, *Asia and Western Dominance: 1498–1945* (London, 1953); also Michael Edwardes, *Asia in the European Age: 1498–1955* (London, 1961).

More specifically, for studies of Asian countries experiencing European intrusion see E. H. Norman, *Japan's Emergence as a Modern State* (New York, 1940), F. C. Jones, *Manchuria Since 1931* (London, 1949), and by far the best treatment of Japanese developments, W. W. Lockwood, *The Economic Development of Japan* (Princeton, 1954). The remarkable rate of growth of the Japanese economy is traced in K. Okawa (and others), *The Growth of the Japanese Economy Since 1878* (Tokyo, 1957).

The literature on Western intrusion into China is immense. See especially J. K. Fairbank, *Trade and Diplomacy on the China Coast: The Opening of the Treaty Ports, 1842–1854*, 2 Vols. (Cambridge, Mass., 1954), Evan Luard, *Britain and China* (Baltimore, 1962), and Saul Rose, *Britain and South-East Asia* (Baltimore, 1962).

There is also a large literature on Indian developments. See Vera Anstey, *The Economic Development of India* (4th ed., London, 1952) and V. A. Smith, *The Oxford History of India* (3rd ed., Oxford, 1958). Critical of British rule is S. C. Jha, *Studies in the Development of Capitalism in India* (Calcutta, 1963). Valuable *Surveys of Indian Industries* are those of B. S. Rao (London, 1957–58), 2V. On the intrusion of the European into North Borneo, I gained much from K. G. Tregonning, *Under Chartered Company Rule: North Borneo, 1881–1946* (Singapore, 1958).

The monumental work on African countries south of the Sahara, during the European era of history, is *An African Survey* edited by Lord Hailey (revised ed. Oxford, 1957). See also the general treatments by C. W. De Kiewiet, *A History of South Africa, social and economic* (London, 1957), R. Robinson (and others), *Africa and the Victorians; the Climax of Imperialism in the Dark Continent* (New York, 1961), Roger Anstey, *Britain and the Congo in the Nineteenth Century* (Oxford, 1962), A. J. Wills, *An Introduction to the History of Central Africa* (London, 1964). Less general is K. O. Dike, *Trade and Politics in the Niger Delta, 1830–1885* (Oxford, 1956). Outstanding is D. S. Landes, *Bankers and Pashas; International Finance and Economic Imperialism in Egypt* (London, 1958), and J. E. Flint, *Sir George Goldie and the Making of Nigeria* (London, 1960).

For theories of imperialism and colonialism and more polemical works (other than those mentioned in the text) see Rosa Luxemburg, *The Accumulation of Capital* (London, 1951), Grover Clark, *The Balance Sheet of Imperialism* (New York, 1936), Richard Pares, 'The Economic Factors in the History of the Empire', *Economic History Review*, vol. 7, no. 2, May 1937, pp. 119–144. Significant are Richard Koebner, 'The Concept of Economic Imperialism', *Economic History Review*, 2nd series vol. 2, no. 1, August 1949, pp. 1–29, and Richard Koebner and H. D. Schmidt, *Imperialism* (Cambridge [Eng.] 1964). See also W. K. Hancock, *Wealth of Colonies* (Cambridge [Eng.], 1950), J. A. Schumpeter, *Imperialism and Social Classes* (New York, 1951), Rudolf Hilferding, *Das Finanzkapital* (Berlin, 1955). Bertrand de Jouvenal, 'Reflections on Colonialism', *Confluence*, vol. 4, October 1955, pp. 249–65, Robert Strausz-Hupé and Harry W. Hazard (eds.), *The Idea of Colonialism* (New York, 1958), which does not define the idea but still provides some valuable essays. Herbert Lüthy's essay, 'Colonization and the Making of Mankind', *Journal of Economic History*, vol. 21, no. 4, December 1961, pp. 483–495 is an important essay. See also M. Blaug, 'Economic Imperialism Revisited', *Yale Review*, vol. 50, no. 3, March 1961, pp. 335–349, and H. M. Wright (ed.), *The 'New Imperialism'* (Boston, 1961).

On the decline of European imperialism see John Strachey, *The End of Empire* (New York, 1960), and S. C. Easton, *The Twilight of European Colonialism* (New York, 1960). The struggle for power within as well as without, during the second half of the nineteenth century is dealt with by A. J. P. Taylor, *The Struggle for Mastery in Europe, 1848–1918* (Oxford, 1954).

CHAPTER III

The special problems associated with population statistics are dealt with in *Statistics of Migration: Definitions–Methods–Classifications*, I.L.O. (Geneva, 1932); see also 'Problems of Migration Statistics', *U.N. Population Studies*, no. 5 (New York, 1949).

In addition to the sources in the text and on the tables (which are not repeated here) for studies dealing primarily with statistical investigations and the chief migratory trends see Emile Levasseur, 'Emigration in the Nineteenth Century', *Journal of the Statistical Society*, vol. 48, March 1885, pp. 63–81, J. J. Spengler and O. D. Duncan (eds.), *Demographic Analyses* (Glencoe, Ill., 1956), OEEC, *Demographic Trends in Western Europe, 1951–1971* (Paris, 1956), R. C. Cook, 'World Migration, 1946–1955', *Population Bulletin*, vol. 13, no. 5, August 1957, pp. 77–95, 'The Future Growth of World Population', *U.N. Population Studies*, no. 28 (New York, 1958), and D. Kirk, *Major Migrations Since World War II* (New York, 1958). A most concise [*The*] *Economic History of World Population* is by C. Cipolla (Harmondsworth, 1962).

On the migration of Europeans to the United States see M. L. Hansen, *The Atlantic Migration, 1607–1860* (Cambridge, Mass., 1940). Economic and industrial aspects are treated by R. T. Berthoff, *British Immigrants in Industrial America, 1790–1950* (Cambridge, Mass., 1953), Brinley Thomas, *Migration and Economic Growth; A Study of Great Britain and the Atlantic Economy* (Cambridge [Eng.], 1954), Charlotte Erickson, *American Industry and the European Immigrant, 1860–1885* (Cambridge, Mass., 1957), and E. P. Hutchinson, *Immigrants and Their Children, 1850–1950* (New York, 1956). The westward movement is dealt with by R. A. Billington, *Westward Expansion* (New York, 1937). On Canadian immigration see Robert England, *The Central European Immigrant in Canada* (Toronto, 1929), Norman Macdonald, *Canada, 1763–1841, Immigration and Settlement* (London, 1939), A. S. Morton, *A History of the Canadian West to 1870–71* (London, 1939), and two articles by D. C. Corbett, 'Immigration and Economic Development', *Canadian Journal of Economics and Political Science*, vol. 17, no. 3, August 1951, pp. 360–368, and 'Immigrants and Canada's Economic Expansion', *International Labour Review*, vol. 77, no. 1, January 1958, pp. 19–37.

Racial intermixture in Latin America is dealt with (in addition to the work of Rosenblat and others mentioned in the tables) by J. Gillin, 'Mestizo America' in R. Linton (ed.), *Most of the World; The Peoples of Africa, Latin America and the East Today* (New York, 1949). See also F. B. de

Avila, *Economic Impacts of Immigration. The Brazilian Immigration Problem* (The Hague, 1954), C. Furtado, *The Economic Growth of Brazil* (Berkeley, 1963), Margaret J. Bates (ed.), *The Migration of Peoples to Latin America* (Washington, 1957), M. Zymelman, 'The Economic History of Argentina 1933–1952', unpublished dissertation, Mass. I. T. (Boston, 1958).

References to African immigration are scattered. Some of the best material is to be found in the book edited by Lord Hailey already mentioned and in the work of Spengler and others in E. A. G. Robinson (ed.), *Economic Development for Africa South of the Sahara*, International Economic Association (London, 1963). Other references will be found in the *South African Journal of Economics* and in *Population Studies*.

On Australian immigration apart from books already mentioned see P. D. Phillips and G. L. Wood (eds.), *The Peopling of Australia* (Melbourne, 1928, especially the historical survey by Herbert Burton), K. H. Bailey (and others), *The Peopling of Australia (further studies)* (Melbourne, 1933), W. D. Forsyth, *The Myth of Open Spaces; Australian, British and World Trends of Population and Migration* (Melbourne, 1942), H. E. Holt (and others), *Australia and the Migrant* (Sydney, 1953), Jerzy Zubrzycki, *Immigrants in Australia*, with statistical supplement (Melbourne, 1960), Charles Price, *Southern Europeans in Australia* (Melbourne, 1964).

An additional source of Russian population figures is F. Lorimer, *The Population of the Soviet Union: History and Prospects* (Geneva, 1946).

There is a large literature on the relation of migration to general economic growth and development, some of which has already been listed. In addition, see Julius Isaac, *Economics of Migration* (London, 1947), and by the same author *The Effect of European Migration on the Economy of Sending and Receiving Countries* (The Hague, 1953). See also J. J. Spengler, 'Population Movements and Investment', *Journal of Finance*, vol. 6, December 1951, pp. 343–360, and vol. 7, March 1952, pp. 10–27, Oscar Handlin (ed.), *The Positive Contribution by Immigrants* (Paris, UNESCO, 1955), and S. Enke, 'Speculations on Population Growth and Economic Development', *Quarterly Journal of Economics*, vol. 71, February 1957, pp. 19–35.

Man has always been haunted by the fear that his numbers would outstrip available food supplies. See Gunnar Myrdal, *Population, a problem for democracy* (Cambridge, Mass., 1940), S. Chandrasekhar, *Hungry People and Empty Lands* (Baroda, 1952), G. F. McCleary, *The Malthusian Population Theory* (London, 1953), E. John Russell, *World Population and World Food Supplies* (London, 1954), and *The Proceedings and Papers of the World Population Conference held at Rome, 1954* (New York, United Nations, 1956).

CHAPTER IV

The principal general references on international investment will be found on the tables accompanying this chapter. In addition, see United

Nations Department of Economic Affairs, *The International Flow of Private Capital, 1946–1952* (New York, 1954) and A. K. Cairncross, 'The Place of Capital in Economic Progress' in L. H. Dupriez (ed.), *Economic Progress*, Papers and Proceedings of a Round Table held by the International Economic Association (Louvain, 1955).

British investments are treated in greater detail by George Paish, 'Great Britain's Capital Investments in Individual Colonial and Foreign Countries', *Journal of the Royal Statistical Society*, vol. 74, January 1911, pp. 167–187, T. H. Boggs, 'Capital Investments and Trade Balances within the British Empire', *Quarterly Journal of Economics*, vol. 29, August 1915, pp. 768–793, R. C. Wyse, 'The Future of London as the World's Money Market', *Economic Journal*, vol. 28, December 1918, pp. 386–397, R. Kindersley, 'British Oversea Investments, 1937', *Economic Journal*, vol. 48, no. 192, December 1938, pp. 609–634, A. R. Conan, *The Changing Pattern of International Investment in Selected Sterling Countries* (Princeton, 1956), and by the same author, 'The United Kingdom as a Creditor Country', *Westminster Bank Review*, August 1960, pp. 16–22, F. W. Paish, 'Britain's Foreign Investments: The Postwar Record', *Lloyds Bank Review*, no. 41, July 1956, pp. 23–39, A. G. Ford, 'The Transfer of British Foreign Lending, 1870–1913', *Economic History Review*, 2nd series, vol. II, no. 2, December 1958, pp. 302–308.

Detailed references to capital movements of other European countries, in addition to those already listed, are Marcel Labordère, 'The Mechanism of Foreign Investment in France and its Outcome, 1890–1914', *Economic Journal*, vol. 24, December 1914, pp. 525–42, and H. D. White, *The French International Accounts, 1880–1913* (Cambridge, Mass., 1933), E. F. Fleetwood, *Sweden's Capital Imports and Exports* (Stockholm, 1947), and Alice Carter, 'Dutch Foreign Investment, 1738–1800', *Economica*, vol. 20, no. 80, November 1953, pp. 322–240.

An outstanding account of the impact of English merchant bankers in the U.S. in the period 1763–1861 is R. W. Hidy, *The House of Baring* (Cambridge, Mass., 1949); also D. L. Kemmerer, 'Financing Illinois Industry' Bulletin, B. H. Soc., vol. 27, no. 2, pp. 97–111. American foreign investments are dealt with by Cleona Lewis and other sources accompanying the tables. See also Ernest Bloch, 'United States Foreign Investments and Dollar Shortage', *Review of Economics and Statistics*, vol. 35, no. 2, May 1953, pp. 154–160, R. F. McKesell, *United States Private and Government Investment Abroad* (Eugene, Oregon, 1962). Valuable on the capital formation and economic growth of the United States is D. C. North, *The Economic Growth of the United States, 1790–1860* (Englewood Cliffs, New Jersey, 1961). Capital investment in Canada is treated by J. Viner, *Canada's Balance of International Indebtedness, 1900–1913* (Cambridge, Mass., 1924), H. C. Pentland, 'The Role of Capital in Canadian Economic Development before

1875', *Canadian Journal of Economics and Political Science*, vol. 16, no. 4, November 1950, pp. 457–474, Penelope Hartland, 'Private Enterprise and International Capital', *Canadian Journal of Economics and Political Science*, vol. 19, no. 1, February 1953, pp. 70–80, and J. A. Stovel, *Canada in the World Economy* (Cambridge, Mass., 1959). Two important fairly recent studies on the interrelation between parts of the North Atlantic economy are J. H. Dunning, *American Investment in British Manufacturing Industry* (London, 1958). Additional references on investments in Latin America are H. S. Ferns, *Britain and Argentina in the Nineteenth Century* (Oxford, 1960), and David Joslin, *A Century of Banking in Latin America* (London, 1963).

The outstanding work on capital investment in Africa (south of the Sahara) is that by Frankel already cited.

Additional sources for Asian countries are H. G. Callis, *Foreign Capital in Southeast Asia* (New York, 1942), G. Ranis, 'The Financing of Japanese Economic Development', *Economic History Review*, 2nd series, vol. 11, no. 3, April 1959, pp. 440–454, and Henry Rosovsky, *Capital Formation in Japan, 1868–1940* (Glencoe, Ill., 1960).

The most important quantitative work to appear on Australian capital developments is that of N. G. Butlin, *Investment in Australian Economic Development, 1861–1900* (Cambridge [Eng.], 1964). See also the earlier works of Gordon Wood, *Borrowing and Business in Australia* (London, 1930) and Roland Wilson, *Capital Imports and the Terms of Trade, Examined in the Light of Sixty Years of Australian Borrowings* (Melbourne, 1931). Some aspects of New Zealand's financial history are dealt with by C. G. F. Simkin, *The Instability of a Dependent Economy* (London, 1951).

Also on foreign investment see Gustav Cassel and others, *Foreign Investments* (Chicago, 1928), Carl Iversen, *Aspects of the Theory of International Capital Movements* (London, 1935), Colin Clark, *Conditions of Economic Progress* (3rd ed. London, 1957), A. M. Imlah, 'British Balance of Payments and Export of Capital, 1816–1913', *Economic History Review*, 2nd series, vol. 5, no. 2, December 1952, pp. 208–239, J. Knapp, 'Capital Exports and Growth', *Economic Journal*, vol. 67, no. 267, September 1957, pp. 432–444.

Articles dealing more specifically with the gains and losses of foreign investment, from the point of view of debtor and creditor countries, are J. F. Cyril, 'Benefits and Dangers of Foreign Investments', *Annals of the American Academy of Political and Social Science*, vol. 150, July 1930, pp. 76–84, C. R. Whittlesey, 'Foreign Investment and National Gain', *American Economic Review*, vol. 23, no. 3, September 1933, pp. 466–470, and H. W. Singer, 'The Distribution of Gains Between Investing and Borrowing Countries', *American Economic Review*, vol. 40, no. 2, May 1950, pp. 473–485.

Since the Second World War a large literature has appeared concerned with the relation between capital investment and the development of the relatively poorer countries of Asia, Africa, and Latin America. In addition to the references already given see Yuan-Li Wu, 'International capital investment and the Development of Poor Countries', *Economic Journal*, vol. 56, no. 221, March 1946, pp. 86–101, United Nations, *Measures for the Economic Development of Under-developed Countries* (New York, 1951), J. M. Hunter, 'Long-term Foreign Investment and Under-developed Countries', *Journal of Political Economy*, vol. 61, no. 1, February 1953, pp. 15–24, and especially two works by Ragnar Nurkse, *Problems of Capital Formation in Underdeveloped Countries* (Oxford, 1953) and 'The Problem of International Investment Today in the Light of Nineteenth-Century Experience', *Economic Journal*, vol. 64, no. 256, December 1954, pp. 744–758, also F. C. Benham, *Economic Aid to Underdeveloped Countries* (New York, 1961), and B. E. Supple, 'Economic History and Economic Under-development', *Canadian Journal of Economics and Political Science* (1961), pp. 460–478.

CHAPTER V

The most up-to-date bibliography on the history of technology is that compiled by E. S. Ferguson, 'Contributions to Bibliography in the History of Technology', *Technology and Culture*, vol. 3, 1961–1962, pp. 73–84, pt. I; *Ibid.*, pt. II, pp. 167–174; *Ibid.*, pt. III, pp. 298–306; *Ibid.*, vol. 4, pt. IV, 1962–1963, pp. 318–330. A recent introductory world survey of *The Geography of Economic Activity* is provided by R. S. Thoman (New York, 1962).

The most reliable *History of Mechanical Inventions* is that by A. P. Usher (Revised ed., Cambridge, Mass., 1954). *A Short* (an English understatement at 782 pages) *History of Technology from the Earliest Times to A.D. 1900* is the work of T. K. Derry and T. I. Williams (Oxford, 1960). A comprehensive [*A*] *History of Technology* is that edited by C. J. Singer (and others) (Oxford, 1954–1958) 5V. Outstanding contributions and indispensable for anyone studying technology are A. R. Hall, 'The Changing Technical Act', *Technology and Culture*, vol. 3, 1962, pp. 501–515, and L. T. White, *Medieval Technology and Social Change* (Oxford, 1962). Rewarding if sometimes obtuse are the works of Oswald Spengler, *Man and Technics* (London, 1932), Lewis Mumford, *Technics and Civilization* (New York, 1934), and especially Sigfried Giedion, *Mechanisation Takes Command* (New York, 1948). *A Short History of Scientific Ideas*, by C. J. Singer (Oxford, 1959), provides an excellent introduction to the history of scientific ideas. See also J. D. Bernal, *Science and Industry in the Nineteenth Century* (London, 1953).

The literature on the sources of invention and innovation is vast. Especially important is the essay by S. C. Gilfillan, *The Sociology of Invention*

(Chicago, 1935). Also by the same author, 'Invention as a Factor in Economic History', *Journal of Economic History*, vol. 5, Suppl. 5, December 1945, pp. 66–85, and *Invention and the Patent System*, United States Congress, Joint Economic Committee (Washington, 1965). Gilfillan shares the view put forward by Ellsworth Huntington, *The Mainsprings of Civilization* (New York, 1945), that mental attitudes depend upon geographical factors. Also valuable are W. F. Ogburn, *Social Change with Respect to Culture and Original Nature* (New ed. New York, 1950), H. G. Barnett, *Innovation: The Basis of Cultural Change* (New York, 1953), and J. U. Nef, *Cultural Foundations of Industrial Civilization* (Cambridge [Eng.], 1958), Nef's book, *War and Human Progress* (London, 1950), is another valuable source. With less stress upon philosophical ideas is the work of John Jewkes and others, *The Sources of Invention* (New York, 1958).

A study of industrial development in recent centuries is best begun by reading G. N. Clarke's essay, *The Idea of the Industrial Revolution*, David Murray Foundation lecture (Oxford, 1953), also T. S. Ashton, *The Industrial Revolution, 1760–1830* (London, 1948), and J. D. Chambers, *The Workshop of the World* (London, 1961). Older works, but still valuable, are William Cunningham, *The Growth of English Industry and Commerce*, first published in 1882, and N. S. B. Gras, *Industrial Evolution* (Cambridge, 1930).

Industrial studies are Herbert Heaton, *The Yorkshire Woollen and Worsted Industries* (Oxford, 1920), J. U. Nef, *The Rise of the British Coal Industry* (London, 1932) 2V., W. H. B. Court, *The Rise of the Midland Industries, 1600–1838* (London, 1938), T. S. Ashton, *Iron and Steel in the Industrial Revolution* (Manchester, 1951), Walther Hoffman, *British Industry 1700–1950* (Oxford, 1955), William Woodruff, *The Rise of the British Rubber Industry* (Liverpool, 1958), L. F. Haber, *The Chemical Industry During the Nineteenth Century* (Oxford, 1958), D. L. Burn, *The Economic History of Steel Making, 1867–1939* (Cambridge [Eng.], 1961), and Archibald and Nan L. Clow, *The Chemical Revolution* (London, 1952). 'The Growth of World Industry' is traced by John Jewkes, *Oxford Economic Papers*, vol. 3, February 1951, pp. 1–15.

Valuable introductions to agricultural developments are N. S. B. Gras, *A History of Agriculture in Europe and America* (New York, 1925), and H. A. Tempany and D. H. Grist, *An Introduction to Tropical Agriculture* (London, 1958).

On economic growth see Simon Kuznets, *Six Lectures on Economic Growth* (Glencoe, Ill., 1959), and A. Maddison, 'Growth and Fluctuation in the World Economy, 1870–1960', *Banca Nazionale del Lavoro Quarterly Review*, vol. 15, June 1962, pp. 127–195; also by Maddison: *Economic Growth in the West* (London, 1964).

The diffusion of technology is dealt with in my article 'Intercontinental

Diffusion of Technology as a Factor in Economic Growth, 1860–1960', Papers and Proceedings of the International Conference of Economic Historians, Munich, 1965, to be published subsequently. See also W. C. Scoville, 'Minority Migrations and the Diffusion of Technology', *Journal of Economic History*, vol. II, no. 4, Fall 1951, pp. 347–360, W. O. Henderson, *Britain and Industrial Europe, 1750–1870* (Liverpool, 1954), S. B. Clough, 'The Diffusion of Industry in the Last Century and a Half', *Studi in Onore Di Armando Sapori* (Milano, 1957), and Walther Hoffman, *The Growth of Industrial Economies* (Manchester, 1958).

The relation between British and American manufacturing technology is examined by H. J. Habakkuk, *American and British Technology in the Nineteenth Century* (Cambridge [Eng.], 1962). See also J. W. Oliver, *History of American Technology* (New York, 1956), J. W. Roe, *English and American Toolbuilders* (New Haven, 1916); also by Roe, 'Interchangeable Manufacture', *Newcomen Society Transactions XVII* (1936–37), pp. 165–174, J. E. Sawyer, 'The Social Basis of the American System of Manufacturing', *Journal of Economic History*, vol. 14, no. 4, 1954, pp. 361–379, H. F. Williamson, 'Mass Production, Mass Consumption, and American Industrial Development', Papers and Proceedings of the 1st International Conference of Economic History, Stockholm, 1960, pp. 137–147, and N. B. Wilkinson, 'Brandy-wine Borrowings from European Technology', *Technology and Culture*, vol. 4, 1963, pp. 1–13.

For an appreciation of the critical nature of the machine-tools industry (in addition to the articles which appear in the Oxford [*A*] *History of Technology* already mentioned) see the four volumes of Robert S. Woodbury published by the Massachusetts Institute of Technology: *History of the Gear-Cutting Machine* (1958), *History of the Grinding Machine* (1959), *History of the Milling Machine* (1960), and *History of the Lathe to 1850* (1961); also L. T. C. Rolt, *A Short History of Machine Tools* (M.I.T., 1965), and C. S. Smith, *A History of Metallurgy* (Chicago, 1965).

On the development of inanimate energy resources see M. Mott-Smith, *The Story of Energy* (New York, 1934), and Hans Thirring, *Energy for Man*, Bloomington, Ind., (1958).

CHAPTER VI

In addition to the references given in the text and on the tables see E. Van Cleef, *Trade Centres and Trade Routes* (New York, 1937), A. W. Kirkaldy and A. D. Evans, *The History and Economics of Transport* [3rd ed., London, 1924), D. P. Locklin, *Economics of Transportation* (5th ed., Homewood, Ill., 1960), K. T. Healy, 'Transportation as a Factor in Economic Growth', *Journal of Economic History*, suppl. 7, 1947, pp. 72–88.

Additional sources on shipping: C. E. Fayle, *A Short History of the World's*

Shipping Industry (London, 1933), S. C. Gilfillan, *Inventing the Ship* (Chicago, 1935), G. S. Graham, 'The Ascendancy of the Sailing Ship 1850–85', *Economic History Review*, Series 2, vol. 9, August 1956, pp. 74–88.

With particular reference to British shipping see William Lawson, *Steam in the Pacific* (Wellington, N.Z., 1909), H. W. Macrosty, 'Statistics of British Shipping', *Journal of the Royal Statistical Society*, vol. 89, May 1926, pp. 452–531, R. G. Albion, 'British Shipping and Latin America, 1806–1914', *Journal of Economic History*, vol. II, no. 4, December 1951, pp. 361–374, F. E. Hyde, *Blue Funnel* (Liverpool, 1956), Sidney Pollard, 'British and World Shipbuilding, 1890–1914: A Study in Comparative Costs', *Journal of Economic History*, vol. 17, no. 3, 1957, pp. 426–444. On American shipping see J. G. B. Hutchins, 'The Declining American Maritime Industries', *Journal of Economic History*, suppl. 6, 1946, pp. 103–122, and on Australia's maritime communications with other continents see Keith Trace, 'Australian Overseas Shipping, 1900–60', an unpublished doctoral thesis, Melbourne University, 1965.

British railways are dealt with by Hamilton Ellis, *British Railway History 1830–1876 and 1877–1947* (London, 1956–1959) 2V. Useful regional studies are J. S. Duncan, 'British Railways in Argentina', *Political Science Quarterly*, vol. 52, no. 4, December 1937, pp. 559–582, Daniel Thorner, 'Great Britain and the Development of India's Railways', *Journal of Economic History*, vol. II, no. 4, Fall 1951, pp. 389–402, J. N. Sahni, *Indian Railways; One Hundred Years, 1853 to 1953* (New Delhi, 1953), B. E. Thomas, 'The Railways of French North Africa', *Economic Geography*, vol. 29, no. 2, April 1953, pp. 95–106, Lin Cheng, *The Chinese Railways* (Shanghai, 1937), I-tu Jên Sun, *Chinese Railways and British Interests, 1898–1911* (New York, 1954), Reinhard Huber, *Die Bagdadbahn* (Berlin, 1943), P. E. Carbutt, 'The Trans-Siberian Railway', *Journal of Transport History*, vol. I, no. 4, November 1954, pp. 238–249, A. W. Currie, *The Grand Trunk Railway of Canada* (Toronto, 1957). S. A. Thomson provides *A Short History of American Railroads* (New York, 1925); S. Thomson and J. H. Edgar deal with *Canadian Railway Development* (Toronto, 1933).

On 'Geographic Factors in the Development of Transportation in South America', see P. E. James, *Economic Geography*, vol. I, July 1925, pp. 247–261. A general treatment of *Communications in the Far East* is the work of F. V. Fellner (London, 1934). G. P. Glazebrook has provided *A History of Transportation in Canada* (New Haven, 1938), and R. J. H. Church has dealt with the 'Geographical Factors in the Development of Transport in Africa', *Transport and Communications Review*, vol. 2, no. 3, July–September 1949, pp. 3–11.

Sources on the Suez and Panama Canals, in addition to those already given, are Lincoln Hutchinson, 'The Panama Canal and Competition for Trade in Latin America, the Orient and Australasia', *Journal of the Royal*

Statistical Society, vol. 76, March 1913, pp. 359–388, William Woodruff and L. McGregor, *The Suez Canal and the Australian Economy* (Melbourne, 1957), A. B. Mountjoy, 'The Suez Canal at Mid-century', *Economic Geography*, vol. 34, no. 2, April 1958, pp. 155–167. For the development of submarine cables consult G. R. M. Garrett, *One Hundred Years of Submarine Cables* (London, 1950). *The Story of the Wheel* has been told by G. M. Boumphrey (London, 1932), *The Story of Flying* by A. Black (New York, 1943).

CHAPTER VII

A good start can be made in the study of international trade with J. B. Condliffe, *The Commerce of Nations* (London, 1951), also William Ashworth, *A Short History of the International Economy* (2nd ed., London, 1963). *International Trade Statistics* are edited by R. G. D. Allen and J. E. Ely (New York, 1953).

Additional references on the composition of international trade are H. C. and A. D. Taylor, *World Trade in Agricultural Products* (New York, 1943), League of Nations, *Industrialization and Foreign Trade* (Geneva, 1945), H. Tyszynski, 'World Trade in Manufactured Commodities 1899–1950', *Manchester School of Economic and Social Studies*, vol. 19, no. 3, September 1951, pp. 272–304, R. E. Baldwin, 'The Commodity Composition of Trade: Selected Industrial Countries, 1900–1954', *Review of Economics and Statistics*, vol. 40, no. 1, Suppl. February 1958, pp. 50–71, P. L. Yates, *Forty Years of Foreign Trade* (London, 1959), A. Maizels, 'Trends in World Trade in Durable Consumer Goods', *National Institute Economic Review*, no. 6, November 1959, pp. 15–36, M. L. Dantwala, 'International Trade in Primary Commodities — A Factual Note', *Indian Economic Journal*, vol. X, no. 2, October 1962, pp. 157–163.

Further references on British trade statistics are A. Maizels, 'The Overseas Trade Statistics of the United Kingdom', *Journal of the Royal Statistical Society*, vol. 112, pt. 2, 1949, pp. 207–223; Elizabeth Schumpeter, *English Overseas Trade Statistics, 1697–1808* (Oxford, 1961). Historical treatments of British foreign trade are A. L. Bowley, *A Short Account of England's Foreign Trade in the Nineteenth Century* (revised ed., London, 1905), William Page (ed.), *Commerce and Industry* (London, 1919) 2V., Werner Schlote, *British Overseas Trade from 1700 to the 1930s* (Oxford, 1952), A. H. Imlah, *Economic Elements in the Pax Britannica; Studies in British Foreign Trade in the Nineteenth Century* (Cambridge, 1958), Phyllis Deane and W. A. Cole, *British Economic Growth, 1688–1959* (Cambridge [Eng.], 1962), and B. R. Mitchell and P. M. Deane, *British Historical Statistics* (Cambridge [Eng.], 1962).

The history of French commerce until the eve of the First World War is covered by Emile Levasseur, *Histoire du Commerce de la France* (Paris, 1911–12) 2V.

Sources dealing with the theory of international trade are voluminous. I gained most from the following works: Jacob Viner, *International Trade and Economic Development* (Glencoe, Ill., 1952), Ragnar Nurske, *Patterns of Trade and Development* (Stockholm, 1959), A. K. Cairncross, 'International Trade and Economic Development', *Kylos*, vol. 13, no. 4, 1960, pp. 545–558, Kenneth Berrill, 'International Trade and the Rate of Economic Growth', *Economic History Review*, 2nd series, vol. 12, no. 3, April 1960, pp. 351–359, and Roy Harrod and Douglas Hague (eds.), *International Trade Theory in a Developing World*, proceedings of a conference held by the International Economic Association (London, 1963).

Studies of trade between Latin America and Europe, and Asia and Europe, were published by the United Nations, Department of Economic Affairs, New York, in 1953.

INDEX

References such as 'v/8' are to tables

POSTSCRIPT

Far from dying in convulsions, as some writers had predicted, by 1960, Europe had returned to the center of the world stage.

Factors helping to explain its recovery were Europe's growing unity, its liberalization of trade (as well as the freer movement of labor, capital and technology), its growing capital resources, its improved methods of production, its shift from agriculture to the manufacturing and service sections, and its monetary stability. Not least important was the outstanding quality of its leaders such as DeGaulle and Adenauer. Other causes assisting European recovery were the quickening of the world economy and the maintenance of a general peace.

However we measure it--whether we turn to the rate of capital accumulation, or increased output, or the rate of investment, or the expansion of trade--Europe's economic recovery after 1950 is obvious. Indeed, it has been estimated that the average annual growth per head in Europe between 1950 and 1973 was twice that of the years 1914-1939. Had there not been a quantum leap (even in real terms) in European production and trade in the twenty years after 1950, Europe could never have raised its general standard of living and welfare as it did.

By 1980, with a population of 250 million, with a productive capacity second to none, with slightly more than half the world's trade, with monetary resources in excess of those held by either the United States or the U.S.S.R., and with the world's largest merchant fleet, the European Economic Community constituted one of the world's most important economic blocks. Only the onset of the world economic recession in the 1970's halted Europe's upward trend.

*

In 1960 Europe was still a world civilization; still the most important part of world history; yet by then the Eurocentric world of 1914 had gone for good. World power had passed to the United States and the U.S.S.R. Significant for the course of future events, the fundamental ideas which had prompted Europe to colonize the world no longer prevailed. Then, as now, there were Europeans who believed in Christianity as a world religion, in the transcendent aspects of European Christian culture, in the idea of Western progress for the human race, in individualism, in the self-determination of peoples, in a liberal economic and political world order, in capitalism, rationalism, egalitarianism, and even in revolutionary socialism--but they were in the minority. Nor did they hold their beliefs with the certainty, fervor and compulsion of earlier times. Almost unawares, since 1945, Europe had increasingly become post-Christian, post-individualistic, post-industrial, and post-capitalistic. European ideas would continue to move the world; European messianism, however, was dead.

Indeed, by 1960, Europe looked not so much to the world as to itself. Its confrontation was not outside, but inside Europe. Out of Europe's growing concern with itself was born the European Economic Community.

*

Europe's recovery in the 1950's does not seem as surprising now as it did then. Europe, after all, with necessity as the spur, was treading known ground. Moreover, on this occasion, she was helped by an enlightened United States economic foreign policy. Just as at an earlier moment in history the Old World had gone to the aid of the New, so now the New World came to the aid of the Old.

What is remarkable is that Europe should have achieved what she did, despite the loss of her vast overseas empires (which suggests that these empires were essentially political rather than economic undertakings--peripheral, not central to European economic strength). In 1939, the colonial empires of Great Britain, France, the Netherlands, Italy, Belgium, Spain and Portugal had spanned the globe. By the 1950's the

European recessional was under way. Twenty years later, all that remained were tiny and unimportant specks of land in and around the oceans of the world. Majestic empires that had taken centuries to build, whose dominions were more extensive than any the world had known, had all been swept away. Whether Europe yielded its power willingly, systematically ridding itself of its overseas possessions one after the other, or fought bitterly to retain what it was convinced was its own, the outcome was the same: European colonization as a state system was dead. Having espoused and spread the principle of revolutionary socialism and self-determination, the Europeans had been hoist with their own petard. Never was power transferred on this scale, so quickly, and relatively speaking, so peacefully. Appropriately enough, the Iberians who had begun Europe's imperial saga, were the last to yield. White minority rule in the world today exists only in South Africa.

The truth is that Europe, having emerged from the worst war the world had known, no longer had the heart to go on. For most Europeans, the imperial idea was dead. The earlier sense of destiny, of duty to others, of Europe's right to govern the world as it saw fit, had all departed. Even when she fought back against those who challenged her rule, as she did at Dien Bien Phu in 1954, and at Suez in 1956, she did so half-heartedly. While the political and especially the economic ties that bound Europe to the other continents could hardly be broken overnight, nothing could disguise the fact that the old imperial fire had gone out. Essentially, Europe lost a great empire because she no longer wanted to keep it.

*

Europe's reluctance to concern itself with the world in the postwar period is borne out by the changes going on in European migration (Appendix Table IV). In contrast to the earlier trans-oceanic exodus, net emigration of Europeans in the 25 years after 1950 amounted to only 2.2 million. By the early 1970's--encouraged by Europe's prosperous economic conditions--more migrants were entering than leaving Europe. By then, four million non-Europeans--chiefly Asians, North Africans and West Indians--were living in northern and western Europe. Even the United Kingdom, the classical country of emigration, while continuing to send numerous emigrants abroad, received equally large numbers of West Indians and Asians. Swelling the inward flow were the large numbers of European nationals being repatriated from the Dutch, French, Belgian, Portuguese and British overseas empires. In the 1960's almost one million French nationals were repatriated from North Africa alone. Portugal's experience was much the same.

Without this influx into Europe, the rate of European population growth--from 1950 to 1970 about 1.1 percent a year against two percent for the world--would have been more modest than it was. With the exception of Ireland, Spain, and to a less extent eastern Europe, the Crude Rate of Natural Increase of most European countries has in fact continued its century-old decline (Appendix Table III). If there has been no falling-off in overall European numbers, it is because the lowering of the European death rate has temporarily extended the life of the population.

Whatever the future of European numbers, European migration is in fact no longer as indispensable to world development as it was. Prompted by new legislation, since 1950 non-Europeans have proceeded to displace Europeans in the major immigration areas of the world. In the 25-year period, 1950-1974, the United States (by far the greatest receiving area) admitted for permanent residence more immigrants from Latin America (about 2.5 million, chiefly from Mexico, Cuba, the Dominican Republic and the West Indies), and Asia (chiefly from the Philippines, China, Korea and India), than from the whole of Europe combined (about three million, chiefly from southern and eastern Europe). Immigrants entering the United States between 1959 and 1979 by region were as follows:

1959		1979
60.9%	Europe	13.4%
8.9%	Asia	41.4%
1.1%	Africa	2.6%
0.5%	Oceania	1.0%
19.8%	Latin America	38.6%
8.9%	Canada	3.0%

Source: U.S. Immigration and Naturalization Service; 1980 estimate by Select Commission on Immigration and Refugee Policy.

In the 10-year period 1965-1974, European immigrants to Canada were also being replaced by migrants from other regions. Between 1965 and 1974 about 250,000 Asian and 170,000 Latin American immigrants entered Canada--traditionally an area of European immigration. Peculiar to Canada and Australia is the number of United States citizens settling there. In 1970-74 the average annual number of immigrants entering Canada from the United States was second only to those coming from the United Kingdom (24,600 against 25,100). In 1970-74 United States immigrants into Australia ranked third after the United Kingdom and New Zealand. Even more surprising in the light of past experience is the number of Asian (Lebanese, Indian, and Turkish) and eastern European (Yugoslav and Greek) immigrants who have entered Australia since 1960.

While the impact of the European migrant in the world these past twenty years has lessened, the number of Europeans migrating within Europe itself has increased. Following the building of the Berlin Wall in 1961, which halted the Westward flow of migrants from the German Democratic Republic, a large, if temporary migration developed between the countries of southern and eastern Europe (Italy, Portugal, Spain and Greece) on the one hand, and western and northern Europe (the Federal Republic of Germany, France, Belgium, Switzerland, the Netherlands and Denmark) on the other. In this movement, European workers migrated from countries where labor was plentiful to countries where (because of economic recovery) it was scarce. So important did this movement become, that by the 1960's intra-European migration had taken precedence over the inter-continental migration of Europeans. In 1960 the number of southern Europeans living in western and northern Europe was estimated at 2.0 million. The figure in 1974 was in the region of 5.5 million. Because of the massive influx of Portuguese, Paris has become the next most important Portuguese city to Lisbon and Oporto. In 1980 guest workers and their dependents in France numbered about four million; the figure for West Germany was about 4.5 million (about 7% of the French and West German population). More than a third of the workers in Switzerland at this time were foreigners. By then, however, the less stimulating European and world economic conditions had lessened the flow of migrants both from Europe to the world and within Europe itself. With unemployment in E.E.C., countries at the beginning of the 1980's estimated at nine millions, the free movement of European labor within the European community was coming to be looked upon with growing disfavor.

*

Europe's increasing preoccupation with itself was as true of finance as it was of migration. By 1945--if not earlier--the United States had unquestionably displaced Europe as banker of the world. By 1960, under American leadership, portfolio investment (chiefly in fixed-interest loans and securities), the classic form of foreign investment until 1914, had been surpassed by United States direct foreign business investment (which, along with other forms of private, long-term, foreign investment, has proved the most effective instrument for the transfer of technology). By then, spurred by the search for greater security and increased profitability, and encouraged by the generally favorable economic and political climate (not least by Europe's growing economic unity), the number of capitalist enterprises with international ramifications had increased rapidly. Between 1960 and 1976, the stock of direct foreign investment of the developed Market Economies (principally European and North American), grew from about $105 billion to approximately $287 billion (Appendix Table VI). The direct foreign investment of the two leading creditor nations in 1980, the United States and the United Kingdom, had risen to $213.5 and $68.9 billion. (Their portfolio investments at this time were $62 billion and $33.6 billion respectively). Despite the onset of the world economic recession in the mid-1970's, the average annual growth rate of world direct foreign investment for the years 1974-79 (measured at current values and by flow rather than by stock), was only slightly less than it had been during the period 1960-73 (11.9 percent against 12.6 percent).

Assisted by favorable exchange rates and its balance of payments position since the early 1970's, no European country increased its share of world investment faster than the German

Federal Republic (from 7.2 percent of the world total in the period 1960-67 to 17 percent in the period 1974-79). In the same period, the French figure increased slightly (from 6.8 to 7.8 percent); the British figure remained fairly stable at nine percent. Throughout the 1960's and 1970's, Europe's importance as a source of funds (i.e., its share of the world stock of direct foreign investment) continued to grow. In broad sectoral terms, the Europeans showed a preference for the same kind of investments as the Americans--with a very gradual shift in emphasis from mining and manufactures, as the leading sectors, to the service-oriented industries.

In contrast to Europe's recovery in world finance, the United States share in world direct business investment was halved (from about 60 percent of the total in the period 1961-67, to approximately 30 percent of a larger total during the years 1974-79). In fact, throughout the 1970's the increasing attractiveness of the United States as a field of direct foreign investment--relative to other areas--caused the stock of direct foreign investment in that country (most of it European) to grow from $13.6 billion in 1971 to $52 billion in 1979. In the period 1961-67 the United States had taken only 2.6 percent of the total flow of direct foreign investment. By 1979, due to an unparalleled growth of European (and Japanese) investment in the United States, the figure was in the region of 30 percent. Contrary to what is generally believed, little of this change can be ascribed to the recent increase in business investments of the major oil-exporting countries. In 1980, direct, long-term business investments of O.P.E.C. countries (which achieved a balance-of-payments surplus in 1980 of more than $100 billion), was only about one percent of the total invested in the western world.

While the flow of business investments across the Atlantic during the 1970's became more balanced, Europe's growing share of world direct foreign investments should not be exaggerated. There has in fact been no absolute fall in the American figure. Inflows into Europe from the United States in the period 1974-79, in current values, were in fact slightly higher than in the years 1968-73. Moreover, recent disinvestments in Europe by the United States have their counterparts in European disinvestments both in Europe and elsewhere. There has not only been a deceleration in the growth rate of United States direct foreign investment; since 1980 there has been a deceleration in the rate of growth of investments generally. More important than Europe's increasing tilt toward America is the slowing down of the entire world economy--a slowing down reflected in the lower rate of growth of world production and international trade.

Since 1960, Europe, along with the United States, has also made available equally large sums (both private and public, including private bank lending) to developing countries and multinational agencies such as the World Bank (Appendix Table

VIII). Aid given by the Market Economies in 1979, relative to their G.N.P. was as follows:

Net Official Development Aid to Developing Countries and Multilateral Agencies in 1979

	As Percent Of GNP	In Millions Of Dollars
Sweden	0.94	956
Norway	0.93	429
Netherlands	0.93	1,404
Denmark	0.75	448
France	0.59	3,370
Belgium	0.56	631
Britain	0.52	2,067
Australia	0.52	620
Canada	0.46	1,025
Germany	0.44	3,350
New Zealand	0.30	61
Japan	0.26	2,638
Switzerland	0.21	205
Finland	0.21	86
U.S.A.	0.20	4,684
Austria	0.19	620
Italy	0.08	273

Source:
U.S. International Development Cooperation Agency

Official development aid was also made available by the Centrally Planned Economies, the bulk of it from the U.S.S.R. (Appendix Table IX). For reasons which are not altogether clear, much more of the aid given by the Market Economies is consumed in the transfer process.

For the Centrally Planned Economies, no area has grown in importance more than Latin America (chiefly Cuba). Until now there is little agreement concerning the extent to which either capitalist or Communist assistance has been a necessary or sufficient condition for the economic development of the developing world. By and large, the underdeveloped countries seek aid for economic reasons; yet aid is often given by Communist and non-Communist governments alike, not for economic but for political reasons.

*

Much of these investment funds and development assistance have been spent throughout the world providing traditional as well as modern forms of technology. In the recent development of micro-computers, micro-electronics, cybernetics, nuclear energy, compound-antibiotics, and, alas, weapons systems, Europe has once more played a leading role. Europe is still the originator of inventions from which others have benefited (the computer industry is an example of the recognition and exploitation by the United States and Japanese companies of theoretical research carried out in Europe).

Europe has also pioneered in aerospace technology. The Soviet Union's launching of the first Sputnik on October 4, 1957 was a landmark in the propulsion and guidance of objects in space. A lesser triumph is the faster-than-sound joint French-British *Concorde* aircraft.

Yet Europe no longer dominates in scientific and technological progress as it once did. Squeezed between the Silicon Valley of California on the one hand, and of Japan, South Korea and Taiwan on the other, Europeans have become customers for products which their own ingenuity and inventive capacity made possible.

Most of the scientific and technological developments of the period 1960-80 were in fact the outcome of a long prior history of incremental effort and achievement of many scientists --European and non-European--throughout the developed world. As the scientific nature of technological development has grown, trial and error invention by an easily identifiable individual has given way to planned, large-scale research with a common world-wide scientific basis. Instead of scientific or technological breakthroughs by a single inventor, we have progressive refinements coming from innumerable laboratories. So costly, so complicated are the scientific processes of modern industry, that progress has only been achieved through the combined efforts not only of many scientists, but of many countries. The growing anonymity of invention is perhaps the most marked aspect of technological progress in the past two decades.

The greater the complexity and cost entailed, the more necessary it has been for governments to intervene in the industrial process. This has always been true of the planned and of certain sectors of the market economies; now it is widespread. A striking example has been the development of nuclear energy in Europe. The more neo-mercantilist European and other governments have become during recent years, particularly since the onset of the world-wide recession in 1973, the more difficult it has been to separate the political from the economic and technological factors at work. Nor have all governments reacted in a similar manner. Faced with greater vulnerability to changes in the Middle East than the United States, European governments have not shown the same antipathy to the development of atomic energy for peaceful purposes. The present dispute in NATO concerning the building of the Siberia-Western Europe pipeline for natural gas is another instance of the political implications of modern technology.

Curiously enough, it is just when science and technology offer new marvels, that their purpose has come to be questioned. Many Europeans feel that their scientific and mechanical genius has left them less secure than they were. The ever-growing gap between technology, which develops cumulatively, and ethics, which relatively speaking, stands still, is clear to all; as is the threat presented by certain branches of modern technology to our very existence.

*

With temporary variations, the value of world trade throughout the 1960's and most of the 1970's increased at a faster rate than world production. Even allowing for inflation, which virtually doubled between 1960-73 and 1973-79, world trade grew at an unparalleled rate. Europe led in both production and trade. Comparing 1960 with 1973, the value of the European Community's total exports (at current prices) increased in an average year by an unprecedented 13-14 percent; the figure for exports within the Economic Community during the same period was about 16 percent. In 1980 Europe's share of world trade, including the U.S.S.R. was more than 50 percent, 40 percent of which was done by the European Economic Community. By then West Germany's share of world trade had long exceeded that of Europe's traditional leading trading nation, the United Kingdom (Appendix Table XXX).

Although there was a considerable increase in the importance of primary produce in international commerce during the past two decades, including a much larger volume of the all-important agricultural trade done within Europe itself, the major expansion was in the trade of manufactures, particularly between European nations. Especially important from a political point of view was the growing inter-relation between the trading (and sometimes bartering) blocks of Western and Eastern Europe. In return for raw material and fuels, exports (chiefly manufactures) from the European Community to the U.S.S.R. alone in 1979 were $8.3 billion. West Germany's exports to the U.S.S.R. a year later were $4.4 billion, up from $3.6 billion in 1979. As a share of G.N.P., West German trade with the U.S.S.R. in 1980 was 16 times higher than the United States trade with the U.S.S.R. Hence, Western Europe's support of detente and the strained transatlantic relations of recent years. The percentage of the U.S.S.R.'s trade with the West in 1980 was as follows:

West Germany	22.0%
Japan	14.0%
Finland	12.6%
France	12.4%
United States	7.6%
Canada	6.6%
Italy	6.4%
Britain	5.3%
Belgium-Luxembourg	3.1%

Source: U.S. Department of Commerce

In 1980 Western Europe also took about half the exports of the developing world and provided it with about 40% of its imports, thus becoming the largest source of trade (as well as aid) to the Third World. Some of it was with the former dependent overseas territories of France, Belgium, Italy, Netherlands, and Britain, whose governments wished to continue the association with the European Community guaranteed them by the Treaty of Rome of 1957 and extended by the Yaoundé Convention signed in the capitol of Cameroon in 1963, and subsequent similar conventions.

The first serious threat to Europe's unparalleled economic expansion and prosperity was the OPEC oil embargo of 1973, which brought a dramatic increase in oil prices. Worse still, as each country sought to protect itself, the oil crisis revealed the fragility of the ties holding the community together. As a result, the hope of a second phase of consolidation expressed at the Summit Conference in Paris in 1972 began to fade. (The first phase of consolidation had come when the Six had completed their Customs Union in 1968 and adopted a common commercial policy in 1970). While the embargo was unsuccessful in changing Western political policy, real oil prices (in terms of manufacturing prices) were much less excessive than they appeared. Yet, the embargo's impact on trade balances was sufficient to cause many Western countries to suffer current account deficits.

Whatever the cause or causes of the deceleration in the growth of world trade, as well as in investment and productivity, since the late 1970's, the earlier cooperative effort to create an interdependent world economy is now in jeopardy. Increasingly, every nation is concerned to look after itself. Beginning with the 1975 Tokyo Round of the General Agreement on Tariffs and Trade (G.A.T.T.), which was far less liberal in outlook than previous trade agreements, a mercantilist attitude threatens to replace the earlier liberal outlook. Moreover, the mercantilism of the present day is much more subtle, than hitherto. Instead of relying on tariffs and quotas, it uses market restrictions, currency manipulations, cartels, direct and indirect subsidies, and voluntary export restraints. A good deal of market sharing and rationalization of industry is also going on; multi-national corporations face new pressures and controls. In consequence, the one-time nominally free-trade area of the European Community is in danger of being turned into a number of inward-looking national economies, all of which threaten to undo Europe's greatest achievement since World War II--its unprecedented economic unity.

*

Yet the idea of a united Europe goes back beyond medieval times and is not likely to die now. If the postwar ardor to set Europe upon a more united, peaceful course has waned, it is because the Soviet Union's military threat and the United States' economic challenge have both lessened. As a consequence the supranational ideas advocated by Jean Monnet and Robert Schuman in the 1950's gave way to the inter-governmental, trans-national outlook of the 1960's, identified with General De Gaulle. Since 1973 the enlarged Economic Community has been concerned with the pragmatic, systematic cooperation of nations. Ironically, nationalism, the idea Europe gave to the world, has prevented Europe's own further union. In place of The Grand Design of Monnet and Schuman there is only fragmentation and aimlessness.

According to some observers, Europe is in fact beset by an incurable, cultural malaise. The psychological readiness to unite which marked the 1950's and 1960's no longer exists. In place of the earlier resolve there is now philosophical turmoil. Cynicism reigns. The transcendent, redemptive aspect of European culture is no longer visible: the moral heritage of Christian centuries has been lost. Little wonder that the democracies are becoming ungovernable; that the so-called European Parliament is no more than a show-place.

Nor are things any better on the economic front. Since the oil crisis of 1973 Europe, with the rest of the world, has drifted into an economic crisis of ever-growing proportions. As production, trade, and monetary difficulties have mounted--more particularly as the armies of unemployed have grown--the doctrine of _sauve-qui-peut_ has gained ascendency once more.

But this is too gloomy a view. Culturally, nothing is proven. True, there has been cultural change since 1960--perhaps decline--but decadence that worsens by the hour? Hardly. Moreover, whatever cultural problems exist, they are not uniquely European. The loss of faith, of beliefs, of enthusiasm, of ties between family, church, and state, is common to the Western World. Europe is passing through one of the many ordeals that it has experienced before. The age-old European dream of a united Europe is not dead, it merely slumbers. As for Europe's political drawbacks, democracies never have been tidy organizations. Mediocracy has often marked their paths in times of peace. It takes a real crisis to bring out their best. The European Parliament may be weak, but it _does_ exist. The foreign policy of the Economic Community has never been more cohesive; there is far more consultation and cooperation between members of the Economic Community concerning foreign affairs today than would have been thought possible a decade ago. To think that everything would be better if Europe were integrated on federal lines like the United States is to think in American terms. If Europe's strength lies in anything, it lies in the variety of its peoples and in the more than two score uniquely different sovereign states.

Europe, like the rest of the Western World, is plagued by the present world-wide economic recession; European monetary and agricultural problems still bar the path to further unity. But consider what Europe has achieved. Out of wartime devastation there emerged (in 1949) the Council for Mutual Economic Assistance (COMECON) and (in 1952) the European Coal and Steel Community of The Six (Belgium, Luxembourg, Netherlands, West Germany, France, and Italy); to be followed in 1957 under The Treaty of Rome by the Economic Community and the Common Market. In 1959 the European Free Trade Area (The Seven) was formed. In 1973 the Economic Community was enlarged to include Britain, Eire, and Denmark (The Nine). The recently established European Monetary System (EMS), while falling short of a full-fledged monetary union, is an important step in that direction. The outcome of Europe's closer union, coupled with the quickening of the world economy, was a period (1950's to the late 1970's) of economic growth and prosperity such as Europe had never experienced before.

Whatever path Europe chooses to follow--national, Atlantic, united, or multi-directional--it will continue to influence the rest of the world as it has done for more than half a millenium. Europe may no longer dominate the world politically, yet its ideas are still at work in every field of thought and action.

APPENDIX TABLE I
(See Table III/1 p. 103)

Estimates of World Population by Continents at Mid-year 1965, 1970, 1975 and 1979
(in millions and percentage of world total)

Year	World	Europe and Asiatic U.S.S.R.	%	North America	%	Latin America	%	Africa	%	Asia	%	Oceania	%	Area of European Settlement	%
1965	3344	676	20.2	214	6.4	247	7.4	311	9.3	1878	56.2	18	0.5	1155	34.5
1970	3678	703	19.1	226	6.1	283	7.7	354	9.6	2091	56.9	19	0.5	1232	33.5
1975	4033	728	18.1	236	5.9	323	8.0	406	10.1	2319	57.5	21	0.5	1308	32.4
1979	4336	746	17.2	244	7.9	359	8.3	456	10.5	2509	57.9	23	0.5	1372	31.6

Source:
United Nations, 1979 Demographic Yearbook
(New York, 1980).

APPENDIX TABLE II

(See Table III/2 p. 104)

Estimates of European Population in Selected European Countries, 1965-1979
(in millions and percentage)

Year	Europe (incl. U.S.S.R.)	United Kingdom	(%)	France	(%)	Germany[1]	(%)	U.S.S.R.	(%)	Italy	(%)	Sweden	(%)	Poland	(%)	Nether-lands	(%)	Spain	(%)
1965	676	54	8.0	49	7.2	76	11.2	231	34.2	52	7.7	8	1.2	32	4.7	12	1.8	32	4.7
1970	703	55	7.8	51	7.3	78	11.1	243	34.6	54	7.7	8	1.1	33	4.7	13	1.8	34	4.8
1975	728	56	7.7	53	7.3	79	10.9	254	34.9	56	7.7	8	1.1	34	4.7	14	1.9	36	4.9
1979	746	56	7.5	53	7.1	78	10.5	264	35.4	57	7.6	8	1.1	35	4.7	14	1.9	37	5.0

Note:
[1] Includes Federal Republic and German Democratic Republic.

Source:
United Nations, 1979 Demographic Yearbook (New York, 1980).

APPENDIX TABLE III

(See Table III/3 p. 105)

Crude Rates of Natural Increase[1] of Selected European Countries, 1961-1979 (Average annual rate per thousand of population)

Country	1961-70	1971-79
United Kingdom	6.0	1.4
Ireland	10.1	11.4
Norway	7.8	4.4
Sweden	4.6	2.0
France	6.4	4.6
Netherlands	11.8	5.7
Federal Republic of Germany	5.3	- 1.5
Austria	4.8	- 0.04
Italy	8.6	4.9
Spain	12.1	10.3
U.S.S.R.	10.1	8.8

Note:
[1]Crude rate of natural increase is equal to crude birth rate less crude death rate.

Source:
United Nations, *1979 Demographic Yearbook*, (New York, 1980).

APPENDIX TABLE IV

(See Table III/4 p. 106)

Emigration[1] from Europe, 1961-1979
(in thousands)

Origin	1961	1962	1963	1964	1965	1966	1967	1968	1969	1970	1971	1972	1973	1974	1975	1976	1977	1978	1979	1961 -70	1971 -79
United Kingdom	91.0	91.2	107.2	226.1	249.3	262.1	265.4	233.5	244.1	237.5	190.8	188.2	195.7	224.5	193.3	166.3	158.8	146.1	147.8	2007.4	1611.3
Sweden	2.6	2.6	3.2	3.2	3.1	3.2	4.0	4.8	4.1	4.9	5.2	6.3	6.7	5.7	4.7	4.9	4.4	4.5	4.9	35.7	47.3
Norway	2.8	3.2	3.2	3.8	3.9	3.8	4.0	4.3	4.1	6.1	3.6	4.2	4.1	4.7	4.9	4.8	5.1	5.4	5.5	39.2	42.3
Finland	0.9	0.6	0.5	0.6	0.5	0.6	0.9	1.5	1.4	2.8	0.7	0.3	0.4	0.5	0.5	0.7	0.9	1.1	1.1	10.3	6.1
Denmark	8.1	8.1	9.1	9.6	10.1	11.2	10.6	13.7	13.7	n.a.	14.2	9.6	12.3	14.1	15.1	13.6	12.2	11.3	12.3	94.2[2]	114.7
France	n.a.	n.a.	n.a.	n.a.	n.a.	n.a.	n.a.	n.a.	n.a.	n.a.	n.a.	n.a.	n.a.	n.a.	n.a.	n.a.	n.a.	n.a.	n.a.	n.a.	n.a.
Belgium	9.2	9.9	10.4	12.1	13.4	12.3	11.6	13.4	12.6	14.0	10.4	11.5	11.2	11.3	11.0	13.2	13.2	13.1	13.2	118.9	108.1
Netherlands	30.4	27.2	20.8	23.3	23.4	25.9	27.2	26.0	24.5	23.7	24.2	23.4	23.6	24.6	23.6	27.8	27.5	27.0	26.7	252.4	228.4
Germany, F.R.	55.3	53.0	59.2	68.5	69.0	73.5	79.7	69.9	64.2	61.3	58.7	64.2	64.2	71.4	71.3	73.4	73.1	74.4	74.3	653.6	625.0
Austria	4.2	2.7	3.6	4.1	4.4	5.5	7.3	12.4	21.5	22.2	11.3	5.0	4.7	3.2	n.a.	n.a.	n.a.	n.a.	n.a.	87.9	24.2[4]
Switzerland	n.a.	n.a.	n.a.	n.a.	n.a.	n.a.	n.a.	n.a.	n.a.	n.a.	n.a.	n.a.	n.a.	n.a.	n.a.	n.a.	n.a.	n.a.	n.a.	n.a.	n.a.
Spain	n.a.	36.2	25.9	24.3	21.4	16.1	19.3	19.4	20.1	16.8	14.4	6.0	5.1	4.6	3.9	3.4	3.2	3.6	4.0	199.5[3]	48.2
Portugal	27.5	24.2	22.4	17.2	17.6	33.3	28.6	27.0	27.4	22.7	22.0	20.1	22.1	25.8	19.3	14.8	14.8	n.a.	n.a.	248.1	138.9[4]
Italy	57.5	56.5	42.5	42.0	50.2	77.1	62.6	57.3	43.1	34.7	34.6	29.9	24.8	25.0	20.6	24.2	22.5	23.6	n.a.	523.5	205.2[4]
U.S.S.R.	n.a.	n.a.	n.a.	n.a.	n.a.	n.a.	n.a.	n.a.	n.a.	n.a.	n.a.	n.a.	n.a.	n.a.	n.a.	n.a.	n.a.	n.a.	n.a.	n.a.	n.a.
Poland	n.a.	n.a.	n.a.	n.a.	n.a.	n.a.	n.a.	n.a.	n.a.	n.a.	n.a.	n.a.	n.a.	n.a.	n.a.	n.a.	n.a.	n.a.	n.a.	n.a.	n.a.

n.a. = not available

Notes:
[1]Because of the lack, the ambiguity, and the incomparability of international, long-term migration statistics, the estimates given here should be treated with caution.
[2]1961-69 only.
[3]1962-69 only.
[4]Incomplete.

Sources:
United Nations, Demographic Yearbook (various).
Europa Yearbook (various).
United Kingdom International Passenger Survey, 1981.
Statistical Tables and Yearbooks of the following countries: Sweden, Finland, Denmark, Belgium, Federal Republic of Germany.
Trends and characteristics of international migration since 1950, United Nations, Demographic Studies No. 64, (New York, 1979).

APPENDIX TABLE V
(See Table III/8 p. 113)

Area and Population of the World by Continent and Region
(1970, 1979)

Continent and Region	Thousands of square kilometers	Adjusted estimates at mid-year (millions)		Density (per square kilometer)		Annual rate of increase (%)	
		1970	1979	1970	1979	1970-69	1970-78
World	135,781	3,678	4,336	27	32	1.9	2.1
Europe[1]	4,936	460	482	94	98	0.9	0.5
Northern & western Europe	2,631	228	235	87	89	0.9	0.3
Central Europe	990	103	109	104	110	0.7	0.6
Southern Europe	1,315	128	138	98	105	1.0	0.9
U.S.S.R.	22,402	244	264	11	12	1.3	1.0
America	42,081	509	603	12	14	2.2	2.0
North America	21,515	226	244	11	11	1.4	0.8
Central America	2,496	67	90	27	36	3.4	3.7
South America	20,566	216	269	11	14	2.9	2.9
Oceania	8,511	19	23	2	3	2.1	1.7
Asia[2]	27,532	2,091	2,509	75	91	2.0	2.5
Southwest Asia	4,506	74	95	17	21	2.4	2.6
South Central Asia	6,771	750	933	113	138	2.5	2.4
South East Asia	4,498	286	359	64	80	2.7	2.7
Eastern Asia	11,757	981	1,122	79	95	1.4	2.4
Africa	30,319	354	456	11	15	2.4	3.6
North Africa	8,525	83	106	10	12	2.7	2.3
Tropical & southern Africa	21,794	271	350	12	16	2.4	4.0

Notes:
[1]Excluding U.S.S.R.
[2]Including Turkey; excluding U.S.S.R.

Source:
United Nations, Demographic Yearbook, (various).

This table confirms the relative, if minor, decline of Europe's share of world population.

APPENDIX TABLE VI
(See Table IV/1 p. 150)

Estimated Stock of Direct Investment[1] Abroad of Developed Market Economies, by Major Country of Origin, 1967-1979

Country of Origin	Billions of Dollars, End of 1967	1971	1973	1975	1976	1979	Percentage Distribution 1967	1971	1973	1975	1976
United States	56.6	82.8	101.3	124.2	137.2	192.6	53.8	52.3	51.0	47.8	47.6
United Kingdom . .	17.5	23.7	26.9	30.8	32.1	51.5	16.6	15.0	13.5	11.9	11.2
Germany, F.R. . . .	3.0	7.3	11.9	16.0	19.9	38.9	2.8	4.6	6.0	6.2	6.9
Japan	1.5	4.4	10.3	15.9	19.4	29.0[2]	1.4	2.8	5.2	6.1	6.7
Switzerland . . .	5.0	9.5	11.1	16.9	18.6	n.a.	4.8	6.0	5.6	6.5	6.5
France	6.0	7.3	8.8	11.1	11.9	14.9[3]	5.7	4.6	4.4	4.3	4.1
Canada	3.7	6.5	7.8	10.5	11.1	13.5[3]	3.5	4.1	3.9	4.1	3.9
Netherlands . . .	2.2	4.0	5.5	8.5	9.8	15.6	2.1	2.5	2.8	3.2	3.4
Sweden	1.7	2.4	3.0	4.4	5.0	5.2	1.6	1.5	1.5	1.7	1.7
Belgium-Luxembourg	2.0	2.4	2.7	3.2	3.6	n.a.	1.9	1.5	1.4	1.2	1.2
Italy	2.1	3.0	3.2	3.3	2.9	n.a.	2.0	1.9	1.6	1.3	1.0
All other (estimate)	4.0	5.1	6.3	15.1	16.8	....	3.8	3.2	3.1	5.7	5.8
Total	105.3	158.4	198.8	258.9	287.2	....	100.0	100.0	100.0	100.0	100.0

Notes:
[1]Because of the lack of reliable and comparable data, figures given here, and on the tables that follow, dealing with international finance, should be treated as no more than rough approximations.
[2]Excluding investment flow for 1977.
[3]In 1978.

Sources:
United Nations Commission on Transnational Corporations, Transnational Corporations in World Development: A Re-examination, (U.N. Economic and Social Council, E/C. 10/38, March 1978).
The Bank of England, Quarterly Bulletin (June issues).
Organization for Economic Development, International Investment and Multinational Enterprises; Recent International Direct Investment Trends (1981).

APPENDIX TABLE VII
(See Table IV/5 p. 158)

Geographical Distribution of Direct Foreign Business Investments[1] of the United Kingdom, the German Federal Republic, and the United States
(Millions of U.S. Dollars)

United Kingdom

to \ from	1968[2]	1978[3]
Developed countries	....	....
Western Europe	2,757.2	12,147.2
E.E.C.	1,760.9	9,270.6
E.F.T.A.	427.6	2,142.8
Other western Europe	568.7	733.8
North America	3,603.3	10,235.7
Canada	1,923.3	2,562.0
U.S.A.	1,680.0	7,673.7
Other developed countries	4,823.3	9,070.2
Australia	2,700.3	5,349.9
Japan	30.8	227.9
New Zealand	391.2	....
South Africa	1,639.7	....
Others	55.7	....
Rest of world	4,455.1	7,745.3
Africa	1,344.8	2,703.8
Asia	1,818.6	3,031.8
Caribbean, Central and South America	1,263.6	2,035.7
Other countries	28.0	-26.1
World	15,638.8	39,198.2
Commonwealth	843.6	13,682.3
Developing countries	4,690.6	8,476.8
Oil exporting countries	476.0	1,611.6

Germany, F.R.

to \ from	1976[4+5]	1979[6]
Developed countries	13,996	90,572
E.E.C.	7,085	37,823
Other European countries	2,525	......
Non-European industrial countries	4,386	......
Canada	780	......
South Africa	421	......
United States	2,815	21,301
Developing countries	4,589	23,760
in Europe	1,191	......
including Spain	843	......
in Africa	379	......
in America	2,684	......
including Brazil	1,918	......
in Asia and Oceania	335	......
OPEC countries	786	3,113
Not classifiable	1,169	......
World	20,540	114,332

United States

to \ from	1968	1978
Developed countries	......	120,471
Canada	19,488	37,071
Europe	19,386	69.553
European communities	8,992	55,228
Other European countries	10,394	14,325
Japan	1,048	4,972
Australia	2,645	6,441
New Zealand	175	467
South Africa	692	1,968
Developing countries	......	40,399
Latin America	11,010	32,662
Other western Hemisphere	1,979	11,196
Africa	1,981	3,175
Middle East	1,803	-2,194
Asia and Pacific	3,645	6,757
International and unallocated	2,705	6,934
World	64,756	167,804

Notes:
[1]See Note 1, Table VI
[2]One pound = \$2.8
[3]One pound = \$2.04
[4]Including secondary direct investment
[5]2.362 DM = U.S. \$1
[6]1.7342 DM = U.S. \$1

Sources:
Business Monitor (U.K.) May 1981.
Bank of England Quarterly Bulletin, June issues
Statistische Beihefte zu der Deutschen Bundesbank, April 1979.
United States Survey of Current Business (various).

APPENDIX TABLE VIII
(See Table IV/7 p. 162)

Development Assistance from Selected Market Economies to Developing Areas
(in millions of U.S. dollars)

Contributing Country	Cumulative Total 1961-1969			Cumulative Total 1970-1978		
	Total	Official	Private	Total	Official	Private
Australia	1,355	1,178	177	4,561	3,441	1,120
Austria	256	152	104	1,434	612	822
Belgium	1,481	905	576	7,863	2,740	5,123
Canada	1,826	1,386	440	13,285	7,577	5,708
Denmark	323	183	140	2,376	1,862	514
Finland	.....	.....	.....	548	349	199
France	11,594	7,758	3,836	31,052	17,094	13,958
Germany, F.R.	7,421	4,064	3,357	26,260	11,585	14,675
Italy	2,563	746	1,817	11,129	3,387	7,742
Japan	4,100	2,651	1,449	35,750	19,428	16,322
Netherlands	1,748	860	888	10,268	4,797	5,471
New Zealand	.....	.....	.....	440	410	30
Norway	195	102	93	2,267	1,425	842
Portugal	452	365	87	681	681	.....
Sweden	746	434	312	6,017	3,893	2,124
Switzerland	960	137	823	10,066	742	9,324
United Kingdom	6,781	3,747	3,034	28,639	7,172	21,467
U.S.A.	41,989	29,851	12,138	84,610	36,201	48,409
Total	83,964	54,641	29,323	281,082	127,621	153,461

Source:
United Nations, Statistical Yearbook (various).

APPENDIX TABLE IX
(See Table IV/8 p. 163)

Development Assistance from Centrally Planned Economies to Developing Areas
(in millions of U.S. dollars)

Contributing Country	Cumulative Total 1962-1969	Cumulative Total 1970-1978
Bulgaria	93	377
China	569	3,670
Czechoslovakia	699	2,142
Germany, D.R.	465	735
Hungary	224	750
Poland	265	858
Romania	261	2,566
U.S.S.R.	3,247	13,420
Total	5,923	24,518
Receiving Areas		
Latin America	297	3,498
Africa	2,221	8,303
Asia	3,405	12,712

Source:
United Nations, Statistical Yearbook (various).

APPENDIX TABLE X
(See Table V/1 p. 200)

Some Important Developments in Agriculture, 1960's-1970's

Approximate date	Development	Usually ascribed to	Area of development	Major effects
1960's-70's	'Green Revolution': propagation of new semi-dwarf, high-yield varieties of wheat and rice for tropical and semi-tropical areas	Norman Borlaug	Widespread, especially in Asia and America	Increased the supply of wheat and rice. Alleviated the threat of famine and encouraged large-scale production.
1960's	Improved crossbred cattle breeds such as Brangus, Santa Gertrudis and Beefmaster	Numerous sources	Widespread	Increased the supply of beef.
1960's	Growing awareness of the dangers of pesticides, especially D.D.T.	North American and Western European environmentalists	Western World	Intensified laboratory research for less harmful pesticides.
1970's	Malathion replaces D.D.T.	Numerous sources	Western World	Reduced toxicity.
1970's	Pest control by genetic selection and integrated pest management	Numerous sources	Western World	Reduced chemical hazards.
1970's	Increase in aquiculture, hydroponics, and fish farming	Numerous sources	Western World	Increased the supply of protein in countries with poor soil.
1970's	Increased use of electrically controlled machines in the cattle, dairy, and poultry industries	Numerous sources	Chiefly in the Western World	Hastened the advent of large-scale agribusiness.
1970's	Increased use of aircraft for fertilizing, seeding, transport, and aerial spraying	Numerous sources	Chiefly in the Western World	Also favors large-scale operations.

APPENDIX TABLE XI

(See Table V/2 p. 204)

Some Important Developments in Mining and Mineralogy, 1960's-1970's

Approximate date	Development	Area of development	Major effects
1960's-1980's	Improved explosives, transport and communication and equipment (e.g., power shovels and rotary drills)	Western World	Higher yield of rock, safer and more economical operation.
1960's	Offshore and additional undersea mining	Western World	Tapping of vast new oil reserves.
1969	First lunar rocks recovered	United States and U.S.S.R.	Further stimulus to scientific research in mineralogy and space exploration.
1970's	Discovery of hitherto unclassified minerals, mainly linked with uranium.	Western World	Made possible technological advances in industries such as supersonic airplanes and television.
1970's	High-pressure jet piercing drills	Europe and North America	Increased efficiency and reduced dust nuisance.
1970's	Use of flame-proof laser beams for mine shaft alignment	Western World	Greater accuracy and faster penetration to greater depths.
1970's	Advance in robotic control of mining operations	Western World	Displaced labor and proved more economical.

APPENDIX TABLE XII

(See Table V/3 p. 207)

Some Important Developments in Textiles, 1960-1980

Approximate date	Technique	Area of development	Major effects
1960-80	Major developments since 1960 have been linked with improvements in chemical synthetics	Europe and United States	The production of wrinkle-free and dirt-resistant fabrics
Late 1970's	The re-introduction of small amounts of cotton and wool into textile fabrics	Europe and United States	The saving of energy-cost materials

APPENDIX TABLE XIII
(See Table V/4 p. 210)

Some Important Developments in Metallurgy Since 1960

Approximate date	Technique	Area of Origin	Major effects
Since 1960	Accompanying the developments in atomic research was the increased use of little-known radioactive metals such as uranium, plutonium, and thorium, as well as the development of other chemical elements such as boron, zirconium, hafnium, cadmium and beryllium used in processing fissionable matter	Western World	Increased the supply of non-ferrous alloys for aircraft and space machines.
" "	Development of heat shields using lead, silver, and gold	Western World including U.S.S.R.	Facilitated space exploration.
" "	Increased use of laser beams in cutting and welding of metals	Western World including U.S.S.R.	Increased efficiency.
" "	Use of laser beams in holography	Western World including U.S.S.R.	Improved the detection of metal fatigue and supplemented radiography.

APPENDIX TABLE XIV
(See Table V/6 p. 219)

Electrical Energy 1970

Continents and Countries	Installed Capacity[1] Total	Hydro	Thermal	Nuclear	Production[2] Total	Hydro	Thermal	Nuclear
World	1,125,948	290,679	817,074	16,614	4,955,977	1,174,940	3,697,593	78,533
Europe								
Austria	7,976	5,467	2,509	......	30,036	21,240	8,796	......
Belgium	6,257	62	6,184	11	30,523	246	30,220	57
Luxembourg	1,157	932	225	......	2,148	887	1,261	......
Czechoslovakia	10,141	1,447	8,694	......	45,163	3,670	41,493	......
France	36,219	14,996	19,577	1,646	146,966	57,399	83,856	5,711
Germany, D.R.	12,067	653	11,339	75	67,650	1,251	65,935	464
Germany, F.R.	47,540	4,700	41,950	890	242,605	17,758	218,817	6,030
Italy	30,408	13,335	16,153	552	117,423	41,300	70,222	3,176
Netherlands	10,114	......	10,065	49	40,859	......	40,491	368
Norway	12,910	12,783	127	......	57,606	57,260	346	......
Poland	13,710	740	12,970	......	64,533	1,887	62,646	......
Spain	17,912	10,883	6,876	153	56,490	27,959	27,607	924
Sweden	15,307	10,862	4,435	10	60,645	41,538	19,051	56
Switzerland	10,540	9,620	570	350	33,173	29,330	1,393	2,450
United Kingdom	62,060	2,153	56,480	3,427	249,016	5,666	217,338	26,012
U.S.S.R.	166,150	31,368	133,830	952	740,926	124,377	612,853	3,696
North America								
Canada	42,826	28,298	14,288	240	204,723	156,709	47,045	969
U.S.A.	360,327	55,752	297,998	6,493	1,639,771	250,699	1,366,750	21,797
Latin America								
Argentina	6,691	609	6,082	......	21,727	1,555	20,172	......
Brazil	11,233	8,828	2,405	......	45,460	39,863	5,597	......
Chile	2,143	1,067	1,076	......	7,550	4,307	3,243	......
Colombia	2,427	1,535	892	......	8,750	6,212	2,538	......
Mexico	7,453	3,320	4,129	......	28,707	15,005	13,701	......
Venezuela	3,172	908	2,264	......	12,708	4,104	8,604	......
Oceania								
Australia	15,584	3,806	11,778	......	53,892	9,175	44,717	......
New Zealand	3,793	2,971	630	......	13,706	11,266	1,255	......
Asia								
China	24,180	8,180	16,000	......	107,000	27,000	80,000	......
India	16,271	6,386	9,465	420	61,212	25,263	33,532	2,417
Indonesia	907	312	595	......	2,300	1,245	1,055	......
Japan	68,262	19,994	46,901	1,336	359,539	80,090	274,625	4,581
Philippines	2,176	549	1,627	......	8,666	2,097	6,569	......
Malaysia	936	293	643	......	3,543	1,202	2,341	......
Singapore	644	......	644	......	2,205	......	2,205	......
Turkey	2,312	724	1,588	......	8,624	3,044	5,580	......
Africa								
Algeria	750	286	464	......	1,979	580	1,399	......
Morocco	582	378	204	......	1,935	1,346	589	......
Egypt	4,357	2,448	1,909	......	7,591	4,705	2,886	......
Nigeria	805	320	485	......	1,550	1,365	185	......
Ghana	665	588	77	......	2,920	2,882	38	......
Zaire	867	809	58	......	3,230	3,152	78	......
Kenya	174	75	99	......	583	336	247	......
Tanzania	143	49	94	......	479	305	174	......
Zimbabwe	1,192	705	487	......	6,410	5,247	1,163	......
South Africa	10,511	14	10,497	......	50,791	25	50,766	......

Notes:
[1]In thousands kW
[2]In millions kWh

Source:
United Nations, 1979 Yearbook of World Energy Statistics (New York, 1981).

APPENDIX TABLE XV

(See Table V/6 p. 219)

Electrical Energy 1979

Continents and Countries	Installed Capacity[1]				Production[2]			
	Total	Hydro	Thermal	Nuclear	Total	Hydro	Thermal	Nuclear
World	1,914,377	440,475	1,349,766	122,590	7,966,344	1,721,239	5,632,190	602,931
Europe								
Austria	13,190	8,200	4,990	....	40,645	27,070	13,575	....
Belgium	10,266	500	8,100	1,666	52,252	580	38,559	13,113
Luxembourg	1,360	1,129	231	....	1,337	325	1,012	....
Czechoslovakia	15,340	2,200	12,700	440	67,900	4,145	61,555	2,200
France	56,671	18,700	30,771	7,200	241,124	68,950	134,266	37,908
Germany, D.R.	18,378	768	16,220	1,390	99,000	1,300	89,700	8,000
Germany, F.R.	81,241	6,510	66,416	8,315	373,618	18,745	313,078	41,795
Italy	44,000	15,700	27,350	552	180,522	48,088	127,194	2,700
Netherlands	17,500	......	16,977	523	62,850	......	58,760	4,090
Norway	18,375	18,213	162	....	88,988	88,803	185	....
Poland	23,900	800	23,100	....	117,460	2,460	115,000	....
Spain	28,728	13,730	13,878	1,120	105,411	42,275	54,100	9,036
Sweden	27,000	14,650	8,450	3,900	94,287	59,779	13,508	21,000
Switzerland	12,850	11,170	650	1,030	42,710	31,955	1,855	8,900
United Kingdom	74,307	2,451	65,258	6,598	299,960	5,464	258,582	35,914
U.S.S.R.	255,000	50,000	195,000	10,000	1,240,000	180,000	1,015,000	45,000
North America								
Canada	78,200	43,570	28,100	6,530	352,304	243,041	75,988	33,275
U.S.A.	616,245	75,626	485,466	54,594	2,323,806	281,432	1,783,028	255,396
Latin America								
Argentina	12,200	3,900	7,930	370	38,000	9,880	24,700	3,420
Brazil	29,020	23,842	4,552	626	122,846	106,904	15,703	239
Chile	2,950	1,480	1,470	....	10,901	7,221	3,680	....
Colombia	4,700	3,130	1,570	....	19,875	13,305	6,570	....
Mexico	16,800	5,725	11,000	....	59,400	23,170	35,530	....
Venezuela	8,500	3,000	5,500	....	27,500	12,500	15,000	....
Oceania								
Australia	23,000	5,700	17,300	....	92,000	15,200	76,800	....
New Zealand	5,800	3,850	1,790	....	22,000	16,500	4,300	....
Asia								
China	52,000	16,000	36,000	....	281,950	73,000	208,950	....
India	28,140	9,908	17,592	640	113,060	42,445	66,370	4,245
Indonesia	2,200	976	1,224	....	7,330	2,807	4,523	....
Japan	140,665	29,258	97,480	13,800	581,441	84,361	435,504	60,506
Philippines	3,795	850	2,795	850	16,713	2,780	13,833	100
Malaysia	1,600	350	1,250	....	8,720	1,220	7,500	....
Singapore	1,650	......	1,650	....	6,448	......	6,448	....
Turkey	5,042	1,882	3,160	....	22,500	9,400	13,100	....
Africa								
Algeria	1,225	330	895	....	5,040	250	4,790	....
Morocco	1,045	430	615	....	4,372	1,582	2,790	....
Egypt	3,928	2,448	1,480	....	14,800	9,510	5,290	....
Nigeria	1,900	600	1,300	....	5,200	3,000	2,200	....
Ghana	900	108	792	....	4,500	4,440	60	....
Zaire	1,694	1,636	58	....	3,775	3,590	185	....
Kenya	500	325	175	....	1,500	1,200	300	....
Tanzania	258	188	70	....	700	525	175	....
Zimbabwe	1,192	705	487	....	4,700	4,000	700	....
South Africa	18,942	505	18,437	....	88,000	2,000	86,000	....

Notes:
[1] In thousands kW
[2] In millions kWh

Source:
United Nations, <u>1979 Yearbook of World Energy Statistics</u> (New York, 1981).

APPENDIX TABLE XVI

Crude Petroleum, Production and Imports
(thousand metric tons)

Continents and Countries	Production 1960	Production 1970	Production 1979	Imports 1960	Imports 1970	Imports 1979
World	1,052,074	2,275,053	3,123,256	382,953	1,166,945	1,702,191
Europe						
Austria	2,448	2,798	1,728	532	3,576	8,612
Belgium	....	....	....	6,781	29,886	33,990
Czechoslovakia	137	203	109	2,255	9,798	19,000
France	1,977	2,309	1,205	31,022	101,344	124,000
Germany, D.R.	....	90	100	1,941	10,334	20,000
Germany, F.R.	5,530	7,535	4,774	23,279	100,347	109,280
Italy	1,998	1,405	1,720	29,466	114,072	114,861
Netherlands	1,918	1,919	1,316	18,873	60,130	60,446
Norway	....	....	18,288	220	6,528	6,320
Poland	194	424	400	714	7,011	16,220
Spain	64	151	895	6,521	30,895	48,300
Sweden	102	....	....	2,646	11,762	16,221
Switzerland	....	....	....	....	5,538	4,633
United Kingdom	148	83	77,628	45,188	102,155	60,384
U.S.S.R.	147,859	353,039	590,917	1,166	3,500	7,000
North America						
Canada	25,509	61,868	73,274	17,749	29,396	30,673
U.S.A.	347,975	475,289	419,907	51,874	66,239	319,659
Latin America						
Argentina	9,138	20,026	24,308	3,315	1,403	1,728
Brazil	3,870	7,837	8,042	5,684	17,366	50,041
Chile	943	1,468	810	513	2,035	3,750
Colombia	7,584	11,327	6,500	......	......	1,350
Mexico	13,889	21,508	74,870	......	......	......
Venezuela	149,372	194,306	123,483	......	......	......
Oceania						
Australia	1	8,494	21,606	11,265	16,208	8,500
New Zealand	1	58	490	......	2,755	2,500
Asia						
China	5,500	23,930	106,150	590	401	....
India	454	6,809	12,785	5,723	11,665	14,700
Indonesia	20,245	42,598	78,256	1,800	......	1,270
Japan	526	770	482	27,056	170,376	239,672
Philippines	....	......	1,300	1,415	9,097	9,400
Malaysia	....	859	12,790	......	9,168	2,500
Singapore	....	....	......	284	10,956	34,221
Turkey	375	3,542	2,620	......	3,845	11,600
Africa						
Algeria	8,632	47,202	54,500	......	......	350
Morocco	92	46	26	90	1,515	3,400
Egypt	3,319	16,404	24,900	2,077	1,617	....
Nigeria	849	54,203	114,500	......	......	....
Ghana	......	......	20	......	846	1,200
Zaire	......	......	1,032	......	675	180
Kenya	......	......	......	......	2,206	2,350
Tanzania	......	......	......	......	732	500
Zimbabwe	......	......	......	......	......	....
South Africa	25	n.a.	n.a.	......	......	....
Libya	n.a.	159,814	99,300	......	......	....
Middle East	261,274	695,081	1,067,068	15,057	24,469	38,580

Sources:
United Nations, World Energy Supplies 1950-1974 (New York 1976).
United Nations, 1979 Yearbook of World Energy Statistics (New York 1980).

APPENDIX TABLE XVII

(See Table V/7 p. 220)

Some Important Developments in Industrial Chemicals Since 1960

Approximate date	Technique	Area of Origin	Major effects
Since 1960	General advance and diffusion of polymer chemistry	Europe, North America	Savings in rare, basic raw materials.
" "	Development of glass, and (later), carbon fibers	United Kingdom, North America	Provided alkali-resistant, anti-corrosive linings for tunnels, pipes, silos etc., and strong, economical material for reinforcing plastics.
" "	Inorganic advances including the manufacture of synthetic cryolite, a rare mineral essential to the production of aluminum	United States; founded on the original fluorine research of Thomas Midgeley in the 1920's	Made aluminum cheaper and more widely available.

(See Table VI/1 p. 253)

World's Railway Mileage, 1979
(in thousand miles and in percentage of world total)

Continent and Country	Mileage	(%)
World	802.43	100.0
Europe	251.54	31.4
Great Britain[1]	11.80	1.5
France	22.83	2.8
Germany[2]	27.50	3.4
Belgium	2.80	0.3
U.S.S.R.	84.50	10.5
North America	252.49	31.5
United States	225.00	28.0
Canada	27.19	3.4
Latin America[3]	82.13	10.3
Mexico	15.29	1.9
Chile	5.18	0.6
Peru	1.60	0.2
Brazil	19.70	2.5
Argentina	28.96	3.6

Continent and Country	Mileage	(%)
Asia	126.16	15.7
India	37.59	4.7
Indonesia	4.15	0.5
Japan	24.96	3.1
Burma	2.59	0.3
China	25.00	3.1
Africa	61.46	7.7
Egypt	2.64	0.3
South Africa	21.39	2.7
Algeria	2.47	0.3
East Africa[4]	6.74	0.8
Rhodesia[5]	2.18	0.3
Australasia	28.14	3.5
Australia	25.06	3.1
New Zealand	3.08	0.4

Notes:
[1]Excluding Ireland.
[2]Federal Republic and German Democratic Republic
[3]Excluding Cuba.
[4]Tanzania, Uganda, Kenya.
[5]Excluding Zambia.

Sources:
World Transport Data, I.R.T.U., Geneva, 1976.
United Nations, Annual Bulletin of Transport Statistics for Europe, 1971-76.

APPENDIX TABLE XIX
(See Table VI/3 p. 255)

Distribution of World Shipping
(1971, 1979)

Gross registered tons and percentages

	'000 tons at mid-1971	%	'000 tons at mid-1979	%
United Kingdom	27,334.7	11.2	27,951.3	6.8
France	7,001.5	2.9	11,945.8	2.9
Germany[1]	9,694.8	4.0	10,114.9	2.4
Netherlands	5,269.1	2.0	5,403.3	1.3
Norway	21,720.2	8.9	22,349.3	5.4
Sweden	4,978.3	2.0	4,636.7	1.1
Italy	8,138.5	3.3	11,694.9	2.8
U.S.S.R.	16,194.3	6.6	22,900.2	5.5
Rest of Europe	31,235.1	12.8[2]	70,133.4	17.0[4]
Europe	131,576.5	53.9	187,169.8	45.3
United States	14,549.3	6.0	17,542.2	4.3
Japan	30,509.3	12.5	39,992.9	9.7
Rest of World	67,316.6	26.4[3]	168,356.2	40.8[5]
World	243,921.2	100%	413,021.1	100%

Notes:
[1]Federal Republic and German Democratic Republic.
[2]Includes Greece 5.4%, Spain 1.6%, Denmark 1.5%.
[3]Includes Liberia 15.8% and Panama 2.6% (chiefly under Flags of Convenience).
[4]Includes Greece 9%, Spain 2%, Denmark 1.3%, Poland 1%.
[5]Includes Liberia 19.7%, and Panama 5.4% (chiefly under Flags of Convenience).

Sources:
Organization for Economic Co-operation and Development, Maritime Transport (various).

APPENDIX TABLE XX

(See Table VI/6b p. 260)

Shipping through the Suez and Panama Canals

Year	Suez Canal (in million metric tons)	Panama Canal (in thousand metric tons)
1969	canal closed	103.0
1970	"	116.5
1971	"	120.5
1972	"	110.0
1973	"	126.2
1974	"	135.7
1975	38.4	135.1
1976	117.6	127.8
1977	128.7	133.4
1978	149.8	157.0

Source:
Organization for Economic Co-operation & Development, _Maritime Transport_ (various).

APPENDIX TABLE XXI
(See Table VI/7 p. 261)

Some Important Developments in Sea Transport, 1960-1980

Approximate date	Technique	Area of Origin	Major effects
1960-1980	Hovercraft and hydrofoil vessels	Europe and United States	Rapid, smooth passage.
1960's	First container ships in trans-Atlantic trade	United States and Europe	Ease of handling, greater security, and saving in manpower.
1970's	Giant oil tankers	United States, Europe and Japan	Transport economies offset by greater financial commitments. Occasioned the deepening of the Suez Canal.
1980's	Super tankers being replaced by medium-sized multi-cargo ships	United States, Europe and Japan	Reduction in freight costs and in risks.

Sources:
Organization for Economic Co-operation and Development, Maritime Transport (various).
Baker, R., New and Improved: Inventors and Inventions That Have Changed the Modern World, British Library Publications Ltd. (London, 1976).

APPENDIX TABLE XXII
(See Table VII/1 p. 302)

United Kingdom
Principal Imports and Exports by Approximate Percentage of Total Value, 1970 and 1979

Imports 1970		Imports 1979	
Basic manufactures	22	Machinery and transport equipment	26
Food and live animals	20	Basic manufactures	22
Machinery and transport equipment	16	Mineral fuels and lubricants	12
Crude materials (except fuels)	14	Food and live animals	12
Mineral fuels and lubricants	10	Miscellaneous manufactures	10
Miscellaneous manufactures	6	Crude materials (except fuels)	8
Chemicals	6	Chemicals and related products	7
Beverages and tobacco	2	Beverages and tobacco	2
Other commodities and transactions	1	Animal fats and vegetable oils	1
Exports			
Machinery and transport equipment	40	Machinery and transport equipment	35
Basic manufactures	24	Basic manufactures	22
Chemicals	10	Chemicals and related products	12
Miscellaneous manufactures	9	Mineral fuels and lubricants	10
Beverages and tobacco	3	Miscellaneous manufactures	9
Food and live animals	3	Food and live animals	4
Mineral fuels and lubricants	3	Beverages and tobacco	3
Crude materials (except fuels)	3	Crude materials (except fuels)	3
Other commodities and transactions	3	Other commodities and transactions	3

Sources:
Europa Yearbook, (various).
United Kingdom, _Statistical Survey_, (various).

APPENDIX TABLE XXIII
(See Table VII/4 p. 303)

France
Principal Imports and Exports by Approximate Percentages of Total Value, 1970 and 1979

Imports

1970		1979	
Machinery and transport equipment	25	Machinery and transport equipment	22
Manufactured and piece goods (including metal)	22	Mineral fuels and lubricants	22
Mineral fuels and lubricants	12	Basic manufactures (paper, textiles, metal)	19
Food (meat, cereals, fruit and vegetables)	11	Food and live animals	10
Crude materials (including textiles)	11	Miscellaneous manufactured articles	10
Chemicals	8	Chemicals	9
Manufactured goods (including clothing)	8	Crude materials (except fuels)	7
Beverages and tobacco	2	Beverages and tobacco	1
Miscellaneous manufactured articles	1	Animal fats and vegetable oils	1
Animal fats and vegetable oils	1		

Exports

1970		1979	
Machinery and transport equipment	33	Machinery and transport equipment	35
Manufactures (including metal and textiles)	24	Basic manufactures (paper, textiles, metal)	21
Food (meat, cereals, fruit and vegetables)	12	Chemicals	12
Chemicals	9	Food and live animals	11
Manufactured goods (including clothing)	9	Miscellaneous manufactured articles (including clothing)	9
Crude materials	5	Crude materials (except fuels)	4
Beverages and tobacco	3	Mineral fuels and lubricants	4
Mineral fuels and lubricants	2	Beverages and tobacco	3
Other unspecified items	1		
Miscellaneous manufactures	1		

Source:
Europa Yearbook, (various).

APPENDIX TABLE XXIV
(See Table VII/7 p. 305)

Federal Republic of Germany
Principal Imports and Exports by Approximate Percentage of Total Value, 1970 and 1979

Imports

1970		1979	
Basic manufactures (including metal, paper, textiles)	24	Mineral fuels	19
Machinery and transport equipment	19	Machinery and transport equipment	19
Food and live animals	15	Basic manufactures	18
Crude materials (except fuels)	13	Miscellaneous manufactures	12
Miscellaneous manufactures (including clothing, instruments)	9	Food and live animals	11
Mineral fuels and lubricants	9	Crude non-edible materials (excluding fuels)	8
Chemicals	6	Chemicals and related products	8
Non-classified commodities and transactions	3	Other commodities and transactions	3
Beverages and tobacco	1	Beverages and tobacco	1
Animal fats and vegetable oils	1	Animal fats, oils and waxes	1

Exports

1970		1979	
Machinery and transport equipment	47	Machinery and transport equipment	44
Basic manufactures	22	Basic manufactures	20
Chemicals	12	Chemicals	13
Miscellaneous manufactures	9	Miscellaneous manufactures	9
Mineral fuels and lubricants	3	Food and live animals	4
Food and live animals	3	Mineral fuels, lubricants etc.	3
Crude materials (except fuels)	2	Crude materials (except fuels)	2
Non-classified commodities and transactions	2	Other commodities and transactions	2
		Beverages and tobacco	1
		Animal fats, oils and waxes	1

Source:
Europa Yearbook, (various).

APPENDIX TABLE XXV

(See Table VII/10 p. 310)

Netherlands

Principal Imports and Exports by Approximate Percentage of Total Value, 1970 and 1979

Imports

1970		1979	
Machinery and transport equipment	25	Machinery and transport equipment	22
Basic manufactures (including textiles and metal)	22	Mineral fuels and lubricants	20
Food and live animals	11	Basic manufactures	16
Mineral fuels and lubricants	11	Miscellaneous manufactures	11
Miscellaneous manufactures (including clothing)	11	Food and live animals	11
Crude materials	9	Chemicals	9
Chemicals	8	Crude materials (except fuels)	7
Beverages and tobacco	1	Other commodities and transactions	2
Animal fats and vegetable oils	1	Beverages and tobacco	1
		Animal fats, oils and waxes	1

Exports

1970		1979	
Food and live animals	22	Mineral fuels and lubricants	19
Machinery and transport equipment	20	Food and live animals	18
Basic manufactures	18	Machinery and transport equipment	17
Chemicals	13	Chemicals	16
Mineral fuels and lubricants	11	Basic manufactures	14
Miscellaneous manufactures	7	Miscellaneous manufactures	6
Crude materials	7	Crude materials (except fuels)	5
Beverages and tobacco	1	Beverages and tobacco	2
Animal fats and vegetable oils	1	Animal fats, oils and waxes	1
Miscellaneous other commodities	1	Other commodities and transactions	1

Source:
Europa Yearbook, (various).

APPENDIX TABLE XXVI
(See Table VII/10 p. 310)

Belgium
Principal Imports and Exports by Approximate Percentage of Total Value, 1970 and 1979

Imports

1970		1979	
Machinery and transport equipment	26	Machinery and transport equipment	24
Non-precious metals	15	Basic manufactures	23
Basic manufactures	13	Mineral fuels and lubricants	14
Ores and minerals	13	Food and live animals	10
Textiles, clothing and accesories	9	Miscellaneous manufactured articles	9
Food and live animals	8	Chemicals	9
Crude materials	8	Crude materials (except fuels)	7
Chemicals	6	Other commodities and transactions	2
Beverages, tobacco and manufactured goods	4	Beverages and tobacco	1
Precious stones and metals	3		

Exports

1970		1979	
Non-precious metals	28	Basic manufactures	34
Clothing and textiles	11	Machinery and transport equipment	23
Vehicles	11	Chemicals	12
Machinery and electrical equipment	10	Food and live animals	8
Chemicals	8	Miscellaneous manufactures	7
Food and live animals	6	Mineral fuels and lubricants	6
Precious stones and metals	4	Other commodities and transactions	6
Ores and minerals	4	Crude materials (except fuels)	3
Beverages, tobacco and manufactured goods	3	Beverages and tobacco	1
Miscellaneous products, instruments and timepieces	3		

Source:
<u>Europa Yearbook</u>, (various).

APPENDIX TABLE XXVII

(See Table VII/10 p. 310)

Switzerland
Principal Imports and Exports by Approximate Percentage of Total Value, 1970 and 1979

Imports

1970		1979	
Unspecified commodities	60	Machinery and transport equipment	24
Machinery	17	Textiles, paper and leather	16
Iron and steel	7	Precision instruments and jewelery	12
Motor vehicles	6	Chemicals	11
Chemicals	5	Petroleum and lubricants	11
Coal, coke and oil	2	Metals	9
Tropical and semi-tropical fruit	1	Agricultural products	8
Raw wool and cotton	1	Miscellaneous manufactures	3

Exports

1970		1979	
Machinery and parts	30	Machinery (including precision instruments and watches)	51
Unspecified commodities	26	Chemicals	20
Chemical dyes and chemical products	16	Miscellaneous manufactures (including paper, jewelery and art)	14
Watches and parts	12	Textiles (including shoes and clothing)	7
Instruments and appliances	5	Food and tobacco	3
Pharmaceuticals	4		
Silk goods	3		
Cotton and embroidered goods	2		
Cheese	1		
Chocolate	1		

Sources:
Europa Yearbook, 1972.
Statistisches Jahrbuch der Schweiz, 1980.

APPENDIX TABLE XXVIII
(See Table VII/10 p. 310)

Sweden
Principal Imports and Exports by Approximate Percentage of Total Value, 1970 and 1979

Imports

1970		1979	
Machinery and transport equipment	30	Machinery and transport equipment	28
Basic manufactures (including textiles and metal)	24	Mineral fuels and lubricants	22
Miscellaneous manufactures	12	Basic manufactures	17
Mineral fuels and lubricants	11	Miscellaneous consumer goods	14
Food and live animals	9	Chemicals	9
Chemicals, dyes, and explosives	8	Food and live animals	6
Raw materials (except fuels)	5	Crude materials (except fuels)	4
Beverages and tobacco	1		

Exports

1970		1979	
Machinery and transport equipment	40	Machinery and transport equipment	43[1]
Basic manufactures (paper, textiles, and metal)	28	Basic manufactures	28[1]
Raw materials (except fuels)	20	Crude materials (except fuels)	13[1]
Miscellaneous manufactures	5	Miscellaneous manufactures	7[1]
Chemicals, dyes and explosives	4	Chemicals and related products	5[1]
Food and live animals	2	Food and live animals	2[1]
Mineral fuels and lubricants	1		

Note:
[1]These percentages based on 1978 figures.

Source:
Europa Yearbook, (various).

APPENDIX TABLE XXIX
(See Table VII/11 p. 312)

Direction of the Foreign Trade
of the Netherlands, Belgium, Switzerland, and Sweden,
by Value, 1970 and 1979

Importing Countries	Year	Principal Sources of Imports					
Netherlands	1970	Germany	Belgium	U.S.A.	France	Britain	Italy
	1979	Germany	Belgium	U.S.A.	Britain	France	Italy
Belgium	1970	Germany	France	Netherlands	U.S.A.	Britain	Congo
	1979	Germany	Netherlands	France	Britain	U.S.A.	Italy
Switzerland	1970	Germany	France	Italy	U.S.A.	Britain	Austria
	1979	Germany	France	Italy	Britain	U.S.A.	Netherlands
Sweden	1970	Germany	Britain	Denmark	Norway	Netherlands	France
	1979	Germany	Britain	U.S.A.	Denmark	Finland	Norway

Exporting Countries	Year	Chief Markets					
Netherlands	1970	Germany	Belgium	France	Britain	Italy	U.S.A.
	1979	Germany	Belgium	France	Britain	Italy	U.S.A.
Belgium	1970	Germany	France	Netherlands	U.S.A.	Italy	Britain
	1979	Germany	France	Netherlands	Britain	Italy	U.S.A.
Switzerland	1970	Germany	Italy	U.S.A.	France	Britain	Austria
	1979	Germany	France	Italy	Britain	U.S.A.	Austria
Sweden	1970	Britain	Germany	Denmark	Norway	U.S.A.	Finland
	1979	Britain	Germany	Norway	Denmark	Finland	U.S.A.

Sources:
Europa Yearbook, 1972, 1981.
United Nations, _1979 Yearbook of International Trade Statistics_, (1980).

APPENDIX TABLE XXX

(See Table VII/12 p. 313)

Growth of World Trade
and Percentage of it held by Europe, Leading European Commercial Countries,
and the United States and Japan
(in millions of U.S. $ and in percentage)[1]

Year	Value of world trade ($ millions)	Europe (%)	United Kingdom (%)	Federal Republic Germany (%)	France (%)	Nether-lands (%)	Italy (%)	Belgium (%)	U.S.A. (%)	Japan (%)
1970	642,583	54	6	10	6	4	4	4	13	6
1979	3,306,255	52	6	10	6	4	4[2]	4	12	7

Note:
[1] See note page 313.
[2] In 1978.

Source:
United Nations, _1979 Yearbook of International Trade Statistics (1980)_.

APPENDIX TABLE XXXI

Exports and Imports of Selected European Countries, 1970 and 1979[1]
(Millions of U.S. Dollars)

	1970		1979	
	Imports	Exports	Imports	Exports
Belgium	11,444.7	11,693.5	62,663.4	58,365.6
France	19,167.9	17,985.6	112,446.2	102,004.0
Germany, F.R.	30,169.6	34,482.8	168,400.5	181.334.0
Italy	14,985.5	13,248.6	57,651.2	57,231.3
Netherlands	13,348.6	11,727.7	70,343.8	66,588.4
Sweden	7,011.8	6,798.8	29,417.2	28,267.5
Switzerland	6,687.5	5,128.6	30,479.3	27,542.2
United Kingdom	21,991.2	19,608.0	106,100.8	93,669.9
U.S.S.R.	11,660.2	12,650.0	51,969.2	53,604.1

Conversion Rates	1970	1979
B/franc	49.64	28.238
F/franc	5.54	4.0653
mark	3.63	1.7342
lira	623.0	829.75
guilder	3.63	1.9167
krona	5.17	4.1796
S/franc	4.32	1.5988
pound	.418	.4531
rouble	.90	.665

Notes:
[1]1978 for Italy and U.S.S.R.

Sources:
Europa Yearbook, (various).
Statistical Yearbook of the United Nations, (various).

APPENDIX TABLE XXXII
(See Tables VII/13, 15, 17, 19 and 21)

Sources of Imports for Selected Countries 1970 and 1979[1]
(approximate percentage, based on value, of total imports per country)

to / from	Belgium '70 (%)	Belgium '79 (%)	France '70 (%)	France '79 (%)	Germany F.R. '70 (%)	Germany F.R. '79 (%)	Netherlands '70 (%)	Netherlands '79 (%)	Sweden '70 (%)	Sweden '79 (%)	Switzerland '70 (%)	Switzerland '79 (%)	United Kingdom '70 (%)	United Kingdom '79 (%)	U.S.S.R. '70 (%)	U.S.S.R. '78 (%)
Afghanistan	..	..	..	..	..	..	..	..	..	..	..	..	..	..	t	t
Algeria	..	..	3	1	..	1	..	..	..	..	..	1	..	..	..	..
Argentina	1	..	t	..	1	..	1	..	t	..	t	..	..	..	t	1
Austria	..	..	t	..	2	3	..	..	..	2	4	4	..	1	1	1
Australia	t	..	1	..	1	..	..	..	..	..	..	..	3	1	..	..
Belgium, Luxembourg	..	..	11	9	10	8	17	12	3	3	3	4	2	5	1	1
Brazil	1	..	1	1	1	1	..	1	1	..	..	..	..	1	..	t
Bulgaria	..	..	..	..	..	..	..	..	..	..	..	..	..	..	9	9
Canada	1	1	1	1	2	1	..	..	..	..	1	..	7	3	..	1
China	..	..	t	..	..	..	..	..	..	..	..	..	..	..	t	1
Cuba	..	..	..	..	..	..	..	..	..	..	..	..	..	..	4	6
Czechoslovakia	..	..	..	..	..	..	..	..	..	..	1	1	..	..	11	9
Denmark	t	..	t	1	1	2	..	1	8	7	1	1	3	2	t	t
Egypt	..	..	t	..	..	..	..	..	..	..	t	..	..	..	3	1
Finland	t	..	t	..	1	1	1	..	5	6	..	1	2	2	3	3
France	17	14	..	..	13	11	8	7	4	4	12	13	4	8	3	3
Germany, F.R.	23	22	22	18	..	..	27	24	19	17	29	29	6	12	3	6
Germany, D.R.	t	..	..	..	2	2	..	..	..	..	..	..	..	..	15	11
Greece	..	..	..	..	..	1	..	..	..	..	..	..	..	..	t	t
Hong Kong	..	..	..	..	..	..	..	..	..	..	..	..	1	1	..	..
Hungary	..	..	..	..	..	..	..	..	..	..	t	1	..	..	7	7
India	t	1	t	..	t	..	..	..	..	..	..	..	1	1	2	1
Indonesia	..	..	..	..	..	..	t	..	..	..	..	..	..	..	t	..
Iran	..	1	t	1	1	1	..	1	..	1	..	..	..	1	1	1
Ireland	..	1	..	..	..	..	..	..	..	..	..	t	4	4	..	..
Iraq	..	..	1	3	..	..	..	..	..	..	..	..	..	..	t	1
Italy	4	4	9	10	10	9	4	4	3	3	9	10	3	5	3	3
Ivory Coast	..	..	1	1	..	..	..	..	..	..	..	..	..	..	..	..
Japan	..	2	1	2	2	3	..	2	..	3	2	..	1	3	3	5
Korea, D.P.R.	..	..	..	..	..	..	..	..	..	..	..	..	..	..	1	1
Kuwait	..	..	1	1	..	..	2	2	..	..	..	..	2	2	..	..
Libya	..	..	..	..	2	2	2	..	..	..	..	1	..	..	..	..
Mongolia	..	..	..	..	..	..	..	..	..	..	..	..	..	..	1	t
Morocco	..	..	1	1	..	..	..	..	..	..	..	..	..	..	..	..
Netherlands	15	17	6	6	12	12	..	..	4	4	3	4	5	7	1	1
New Zealand	..	..	t	..	..	..	..	..	..	..	..	..	2	1	..	..
Nigeria	..	..	..	1	..	1	..	4	..	1	t	t	1	t	..	..
Norway	1	..	t	1	2	2	..	..	6	5	..	1	2	3	t	t
Poland	..	..	t	..	..	1	..	..	..	1	..	t	..	..	11	10
Portugal	..	..	t	..	..	..	..	..	..	1	..	t	..	1	..	..
Romania	..	..	..	..	..	..	..	..	..	..	..	..	..	..	5	3
Saudi Arabia	..	3	..	5	..	1	2	4	..	3	..	..	..	2	..	..
South Africa	..	1	1	1	1	1	..	..	..	..	..	t	3	1	..	..
Spain	..	1	1	3	1	1	..	1	..	..	1	1	1	1	..	..
Sweden	2	2	2	2	3	2	2	2	..	..	3	2	4	3	1	1
Switzerland	1	2	3	2	3	4	1	1	3	2	..	..	2	5	..	..
Tunisia	..	..	t	..	..	..	..	..	..	..	..	..	..	..	..	..
Turkey	..	..	..	..	..	..	..	..	..	..	..	..	..	..	t	t
United Arab Emirates	..	..	..	1	..	t	..	1	..	..	..	..	..	1	..	..
United Kingdom	6	8	5	6	3	6	6	8	14	12	8	8	..	..	2	2
U.S.A.	9	6	10	8	11	7	10	8	9	7	8	6	13	10	1	5
U.S.S.R.	1	1	1	2	1	3	..	1	2	4	..	3	2	2	..	..
Vietnam	..	..	..	..	..	..	..	..	..	..	..	..	..	..	t	t
Yugoslavia	..	..	..	..	..	t	..	..	..	..	..	1	..	..	2	3
Zaire	4	2	t	..	..	..	..	..	..	..	..	..	..	..	..	..
Zambia	..	..	..	..	..	..	..	..	..	..	..	..	1	..	..	..
Unspecified	12	11	12[2]	10	14	12	17	16	19	14	13	6	25	10	2	0

t = trace (less than .5%)

Notes:
[1]1978 for U.S.S.R.
[2]Including 4% from other African countries.

Sources:
Europa Yearbook (various).
Statistisches Jahrbuch der Schweiz (1980).
Britain 1981: An Official Handbook (London, 1981).

APPENDIX TABLE XXXIII
(See Tables VII/14, 16, 18, 20 and 22)

Destination of Exports of Selected Countries 1970, 1979[1]
(approximate percentage, based on value, of total exports per country)

from / to	Belgium '70 (%)	Belgium '79 (%)	France '70 (%)	France '79 (%)	Germany F.R. '70 (%)	Germany F.R. '79 (%)	Netherlands '70 (%)	Netherlands '79 (%)	Sweden '70 (%)	Sweden '79 (%)	Switzerland '70 (%)	Switzerland '79 (%)	United Kingdom '70 (%)	United Kingdom '79 (%)	U.S.S.R. '70 (%)	U.S.S.R. '78 (%)
Afghanistan	..	..	..	..	..	..	..	..	..	..	..	..	..	..	t	t
Algeria	..	1	3	2	..	t	..	..	..	..	..	1	..	..	..	..
Argentina	t	..	t	..	1	..	..	..	1	..	1	1	..	..	t	t
Austria	..	1	t	1	5	5	1	1	..	1	5	5	..	1	1	1
Australia	t	..	t	..	1	..	..	..	..	1	..	1	4	2	..	..
Belgium, Luxembourg	..	..	11	10	8	9	14	15	3	3	2	3	4	6	1	1
Brazil	t	..	t	..	1	1	..	..	1	1	1	1	..	1	..	t
Bulgaria	..	..	..	..	..	..	..	..	..	..	..	..	..	..	7	9
Canada	t	..	1	1	1	t	..	..	..	1	1	1	4	2	..	t
China	..	..	t	..	..	1	..	..	..	..	t	..	..	..	t	t
Cuba	..	..	..	..	..	..	..	..	..	..	..	..	..	..	5	6
Czechoslovakia	..	..	..	..	..	..	..	..	..	..	..	..	..	..	9	8
Denmark	1	1	1	1	2	2	1	2	10	9	2	1	3	2	t	1
Egypt	..	..	t	1	..	..	..	..	..	..	t	1	..	..	3	t
Finland	1	..	t	..	1	1	..	..	6	6	..	1	2	1	2	3
France	20	19	..	..	12	13	10	11	5	6	8	9	4	7	1	2
Germany, F.R.	25	23	21	17	..	..	33	30	12	11	15	20	6	11	2	4
Germany, D.R.	t	..	..	..	2	2	..	..	..	..	..	1	..	..	15	11
Greece	..	..	t	1	..	1	..	..	..	..	..	1	..	1	t	1
Hong Kong	..	1	..	..	..	..	..	..	..	..	..	..	1	1	..	..
Hungary	..	..	..	..	..	t	..	..	..	..	1	1	..	..	7	7
India	t	1	t	..	1	..	..	..	..	..	..	..	1	1	1	1
Indonesia	..	..	..	..	..	..	..	..	..	..	..	..	..	..	t	..
Iran	..	t	t	1	1	1	..	1	..	..	..	2	..	1	2	1
Ireland	..	..	..	..	..	..	..	..	..	..	..	..	4	6	..	..
Iraq	..	..	..	1	..	t	..	..	..	..	..	..	..	..	1	2
Israel	..	..	t	..	..	..	..	..	..	..	..	2	..	1	..	..
Italy	5	5	8	11	9	8	5	5	3	3	9	7	3	3	2	3
Ivory Coast	..	..	1	1	..	..	..	..	..	..	..	..	..	..	..	..
Japan	..	..	1	1	2	1	1	..	..	1	3	3	2	1	3	2
Korea, D.P.R.	..	..	..	..	..	..	..	..	..	..	..	..	..	..	2	1
Kuwait	..	..	..	..	..	..	..	..	..	..	..	..	t	1	..	..
Liberia	..	..	..	..	..	..	..	..	..	1	..	..	..	..	..	..
Libya	..	..	..	1	t	t	..	..	..	..	..	..	..	..	..	..
Mongolia	..	..	..	..	..	..	..	..	..	..	..	..	..	..	2	2
Morocco	..	..	1	1	..	..	..	..	..	..	..	..	..	..	..	..
Netherlands	19	16	5	5	11	10	..	..	4	5	3	3	5	7	1	1
New Zealand	..	..	..	..	..	..	..	..	..	..	..	..	2	1	..	..
Nigeria	..	1	..	1	..	t	..	1	..	..	..	1	1	2	..	..
Norway	1	1	1	1	2	1	1	1	11	10	..	1	2	2	t	t
Poland	..	..	t	1	..	1	..	..	..	1	..	1	..	..	11	10
Portugal	..	..	1	..	..	..	..	..	..	..	1	1	..	1	..	..
Romania	..	..	..	..	..	..	..	..	..	..	..	..	..	..	4	3
Saudi Arabia	..	1	..	1	..	1	..	..	..	..	..	2	..	2	..	..
Singapore	..	..	..	..	..	..	..	..	..	..	..	..	..	1	..	..
South Africa	..	..	1	1	2	1	..	..	..	..	..	1	4	2	..	..
Spain	..	1	2	3	2	1	1	1	..	1	2	2	2	1	..	..
Sweden	2	2	1	1	4	3	3	2	..	..	3	2	4	4	1	1
Switzerland	2	3	4	4	6	5	2	2	3	2	..	..	3	6	..	..
Tunisia	..	..	t	1	..	..	..	..	..	..	..	..	..	..	..	..
Turkey	..	..	..	..	..	..	..	..	..	..	..	..	..	..	1	t
United Arab Emirates	..	..	..	..	..	..	..	..	..	..	..	..	..	1	..	..
United Kingdom	4	8	3	8	4	7	7	8	13	12	7	7	..	..	4	2
U.S.A.	6	4	4	5	9	7	4	3	6	6	9	7	11	10	1	1
U.S.S.R.	1	1	1	2	1	2	t	..	2	1	..	1	1	1	..	..
Vietnam	..	..	..	..	..	..	..	..	..	..	..	..	..	..	1	1
Yugoslavia	..	..	..	1	..	2	..	..	..	..	..	1	..	..	3	3
Zaire	1	t	..	..	..	..	..	..	..	..	..	..	..	..	..	..
Zambia	..	..	..	..	..	..	..	..	..	..	..	..	t	..	..	..
Unspecified	10	9	23[2]	14	12	12	17	17	20	18	27	8	27	10	4	9

t = trace (less than .5%)

Notes:
[1] 1978 for U.S.S.R.
[2] Including 4% to other African countries.

Sources:
<u>Europa Yearbook</u> (various).
<u>Statistisches Jahrbuch der Schweiz</u> (1980).
<u>Britain 1981: an Official Handbook</u> (London, 1981).